A QUEER READER

A QUEER READER

EDITED BY
PATRICK HIGGINS

THE NEW PRESS · New York

For
Julian Jackson

Published in the United States by
The New Press, New York
Distributed by W. W. Norton & Company, Inc.,
500 Fifth Avenue, New York, NY 10110

Originally published in Great Britain in 1993 by
Fourth Estate Limited, London, England.

The acknowledgments on p. 362 constitute an
extension of this copyright page.

ISBN 1-56584-210-3
LC 94-67359

Established in 1990 as a major alternative to
the large, commercial publishing houses, The
New Press is the first full-scale nonprofit
American book publisher outside of the
university presses. The Press is operated
editorially in the public interest, rather than
for private gain; it is committed to publishing
in innovative ways works of educational,
cultural, and community value that, despite
their intellectual merits, might not normally be
"commercially" viable. The New Press's
editorial offices are located at the City
University of New York.

Printed in the United States of America

PB   95 96 97 98   9 8 7 6 5 4 3 2 1

Contents

Preface

This book is a history. It tells, or rather attempts to tell, the story of male homosexuality from the time of the Greeks, over 2,500 years ago, to the present day. It does this through the use of documentary extracts, anecdotes and stories.

The history of sexuality is a fashionable and growing subject within the academy, particularly within the American academy – a product of the social revolution experienced throughout the West during the 1960s, when it became possible to explore aspects of the past that had been off limits for generations, the preserve of the pornographer. Historians could at last colonise the forbidden shore, extending our understanding of the past. Among the obvious benefits was an appreciation of the role of women, largely a Cinderella subject before the 1960s. It became possible to situate people in the past in a more plausible universe. The benefits have greatly enhanced the quality of the discipline and have increased the opportunities for historical ingenuity and imagination.

The material collected in this volume has been drawn from many different sources, and I am grateful to a huge number of writers and commentators for allowing me to plunder their work. The book was constructed in the efficient and convivial atmosphere of the University Library at Cambridge – a unique library, in my experience, in that it seems genuinely designed for the convenience of the reader. Many of my fellow inmates there provided much encouragement as I hunted the catalogues and the shelves for my elusive quarry. They also drew my attention to particular items which they encountered in their own reading. For their company and their help I should like to thank Jon Parry, Miri Rubin, Julian Hoppit and Helen Phillips.

I owe a considerable debt of gratitude to my friends who so generously encouraged me while I tried to make sense of a puzzling subject. Carol Macready has been a wonderful support; her good humour and charm continually lifted my spirits. Her mastery of the practical side of life has been a continual source of amazement to me, and I have often benefited from her help. To the other members of her clan, to James Laurenson elder and younger, and to Lucy Akrill, many thanks for numerous services. Christopher Parsons has been a wise counsellor, a tower of strength and a source of many interesting ideas. He placed his considerable knowledge of literature at my disposal and pointed me in many fruitful directions as well as saving me from many errors. My agent, Mike Shaw, has been a tremendous source of inspiration throughout; I never cease to be amazed by his patience and industry and count myself lucky to be one of his clients. I have been fortunate also in that Christopher Potter, my editor at Fourth Estate, has devoted so much time to the project and made so many valuable suggestions that have, I think, greatly improved the book.

Akbar Shamji made it all possible by creating a situation in which I could make the book – a true liberator and a good friend. Without Rob Davies the book would never have been finished; I have greatly valued his support and encouragement. His brutal honesty has been a source of infuriation and delight, but his comments have greatly improved the final text.

This book really began in 1980 in conversations with Julian Jackson when we were fellow students at Peterhouse. Many projects have perished since then, but this has remained. Julian's wisdom, company and friendship have been a wonderful source of pleasure and delight over many years, and he has been the testing-ground for the interpretation offered in this book. His love of stories, anecdotes and gossip has matched my own, and it seems appropriate that the book should be dedicated to him as so much of it was collected simply (in the beginning at least) to amuse him.

Patrick Higgins
May 1993

The homosexual has been a significant part of human sexual activity ever since the dawn of history primarily because it is an expression of capacities that are basic to the human animal.

Alfred Kinsey

It is by the power of names, of signs originally arbitrary and insignificant, that the course of the imagination has in great measure been guided.

Jeremy Bentham

A man is least himself when he talks in his own person. Give him a mask and he will tell you the truth.

Oscar Wilde

Since our Desire cannot take the route which is straightest, Let us choose the crooked.

W. H. Auden

I think rigid heterosexuality is a perversion of nature.

Margaret Mead

The whole trouble with Western society today is the lack of anything worth concealing.

Joe Orton

Introduction:
The Power behind the Mask

Homosexuality shocks less, but continues to be interesting; it is still at that stage of excitation where it provokes what might be called feats of discourse. Speaking of homosexuality permits those who aren't to show how open, liberal and modern they are; and those who are to bear witness, to assume responsibility, to militate. Everyone gets busy, in different ways, whipping it up.

Roland Barthes

A man is homosexual if he says he is.
Or if he is caught in the act.
Suppose it's the first time he's performed the act?
Who makes the rules?

Ned Rorem

I don't want to be labelled as either a pansy or a heterosexual. Labelling is so self-limiting. We are what we do – not what we say we are.

Montgomery Clift

Homosexuality is not difficult to explain. It is the erotic attraction of a member of one sex for a member (or more usually members) of his (or her) own sex – an activity or feeling that is perfectly compatible with erotic attraction to members of the opposite sex. Individuals can also be exclusively erotically interested in members of their own sex. There are many different manifestations, and homosexuality is not necessarily restricted to a particular physical act, such as sodomy. It is possible for an individual to have homosexual feelings and never act upon them.

The problem comes with use, by a whole range of commentators, of the word 'homosexual' as a noun. The writer Gore Vidal and the composer and diarist Ned Rorem have both fought a long campaign against such a usage. In an interview with the Australian gay activist Denis Altman, Vidal outlined his objections to the use of the word homosexual:

ALTMAN: You've said that the word homosexual should be used as an adjective and never as a noun. Yet, the homosexual movement is based on the assumption that there are homosexuals, that there is a homosexual identity. Do you agree?

VIDAL: If there is such a thing as a homosexual identity, you must then admit that there is such a thing as a heterosexual identity. You must find a significant likeness between the late Bertrand Russell and the late Lyndon Johnson, two men who had absolutely nothing in common except that they both liked to go to bed with women. And death, of course. They're both 'into' that now. Since I don't recognize such a thing as a heterosexual personality how can I define or detect a homosexual personality? Homosexual is just an adjective that describes a sexual act between members of the same sex, an act as normal, whatever that may mean, or natural – clearer meaning – as that between two members of the opposite sex. Nothing more. If there is such a thing as 'gay sensibility', then why not a 'realtor's sensibility' or a 'White Plains, New York sensibility'?[1]

Like Vidal, Rorem was among the first generation of intellectuals to acknowledge publicly that his personal sexual proclivities took a homosexual twist. He objects, though, to the process that labels him as a 'homosexual'. 'I do', he writes, 'make an issue of how I don't make an issue of homosexuality.'[2] Some activists try to create a sort of rainbow coalition of persecuted 'minorities', of blacks, women and homosexuals. Such a coalition, of course, almost certainly encompasses a majority of the human race. This objection may be dismissed as pedantry, but Rorem, however, draws an important contrast between homosexuality and negritude that makes a nonsense of homosexual as a noun:

Unlike negritude, homosexuality is not physically spottable . . . A black when he is not Uncle Tomming is still black, and he's still black when he solves an algebraic equation. Is a queer queer when out of bed? When solving equations? Homosexuals have options: like heretics they can repent. A black cannot repent: he can only regret, or be proud.[3]

People have probably always attached some broader meaning to sexual thoughts and actions. Plato, in The Symposium, advanced the idea that men who preferred their own sex were more manly; many modern doctors have suggested the reverse. In the Middle Ages the Catholic Church popularised the idea that men who practised homosexuality were invariably heretics. It is this which explains the description of such men as 'buggers', a word which was at one time applied to all heretics irrespective of their sexual tastes.

The search for meaning intensified during the nineteenth century. Many more connections were established between sexual acts and preferences and personality and character. Scientists invested heavily in the idea of the norm, and expended much effort in cataloguing deviance. They employed an idea which had long shaped discussion of homosexuality: Aristotle's division of actions, feeling and behaviour into those which were 'natural' and those which were 'unnatural'. 'Natural' and 'normal' in the hands of the scientist became interchangeable. What most people did, or rather seemed to do or aspired to do, became defined as the most 'natural' act. Thus ancient philosophy received the imprimatur of science, and these notions were widely disseminated: a development which has done much to pollute modern thought.

For several centuries the words 'sodomite' and 'catamite', with a variety of variants, have served as labels to identify men who preferred their own sex. Sodomy covered a multitude of sins, which sometimes included bestiality. The word 'sodomite' comes down to us from the spectacular dramas described in the nineteenth chapter of Genesis. 'Catamite' comes from the Greek, a corruption of 'Ganymede', the name of the young shepherd plucked by Zeus from a hillside to become the cup-bearer to the gods; it could also mean 'bright penis'. 'Homosexual' appeared on the scene in 1869, and within a short period of time banished all other rivals from the field to become the word most used in public and scientific discourse. Like so much of the new vocabulary of the nineteenth century, the word was the invention of a German, so busy was German society in trying to classify the human and natural world. The stem 'homo' was from the Greek rather than the Latin, meaning 'same' rather than 'man', thus allowing 'homosexuality' to be employed to cover female homosexuality as well. There were of course rivals from the gutter, and as homosexuality became more visible so the terms of abuse multiplied.

ii

If a sexuality is to be disclosed, what will be taken as the true determinant of its meaning: the phantasy structure, the act, the orifice, the gender, the anatomy?

Judith Butler

The idea of a distinctive homosexual type or personality has a long pedigree. It is, however, a myth. It would be impossible to find significant common characteristics (as Vidal suggests some common characteristics must also be shared by the 'heterosexual' as well) in a group of men who practise homosexual sex. Yet the idea of shared homosexual characteristics is a myth which supports many social doctrines. A whole series of experts (scientists, psychologists, psychiatrists, lawyers, policemen) subscribe to, and trade in, the idea of a division of mankind into homosexuals and heterosexuals. The myth also has wide popular currency. It is a fiction that is difficult to dislodge.

In the Western tradition, homosexuality has often been depicted as a subversive practice. Philip IV of France in the early fourteenth century employed the 'homosexual' smear to destroy the powerful order of crusading knights, the Knights Templar.[4] In the sixteenth century Henry VIII and his chief minister Thomas Cromwell used a similar tactic while they were dissolving the English monasteries, in order to discredit the monks.[5] In our century, Senator Joe McCarthy used this weapon in his battle against American liberalism. It remains a powerful political card. In the 1980s a small gang of British Conservative MPs, with allies in the popular press, used the smear to make their party seem virtuous and to score political points against their opponents. Norman Tebbit as Tory Party Chairman in 1987 showed a photograph of some books on homosexual love which had found their way into a couple of London schools: 'Labour's idea of comprehensive education,' he sneered.

A peculiar feature of modern society has been the way in which some individuals label themselves as 'homosexual'. Such people believe that because they perform homosexual acts or have homosexual thoughts this makes them somehow different from the rest of their fellow citizens. It is a reaction to the division of sexuality into hetero and homo, an acceptance of the prevailing social doctrine. Theatrical knight Sir Ian McKellen, the hero of the *Guardian* liberals and the conscience of British homosexuality, told one interviewer in 1988, 'I do happen to be gay and that makes a difference.' This is an interesting idea, and it would be intriguing to get McKellen to elaborate on that difference. Sometimes self-styled homosexuals suggest that they are superior in some way – more creative possibly.

Such self-identification can be traced back at least to the nineteenth century. A homosexual tradition was established in the West, inspired, I suspect, by the German art historian Johann Winckelmann, who appropriated and celebrated a peculiarly homosexual aesthetic which shaped the development of a homosexual identity in the nineteenth century.

In recent decades many of those who identify themselves in this way have rejected the word 'homosexual' because of its association with science and medicine and they have adopted instead the word 'gay'. In an important exploration of the American homosexual subculture published in 1950, D. W. Cory traced the ancestry of this word back to the slang of the 1920s.[6] In 1950 the word was used as part of the elaborate code that men, attracted to other men, adopted in an effort to escape detection by others who did not share their interest. 'Gay' is now almost universally accepted and seems to have stuck.

The curious feature of this self-identification is that it has in the last quarter of a century generated a political and social movement which has had immense success in making homosexuality the subject of popular discourse in a way that would have been impossible before the 1960s. The aims of such a movement are primarily political. They seek to pass laws to remove social hostility directed towards homosexuality and people who choose to identify themselves as homosexuals. In America, in a political culture accustomed to the existence of single-issue pressure groups and with a political tradition which accords some significance to the idea of rights, such a movement seems to have had some success. Laws have been passed that outlaw discrimination against homosexuals at work and in the allocation of housing. Elsewhere, success has been more limited. Activists have also campaigned for the decriminalisation of homosexual sex and the right for individuals to identify themselves as homosexuals without suffering any disagreeable consequences as a result. This campaign has often focused on the armed services, which in some countries retain the power to remove individuals caught performing homosexual acts or identifying themselves as homosexuals. Such a movement is an interesting phenomenon and acquires much of its power from the fact that in the late twentieth century some people believe that sexual inclination is so fundamental to their existence that they choose to organise their life accordingly and believe that it is this aspect of their personality which primarily defines them.

The Gay Movement is, of course, rooted in a radical tradition, and much has been made of its association with the Left. The Movement has a touching faith in the power of the state to change popular prejudices and attitudes. Laws outlawing racial discrimination have been on the statute-book in Britain since the 1960s, but racial discrimination, hatred and tension continue. If anything they have grown since the passage of such acts (which is not to suggest any connection between the legislation and this development). In Northern Ireland, successive administrations have since 1969 legislated continually to outlaw discrimination based on religion, but with little success. Laws rarely change people's opinions. Yet the activists spend much time agitating on this front, believing that it offers them a way of creating a climate of opinion more favourable to homosexuality.

In the early days of the Gay Movement a sort of messianic faith among its leaders generated a belief that one day all people involved in homosexual acts or thinking homosexual thoughts would identify themselves as homosexual – as members of a common brotherhood, as it were. To this end they set about creating a homosexual community which would receive all those identifying themselves in this way. Such individuals performed the act of what was called 'coming out'. This became a critical rite of passage through which the individual began his life again, this time honestly acknowledging his sexual tastes and proudly announcing them to family, friends, neighbours and workmates – an experience not unlike the conversion which many evangelical Protestants undergo in their religious lives.

Unfortunately the numbers who rallied to the flag were disappointingly small. The activists denounced those who failed to come out as cowardly, as collaborators in a system which oppressed all deviants. Particular venom was directed against married men who practised homosexual acts. The Movement has never really believed in bisexuality and has done much to marginalise such activity, and in this it made common cause with the heterosexual moralists who also abuse the bisexuals. Indeed the agreement on a basic division into heterosexuals and homosexuals is sufficient to make many homosexual apologists mirror conventional sexual theories. As a consequence of this attitude – the desire to divide mankind into sheep and goats – the concept of bisexuality and the evolution of sexual preferences have remained largely unstudied, chiefly because they undermine the rigid categories employed by the zealots on both sides.

iii

The study of the history of homosexuality developed from within the Gay Movement. It began as an attempt by activists to reclaim a homosexual heritage. In this action such historians were imitating the way in which feminists had created a flourishing subdivision of social history which they christened 'women's history'. 'Gay history' (or 'gay and lesbian history') has never been able to match its more robust and powerful elder sibling: it is still a fairly sickly offspring, making as yet only limited impact on what one might call 'mainstream history'.

There is a proper suspicion of 'homosexual history' among traditional practitioners of all branches of history. A tendency to employ a specialised and highly theoretical language has not helped its cause. Theories manufactured in Paris and exported with all their paradoxes and puzzles to North America and Britain provide a starting-point for much of the history of sexuality. Academic history has as a discipline resisted the sort of ideological penetration that has affected (and undermined?) some other humanistic disciplines. It has done so through a strong scepticism about theory. After fighting a long war against Marx and his followers and having successfully resisted their designs, it is unlikely to surrender without a struggle to the philosophies of Michel Foucault.[7] Foucault had a tendency to depict history as a succession of major changes or turning-points which completely transformed human society. There has always been much greater continuity in human feelings and social institutions than his scheme of things seems to allow; change, when it occurs, occurs less cataclysmically. There are also massive and insurmountable difficulties in the cavalier fashion with which Foucault deals with evidence.

One of the greatest acts of folly of this new school of 'homosexual historians' has been to focus its attention so overwhelmingly on 'ordinary people' in the past. It rejects what it regards as the élitist approach of other scholars and their concentration on individuals about whom most evidence survives. The problem is that for most centuries the amount of evidence that survives for 'ordinary people' is extremely limited, and much that remains has been filtered through the eyes of the very people the radicals so despise, the élite. The results are historical accounts which owe more to twentieth-century prejudices than to the proper pursuit of the historical technique perfected by Western scholars since the Enlightenment.

A key ingredient in this historical fantasy is the prominence of the 'homosexual-as-victim' thesis. Jonathan Katz in an early work in this genre told his readers that over the centuries:

> American homosexuals were condemned to death by choking, burning, and drowning; they were executed, jailed, pilloried, fined, court-martialled, prostituted, fired, framed, blackmailed, disinherited, declared insane, driven to insanity, to suicide, murder, and self-hate, witchhunted, entrapped, stereotyped, mocked, insulted, isolated, pitied, castigated and despised. They were also castrated, lobotomized, shock-treated and psychoanalyzed.[8]

Louis Crompton, a 'gay' historian, contributed an essay on 'Gay Genocide' to a collection of essays entitled *The Gay Academic*.[9] 'The term genocide', Crompton writes, can 'properly be applied to society's treatment of gay people . . . For a remarkable length of time – not less than 1400 years – the homosexual men and women in western society stood under formal sentence of death, and were in consequence, systematically killed or mutilated.' The crime has been compounded by the silence of historians: 'there has been no public account of this astonishing crime against humanity, all but unparalleled in its relentless use of sanctified legal traditions, and in its continuance in this century.'[10]

Crompton feels there has been a conspiracy. The evidence presented is flimsy – chiefly the comments and sermons of the moralists and the draconian laws of the state. The problem is that such laws were rarely used. Even Katz, who behind the emotional language is a good historian, accepts that in colonial America despite vicious laws only three men were ever executed for sodomy.

There can be no doubt that during the Third Reich men were killed because they practised homosexual sex. The liberal regime that prevailed in Germany before 1933 had allowed men to identify themselves as homosexual, making it easier for the Nazis subsequently to round them up to be killed. Almost every other period of persecution that we can document was much less lethal. The Third Reich was remarkable for the ferocity with which the modern state could be mobilised in the destruction of particular enemies. The revival of interest in the Homosexual Holocaust occurred at a moment in the history of the Gay Movement when that Movement felt itself under attack and sought a suitably apocalyptic parallel with which to galvanise its supporters. The threat never materialised; Anita Bryant proved to be a much less formidable foe than Adolf Hitler.

Most 'homosexual history' is the product of the ghetto and largely speaks to that audience. It usually leads to a dead end.

This is a pity. The last quarter of a century has witnessed a major change in the subjects that can now be discussed in media of all kinds – a triumph in part due to the Gay Movement. The removal of the restrictions that once led scholars to ignore material on homosexuality has produced an explosion in the amount of material now available, which allows us to understand this curious phenomenon and to destroy well-entrenched myths. Much of this material has appeared in a succession of biographies, beginning with the publication of Michael Holroyd's *Lytton Strachey* in 1967–8. Since then, scores of scholars have uncovered a rich vein of documentation which has many implications for the history of society. The high standards of scholarship and the degree of detective work employed make such works among the glories of the age.

Such efforts have largely been confined to the modern period, though the efforts of an American scholar, Thomas Stehling, reveal the rich prizes that can be won through the application of such techniques to earlier periods. Stehling translated over two hundred poems to produce a powerful anthology of male love poems from the Middle Ages.[11] Many of the poems were already known and published, but they had invariably been mistranslated in a deliberate effort to obscure their meaning – a reticence often defended by its practitioners as an attempt not to upset or embarrass their readers. Readers need to be upset. Historians would do well to heed the advice of the journalist and writer J. R. Ackerley on this subject in a letter to Stephen Spender:

> To speak the truth, I think people ought to be upset, and if I had a paper I would upset them all the time; I think that life is so important and, in its workings, so upsetting, that nobody should be spared, but that it should [be] rammed down their throats from morning to night. And those who cannot take it die of it; it is what we want.[12]

iv

One reason that might explain the emphasis by 'homosexual' historians on suffering is the attempt to make common cause with other social groups which are increasingly presented as having suffered across the centuries, sometimes for their beliefs but usually for the colour of their skin or the fact of their gender. Jonathan Katz and his cronies can therefore present the homosexual as a fellow sufferer.

Of course the differences are considerable. Homosexuals do not have to identify themselves; women, Blacks and Jews cannot so easily escape the persecutor. It is in any case never easy to measure the extent of suffering. It is a commodity in which historians do not ordinarily deal, not because they have no sympathy for the sufferings of people in the past (or for that matter in the present) but because the type of evidence which survives rarely allows them to speculate in this way.

Since the beginning of time (or so it sometimes seems), moralists have attacked homosexuality; sometimes along with much else. This does not appear to have prevented some men from feeling attracted towards other men and occasionally acting upon such an impulse. Some may have been put off acting on their fantasies; others may have even suffered guilt. Many others may have done what most people seem to do: pay lip-service to the prevailing moral views of those in power while acting differently in the privacy of the bedroom.

Probably the most hopeless of all these moralists was an eighteenth-century Spanish priest who found himself in what the Spanish called California. The priest was appalled at how openly homosexuality flourished amongst the natives and dedicated his life to the eradication of this vice: 'The abominable vice will be eliminated to the extent that the Catholic faith and all the other virtues are firmly implanted there, for the glory of God and the benefit of those poor ignorants.'[13] California never lived up to his hopes of a virtuous land.

Legislators have passed laws without number prohibiting homosexual acts. Yet while the records of law courts survive throughout Europe over a long period of time, all seem to report few prosecutions for such crimes – the rate of detection and prosecution is unlikely to have deterred the seriously interested.

Courts faced major problems in prosecuting for homosexual activity. In the period before organised police forces, most prosecutions depended on information offered by ordinary citizens. In Renaissance Italian cities, convenient postboxes were provided by the state for citizens to pass on such information anonymously. Leonardo da Vinci was the victim of one such denunciation. The problem was that anonymity offered a wonderful opportunity for the operation of plain malice and jealousy, and much court time was in consequence wasted on cases that were difficult to prove. Most communities usually preserved the accused men's right to face or question those who had accused them of these crimes. In an effort to eliminate frivolous complaints, the magistrates of fifteenth-century Dubrovnik passed a law which visited on the accuser the same punishment (incineration) as that which was meted out to a convicted sexual criminal if the accusation did not produce a conviction. This would certainly make an accuser think twice before presenting an accusation, and as a consequence trials for homosexual offences were extremely rare in the Dalmatian port. In most countries the act of sodomy carried the death penalty. An enmity would therefore have to be particularly strong for one citizen to accuse another. The accuser in his turn would be faced with the enmity of those who had suffered the loss of a family member and might therefore prefer to revenge himself on an enemy in a different manner, which would not escalate into a large-scale feud.

Homosexual scandals are no respecters of persons, and powerful groups may prefer to turn a blind eye to the peccadilloes of their friends and relatives rather than risk the damage that might accrue to the family or institutions to which the accused might be attached. There might even be some damage to the ruling élite itself. It is interesting that many of the great homosexual scandals of the late nineteenth and early twentieth centuries were the results of the efforts of radical elements keen to advertise the corruption and decadence of the upper classes. The scandals that surrounded Fritz Krupp and Philipp von Eulenburg in Wilhelmine Germany were deliberately orchestrated by the Social Democrats in order to damage the Kaiser and the rulers of Imperial Germany.[14] Even the Wilde trial in England (which grew out of a family quarrel) generated fears of a wider attack on fellow-travellers. The government made every effort to contain the trouble; the Irishman was fed to the wolves while others escaped. Yet Wilde was given the opportunity to escape – the warrant for his arrest was issued only after the boat train had left London. Wilde foolishly did not take this opportunity. Men who indulge in homosexual acts enjoy many advantages denied to other members of the radical rainbow constructed by 'homosexual' historians.

One problem has been the definition of a homosexual act. Who, as Ned Rorem asks, decides what constitutes such an act? Two men wrestling in the privacy of their bedroom may seem to be engaged in a homosexual act, but if the same two men wrestled at an organised tournament few people would be prepared to accept that the act was any longer homosexual. Alfred Kinsey in his famous report recorded the curious way that some men stalinised their sex lives, in the process evading any stigma that might be attached to the label 'homosexual':

> . . . the homosexuality of certain relationships between individuals of the same sex may be denied by some persons, because the situation does not fulfill other criteria that they think should be attached to the definition. Mutual masturbation between two males may be dismissed, even by certain clinicians, as not homosexual, because oral or anal relations or particular levels of psychic responses are required, according to the concept of homosexuality . . . There are persons who insist that the active male in an anal relation is essentially heterosexual in his behaviour, and that the passive male in the same relation is the only one who is homosexual. Some males who are being regularly fellated by other males without, however, performing fellation themselves, may insist that they have never been involved in a truly homosexual relation. Their consciences are cleared and they may avoid trouble with society and with police by perpetuating the additional fiction that they are incapable of responding to a relation with a male unless they fantasize themselves in contact with a female.[15]

Human beings have a wonderful capacity to deceive themselves and others. All sorts of elaborate covers have been created to disguise the need many men feel for sexual contact with other men – what some scholars call the 'homosocial'. Proper 'homosexual history' should be about those tactics and strategies that people devise to negotiate life. The idea of honesty – a word which occupies too prominent a place in the gay lexicon – does not always help the historian decode the past.

Most legislation, before the nineteenth century at any rate, was mainly focused on the act of sodomy. All sorts of evidence suggests that this is not necessarily the defining characteristic of homosexuality: many men who consider themselves homosexual might never perform this act. For the courts, sodomy provided many problems of proof and allowed men to perform other acts without themselves or their partners risking prosecution, so evading the label 'sodomite' or 'homosexual'. The law usually demanded proof of penetration, which was difficult to secure. Sometimes a witness or witnesses might come forward, but generally, and rather sensibly, individuals indulging in such acts would do so away from witnesses. Sometimes one partner might confess his crime, but he was often liable to prosecution as well.

The emergence of a police force in most cities during the nineteenth century changed the types of sex crimes which came before the courts and on to the statute-books. The police found, then as now, that if they stationed themselves in districts where men cruised other men they not only might witness sexual acts (which they could prosecute as offences against public decency) but might also be approached by men soliciting them to commit sexual acts (enabling them to bring charges for soliciting and a whole range of other offences). They might even attract more victims if the policeman involved was young and attractive. In this way the police might secure many convictions and justify their existence as the guardians of public decency.

The use of expert witnesses by the courts also secured more convictions for sex crimes. Doctors might examine the accused and produce the necessary technical evidence that would supply a conviction. It was, indeed, from among the ranks of doctors employed in this task that the first scientific literature on the subject of homosexuality emerged. This was aided by a degree of national rivalry as well. Ambroise Tardieu, a doctor working in Paris, came to the conclusion in the mid-nineteenth century that he could identify homosexuals by the distinctive shape of their penises.[16] Johann Ludwig Casper, a German doctor working in the same line, refuted his argument, presenting an impressive array of evidence to disprove the Frenchman. 'This "horrible mystery", he wrote, 'as it was properly psychologically termed by an ingenious public prosecutor in his speech at a trial . . . is found still more mysterious when its depths have been probed . . . The crime has not, however, been put an end to, either by Christianity, by civilization, or by penal codes, and even capital punishment . . . has failed to eradicate it.'[17] In this way homosexuality became a 'scientific problem'.

Without doubt men suffered, but suffering is not a monopoly of the homosexual: it is the prerogative of all men. A history of homosexuality told as the story of oppression cannot convince or persuade.

V

It is scarcely understood by the minds of men

Michelangelo

It is a characteristic of human nature to be inclined to regard anything which is disagreeable as untrue, and then without much difficulty to find arguments against it.

Sigmund Freud

History written by radicals usually contains fairly easily identified heroes and villains. In 'homosexual history' the hero is of course the poor downtrodden guy who wants the same right to live his own life, on his own terms, as his brother in late-twentieth-century Greenwich Village or in the Castro district of San Francisco. There were many villains stopping him from enjoying his birthright.

The scientists and their allies in medicine, psychiatry and psychology are usually presented as important foes. Many of the most negative images of homosexuality can be traced back to the men of science, who have rarely had a good word to say on the subject. As the twentieth century has advanced, social scientists have also enlisted in the great quest both to discover the cause of homosexuality and to define the word 'homosexual' – to discover, indeed, a homosexual personality'. It must be said that much ingenuity has been shown in the quest, and many hours of effort have been devoted to the task. At regular intervals a team of scientists will announce to the world that it has located the cause and that it can explain homosexuality. Articles in newspapers and magazines appear heralding this great advance in science; occasionally the successful scientists might even appear on television. Not everyone is convinced, though, and the explanation quickly falls apart, so the quest continues. A new group makes a breakthrough which is heralded in its turn. The literature on this subject is as a consequence enormous and massively contradictory.

One breakthrough which attracted more than the usual amount of media attention came from Finland (for this is a game that is played right across the planet) in the 1970s. Knut Freund and his team invented a splendid little gadget which the Finns assured the credulous journalists could determine within a matter of minutes if someone was or was not a homosexual. The device was called by the Finns the plethysmograph. A recent textbook has described this advance:

> The work of Knut Freund and his associates is perhaps the most rigorous work in this area. Freund invented a device . . . that fits over the penis and directly measures its blood volume . . . Sexual orientation – or, in Freund's terminology, 'erotic orientation to body shape' – is observed by recording genital blood volume responses when the subject is shown photographs of naked people of various ages, appearances, and sexes. Numerous studies have demonstrated the fundamental reliability and validity of this technique . . . Not surprisingly, plethysmography does not work well with involuntary subjects. It is therefore impractical to use it to determine the incidence of sexual orientation in the population at large.[18]

Freund has had many imitators in the Heath Robinson world of science. Future generations may not be able to take as seriously as we the image of men in white coats attaching wires and appliances to the genitals of human guinea-pigs and measuring their reactions while showing them pornographic images on a slide projector. It might tell us much about the psychology of the 'neutral' scientists monitoring the exercises.

What the historian finds most amusing in these efforts is the presentation of evidence outside a sociological context. The assumption is that class and education do not really make much difference; scientists rarely address the problems posed by different levels of articulacy and education among those they choose to interview and test. The samples are also so incredibly small. Irving Bieber's study of 1962,[19] which is one of the most widely cited modern surveys, was based on 200 men. On this study, chapters in textbooks rest their explanation for homosexuality, since Bieber found that the cause was Mother – a welcome support for the Freudians!

Most surveys draw their samples either from college students (earning an extra buck) or from patients and prisoners locked up in institutions where such efforts might be presented as part of their treatment. Inadvertently, what these scientists have supplied to some future historian is the material to examine the sexual attitudes of college students, mental patients and prisoners (presuming, of course, that they all told the doctors the truth – another whole can of worms, that just might muck up the results of the survey!).

The ingenuity of the scientists never ceases to amaze. One team in 1991 contrasted the brains of a number of victims of Aids against the brains of a group of men who died from other causes. A grisly business.

While such efforts may help to oppress men who are attracted to their own sex, they may also simply confuse them, as they provide no single answer. The more the 'problem' is studied, the less certain the conclusions become. The scientific and medical community is still divided along the old nurture and nature lines, with one party claiming biological determination while another suggests that homosexuality is environmentally determined. Most depends on what type of doctor you talk to. Psychologists have traditionally backed nurture; after all, if the matter was fixed ahead of time it might put them out of a job. The Gay Movement prefers nature, for obvious reasons. The entire thing is an enormous pantomime. If there has been a victim, it might most logically be the mothers of the men who turn out to have homosexual urges. A lot of the literature blames them, and if anyone has been made to feel guilty it is undoubtedly Mother. In those critical first few months, psychologists told her, she dare not make a single mistake or the consequences would be truly awful. If she loved baby too much it was wrong; if she loved him too little it could also be wrong. Dad got off scot-free. Occasionally allowed to play a supporting role, he was usually acquitted of the consequences of any absence from the family nest as he earned the money to keep Mom and junior in the style to which all soon became accustomed. The absent father was never really a suspect – not in a profession overwhelmingly dominated by men.

Science might also liberate, however. An individual shopping around for a justification of his thoughts and actions might find that Freud and the doctors had lifted the burden of responsibility from his shoulders. He was simply the victim of circumstances that might have been determined even before he was born or even before he first began to walk.

During the 1940s, when science seemed particularly persuasive, there were occasions when some doctors advocated surgery to deal with homosexuality, but the numbers involved were tiny. Most parents, if junior was caught in the act or revealed insufficient interest in the opposite sex, sent him off to therapy. There were doctors then as now who offered to cure such cases. Science and medicine did not speak with one voice: the doctors were no more co-ordinated in their efforts than the agents of the state.

vi

Cambridge never fails to provide an outlet whatever the bent may be
. . .

E. A. R. Ennion

. . . queers stick together like glue.

Juvenal

The city is the human market-place that allows strange people to seek out those of fellow-feeling, it offers economic independence, the anonymity and randomness needed to sponsor original styles of life.

Edmund White

It is possible to argue that the social organisation of Western society promotes homosexuality, or at least makes such activity possible. Most social, political and educational institutions (with the exception of the family) have been organised along strict division of the sexes. In some ways this has changed since the 1960s, though it is still largely true. The Catholic Church in the West has traditionally been organised in this way. Monasteries and clerical celibacy brought together men, who were kept away from women, under the same roof. As a consequence, it is possible to provide evidence in almost all centuries of homosexual misdemeanours and accusations involving clerics. The same may also be true of the armed forces, of all kinds of navies, and of schools and universities. If one wanted to design a system better calculated to promote opportunities in which to foster homosexual affection and activity, it would be difficult to improve upon the system which has operated in the West across many centuries.

What has added to the opportunities available has been the virtual unbroken existence, in large Western cities since antiquity, of an urban homosexual subculture, usually attached to one particular district. Such districts draw men to them, and no amount of police activity has been able totally to eradicate such places. *Spartacus*, a guidebook designed for the traveller interested in exploring such areas, offers information of this sort on almost every country in the world. In its 1977 edition it informed travellers to Cuba that the Havana scene was organised around an ice-cream stall in the centre of the city! The emergence of a Gay Movement obviously increased the size of such subcultures, and it has been one of the continuing frustrations of the activists that all the new clubs, bars and shops which grew up as a result of their hard work, demonstrating and witnessing, attracted clients who rejected every attempt made to politicise them, who saw in this New Model Ghetto the opportunities to seek sexual partners, make and meet friends, and enjoy themselves. More men went on the demos, but they always remained a small fraction of those who used the ghetto to enhance the quality of their own life.

Casper, the German forensic scientist writing in the 1860s, suggested that 'in all the large towns of Europe this vice glides about enshrouded in darkness, impenetrable to the uninitiated; but there seems to be no inhabited spot where it is not to be found.'[20] Writers since ancient times have, he claims, specified 'certain peculiarities in the walk, look, demeanour and voice' by which such men 'may be recognised'. He reported that one informant, who seems to have been exaggerating just a little bit, told the curious doctor that 'We discover each other at once, at a single glance, and by exercising a little caution, I have never been deceived. Upon the Righi, at Palermo, in the Louvre, in the Highlands of Scotland, in St. Petersburg, on the landing at Barcelona I observed parties whom I had never seen, and whom I recognised in a second.' It takes one, as the old saying goes, to know one. Cruising is a venerable tradition, and the city offers anonymity and opportunity, in this way cradling diversity and providing additional opportunities for the interested.

vii

Jews and homosexuals are the two outstanding creative minorities in contemporary western culture – creative that is, in the truest sense; they are creators of sensibilities.

Susan Sontag

Might I remind you that the greatest artists and philosophers did not enjoy the benefits of heterosexuality.

Philip Larkin to Kingsley Amis

How tired I am of keeping a mask on my countenance. How tight it sticks – it makes me sore.

William Beckford

In the 1970s a new market for more positive descriptions of homosexuality began to emerge. A staple in such apologies for homosexuality, designed primarily for the young and their parents' 'coming to terms with homosexuality', was the ritual list of the great homosexuals in history. In one of the most popular works of this genre (a bestseller), Laura Hobson's *Consenting Adult*, the hero, Jeff Lynn, an all-American boy, reconciles himself to his sexual tastes through a fairly standard form of consciousness-raising. 'There were', he told himself,

> people who were homosexual that you could be proud of, Leonardo and Michelangelo and Plato and Tchaikovsky and also plenty of living people, famous playwrights and composers and conductors and authors. The string of names came quickly because he had so often gone over them. Telling my beads, he had once thought, a sour smile down inside somewhere. Maybe someday he would do some research, call it 'Great Homosexuals down the Ages', a thesis for a college award or advanced degree. Except you never could do a thesis like that; if you sounded interested in being homosexual, people knew right away about you.[21]

Jeff is suffering. He is only in Chapter 2; he has thirteen more chapters to endure before everything comes right and he can bring his lover – another identikit all-American boy, suitably wholesome – home to meet Mom (Dad having met his just reward with only a few pages to go). In his hour of need, Jeff brought the great homosexuals of history to mind. Scott Fitzgerald, another all-American boy, scoffed at such activity in his notebook: 'The great pansy thesis – that all great pansies were pansies.'[22]

These days it is not politically correct to construct such a list – such is the drive to embrace the Common Man; such is the proletarianisation of 'homosexual history'. What is odd, however, is that recent scholarship has reinforced and multiplied such lists. Jeff Lynn's 1993 model would have many more names to choose from. What the research has done is to create a more interesting puzzle. What, if anything, is the connection between homosexuality and genius, and, more importantly, what role has homosexuality played in the making of modern culture? In an interesting essay placing the spy and art historian Anthony Blunt in his cultural milieu, critic and thinker George Steiner offered the following reflection:

> Neither sociology nor cultural history, neither political theory nor psychology has ever begun to handle authoritatively the vast theme of the part played by homosexuality in Western culture since the late nineteenth century. The subject is so diffuse and of such methodological and emotional complexity that it would require a combination of Machiavelli, de Tocqueville, and Freud to produce the great missing book. There is hardly a branch of literature, of music, of the plastic arts, of philosophy, of drama, film, fashion, and the furnishings of daily urban life in which homosexuality has not been crucially involved, often dominantly. Judaism and homosexuality (most intensely where they overlap, as in a Proust or a Wittgenstein) can be seen to have been the two main generators of the entire fabric and savour of urban modernity in the West. In ways that C. P. Snow did not even hint at in his argument on 'the two cultures', it is, by and large, the striking absence of any comparable homosexual presence in the exact and applied sciences which has helped bring on the widening gap between the general culture and the scientific.[23]

This is the agenda which should shape the form and the content of 'homosexual history'. Here are puzzles that demand some sort of answer and tell us much about Western society and culture.

It is surely in the imagination of the West that homosexuality has revealed its greatest power. One might range across many centuries and many different countries and produce an impressive list of canonical texts, works which have offered young and old expressing their homosexuality a rich source from which to construct their identity. The pen has in this proved far mightier than the sword, the sermon, the law or even the discoveries of the scientist.

Over time, homosexuality has created a fascinating series of codes and symbols which testify to the powerful emotions that sexuality can generate. For a long time such codes and symbols have remained restricted to small groups of the initiated, for the 'love that dared not speak its name', in Wilde's famous phrase, has been so long condemned to remain hidden by masks. The uncovering of such 'hidden things' promises to be a rewarding experience.

CHAPTER ONE

Antiquity

The heroic age. Among artists and writers, the civilisations of Greece and Rome have been much celebrated for their homosexuality, illuminating the repressions and restrictions of the present against the permissive wisdom of the ancients.

In the eighteenth century, the German classicist Johann Winckelmann articulated a celebration of the Greeks which became a standard item in the making of the modern homosexual identity. 'To the Greek climate', he wrote,

> we owe the production of taste, and from thence it spread at length over all the politer world. Every invention, communicated by foreigners to that nation, was but the seed of what it became afterwards, changing both its nature and size in a country, chosen, as Plato says, by Minerva, to be inhabited by the Greeks, as productive of every kind of genius . . . There is but one way for the moderns to become great, and perhaps unequalled; I mean, by imitating the ancients . . . The most beautiful body of ours would perhaps be as much inferior to the most beautiful Greek one, as Iphicles was to his brother Hercules.

The bodies that Winckelmann and his followers celebrated were male:

> I have observed that those who are only aware of beauty in the female sex and are hardly or not at all affected by beauty in our sex, have little innate feeling for beauty in art in a general and vital sense.

Thus the homosexual commentator is provided with a monopoly of understanding, while his heterosexual brother labours under the handicap of his narrow proclivities.

Winckelmann noted with evident approval the practice at Sparta by which young athletes 'were bound to appear every tenth day naked before the ephors' in order to ensure the perfection of the young male physique, and 'when they perceived any inclinable to fatness, ordered a scantier diet'. Writings about antiquity have often allowed author and reader to indulge their own personal fantasies of a long-departed golden age. Winckelmann was, of course, a spiritual ancestor of the youth and nature movements which developed in nineteenth-century Germany, encouraging the young male to exercise and expose himself to nature. Walt Whitman, the American poet, who has been described by one modern literary critic as 'the first homosexual', wrote an essay celebrating Greek culture which suggested that 'the highest height and deepest depths known to civilization . . . came from their natural and religious idea of Nakedness.'

The image of the ancient world as a homosexual paradise has been passed down chiefly through the study of classical literature. Plato's famous work *The Symposium* is still possibly one of the most powerful testimonies in defence of homosexual love available in any language. In an educational system in which classical literature has until recent decades played a significant role, the discovery of Plato's work offered an important release for the young homosexual. It was a major source of empathy and provided the blessing of one of the greatest philosophers who has ever lived. In E. M. Forster's novel *Maurice*, the hero finally understands his passion for his friend Clive when he reads *The Symposium*. It allows him to articulate his inclinations and makes as a consequence an appropriate present for the more worldly Clive to give him. Plato suggested, long before Hollywood, to all anxious young lovers that out there, somewhere, there is a perfect partner for everyone.

The Symposium reveals a world constructed around very different principles from our own. Homosexual love is presented as superior to heterosexual passion, and all the speakers in the dialogue are chiefly interested in young men. Greek society at that time supported institutions and practices which fostered relationships between older and younger men as an important element in what modern social scientists would call 'the socialisation of the young citizen'. Physical beauty and athletic prowess were highly prized, and many men regularly visited the gymnasium to spy out the talent. Younger men, in the manner of the starlet, used their beauty to capture the affections of powerful and influential older men.

Greek legends and myths vindicated this worldview, for even the king of the gods, Zeus, was not immune from the attractions of the male adolescent. His abduction of the young Trojan shepherd Ganymede is a story that has been frequently depicted in painting and poetry down the centuries. In our own age W. H. Auden cast his cold and cynical eye on the tale, presenting the young shepherd as the sort of difficult-to-please hustler he himself had met in his travels around Weimar Berlin.[1] Auden believed that Zeus would have had his work cut out keeping his young lover entertained.

Plato suggested spitefully that the Ganymede story had been invented by the Cretans. Crete had the reputation of being a peculiarly homosexually inclined community, even by the standards of the Greeks. Plato's pupil Aristotle suggested that the Cretans' dissemination of the story was a device to control the island's population.

A pair of homosexual lovers, Harmodius and Aristogiton, were credited with preserving Athenian democracy by challenging the Athenian tyrant Hippias in 514BC. The Theban band (see pages 33–4) furnished another example of the power of homosexual love, and Philip of Macedon's comment on the dead comrades and lovers on the battlefield at Chaeronea is an epitaph that became a motto of the homosexual cause: 'Perish miserably they who think that these men did or suffered aught disgraceful.' In the moment of their defeat they too passed into the legends of antiquity.

The ideal was not the norm, for, as the relationship between Alexander the Great (356–323BC) and his friend Hephaiston suggests, some adult males continued their connections long after either of the partners could be cast as the young beloved adolescent. The effeminate man, exclusively homosexual in interest, was a stock figure of Greek comedy always likely to produce a laugh from a Greek audience: a tradition which continues.

The Romans were much less idealistic about love and sex than the Greeks, and homosexuality was extremely common in Roman society. The state taxed male prostitutes, who also enjoyed an official holiday each year, allowing them to take a short rest from their labours. The cities of the Roman empire contained large and flourishing homosexual subcultures, evidence of which has been preserved in the case of the city of Pompeii, where the modern archaeologist has been able to find plenty of material to corroborate our image of the licentiousness and promiscuity of the Roman male. In one district, homosexual graffiti – much of it highly graphic – still survives:

Phoebus the perfume-maker fucks excellently.

I want to be fucked by a male.

Autus fucked Quintius here.

Many of these were found in the bathing areas, for in the Roman world the bathhouse eclipsed the gymnasium as the arena for homosexual encounters.

The Romans took an indulgent attitude to pleasure. Gibbon records the fact that, of the first twelve emperors of Rome, only one was exclusively heterosexual in his sexual interest: the odd one out being that curious freak of nature Claudius, who has excited much sympathy in the twentieth century. Bisexuality was common, and frowned upon only by the moralists, who were unwilling to join in the fun.

Roman literature supplies many examples of homosexual love, most notably in the works of Horace, Propertius, Petronius, Catullus and Juvenal. In Petronius's *Satyricon* we possess one of the earliest pornographic novels which can still excite the interests of a modern reader.

The Romans too had homosexual heroes. They borrowed from the Greeks the myths of Olympus, and added more. Julius Caesar was never allowed to forget his youthful experiments when he had gone out East and fallen under the spell of King Nicomedes. In the attachment of the Emperor Hadrian for the young Greek Antinous they found a contemporary story of the ennobling qualities of homosexual love. Hadrian made his lover a god after the young man was drowned in the Nile in AD130, and statues were erected throughout the empire, making him the focus of a short-lived cult.

Quid Pro Quo

In Athens, in the second half of the sixth century, pederastic scenes became very popular on vases, a fashion that enables us to trace the history of Athenian pederasty in some detail. On those vases, which circulated in the aristocratic symposia, we see adult men offering a boy a present with one hand and freely reaching for the boy's penis with the other — clearly, *quid pro quo* . . . The Athenian vases clearly show that only the adults were considered to derive satisfaction from pederastic intercourse; the boy usually looks as if he is solving some academic problem. Evidently he was not allowed to take pleasure in the sexual aspect of the relationship. The apparent one-sidedness of the affair accords with its probable origin in initiation rites, which also aimed at teaching youngsters to respect their elders.

from an article by the classical scholar Jan Bremmer

Harmodius and Aristogiton

The coup of Harmodius and Aristogiton (514 BC) arose out of a love affair . . . Pisistratus [tyrant of Athens] died at an advanced age in possession of the tyranny, and was succeeded in his power . . . by Hippias, his eldest son. Harmodius was in the flower of youth, and Aristogiton, a citizen of the middle class, became his lover. Hipparchus [the brother of Hippias] made an attempt to gain the affections of Harmodius, but he would not listen, and denounced him to Aristogiton. As a lover he was tormented at the idea and, fearing that Hipparchus in view of his power would resort to violence, at once formed such a plot as a man in his station might for the overthrow of the tyranny. Meanwhile, Hipparchus made another attempt; he had no better success, and thereupon he determined not indeed to take any violent step but to insult Harmodius in a way that would not reveal his motive. For in the rest of his government, he was not oppressive to the majority, but had ruled without incurring unpopularity . . . When Hipparchus found his advances repelled by Harmodius, he carried out his intention of insulting him. There was a young sister of his whom Hipparchus and his friends first invited to come and carry a sacred basket in a procession; and then they rejected her, declaring that she had never been invited by them at all because she was unworthy. Harmodius was very angry and Aristogiton, for his sake, more angry still. They had already laid their preparations with those who were to share in their coup, but were waiting for the festival of Panathenea, when the citizens were to take part in the procession assembled in arms; for to do so on any other day would have aroused suspicion. Harmodius and Aristogiton were to begin the attack and the rest were immediately to join in and engage the guards . . . The day of the festival arrived, and Hippias went out of the city with his guards to the place called Ceramicus, where he was occupied in marshalling the procession. Harmodius and Aristogiton, who were ready with their daggers, stepped forward to do the deed. But seeing one of the conspirators in familiar conversation with Hippias, who was readily accessible to all, they took alarm and thought that they had been betrayed and were on the point of being seized. They therefore determined to take their revenge first on the man who had offended them on whose account they were putting everything in peril. So they rushed, just as they were, within the gates. They found Hipparchus near the Leocorium, as it was called, and then and there falling upon him with all the blind fury of an injured lover or of a man smarting under an insult, they stuck and killed him. The crowd ran together, and so Aristogiton for the present escaped the guards: but he was afterwards taken and not very gently handled. Harmodius perished at once on the spot . . .

Such was the conspiracy of Harmodius and Aristogiton, which began in the resentment of a lover; the reckless attempt which followed arose out of a sudden fright. To the people at large, the tyranny became more oppressive afterwards; Hippias became more apprehensive, put many citizens to death and also began to look abroad in hope of securing an asylum . . . Hippias ruled three years longer over the Athenians. In the fourth year (510) he was deposed.

from The Peloponnesian War, *by the Athenian historian Thucydides (c. 460–c. 395 BC)*

The Desire and Pursuit of the Whole

First of all, you must learn the constitution of man and the modifications which it has undergone, for originally it was different from what it is now. In the first place there were three sexes, not, as with us, two, male and female: the third partook of the nature of both the others and has vanished, though its name survives. The hermaphrodite was a distinct sex in form as well as in name, with the characteristics of both male and female, but now the name alone remains, and that solely as a term of abuse. Secondly, each human being was a rounded whole, with double back and flanks forming a complete circle; it had four hands and an equal number of legs, and two identically similar faces upon a circular neck, with one head common to both the faces, which were turned in opposite directions. It had four ears and two organs of generation and everything else to correspond. These people could walk upright like us in either direction, back-wards or forwards, but when they wanted to run quickly they used all their eight limbs, and turned rapidly over and over in a circle, like tumblers who perform a cart-wheel and return to an upright position. The reason for the existence of the three sexes and for their being of such nature is that originally the male sprang from the sun and the female from the earth, while the sex which was both male and female came from the moon, which partakes of the nature of both sun and earth. Their circular shape and their hoop-like method of progression were both due to the fact that they were like their parents. Their strength and vigour made them very formidable, and their pride was overweening; they attacked the gods . . .

So Zeus and the other gods debated what was to be done with them. For a long time they were at a loss, unable to bring themselves either to kill them by lightning, as they had the giants, and extinguish the race – thus depriving themselves for ever of the honours and sacrifices due from humanity – or to let them go on in their insolence. At last, after much painful thought, Zeus had an idea. 'I think,' he said, 'that I have found a way by which we can allow the human race to continue to exist and also put an end to their wickedness by making them weaker. I will cut each of them in two; in this way they will be weaker, and at the same time more profitable to us by being numerous. They shall walk upright upon two legs. If there is any sign of wantonness in them after that, and they will not keep quiet, I will bisect them again, and they shall hop on one leg.' With these words he cut the members of the human race in half, just like fruit which is to be dried and preserved, or like eggs which are cut with a hair. As he bisected each, he bade Apollo turn round the face and the half-neck attached to it towards the cut side, so that the victim, having the evidence of bisection before his eyes, might behave better in future. He also bade him heal the wounds. So Apollo turned round the faces, and gathering together the skin, like a purse with draw-strings, on to what is now called the belly, he tied it tightly in the middle of the belly round a single aperture which men call the navel. He smoothed out the other wrinkles, which were numerous, and moulded the chest with a tool like those which cobblers use to smooth wrinkles in the leather on their last. But he left a few on the belly itself round the navel, to remind man of the state from which he had fallen.

Man's original body having been thus cut in two, each half yearned for the half from which it had been severed. When they met they threw their arms around one another and embraced, in their longing to grow together again, and they perished of hunger and general neglect of their concerns, because they would not do anything apart. When one member of a pair died and the other was left, the latter sought after and embraced another partner, which might be half either of a female whole (what is now called a woman) or a male. So they went on perishing till Zeus took pity on them, and hit upon a second plan. He moved their reproductive organs to the front: hitherto they had been placed on the outer side of their bodies, and the processes of begetting and birth had been carried on not by the physical union of the sexes, but by emission on to the ground, as is the case with grasshoppers. By moving their genitals to the front, as they are now, Zeus made it possible for reproduction to take place by the intercourse of the male with the female. His object in making this change was twofold; if male coupled with female, children might be begotten and the race thus continued, but if male coupled with male, at any rate the desire for intercourse would be satisfied, and men set free from it to turn to other activities and to attend to the rest of the business of life. It is from this distant epoch, then, that we may date the innate love which human beings feel for one another, the love which restores us to our ancient state by attempting to weld two beings into one and to heal the wounds which humanity suffered.

Each of us then is the mere broken tally of a man, the result of a bisection which has reduced us to a condition like that of flat fish, and each of us is perpetually in search of his corresponding tally. Those men who are halves of a being of the common sex, which was called, as I told you, hermaphrodite, are lovers of women, and most adulterers come from this class, as also do women who are mad about men and sexually promiscuous. Women who are halves of a female whole direct their attention towards women and pay little attention to men; Lesbians belong to this category. But those who are halves of a male whole pursue males, and being slices, so to speak, of the male, love men throughout their boyhood, and take pleasure in physical contact with men. Such boys and lads are the best of their generation, because they are the most manly. Some people say they are shameless, but they are wrong. It is not shamelessness which inspires their behaviour, but high spirit and manliness and virility, which lead them to welcome the society of their own kind. A striking proof of this is that such boys alone, when they reach maturity, engage in public life. When they grow to be men, they become lovers of boys, and it requires the compulsion of convention to overcome their natural disinclination to marriage and procreation; they are quite content to live with another unwed. In a word, such persons are devoted to lovers in boyhood and themselves lovers of boys in manhood, because they always cleave to what is akin to themselves.

Whenever the lover of boys – or any other person for that matter – has the good fortune to encounter his own actual other half, affection and kinship and love combined inspire in him an emotion which is quite overwhelming, and such a pair practically refuse to be separated even for a moment. It is people like these who form lifelong partnerships, although they would find it difficult to say what they hope to gain from one another's society. No one can suppose that it is mere physical enjoyment which causes the one to take such intense delight in the company of the other. It is clear that the soul of each has some other longing which it cannot express, but can only surmise and obscurely hint at . . . The reason is that this was our primitive condition when we were wholes, and love is simply the name for the desire and pursuit of the whole.

Aristophanes' account of sexual attraction, from The Symposium, *by the Greek philosopher Plato (427–347 BC)*

Fruitless Labours

The Socrates whom you see has a tendency to fall in love with good-looking young men, and is always in their society and in an ecstasy about them . . . [yet] he wears these characteristics superficially, like the carved figure, but once you see beneath the surface you will discover a degree of self-control of which you can hardly form a notion . . . Believe me, it makes no difference to him whether a person is good-looking – he despises good looks to an almost inconceivable extent – nor whether he is rich nor whether he possesses any of the other advantages that rank high in popular esteem; to him all these things are worthless, and we ourselves of no account, be sure of that. He spends his whole life pretending and playing with people . . .

Believing that he was serious in his admiration of my charms, I supposed that a wonderful piece of good luck had befallen me; I should now be able, in return for my favours, to find out all that Socrates knew; for you must know that there was no limit to the pride that I felt in my good looks. With this end in view I sent away my attendant, whom hitherto I had always kept with me in my encounters with Socrates, and left myself alone with him. I must tell you the whole truth; attend carefully, and do you, Socrates, pull me up if anything I say is false. I allowed myself to be alone with him, I say, gentlemen, and I naturally supposed that he would embark on conversation of the type that a lover usually addresses to his darling when they are *tête-à-tête*, and I was glad. Nothing of the kind; he spent the day with me in the sort of talk which is habitual with him, and then left me and went away. Next I invited him to train with me in the gymnasium, and I accompanied him there, believing that I should succeed with him now. He took exercise and wrestled with me frequently, with no one else present, but I need hardly say that I was no nearer my goal. Finding that this was no good either, I resolved to make a direct assault on him, and not to give up what I had once undertaken; I felt that I must get to the bottom of the matter. So I invited him to dine with me, behaving just like a lover who has designs upon his favourite. He was in no hurry to accept this invitation, but at last agreed to come. The first time he came he rose to go away immediately after dinner, and on that occasion I was ashamed and let him go. But I returned to the attack, and this time I kept him in conversation after dinner far into the night, and then, when he wanted to be going, I compelled him to stay, on the plea that it was too late to let him go.

So he betook himself to rest, using as a bed the couch on which he had reclined at dinner, next to mine, and there was nobody sleeping in the room but ourselves . . . when the light was out and the servants had withdrawn, I decided not to beat about the bush with him, but to tell him my sentiments boldly. I nudged him and said: 'Are you asleep, Socrates?' 'Far from it,' he answered. 'Do you know what I think?' 'No, what?' 'I think that you are the only lover that I have ever had who is worthy of me, but that you are afraid to mention your passion to me. Now, what I feel about the matter is this, that it would be foolish of me not to comply with your desires in this respect as well as in any other claims that you might make on my property or on that of my friends. The cardinal object of my ambition is to come as near perfection as possible, and I believe that no one can give me such powerful assistance towards this end as you. So the disapproval of wise men, which I should incur if I refused to comply with your wishes, would cause me far more shame than the condemnation of the ignorant multitude if I yielded to you.'

He listened to what I had to say, and then made a thoroughly characteristic reply in his usual ironical style: 'You must be a very sharp fellow, my dear Alcibiades, if what you say about me is true, and I really have a power which might help you to improve yourself. You must see in me a beauty which is incomparable and far superior to your own physical good looks, and if, having made this discovery, you are trying to get a share of it by exchanging your beauty for mine, you obviously mean to get the better of the bargain; you are trying to get beauty in return for sham; in fact, what you are proposing is to exchange dross for gold. But look more closely, my good friend, and make quite sure that you are not mistaken in your estimate of my worth. A man's mental vision does not begin to be keen until his physical vision is past his prime, and you are far from having reached that point.'

'Well,' I said, 'I have done my part; what I have said represents my real sentiments and it is now for you to decide what you think best for me and for yourself.'

'Quite right,' he answered, 'we will consider hereafter, and do whatever seems to be best in this as in other matters.'

I had now discharged my artillery, and from the answer which he made I judged that I had wounded him; so, without allowing him to say anything further, I got up and covered him with my own clothes – for it was winter – and then laid myself under his worn cloak, and threw my arms round this truly superhuman and wonderful man, and remained thus the whole night long. Here again, Socrates, you cannot deny that I am telling the truth. But in spite of all my efforts he proved completely superior to my charms and triumphed over them and put them to scorn, insulting me in the very point on which I piqued myself, gentlemen of the jury – I may call you that, since you have the case of Socrates' disdainful behaviour before you. I swear by all the gods in heaven that for anything that had happened between us when I got up after sleeping with Socrates, I might have been sleeping with my father or elder brother . . . I realized I had been slighted, but I felt a reverence for Socrates' character, his self-control and courage . . . in the one point in which I had expected him to be vulnerable he had eluded me. I was utterly disconcerted, and wandered about in a state of enslavement to the man the like of which has never been known.

Alcibiades' account of his attempt to seduce Socrates, from Plato, The Symposium

Divine Invention

The pleasures of males with males, or females with females, is contrary to nature and a boldness of the first rank in the surrender to pleasure. And we all charge the Cretans that they made up the tale of Ganymede; they were convinced, we say, that their legislation came from Zeus, so they went on to tell this story against him that they might, if you please, be following his example when they indulged in this pleasure too.

from Plato, The Laws

Not Just a Pretty Face

What a handsome face he has: but if he were naked you would forget he had a face, he is so beautiful in every way.

from Plato, Charmides

Contemptuous Partner

Why should the boy return his affection? Because he assigns to himself the gratification of his passion, leaving to the boy the extremity of shame? Or because the favour that he is eager to exact cuts the favourite off completely from his family and friends? Then again the very fact that he uses not force but persuasion makes him more detestable, because a lover who uses force proves himself a villain, but one who uses persuasion ruins the character of the one who consents. Again, is one who sells his youth for money any more likely to love the purchaser than one who trades in the market? Certainly the fact that he is young and his partner is not, or that he is beautiful and his partner is no longer, or that he is not in love and his partner is – this will not stir his affection. A boy does not share the man's enjoyment of sexual intercourse as a woman does: he is a sober person watching one drunk with sexual excitement. In view of all this it is no wonder if he develops an actual contempt for his lover.

from Xenophon, The Symposium. Xenophon (c.430–352 BC) was a Greek historian. A disciple of Socrates, he tried to present his teacher's ideas but misunderstood Socrates' philosophy. A soldier turned intellectual, he had fallen under Socrates' spell after the older man had picked him up on an Athenian street. Socrates asked him, 'Where can you get brave and virtuous men?' Xenophon was puzzled, and Socrates took him home and began his philosophical education.

Alexander and Hephaiston

Hephaiston was the man whom Alexander loved, and for the rest of their lives their relationship remained as intimate as it is now irrecoverable: Alexander was only defeated once, the Cynic philosophers said long after his death, and that was by Hephaiston's thighs . . . Hephaiston's age is not known and its discovery could put their relationship in an unexpected light; he may even have been the older of the two . . . At the age of thirty Alexander was still Hephaiston's lover although most young Greeks have grown out of the fashion by then and an older man would have given up or turned to a younger attraction. Their affair was a strong one: Hephaiston grew to lead Alexander's cavalry most ably and to become his Vizier before dying a divine hero, worthy of posthumous worship.

'Sex and sleep', Alexander is said to have remarked, 'alone make me conscious that I am mortal.'

from Robin Lane-Fox, Alexander the Great (1975)

The Death of Orpheus

. . . the son of Oeagrus, Thracian Orpheus, loved from his heart Calais, the son of Boreas, and many times in the shady groves he sat, singing of his love: nor was his soul at peace, but he was always devoured by sleepless cares through the agency of his soul, seeing youthful Calais. Gathering around him, the evil women of

Thrace, having sharpened their keen-edged swords, killed him, because for the first time amongst the Thracians he made known love between men, nor did he praise the love of women. They cut off his head, with their swords, and immediately it became submerged, because they threw it into the Thracian sea, fastening it to the lyre by means of nails, so that they both were carried by the sea, moistened by the blue waves. The white-crested sea brought them to sacred Lesbos. And thus the sound of the harmonious lyre filled both the sea and the isles, and the sea-beaten shores. It is here that men buried with due honours the melodious head of Orpheus, and placed into the tomb the sweet-sounding lyre which charmed the speechless stones and the hateful water of Phorcus. It is because of him that songs and the lovely lyre possess the island, which is of all the most melodious. But when the war-like Thracians learnt of the cruel deeds of their women, a dreadful pain entered them, and they tattooed their women, so that, having on their skin the dark-blue marks, they should never forget their dreadful labour. Even to this very day, as a punishment for the murder of Orpheus, they inflict marks on their women, because of that misdeed.

from Phanocles, Hellenistic poet

The Fragmentation of Greece

The best we can do is first, to make the reasonable assumption that Greek homosexuality satisfied a need not otherwise adequately satisfied in Greek society, secondly, to identify that need and thirdly, to identify the factors which allowed and even encouraged satisfaction of the need by homosexual eros in the particular form which it took in the Greek world. It seems to me that the need in question was a need for personal relationships of an intensity not commonly found within marriage or in the relations between parents and children or in those between the individual and the community as a whole. The deficiencies of familial and communal relationships can be derived from the political fragmentation of the Greek world. The Greek city-state was continuously confronted with the problems of survival in competition with aggressive neigh-bours, and for this reason the fighter, the adult male citizen, was the person who mattered. The power to deliberate and take political decisions and the authority to approve or disapprove of social and cultural innovation were strongly vested in the adult male citizens of the community; the inadequacy of women as fighters promoted a general devaluation of the intellectual capacity and emotional stability of women; and the young male was judged by such indication as he afforded of his worth as a potential fighter . . .

The Greeks neither inherited nor developed a belief that a divine power had revealed to mankind a code of laws for the regulation of sexual behaviour; they had no religious institution possessed of the authority to enforce sexual prohibitions. Confronted by cultures older and richer and more elaborate than theirs, cultures which none the less differed greatly from each other, the Greeks felt free to select, adapt, develop and – above all – innovate. Fragmented as they were into tiny political units, they were constantly aware of the extent to which morals and manners are local. This awareness also disposed them to enjoy the products of their own inventiveness and to attribute a similar enjoyment to their deities and heroes.

from Kenneth Dover, Greek Homosexuality *(1978)*

A Time and a Place

Pericles was right in what he said to Sophocles, when the latter was his colleague as a General, at a meeting with him on common business. A beautiful boy happened to go by and Sophocles remarked: 'What a pretty boy, Pericles!' 'A general', Pericles replied, 'should keep his eye from trespassing as well as his hands.' But if Sophocles had made the same remark during a trial of athletes, he could not fairly have been blamed. Such is the force of time and place.

from On Duties, *by the Roman orator and statesman Cicero (106–43 BC)*

A Favour and a Threat

My love and I are yours to command
Aurelius –
    with the following 'modest' reservation:
if ever at any time you've held
a chaste good in your mind,
    unmarred by whatever desires,
modestly keep this boy of mine in like state.
I do not refer
    to the menace of common contacts,
to those set on their business
coming and going in the streets,
it is you
    and your punitive penis
I fear –
    a threat to all sorts and conditions of youth.
Wag this maleficent instrument
where, when and as much as you may
on whatever occasions occur
outside your domestic circle,
only withhold one item from its attentions . . .
I present this modest request. But should
a congenital turpitude
    take you and prick you into besetting Catullus's love with pitfalls
of seduction
look for the luckless fate of the common adulterer:
he who
    with ankles clamped

and door open
    feels the horse-radish
(suitably cut for withdrawal)
    splitting him,
or the mullet's fins.
      a poem by the Roman poet Catullus (c. 84–c. 54 BC)

Memories

Yes, Memmius, once
you filled me truly
slowly – daily –
with the length
of your great beam
and supine I
received it duly.
      a poem by Catullus

Enslaved

Love of Lyciscus holds me now, who prides himself
that his tenderness surpasses that of any girl,
from whom no frank advice or urgent contumely
on the part of my friends can set me free,
but only another blaze of desire, for a fair girl
or a sleek boy, long hair put up in a knot.
      from Horace, Epode 11. Horace (65–8 BC) was a Roman soldier who became a poet and
      won both fame and fortune in his lifetime.

Pliant Boys

If ever I have an enemy, let him love girls; let him delight in a boy if ever I have a
friend! Down a smooth stream in a safe skiff you glide: for how can the waves of a
tiny channel hurt you? A boy's heart is often mollified by a single word, whereas
a girl will scarce relent though your blood be shed.
      a poem by the Roman lawyer turned poet Propertius (c. 50 – after 16 BC)

The Abduction of Ganymede

The King of Heaven once was fired with love
Of Ganymede and something was devised
That Jove would rather be than what he was.
Yet no bird would he deign to be but one

That had the power to bear his thunderbolts.
At once his spurious pinions beat the breeze
And off he swept the Trojan lad; who now,
Mixing the nectar, waits in heaven above
(Though Juno frowns) and hands the cup to Jove.

> *from* Metamorphoses, *by the Roman poet Ovid (43* BC – AD *18). The work collected together the myths, legends and fables of the ancient world and exercised an enormous influence over future generations of writers and artists in Europe.*

Telling Father

'When I was in Asia,' Eumolpus began, 'on work connected with the administration of finance there, I was billeted in a private house in Pergamum. My stay there was a delightful one. Not only were my accommodations both comfortable and civilised, but my host's son was a boy of extraordinary beauty. Under the circumstances, my strategy as you may have guessed, was to become the boy's lover without in any way arousing the father's suspicions. So whenever the conversation at dinner happened to touch on pederasty, I affected to be so scandalised and protested so vigorously that my modesty was offended even by the mere mention of such things, that everyone, and especially the boy's mother, took me to be a philosophical saint. In no time at all, on the pretext of keeping possible seducers from setting foot in the house, I was soon chaperoning the boy on his way to the gymnasium, supervising his studies, and acting as his adviser and moral tutor.

'One day, as it happened, we were taking our rest in the dining room, since a public holiday had cut short our studies and the fatigue that comes from too much merry-making had left us too tired even to climb upstairs to bed. With a trembling voice I made my prayer to Venus: "O goddess," I whispered, "if I can kiss this sleeping boy without his noticing it, tomorrow I will present him with a pair of doves." Tempted by the price I put on my pleasure, the little impostor started to snore away. For my part, I crept close to him and stole several kisses. Pleased with this auspicious beginning, I rose early the next morning, brought back a pair of doves to the waiting boy and so fulfilled my vow.

'The following night the same opportunity presented itself, but this time I made a slight change in the form of my vow. "O goddess," I whispered, "if I can caress this boy's body with a free hand, tomorrow I will bring him a pair of the finest fighting-cocks in the world. But he must not feel anything at all." At this the boy quickly snuggled closer, half-afraid, I think, that I might fall asleep before I touched him. I swiftly relieved him of his fears and with roving hands took my pleasure of his whole body, all but the supreme bliss. The following morning, to his delight, I brought him back the gift I had promised.

'Once again on the third night, I seized my chance. By this time the boy barely pretended to be asleep, and I rose and whispered in his ear: "O immortal gods, if I may take from this sleeping boy the perfect pleasure of my dreams, I will bring him tomorrow a splendid Macedonian stallion. But on one condition only: he must not feel a thing." Never did the boy sleep more soundly. Filling my hands with his milk-white skin, I bound my lips to his, and with one supreme effort, fulfilled my every dream. The next morning he sat eagerly waiting for me in his room. As you can perhaps imagine, it is one thing to buy doves and fighting-cocks, but quite another to buy a stallion. Besides, I was apprehensive that the sheer size of such a gift might make my generosity suspect. So I strolled about for a few hours and then came back, giving the boy nothing more than a kiss. Bewildered, he looked about everywhere, then threw his arms around my neck and said, "Please, sir, where's the stallion?"

'This breach of my word, of course, shut the door against me, but it was not long before I had my way with him again. In fact, several days later, another festival gave me my opportunity once more. As soon as I heard his father snoring away, I begged the boy to make it up with me, or rather, to let me make love to him; in short, I used all those arguments which only a frustrated lover knows how to use. He was still angry, however, and to all my pleas he said nothing but, "Go back to sleep or I'll tell my father." But there is no refusal so final that a determined lover cannot somehow get around it. So, quite ignoring his refrain about waking his father, I slipped into bed beside him, and after a brief and none too convincing resistance on his part, I had my way with him. Apparently this high-handed treatment did not in the least displease him. True he reproached me for breaking my word and told me that he had suffered from the jeers of his friends to whom he had boasted of my generosity, but then he said: "Just to show you I'm not like you, you can do it again if you want.' So we made it up, and after enjoying myself a second time at his own invitation, I fell off into a deep sleep. But the boy with all the passive ardour of his age, was still dissatisfied even with my double proof of affection, and in a short while he prodded me awake, whispering, "Don't you want to do it again?" The offer was by no means unwelcome and I accepted with pleasure. Finally after a great deal of panting and sweating, I managed to oblige him and immediately dropped off to sleep, completely exhausted. In less than an hour he was pinching me again: "Why don't we do it some more," he asked. I was furious at being constantly reawakened and angrily turned his own words against him. "Go back to sleep," I cried, "or I'll tell your father." '

from The Satyricon *by Petronius (d. AD 69). A courtier of the Emperor Nero – Tacitus suggested indeed that for a while he was the Emperor's 'arbiter of taste' – Petronius committed suicide, and the note he left detailed the Emperor's vices.*

Make your Lover a Friend

Every friend loves, but not all men
Who love are friends. You'll find this true,
Then, whomsoever you may love,
Be his friend too.

an epigram by Martial (c. AD 40–104), a Spanish poet who earned his living in Rome from his poetry. He never married.

A Change of Heart

Young Hyllus, why refuse today
What yesterday you freely granted,
Suddenly harsh and obdurate,
Who once agreed to all I wanted?

You plead your beard, your weight of years,
Your hairy chest in mitigation?
To turn a boy into a man,
How long was last night's duration?

Why Hyllus, do you mock at me,
Turning affection into scorning?
If last night you were still a boy,
How can you be a man this morning?

an epigram by Martial

Crystal-Clear

Your lad is sore in front
And you itch at the rear;
I'm no clairvoyant but
I see things crystal-clear!

an epigram by Martial

The Twins

Down to a different crotch goes each twin brother:
Are they more alike or less like each other?

an epigram by Martial

Off the Guest List

At public baths you pick each dinner guest
And muster up the evening's company;
I've never been invited, I protest:
Perhaps, when naked, I don't please your eye.

an epigram by Martial

Butch Bride

Do you see that man, Decianus, with unkempt hair, of whose stern brow even you are afraid, and who keeps talking of the Curii and our champions the Camilli? Put no faith in his appearance: yesterday he got married – to a man.

an epigram by Martial

Tell-Tale Glances

That lover of gloomy cloaks, all Baetic-covered and ash-coloured, who thinks that scarlet-dressed folk are not real men, and calls amethyst-coloured garments women's clothes, and praises everything that is in its natural state, although he may always go in for dark colours, he's got greenery-yallery morals. He'll ask why I suspect him of being effeminate. We bathe together: he never looks at anything up above, but gazes with guzzling eyes at the he-men, and looks at their pricks with twitching lips. Do you ask who he is? The name's gone out of my mind.

an epigram by Martial

Disappointed Shopper

The slave-dealer asked me 100,000 sesterces for a boy: I just laughed, but Phoebus handed it over at once. My prick is sorry about this and complains to itself about me, and Phoebus gets congratulated at my expense. Ah, but Phoebus' prick presented him with two million sesterces: if you give me that much, I'll be able to pay more.

an epigram by Martial

The Theban Band

The sacred band, we are told, was first formed by Gorgidas, of three hundred chosen men, to whom the city furnished exercise and maintenance, and who encamped in the Cadmeia; for which reason, too, they were called the city band; for citadels in those days were properly called cities. But some say that this band was composed of lovers and beloved. And a pleasantry of Pammenes is cited, in which he said that Homer's Nestor was no tactician when he urged the Greeks to form in companies by clans and tribes . . . since he should have stationed lover by beloved. For tribesmen and clansmen make little account of tribesmen and clansmen in times of danger; whereas, a band that is held together by the friendship between lovers is indissoluble and not to be broken, since the lovers are ashamed to play the coward before their lovers, and both stand firm in danger to protect each other. Nor is this a wonder, since men have more regard for their lovers even when absent than for others who are present, as was true of him who, when his enemy was about to slay him where he lay, earnestly besought him to run his sword through his breast, 'in order', as he said, 'that my beloved may not have to blush at the sight of my body with a wound in the back'. It is related, too, that Iolaus who shared the labours of Hercules and fought by his side was beloved of him. And Aristotle says that even down to his day the tomb of Iolaus was a place where lovers and beloved plighted mutual faith. It was natural, then, that the band should also be called sacred, because even Plato calls the lover a friend 'inspired of God'. It is said, moreover, that the band was never beaten, until the battle of Chaeronea; and when, after the battle, Philip [of Macedonia] was surveying the dead, and stopped at the place where the three hundred were lying, all where they had faced the long spears of his phalanx, he was amazed, and on learning that this was the band of lovers and beloved, burst into tears and said: 'Perish miserably they who think that these men did or suffered aught disgraceful.'

from the Greek writer Plutarch (AD c. 46–c. 120).

Slut

And as to the loves of Hercules, it is difficult to record them because of their number.

from Plutarch

Caesar's Past

The only specific charge of unnatural practices ever brought against him was that he had been King Nicomedes' bedfellow – always a dark stain on his reputation and frequently quoted by his enemies. Licinius Calvus published the notorious verses:

> The riches of Bithynia's King
> Who Caesar on his couch abused.

Dolabella called him 'the Queen's rival and inner partner of the royal bed', and Curio the Elder: 'Nicomedes' Bithynian brothel'. Bibulus, Caesar's colleague in the consulship, described him in an edict as 'the Queen of Bithynia . . . who once wanted to sleep with a monarch, but now wants to be one.' And Marcus Brutus recorded that, about the same time, one Octavius, a scatterbrain creature who would say the first thing that came into his head, walked into a packed assembly where he saluted Pompey as 'King' and Caesar as 'Queen'. Moreover, Gaius Memmius directly charges Caesar with having joined a group of Nicomedes' debauched young friends at a banquet, where he acted as a royal cup-bearer; and adds that certain Roman merchants, whose names he supplies, were present as guests. Cicero, too, not only wrote in several letters:

> Caesar was led by Nicomedes' attendants to the royal bedchamber, where he lay on a golden couch, dressed in a purple shift . . . So this descendant of Venus lost his virginity in Bithynia

but also once interrupted Caesar while he was addressing the House in defence of Nicomedes' daughter Nysa and listing his obligations to Nicomedes himself. 'Enough of that,' Cicero shouted, 'if you please! We all know what he gave you, and what you gave in return.' Lastly, when Caesar's own soldiers followed his decorated chariot in the Gallic triumph, chanting ribald songs, as they were privileged to do, this was one of them:

Gaul was brought to shame by Caesar;
    By King Nicomedes, he.
Here comes Caesar, wreathed in triumph
    For his Gallic victory!
Nicomedes wears no laurels,
    Though the greatest of the three.

from The Twelve Caesars, *by the Roman historian and gossip Suetonius (*AD *c. 70–c. 140).*
Suetonius was for a time secretary to the Emperor Hadrian, but was banished from the
court for an indiscretion with the Empress.

Tiberius

On retiring to Capreae he made himself a private sporting-house, where sexual extravagances were practised for his secret pleasure. Bevies of girls and young men, whom he collected from all over the Empire as adepts in unnatural practices, and known as *spintriae*, would copulate before him in groups of three, to excite his waning passions. A number of small rooms were furnished with the most indecent pictures and statuary obtainable, also certain erotic manuals from Elephantis in Egypt; the inmates of the establishment would know from these exactly what was expected of them. He furthermore devised little nooks of lechery in the woods and glades of the island, and had boys and girls dressed up as Pans and nymphs prostituting themselves in front of caverns or grottoes . . . The story goes that once, while sacrificing, he took an erotic fancy to the acolyte who carried the incense casket, and could hardly wait for the ceremony to end before hurrying him and his brother, the sacred trumpeter, out of the temple and indecently assaulting them both. When they jointly protested at this disgusting behaviour he had their legs broken.

from Suetonius, The Twelve Caesars

Caligula

He had not the slightest regard for chastity, either his own or others', and was accused of homosexual relations, both active and passive, with Marcus Lepidus, also Mnester the comedian, and various foreign hostages; moreover, a young man of consular family, Valerius Catullus, revealed publicly that he had buggered the Emperor, and quite worn himself out in the process.

from Suetonius, The Twelve Caesars

The Vain General

Otho, who peeked at himself to see how his armour looked
Before riding into battle. A fine heroic trophy
That was indeed, fit matter for modern history books,
A civil war where mirrors formed part of the fighting kit!

To polish off a rival *and* keep your complexion fresh
Demands consummate generalship; to camp in palatial splendour
On the field of battle *and* give yourself a face pack
Argues true courage. No Eastern warrior queen,
Not Cleopatra herself aboard that unlucky flagship,
Behaved in such a fashion.

> from Juvenal's Satires. The most famous satirist of his age, Juvenal (c. AD 60–136) was a
> contemporary of Martial, and placed Roman society under his sharp gaze.

A Sinecure

You remember that actor they called 'the Danube Basin'?
Everyone knows why during his married life
He showered gifts on his wife – yet left both house and fortune
To a favoured freedman. Girls can do well for themselves
If they don't mind sleeping third in the marriage bed.

> from Juvenal's Satires

Unnatural Contracts

A wealthy, well-born
Man is betrothed in marriage to another man
And you do nothing! Not a shake of the helmet, no pounding
The ground with your spear, not even a complaint
To your father! Away with you then, remove yourself
From the broad Roman acres that bear your name, and suffer
Neglect at your hands! This is the kind of talk
We shall hear: 'I must go down tomorrow
First thing: a special engagement.'
'What's happening?' 'Need you ask?
I'm going to a wedding. Old So-and-so's got his boyfriend
To the altar at last – just a few close friends are invited.'
We have only to wait now: soon such things will be done,
And done in public: male brides will yearn for a mention
In the daily gazette. But still they have one big problem
Of a painful kind: they can't keep their marriages solvent
By producing babies. Nature knows best: their desires
Have no physical issue.

> from Juvenal's Satires

Dishonest Romans

Appearances are deceptive
Every back street swarms with solemn faced humbuggers
You here – have *you* the nerve to thunder at vice, who are
The most notorious dyke among all our Socratic fairies?

Your shaggy limbs and the bristling hair on your forearms
Suggest a fierce male virtue: but the surgeon called in
To lance your swollen piles dissolves in laughter
At the sight of the well-smoothed passage. Such creatures talk
In a clipped, laconic style, and crop their hair crew-cut fashion,
As short as their eyebrows. I prefer the perverted
Eunuch priest of the Mother Goddess: at least he's open
And honest about it. Gait, gestures, expression, all
Proclaim his twisted nature. He is sick, a freak of fate,
Not to be blamed. Indeed, his wretched self-exposure,
The very strength of his passion, beg pity and forgiveness.
Far worse is he who attacks such practices with hairy
Masculine fervour, and after much talk of virtue
Proceeds to cock his dish like a perfect lady.

> *from Juvenal's* Satires

Lament of the Ageing Hustler

JUVENAL: Why do you look so gloomy, Naevolus?
     You used to take life as it came –
     The provincial squire in person, a dinner-table wit
     Whose jokes had an edge of urban sophistication.
     What a change today – that sick-hand look, that unkempt
     Bush of dry hair! Your complexion's lost all the glow . . .
     You've lost weight too,
     You seem to have transformed . . .
     It's not so long, I recall, since you used to hang around
     The temples of Ceres and Isis, or Ganymede's little shrine
     . . . all such places are hot spots for easy women.
     You laid them by dozens then, and something you don't mention
     More often than not you had their husbands, too.
NAEVOLUS: Many have made a packet from my way of life, but it's never
     Brought me any decent pickings. Sometimes I'll collect
     A greasy street-cloak, coarse and crudely dyed,
     Cut from a bolt of loose-woven Gallic cloth, or
     Some silver-plated gewgaw, lacking a hallmark.
     Mankind is ruled by the Fates, they govern those private
     Parts that our clothes conceal. If your stars go against you
     The fantastic size of your cock will get you precisely nowhere
     However much Virro may have drooled at the spectacle
     Of your naked charms, though love-letters come in by the dozen
     Imploring your favours, though – quote –
     A man is attracted
     By the very sight of – a pansy. Yet what could be lower
     Than a close-fisted queer? 'I paid you so much then,'

He says, 'and a bit more later, and more that other time –'
Working it out by piece-rates.
'Well,' I say, 'fetch the accountant
With his reckoner and tables, tot up the total figure:
A miserable five thousand. Now list my services. Do you
Suppose it's easy, or fun, this job of cramming
My cock up into your guts till I'm stopped by last night's supper?
The slave who ploughs his master's field has less trouble
Than the one who ploughs him.'
'But you used to fancy yourself
As a pretty young boy,' he says, 'a latter-day Ganymede.'
'Can't your sort ever show kindness to your minions, your humble
Ploughboys of pleasure? Are you so tight in purse
That you even grudge the expense of your peculiar vices?'
What a creature! But you are obliged to send him presents . . .
JUVENAL: Indeed,
You have cause for complaint here, Naevolus. But what
Does he say on the other side?
NAEVOLUS: Takes no notice at all,
He's so busy looking around for another two-legged donkey
As my replacement . . .
What's my best move now, after all these wasted years
And disappointed hopes? The bloom of life will wither
Too soon, our miserable span on earth is running out . . .
JUVENAL: Never fear: so long as these Seven Hills stand fast
You'll always have friends in the trade, they'll still come flocking
From near and far, by ship or by coach.
from Juvenal, Satire IX

Toy Boy

Trajan was much shrewder and more tactful than some of the group of pederasts who surrounded him. His fellow Spaniard, the champion and confidant of the young Hadrian, Licinius Sura, so loaded his bed-fellows with wealth that the scandal was recounted by the exiled philosopher Epictetus to Arrian in far-off Nikopolis. More embarrassing and instructive still to Trajan of the limits of tolerable pederastic behaviour in those holding high positions was the fate of his cultivated friend, Vibius Maximus, whom he had appointed Prefect of Egypt from 103 to 107. The Prefect was accused by some Alexandrian dignitaries of financial corruption, extortion, interfering with magistracies and bribing the father of a handsome seventeen-year-old, Theon, whom he then proceeded to corrupt in another way. The Prefect's attentions went beyond all acceptable bounds of propriety and had the disastrous effect of turning his beloved's head. The boy not only slept with him in the state bed but emerged from it among the morning suitors in the palace and flagrantly flaunted the signs of the previous night's intercourse. He sat next to the Prefect on the magistrate's rostrum, was paraded at official banquets and at prefectorial reviews and inspections. He cheeked the court chamberlain to his face in public, mocked the grovelling clients and gaily missed both his school and training in the palaestra. Ironically, the trial and condemnation of Vibius Maximus (on financial not sexual charges) took place in Rome before his friend Trajan himself, who must have found the whole episode painfully embarrassing, resolving even more to avoid such appalling and destructive indiscretions himself.

from Royston Lambert, Beloved and God: The Story of Hadrian and Antinous (1984)

CHAPTER TWO

The Middle Ages

It was, curiously, the impact of the ideas of a Greek philosopher – Aristotle – on Christian thought during the twelfth and thirteenth centuries that led to the wholesale persecution and condemnation of men who indulged their homosexual desires. Before that time it has been suggested that European society remained reasonably tolerant of homosexual behaviour, despite the extraordinarily puritanical ethics proposed by many early Christian thinkers such as St Paul and St Augustine. Aristotle based his philosophy on the idea that human behaviour ought to be in harmony with nature, and this became a fundamental feature of Christian thought at a time when theologians began to impose a more legalistic and rigid interpretation on Christianity. This fitted in with an attempt by the ecclesiastical authorities to eliminate local customs and practices in an effort to impose uniform standards across the whole of Christendom. This systematisation of the faith was led by the papacy, which increased its power over the Church during the eleventh century. The Inquisition was one agent in this process, leading the hunt for heresy which became a major preoccupation of the Church. The Dominican friars staffed the tribunals to investigate contemporary deviance, and became notorious for their intolerance. Such developments provided splendid opportunities for moralists to sound off about the iniquities of man and his sexual depravity. Peter Damian, who appears from his writings to have been quite unhinged,[1] was one of those who adapted Aristotle's idea of nature as a way of condemning homosexuality for its supposed unnaturalness. But it was in a twelfth-century work by Alan of Lille, *The Complaint of Nature*,[2] that such an idea was fully developed, and this provided a model for later writers.

The word 'bugger' has its origins in this period. Heresy had flourished during the tenth century in Bulgaria, and each new manifestation of unorthodoxy throughout Europe was described as one more branch of the Bulgarian heresy. Heretics were believed to be addicted to every vice, and their sexual practices were much sensationalised from the pulpits by friars as keen to draw an audience for their ideas by these means as any contemporary tabloid editor engaged in the same enterprise. 'Bugger' is just one corruption of the word 'Bulgar' that has passed down to our age, a pejorative label that has stuck.

The numbers of men who burned for their sins remained small. The medieval Church and its allies in the state were no more effective than other authorities in crushing homosexual behaviour and desire.

Two American scholars, John Boswell and Thomas Stehling, have recently exposed the existence of a powerful homosexual culture throughout the Middle Ages.[3] Much of the evidence for such a culture has long been suppressed by generations of pious and reticent medievalists eager to maintain the purity of both their medieval heroes and their modern readers.

Medieval ecclesiastical institutions were sexual hothouses in which priests and monks often fell under the spell of other members of their own sex. Many religious orders tried to curb such passions, but without success. Under some monastic rules much attention was devoted to the organisation of the dormitory. A light would often shine all night, and the younger monks were divided up throughout the dormitory (though this may simply have been a measure designed to keep the older monks happy!). Priests played a major role in education, and scholars in the universities and cathedrals often found themselves sharing beds with their tutors.

In his travels in the underworld, Dante encountered his old teacher Brunetto among the inhabitants of hell condemned to spend eternity in the company of clerics and scholars who had, like him, been guilty of the sin of Sodom.[4] Nobles, gentlemen, and knights were segregated from these clerical sinners, though their crime was the same. Dante draws an important distinction that existed in medieval society between the homosexuality of the cloister and that of the court. Warriors have left fewer literary remains of their desire, though the twelfth-century romance Eneas provides some evidence of this milieu. Ordericus Vitalis, a churchman, was one of those who depicted the court of King William Rufus (r. 1087–1100) as a place given over to almost every sexual vice. Richard the Lionheart was often warned by churchmen about his homosexual behaviour, though he found it difficult to keep his promises of restraint. A Crusader, Richard spent almost all his life in the company of other warriors. Crusading society had the reputation of encouraging the homosexual interests of participating knights. The King of France in the fourteenth century used such stories to destroy the most powerful order of crusading knights, the Knights Templar.[5]

In some ways the most interesting surviving evidence of these centuries is the interrogation of Arnold Verniolle and his sexual partners in 1323. This evidence is remarkable in that it is so complete. Arnold was clearly a man whose tastes were exclusively homosexual, and his tales of seducing his young friends should make us wary of accepting traditional interpretations which turn medieval society into a place where sexual deviance was well-nigh impossible to practise. Arnold would probably have survived had he not been caught up in a hunt for heretics in his local district. The court devoted most of its time to questioning him about his successful attempt to impersonate a priest, which was a much more serious offence than his sexual delinquency. As it was, two of his judges pleaded for a more lenient punishment, though they failed to persuade a majority of the judges, who passed a sentence imprisoning him for life.

Biblical Foundations

And there came two angels to Sodom at even; and Lot sat in the gate of Sodom: and Lot seeing them rose up to meet them; and he bowed with his face toward the ground; And he said, Behold now, my lords, turn in, I pray you, into your servant's house, and tarry all night, and wash your feet, and ye shall rise up early, and go on your ways . . . But before they lay down, the men of the city, even the men of Sodom, compassed the house round, both old and young . . . And they called upon Lot, and said unto him, Where are the men which came in to thee this night? bring them out unto us, that we may know them. And Lot went out at the door unto them, and shut the door after him, And said, I pray you, brethren, do not so wickedly. Behold now, I have two daughters which have not known man; let me, I pray you, bring them out unto you, and do ye to them as is good in your eyes: only unto these men do nothing . . . Then the Lord rained upon Sodom and upon Gomorrah brimstone and fire from the Lord out of the heaven; And he overthrew those cities, and all the plain, and all the inhabitants of the cities, and that which grew upon the ground.
> Genesis 19: 1–25

If a man also lie with mankind, as he lieth with a woman, both of them have committed an abomination: they shall surely be put to death; their blood shall be upon them.
> Leviticus 20: 13

I am distressed for thee, my brother Jonathan: very pleasant hast thou been unto me: thy love for me was wonderful, passing the love of women.
> 2 Samuel 1: 26

Know ye not that the unrighteous shall not inherit the kingdom of God? Be not deceived: neither fornicators, nor idolaters, nor adulterers, nor effeminate, nor abusers of themselves with mankind.
> 1 Corinthians 6: 9

Double Agent

There is a constant deception at play in his double sex:
He's a woman when passive, but when active in shameful deeds, he's a man.
> from a poem by Ennodius (c. 473–521), a French priest who became Bishop of Pavia

Unyielding Victim

Horace composed an ode about a certain boy
Who could easily enough have been a pretty girl.
Over his ivory neck flowed hair
Brighter than yellow gold, the kind I have always loved.
His forehead was white as snow, his luminous eyes black as pitch;

His unfledged cheeks full of pleasing sweetness
When they gleamed bright white and red.
His nose was straight, lips blazing, teeth lovely,
Chin shaped after a perfectly proportioned model.
Anyone wondering about the body which lay hidden under his clothes
Would be gratified, for the boy's body matched his face.
The sight of his face, radiant and full of beauty,
Kindled the observer's heart with the torch of love.
But this boy — so beautiful, so extraordinary,
An enticement to anyone catching sight of him —
Nature has moulded wild and stern:
He would sooner die than consent to love.
Rough and thankless, like a tiger cub,
He only laughed at the gentlest words of a suitor,
Laughed at attentions doomed to have no effect,
Laughed at a sighing lover's tears.
He mocked those he himself caused to die.
Wicked indeed this one, and as cruel as wicked,
Who with this vice in his character keeps his body from being his glory.
A handsome face demands a good mind, and a yielding one,
Not puffed up but ready for anything.
The little flower of youth is fleeting and too brief;
It soon withers, falls, and knows not how to revive.
This flesh is now so smooth, so milky, so unblemished,
So good, so handsome, so slippery, so tender.
Yet the time will come when it will become ugly and rough,
When this flesh, dear boyish flesh, will become worthless.
Therefore while you flower, take up ripe practices.
While you are in demand and able, be not slow to yield to an eager lover.
For this you will be prized, not made less of.
These words of my request, most beloved,
Are sent to you alone; do not show them to many others.

A poem by Marbod of Rennes (c. 1035–1123), a French priest who taught for most of his life at Angers cathedral, where he was master of the cathedral school. He became Bishop of Rennes in 1096, and was the author of a large amount of homosexual verse.

A Wicked Sin

There are a hundred thousand sins invented by the devil,
And with them he drags this world to punishment's abyss
Where those who are imprisoned die by being unable to die —
Indeed, they would rather die because no death could equal their pain.
There that wretch rages, roasted by eternal flames:
Brow, eyes, nostrils, neck, ears,
Mouth, throat, and breasts become fodder for flames.

Back, sides, and belly blaze without relief;
Guilty hips and cock never cool.
O how sad the man to be handed over to those flames!
How gloomy he becomes, now that he has become food for snakes;
He can scarcely sustain the powerful stench hour after hour.
He is beaten on all sides with the lashes of his savage tormentors.
And though the vengeance of Dis is hard on everyone,
There are, nonetheless, degrees of punishment.
As sins are weighed so are they punished:
Greater punishments for greater sins, and lesser for lesser.
Thus copulation performed by members of a single sex,
A crime less serious than none, is punished more severely than any other.
Therefore, anyone fearing punishment who has not eased his reins to sin
Should not ease them now. And anyone guilty of this disgrace should draw his
    back in.
O wicked sin! it is as if a billy goat went after a kid
When there was no lack of female goats; to him the world's grief clings.
Less serious than none, it is punished more severely than all.
    a poem by Marbod of Rennes

Unpromising Terrain

I hate your disdain, your intractable heart;
I hate a hard heart, along with rude manners;
I hate pompous young men, hard as flint.
A pliant tree is pleasing; I hate an inflexible oak.
    a poem by Baudri of Bourgueil (1046–1130), a French Benedictine monk who had been a
    pupil of Marbod of Rennes at Angers. He rose to become abbot and was made Archbishop
    of Dol in 1107. Thomas Stehling, who has studied his poetry, writes that 'in reading Baudri
    we get the impression he fell in love with everyone, both men and women.'

Divine Creation

What we are is a crime, if it is a crime to love,
For the God who made me live made me love.
    from a poem by Baudri of Bourgueil

Caprice

. . . all youth is inconstant . . .
    from a poem by Baudri of Bourgueil

Unsafe

A boy is hardly a safe thing; don't trust yourself to some of them.
    Hildebert of Lavardin (c. 1055–1133), Archbishop of Tours

The Sins of the Florentines

In the whole world I don't think two sins are more abominable than those the Florentines commit. The first is usury and infidelity and the second is so abominable I don't dare mention it.

a statement by Pope Gregory XI (Pope, 1073–85)

The Court of King William Rufus

At that time effeminates set the fashion in many parts of the world: foul catamites, doomed to eternal fire, unrestrainedly pursued their revels and shamelessly gave themselves up to the filth of sodomy. They rejected the traditions of honest men, ridiculed the counsel of priests, and persisted in their barbarous way of life and style of dress. They parted their hair from the crown of the head to the forehead, grew long and luxurious locks like women, and loved to deck themselves in long, over-tight shirts and tunics. Some of them frivolled away their time, spending it as they chose without regard for the law of God or the customs of their ancestors. They devoted their nights to feasts and drinking-bouts, idle chatter, dice, games of chance and other sports, and they slept all day . . . Our wanton youth is sunk in effeminacy.

from Ordericus Vitalis (1075–1143?), The Ecclesiastical History (1141)

Clerical Crimes

I will bring into the light what was fashioned secretly in the workshop of ancient wickedness. I do not accept that this hidden thing should go on, namely, that certain ones who are filled with the poison of this crime, as if taking heart, should confess to one another to keep the knowledge of their guilt from becoming known to others. While they shame the face of men, the authors of this guilt become the judges. The indiscreet indulgence which each desires to be applied to himself, he rejoices to bestow on the other through a delegated change of roles. So it happens that although they ought to be penitents for their great crimes, nonetheless their faces do not pale with fasting, nor do their bodies waste away with thinness. While the belly is in no way restrained from the immoderate reception of food, the spirit is shamefully inflamed to the ardour of habitual lust, with the result that the one who had shed tears for what was committed continues to commit more seriously what should be mourned.

from The Book of Gomorrah (c. 1056), by Peter Damian (c. 1007–72)

Homage to Beauty

Who acts out of modesty to handsome men?

Hilary the Englishman (twelfth century), a student of Abelard's

Burning Desire

Venus is kindled by anything, but her greatest heat
Comes from the sin of sodomy, as anyone who has tried it knows.
  Twelfth-century graffiti

An Unsuitable Attachment

The Queen addresses her daughter Lavine, who has just confessed her love for the knight Eneas.

What have you said, foolish madwoman? Do you know to whom you have given yourself? This wretch is of the sort who have hardly any interest in women. He prefers the opposite trade: he will not eat hens, but he loves very much the flesh of a cock. He would prefer to embrace a boy rather than you or any other woman. He does not know how to play with women, and would not parley at the wicket-gate; but he loves very much the breech of a young man. The Trojans are raised on this. You have chosen very poorly. Have you not heard how he mistreated Dido? Never did a woman have any good from him, nor do I think you will have, from a traitor and a sodomite. He will always be ready to abandon you. If he finds any sweet boy, it will seem fair and good to him that you let him pursue his love. And if he can attract the boy by means of you, he will not find it too outrageous to make an exchange, so that the boy will have his pleasure from you, while in turn sufficing for him. He will gladly let the boy mount you, if he in turn can ride him: he does not love coney fur.

It would quickly be the end of this life if all men were thus throughout the world. Never would a woman conceive; there would be a great dearth of people; no one would ever bear children, and the world would fail before a hundred years. Daughter, you have completely lost your senses, since you have taken as your love such a man, who will never care for you, and who acts so against nature that he takes men and leaves women, undoing the natural union. Take care that you never speak to me of him again. I wish you to give up the love of this sodomite wretch. Turn your heart in another direction.
  from the twelfth-century French romance Eneas, *by an unknown Norman poet*

To Beguile is not to Love

That you pursue boys, love them, and are loved by them
Is worthless activity, not for a man; it's bird-hunting for a fool.
Did I say you love them? Yes, if hate can manifest love,
Or if deluding them with clever traps is love.
You teach sin and put curbs on sinning;
Sinning's season begins with you, Tatius.
To enter into sin, they always pay with a gift,
And to get you to conceal the deed, they pay again with a gift.

The fault is yours that their lives and reputation suffer;
Your fault that they lose their good name and esteem.
Wounds must be added to wounds, labour to labour –
To succeed, inflict new wounds on old.
To get the better of him, let him feed on scant oats;
Then he'll never get enough, so you can get the better of him.
This delicate diet, dear, has already kept yours in line for you,
And my colt has yielded to a strong horse.

a poem by Geoffrey of Winchester (d. 1107)

Subversion

Men make women of themselves, and stallions become mares.

Walter of Chatillon (c. 1135–after 1184)

Richard the Lionheart

During these years another, a darker side of Richard's character began to take shape. Contemporary writers furnish us with no details, but Richard we know chose men, rather than women, as his usual sexual partners. As a boy he had been very close to Queen Eleanor [his mother] and was always her favourite son, brought up in the predominantly feminine environment of the queen's court at Poitiers . . . Richard's aversion to women was manifested at the outset of his reign: his coronation banquet was a bachelor party . . . Richard by preference spent almost all of his life in male company [chiefly with soldiers] . . . We simply do not know who his sexual partners were, except possibly for Philip Augustus [King of France] . . . At some point during the period around Christmas 1190 [which he spent at Messina in Sicily on his way to the Holy Land], Richard faced a crisis in his personal life. To what extent he had been an active homosexual, we do not know; but stories about his abnormal sexual preferences were widely current. These suspicions were potentially serious in their implications. The Church took an extremely dim view of homosexual behaviour and classed it among the most serious types of sexual offences . . . [At that time, possibly as a result of ecclesiastical pressure, Richard] apparently decided to abjure his preferences for male sexual partners. He called the eminent churchmen who were with the army to meet privately with him in the chapel of Reginald de Moyac. There in the presence of his spiritual fathers Richard appeared barefoot, carrying three bundles of branches made up as scourges. Falling to his knees in the chapel, surrounded by his bishops and clerics, Richard confessed his past misbehaviour and asked the clergy to assign him a suitable punishment for his sins. They pronounced him absolved . . . Richard did apparently make considerable efforts for a time to live up to the commitment he made at Messina and it is surely not coincidental that he was married only a few months after this episode . . . in 1195 Richard was visited by a hermit . . . he had again fallen in with homosexual companions [while on Crusade in the Holy Land]. The hermit who visited the king chose the occasion to excoriate Richard's sexual diversions and warned him of the vengeance that God would take on him if persisted in imitating the wantonness of Sodom. The immediate effect of the hermit's warning was negligible. Richard was annoyed and not at all inclined to change his habits or his friends. The hermit found it prudent to withdraw from the court as soon as he had preached his sermon and, indeed, went into hiding. Presumably he had reason to think that Richard might repay him rudely for the remarks that he had made. At the end of March, however, Richard fell gravely ill and on his sickbed the hermit's warning suddenly hit him with great force. He called the clergy to his bedside, confessed the details of his misdeeds, and received absolution for his sins. Queen Berengaria [his wife] was summoned from Poitiers where she had been living in seclusion . . . [and Richard for a time turned over a new leaf].

from J. A. Brundage, Richard the Lionheart (1974)

Saladin

Ranking with Alexander, Caesar, and Bonaparte, the eminent and glorious Saladin (Sellah-ed-Deen), Sultan of Egypt and Syria, was like Rome's greatest emperor 'the husband of all women and the wife of all men', a habitual pederast. Arab historians of the twelfth century cited him as being wise, noble and courageous, coping with the invading Crusaders with martial prudence but, when it came to fair beardless youths, more salacious than a he-goat. They attributed this to early impotence.

from Allen Edwardes, The Jewel in the Lotus (1961)

Plain Speaking

'Alas!' says Helen, 'I grieve over you:
You openly despise sex with women.
Through you the right order of things is overturned and law perishes.
Since you do not procreate, why did your father beget you?'
[GANYMEDE:] 'Let old men eager for children beget sons;
　　Let tender youth play freely in their lust.
　　The sport we play was invented by the gods,
　　And is still played by the worthiest men.'
[HELEN:] 'Your face, that beauty of beauties,
　　Will die along with the rest of you since
　　You won't ever marry; if by some chance you do marry,
　　Your son will preserve his father's beauty.'
[GANYMEDE:] 'I don't want my face duplicated;
　　I'd rather have it attract men with its uniqueness.
　　I hope your face will sag with age
　　Since I can see it makes me less loved.'

[HELEN:] 'O how happy is the love of the opposite sexes
 When a man caresses a woman in mutual embrace.
 He and she are drawn together in natural inclination;
 Birds, wild beasts, and cattle are happy in this bond.'
[GANYMEDE:] 'Man shouldn't imitate birds or cows;
 Man has been given the power to reason.
 Peasants, who can be called cattle,
 They're the ones who should be fouled with women.'
[HELEN:] 'No love of a boy ever touches the heart,
 But when one bed joins man to woman,
 This is a bond that is productive, this is right order,
 For between opposite sexes there can be equal affection.'
[GANYMEDE:] 'Opposites always disagree; the right way is like with like.
 Man can be fitted to man by elegant conjunction.
 If you don't know this, look at the gender of their articles:
 Masculine should be coupled with masculine by the rules of grammar.'
[HELEN:] 'When man's creator fashioned mankind,
 He made sure that he made women more beautiful than men
 So that men would be enticed to bond with women
 And not love men more than women.'
[GANYMEDE:] 'I might agree that it would be right to love women
 If the honesty of their behaviour corresponded to their appearance.
 But wives pollute the marriage bed
 And unmarried women make cheap marketplaces of themselves.'
[HELEN:] 'Let men blush; let nature grieve.
 Men don't care about the restraints of nature.
 Venus joins men in sterile unions;
 Boys disregard their sex and sell their legs.'
[GANYMEDE:] 'We know that honourable men approve of this act,
 For the men who run the world's government, hold its highest offices,
 And pass judgement as censors on behaviour and sin,
 They do not shun the slippery thighs of boys.'
[HELEN:] 'Let me skip over those who are inflamed by madness to do such things.
 You boys, no rational faculty defends you.
 This boy isn't acting out of pleasure;
 Therefore, he sins and offends all the more seriously.'
[GANYMEDE:] 'The smell of money is good; nobody turns down money.
 Wealth, I admit, attracts us.
 The boy who wants to get rich won't give up this sport;
 It helps boys get ahead; it makes them rich.'
[HELEN:] 'Even if we grant that boys shouldn't be blamed for this,
 No rationalization can excuse older men.
 When I see a persistent old man, I laugh at him.
 This sport is sin for grey hairs.'
[GANYMEDE:] 'I don't excuse old men reproached by their own old age.
 When they see their bristles already turning white, it's disgraceful

That they throw themselves into these games and usurp these joyful
   pleasures.
But these old men don't limit what boys can do.'
[HELEN:] 'Tell me this, boy: when a boy's looks change,
   When fleece comes on his cheeks and his face gets wrinkled,
   When a bush grows on his chest and his belly becomes rough,
   What does a cocky boy used to rubbing men think of himself?'
[GANYMEDE:] 'Maiden, you tell me, when a virgin's beauty wastes away,
   When her lips harden and her skin dries up,
   When her eyebrows get bristly and her eyes runny,
   Won't her lover then, even though he's eager, droop?'
[HELEN:] 'I only wish that you would become smooth and hairless down below
   And a woman's chamber appear there,
   So that you would become a girl, and nature take her revenge,
   Since you've wickedly declared war on her.'
[GANYMEDE:] 'I'd like to be smooth and hairless under my groin,
   But please, no woman's chamber.
   It happens that I reject women because I hate them;
   For what's the difference between a woman and a she-ass?'
[HELEN:] 'Oh! if I weren't restrained by a delicate sense of modesty,
   I'd speak now without the colours of rhetoric,
   But I am ashamed to use foul language.
   Foul things sit badly in the mouth of a maid.'
[GANYMEDE:] 'We came here prepared to talk about foul things;
   This is not the time for respectability.
   We should put religion and modesty behind us.
   Let me spare neither maiden nor truth.'
[HELEN:] 'I don't know where I should turn, for if I don't say foul things
   In this exchange, it will be said I lost,
   But if I try to match your words,
   It will savour of a slut's foul language.'
[GANYMEDE:] 'Find some stranger to fool.
   I know the boy you offered your lap to, lying flat on your back.
   Where was your dove-like innocence then?
   Suddenly you are transformed from Thais into a Sabine woman.'
[HELEN:] 'O you men who lie on top of men and let them lie on you,
   Who deprive men unnaturally of masculinity,
   You shamefully pollute yourselves and boys at night,
   And in the morning – but I'll be silent – there is wickedness in your sheets.'
[GANYMEDE:] 'O you men who have concubines sleeping in your little beds
   And who love to get wet in their female slop,
   When Thais lies on her back and opens herself to you,
   You know what her bilge smells like.'
[HELEN:] 'Thais smells like Thais because of her habits,
   But a girl smells sweeter than balsam:
   On her lips there is honey, a honeycomb in her mouth;

Happy is the man who gets to enjoy sleeping with a virgin.'
[GANYMEDE:] 'When Jupiter lies in the middle of his bed and divides his attention
    Between the two of us, turning now to Juno and now to me,
    He prefers a boy's game to a woman's when he tries it:
    Every time he is turned towards her, he either argues or snores.'
[HELEN:] 'Your Venus is sterile, unfruitful,
    And insulting to women –
    One man submitting to another in shameful transaction:
    This monstrous Venus counterfeits a woman.'
[GANYMEDE:] 'It's not monstrous to avoid a monster –
    The gaping cave with its sticky bush,
    The cave whose stink is worse than anything,
    The cave you wouldn't touch with a pole or oar.'
[HELEN:] 'Stop speaking so basely or roughly;
    Speak more modestly, filthy boy!
    If you don't care to show respect to a maiden,
    At least respect Nature and the gods.'
[GANYMEDE:] 'If things are cloaked in the trappings of fine words,
    Dressed-up filth can deceive us.
    But I will not gild dross;
    It is good for words to be akin to their substance.'

an anonymous poem from the early thirteenth century. A considerable number of such debates between Ganymede and Helen discussing the merits of homosexuality and inclining against heterosexuality survive from this period.

Contagion

Love of boys is a violent plague.

from an anonymous poem of the thirteenth or fourteenth century

Chartres

If anyone in this life wants to live not as a sodomite,
He'd better get out of Chartres, unless he wants to be
    transformed from a man into a woman.

an anonymous poem of the thirteenth or fourteenth century

Wasted Seed

Damn the semen from which no offspring come,
Which flows for nothing and produces nothing useful.

an anonymous thirteenth-century poem

Mutual Exchanges

A maid loved Graecinus, Graecinus loved a boy,
And that boy was taken only with the maid.
Graecinus handed her over to the boy, the boy gave himself to Graecinus,
And both enjoyed the fruits of their desires.

an anonymous poem of the thirteenth or fourteenth century

Edward II

It is more than likely that Edward of Caernarvon was a homosexual, but that does not mean that he was *ipso facto* incompetent or stupid, or that he could not also lead a normal heterosexual life. As a homosexual he is in very distinguished historical company, as a heterosexual he was father of one of our most spectacular kings and a remarkable family. The choice of Gaveston as his youthful companion was in the first place not his – it was the choice of his respected father, and Gaveston came to be hated by a jealous baronage not for his viciousness but for his waspish wit at their expense, his tactless pride in flaunting his royal favours, and a skill at the manly art of jousting which they could not equal. Only one chronicler specifically refers to sodomy between Edward and Gaveston – the Cistercian monk of the abbey of Meaux in the East Riding of Yorkshire – and his knife is somewhat blunted in that he does not complain of sodomy, but of 'too much sodomy'. Edward's contemporary biographer in referring to Gaveston quotes David and Jonathan and 'a love which is said to have surpassed the love of women', but he was anxious to point out that Gaveston's unpopularity was mainly due to the fact that he was both a foreigner and an upstart. Victorian historians have for the most part politely glossed over the issue – the relationship was 'innocent though frivolous' wrote Hume and 'it was reserved for a later generation to discover an element of vice in what his contemporaries viewed with pitying indignation as a stupid but faithful infatuation' wrote the benign Bishop Stubbs. Most of the chroniclers, too, hesitated to be frank – they referred to Gaveston's 'loving the king's son inordinately', Edward 'so much loved him that he called him brother', and by 'exalting overmuch a man that he had loved' he caused 'slander to the people and damage to the realm', and similar phrases which can mean much or little as the reader is inclined. Modern historians until recently have been equally hesitant. Professor Tout maintained surprisingly that 'it is impossible to take these vague charges seriously.' Professor Vickers stated that 'Edward was more unbusinesslike than vicious.' Dr Conway Davies suggested that the charges 'should be ignored' because 'they are insubstantiated.' Professor Hilda Johnstone in quoting a medical critic of 1910, politely wrote 'still less need we go so far as to find the explanation . . . in the assumption that he suffered from what "medical science recognizes under the general name of degeneracy" caused by "a diseased condition of the brain".' Maddicott, on the other hand, has no doubt that a homosexual relationship did exist . . . The truth would seem to be that Edward of Caernarvon was far from incompetent, and if, in the choice of intimate friend, there is strong evidence of homosexuality, there is no evidence that that homosexuality impaired his competence as head of state.

from H. F. Hutchinson, Edward II: The Pliant King (1971)

The Lombards

The Commons beg that all the Lombards who follow no other calling but that of merchant be made to leave the country . . . They are wicked usurers and employ all the subtle wiles of such men . . . They have now lately introduced into the land a very horrible vice which is not to be named, because of which the Realm cannot fail to be destroyed if swift punishment be not ordained.

from a parliamentary statute of the reign of Edward III (1327–77)

Medieval Slang

Like that of the modern West, the gay subculture of the High Middle Ages appears to have had its own slang, which gradually became diffused among the general population. The equivalent of 'gay', for example, was 'Ganymede'. The similarity of the word to gay in its cultural setting is striking. In an age addicted to classical literature, the invocation of Greek mythology to describe homosexual relationships not only tacitly removed the stigma conveyed by the biblical 'sodomite', the only word in common use before or after this period, but also evoked connotations of mythological sanctions, cultural superiority, and personal refinement which considerably diminished negative associations in regard to homosexuality. Although 'Ganymede' was also used derisively, it was basically devoid of moral context and could be used by gay people themselves without misgivings . . . The word 'ludus' ('game') also seems to have acquired a specialized meaning in certain circles: its use in oblique or punning references to homosexuality in many different literary contexts suggests that it was widely used with specifically gay connotations. 'Hunting' and terminology related to it figure prominently in poetry by or about gay people, and it is possible that it represented what 'cruising' describes in the gay subculture of today . . . The rich irony of Ganymede having been hunting himself when the eagle swooped down upon him doubtless added to the effectiveness of the metaphor, as did the residual association of hares with homosexuality.

Many other gay expressions are now lost or indecipherable: 'wood' may have had some sexual significance at the time, and the Roman 'mule' is contrasted in one poem with a horse, a distinction with no discernible analogy to gay slang before or after.

from John Boswell, Christianity, Social Tolerance and Homosexuality (1980)

The Trial of Arnold Verniolle

On 13 June 1323, Guillaume Roux . . . a student in the liberal arts at Pamiers, slightly over sixteen years of age . . . testified as follows . . . [After meeting Guillaume in the street] Arnold then suggested that Guillaume come to his house where he would show him books and he could stay. The two then went to Arnold's house and entered an upper room. When they were alone, Arnold showed him a book, saying it contained decretals, and after reading a bit told the speaker, 'See what these decretals say here!' When the speaker said that he didn't understand the words of the decretals, Arnold told him in the vernacular [Provençal] that it was written that if a man plays with another, and because of the warmth of their bodies semen flows, it is not as grave a sin as if a man carnally knows a woman; because, so he said, nature demands this and a man is made healthier as a result . . .

When Guillaume said he didn't believe that it was a lesser sin to so behave with a man than to know a woman carnally, Arnold told him that it is a lesser sin and that the decretal said so. Arnold then threw the speaker down on the ground, placed his hands on his back, and lay on Guillaume. He then removed the speaker's clothes and told him to spread his thighs or some evil would befall him. The speaker then spread his thighs, and Arnold got completely undressed, embraced the naked youth, kissed him, placed his penis between Guillaume's buttocks, and, moving himself as with a woman, his semen flowed between the speaker's legs. When this was accomplished, Arnold told Guillaume to do likewise to him and that he could not leave the room until he had done so. Guillaume then likewise let his semen flow out between Arnold's buttocks, and Arnold then made a similar movement.

When this was over, Arnold said that they must mutually swear never to do this again, either with each other or with anyone else. They swore on the Gospels.

[Despite their oaths, they met a number of times in the following weeks and similar acts took place again, once in a field owned by Arnold's brother outside the town] . . . Arnold had twice committed sodomy with him . . . and vice versa . . . He added that Arnold promised to lend him books and give him a knife if he would consent to commit this crime . . .

On another occasion, in the portico connecting the dormitory and latrines of the Franciscan convent of Pamiers, to which he had come to confess about his aforementioned sins, Arnold solicited him to commit sodomy, telling him that he would introduce him to a friar of the same house who would lighten his penance and would absolve him of the oath they had sworn about not committing that crime . . .

That same year, around the Feast of the Ascension on a rainy day between noon and three p.m., and on another day and time which he didn't recollect, when the speaker was at the school situated near the Carmelite house in Pamiers, Arnold of Verniolle came to him. He said that if Guillaume would come along with him, he would give him a writing tablet. The two of them came to a house situated near the home of the Minorissi family of Pamiers, although he didn't know whose house it was. In a box Arnold found four small tablets that he wanted to give to Guillaume and that Guillaume wanted to take, saying that they weren't particularly valuable. Next, Arnold shut the door, and on the ground floor room in which a bed was situated, Arnold lay down with his clothes on and asked Guillaume to lie down beside him. He did so in the manner described . . . Arnold committed sodomy on the speaker as they lay side by side. Arnold then told Guillaume to do the same to him, which he did. When that was done, they separated and Guillaume returned to school . . .

[Others testified to similar activities: Guillaume Bernard, aged fifteen and a half, also described as a student of liberal arts; Guillaume Boyer, eighteen; Guillaume Pech, nineteen – all students of art living in Pamiers. A Carmelite friar, Pierre Recort, had been a cell-mate of Arnold's while he had been waiting to appear before the inquisitors. He reported the following.]

Arnold used to go with one or another of the aforementioned youths, bringing along some wine, silver cups, and food to a field . . . When they were there, they sometimes used to spread out a robe, dance, and wrestle, and afterwards commit sodomy with each other. The boys would even come to his home and there, in an upper chamber, which was his study, they committed sodomy with him and he with them. And in that way one day the three youths fooled around with Arnold, lying down together on the bed, one of them committing sodomy with the other as the third watched . . .

He told Pierre that he believed that sodomy is a mortal sin, although it is equal to simple fornication or fornication with prostitutes . . .

Arnold had said that the bishop would have enough on his hands if he were to apprehend everyone in Pamiers who had been infected with that crime because there were more than three thousand persons . . .

[At the end of this remarkable document is recorded the confession of Arnold himself, a clerk in minor orders in his early thirties.] About twenty years ago, although he didn't remember when, when he was about ten or twelve, his father sent him to study grammar in Pamiers. . . . At this school he boarded with Master Poncius . . . [and others. Among them was] Arnold Auriol, son of Pierre, a knight near Bastide de Serou, who already shaved his beard and is now a priest . . . for about six weeks he shared a bed with Arnold Auriol. After they had been together for about two or three nights and Arnold Auriol thought Arnold was asleep, he started to kiss the speaker and placed himself over Arnold's thighs. He then placed his penis between Arnold's thighs and moving himself about as with a woman, he ejaculated between Arnold's thighs. He continued this sin all night, as long as the speaker slept with Arnold Auriol. Because Arnold was still a boy, this act was displeasing to him; but because of shame, he didn't dare to reveal it to anyone. At that time, he didn't even have the will or desire to commit that sin, for, so he said, he did not yet have such desires . . . [After six weeks he moved into the bed of his tutor, Master Poncius] who solicited Arnold to commit that vice.

[He recited a long list of his sexual misdemeanours. His account of his meeting with Guillaume Roux was that the youth had sought him out and Arnold had asked him if he was willing to have sex with a cleric.] Guillaume answered that he was willing; Arnold then asked if he had committed this sin with someone else. Guillaume replied that he had done so with a certain squire of his country, who had shared his bed; he added that he knew well how to commit that crime . . . They then undressed, lay down nude on the bed and, in the aforementioned way, first one and then the other committed sodomy; they then swore on the Gospels never to reveal anything about this sin to anyone. Arnold then borrowed from Guillaume a book by Ovid, whose title he didn't know. Guillaume then asked Arnold to give him a knife which he carried with his knives but Arnold refused, and said he would give him a different one.

. . . it seems that he [Guillaume] enjoyed it as much as Arnold did, to tell from his words and deeds . . . He [Arnold] had said that he believed simple fornication and sodomy were equal sins; he said that he truly believed that sodomy and simple fornication were equal sins and that rape, deflowering of a virgin, adultery, and incest were greater and graver sins than sodomy . . . he had told Guillaume Roux that in some men nature demands that they perform this act or know women carnally; and, he said that he very much felt in himself that his body would suffer if he should abstain for more than eight or fifteen days if he did not have sex with a woman or didn't commit that crime with a man . . .

[At the end of the trial the Bishop dressed 'in his pontifical robes with his pastoral staff and his cap without a mitre' delivered his verdict.] You, Arnold of Verniolle, have fallen into the horrible and damnable crime of sodomy, as is noted above in your full confession, and because of which you are to be gravely and harshly punished . . . You should therefore be degraded and placed in iron chains in the strictest prison, to be fed a diet of bread and water for life . .

from the Inquisition registers of Jacques Fournier, Bishop of Pamiers (1317–26)

CHAPTER THREE

The Renaissance

Italy was by the thirteenth century once more the dominant cultural and economic force in Europe. The peninsula was the most highly urbanised part of Europe, supporting a large network of towns and cities which included Florence, Venice and Rome – all with populations in excess of 100,000 by the fourteenth century. Historians have been able to identify in most of these Italian cities a lively and active homosexual subculture.[1] It was in this milieu that the great artists of the Italian Renaissance lived and worked, and it is difficult to refute their contemporaries' powerful evidence that in so many cases their sexual proclivities were directed towards men. In any catalogue of homosexuals through the ages, Leonardo and Michelangelo occupy a prominent place.

Homosexual desire obviously informed the work of many of these artists. Michelangelo's statue of David has over the centuries been turned into a homosexual icon. In an important study,[2] Professor James Saslow has traced the way in which Renaissance artists used a whole set of images with homoerotic overtones in their art. The story of Zeus's abduction of Ganymede is possibly the most famous such image, as it provided painters and sculptors with the opportunity to depict a particularly attractive young man.

It is also beginning to be possible to identify the existence of a homosexual subculture in Elizabethan London.[3] The works of William Shakespeare have been carefully combed by scholars for clues to the playwright's sexual tastes,[4] but as with so much in his work, no firm conclusions can be drawn: he remains as elusive as ever. Perhaps it is best that the dominant figure should remain an enigma safe from the biographical busybodies.

Shakespeare's contemporary Christopher Marlowe was certainly a man who was driven by homosexual passions, a fact reflected in the subject-matter of his plays, most famously in *Edward II*. Marlowe was a rebel who became caught up in the dangerous world of Elizabethan espionage and whose murder in a brawl at a tavern in Deptford remains a mystery.

Moralists flourished and the Counter-Reformation turned the attention of the Catholic Church to the business of artistic censorship, and from the last decade of the sixteenth century artists and writers in Catholic Europe had to become more circumspect in the subjects they depicted in their art. The century supported one extraordinarily camp monarch, Henri III of France, who was probably a transvestite. Henri created a flamboyant court in Paris and surrounded himself with a bevy of male favourites who were known as *mignons*.[5]

Renaissance Venice

Indicative of the growth of this [homosexual] subculture was the Ten's growing awareness that homosexuality was associated with particular activities and areas of the city. Certain schools were seen as especially suspicious. For example, in 1444 the Ten noted that 'certain teachers of musical instruments, singing and gymnastics keep their schools open until two or three hours after dark.' This, they argued, was dangerous for the many young boys gathered in such schools 'because it might lead some of these youths to commit prohibited deeds'. They ruled, therefore, that no master of those arts could hold classes after sunset under penalty of six months in jail and a one-year banishment. In addition they offered a 100-lire reward for anyone who turned in a master for breaking the curfew.

A continuity in the Ten's suspicion of these schools is revealed in a *parte* [decree] of 1477 that reinforced the earlier ruling with an eye to 'eliminating this abominable vice which we are told is committed daily and publicly in this our city'. To the other schools were added those devoted to the study of the abacus and fencing. All were prohibited from meeting after the twenty-second hour in the summertime and after the twenty-third hour in wintertime. In addition, these classes were ordered confined to the areas around San Marco and the Rialto. As both areas had the most elaborate patrolling apparatus in the city, this latter provision seems to have been designed to improve surveillance of their activities. Also, as the economic and political centers of the city, they had high densities of people and movement that would have made privacy difficult even without extensive patrols. Finally, the Ten ordered that no school could have any private or secret rooms for instruction; all teaching had to be done with groups in public halls. The Ten clearly felt that homosexual activity with young boys was often initiated in these settings and that these schools were dangerous head-quarters for sodomy – literally schools for sodomy.

Another danger area that this *parte* referred to was apothecary shops throughout the city often run by barber-surgeons. Such shops were also forbidden to keep private rooms for games or exercises for the young. Prosecution reveals a strong relationship between barbers and homosexuality, suggesting that they may have provided important links to the subculture . . .

Certain secluded public places seemed especially threatening. Young men tended to gather after dark under the portico of the drapers near the Rialto and in the doorway of the Church of San Martino . . . More general danger areas feared by the Ten were the shops of pastrymakers. They warned that 'in the shops of the pastrymakers in this our city many youths and others of diverse age and condition come together day and night; there they hold games, drink and commit many dishonesties and sodomy.' Games and drinking that might lure young men into the subculture were forbidden; presumably one was to buy one's pastry and leave . . .

The Ten discovered it everywhere . . . the Ten found that all their rhetoric and stern penalties seemed to have little impact . . .

The Venetian ecclesiastical community was seen as an important part of the homosexual subculture legally outside the disciplining jurisdiction of the Ten.

The dangers of clerical homosexuality, especially in monasteries, were recognized . . . [the Ten felt] that the Church was much too lenient and ready to protect its own in such matters . . .

That subculture, whether a product of the fifteenth century or a product of that century's fears, or both, elicited the Ten's aggressive attention. Representing the most influential families of Venice, the Ten devoted an inordinate amount of time and expense to repressing sodomy. It seems, however, that rather than limiting the crime, the more they pursued the matter, the more sodomy they uncovered . . . their records indicate that the homosexual subculture became a well-entrenched part of Venetian society at all social levels.

from Guido Ruggiero, The Boundaries of Eros *(1985)*

Passing Through

The sculptor Donatello took particular delight in having beautiful apprentices. Once someone brought him a boy that had been praised as particularly beautiful. But when the same person then showed Donatello the boy's brother and claimed that he was even prettier, the artist replied, 'the less long will he stay with me!'

from the Facetiae, *a late-fifteenth-century Florentine account of Donatello*

Call to Arms

In a sermon on November 1, 1494, Savonarola railed at the priests of Florence: 'Abandon your pomp and your banquets and your sumptuous meals. Abandon, I tell you, your concubines and your beardless youths. Abandon, I say, that unspeakable vice, abandon that abominable vice that has brought God's wrath upon you, or else: woe, woe to you!'

from James Saslow, Ganymede in the Renaissance *(1986)*

The Little Devil

One day in the summer of 1490, while he was in Pavia, Leonardo encountered an appealing ten-year-old boy and promptly adopted him. The boy had thick hair, which was naturally curly, a low forehead, large eyes with fine eyelashes, a somewhat sharp nose, thick lips, a delicately formed chin, and a short neck. His name was Gian Giacomo Caprotti, his parents were poor, and it was not difficult to arrange that the boy should enter his household as a servant. A small amount of money would be given to the parents, a legal deed would be drawn up, and thereafter the boy would remain with him until he came of age, the property of his master. The boy proved to be a talented thief, and Leonardo sometimes regretted employing him. Soon he was given the nickname of Salai, meaning the 'little devil' . . . For nearly twenty-six years Salai remained at his side.

By Leonardo's account Salai was a 'thievish, lying, obstinate glutton'. He was also handsome, vigorous, impudent, and charming. His upkeep was considerable, he demanded and received an unusually large wardrobe and a quite fantastic number of pairs of shoes . . . He was self-indulgent and Leonardo evidently pampered him. He appears to have been simultaneously amused and incensed by the boy's behaviour . . . There arose in the nineteenth century the legend that Salai became an apprentice and was in fact introduced into the studio in order to learn painting . . . A particularly bad copy of the Mona Lisa was attributed to him, and even in our own century there have been scholars who cheerfully attributed to him a large number of paintings. Yet there is no evidence that Salai painted anything or even assisted Leonardo in grinding his colors. He was a charming little devil, and perhaps nothing more.

Nevertheless Leonardo developed a great affection for him and later gave him half of the small property he owned in Milan, confirming the gift in his will. The painter and the charming boy were inseparable; they traveled together through Italy; and when in his last years Leonardo became the pensioner of King Francis I [of France] with a palace of his own at Amboise, Salai came to stay with him . . . he was never in a strict sense a servant. Bodyguard, gatekeeper, majordomo, adopted son, he occupied an ambiguous position in the household, and it may have been this ambiguity that gave pleasure to Leonardo, who depended upon him for all those services that are not provided by servants.

from Robert Payne, Leonardo *(1978)*

The Rod

Concerning the Rod. It holds conference with the human intelligence and sometimes has intelligence of itself. When the human will desires to stimulate it, it remains obstinate and follows its own way, sometimes moving of itself without the permission of the man or of any mental impetus. Whether he is awake or sleeping, it does what it desires. And often the man is asleep and it's awake, and often the man is awake while it sleeps, and often when the man wishes to use it, it desires otherwise, and often it wishes to be used and the man forbids it.

Therefore it appears that this creature possesses a life and an intelligence alien from the man, and it seems that men are wrong to be ashamed of giving it a name or of showing it, always covering and concealing something that deserves to be adorned and displayed with ceremony as a ministrant.

an entry in one of Leonardo's notebooks for 1508, when the painter was fifty-six years old

The Rule of Law

I have yet to speak of another wicked and pernicious vice, which was widely practised and highly esteemed in this city [of Venice], and this was the unnatural vice called sodomy, for which, as we read in ancient writings, the great God sent down fire upon the two cities so notorious to all. This vice was openly practised in

Venice without shame; indeed it had become so habitual that it was more highly regarded than having to do with one's own wife. Young Venetian nobles and citizens tricked themselves with so many ornaments, and with garments that opened to show the chest, and with so many perfumes, that there was no indecency in the world to compare with the frippery and finery of Venetian youth and their provocative acts of luxury and venery. Truly they may be called not youths, but women. They were tolerated by their fathers and relatives although they deserved punishment; had [their elders] taken action, and forbidden this indecent clothing, this lascivious and dishonourable behaviour, this effeminacy on the part of their sons and relatives, perhaps things would have gone differently and the heavens would not have allowed such a catastrophe [the defeat of the Venetians at the battle of Agnadello] to fall upon us. But such was the love of fathers for their children that they were blind to their ruin, sunk and drowning as they were in this accursed vice, and they neither saw nor realized it. By the power of money these [young people] turned from men into women, and now that after this disaster money must needs be in shorter supply they will do far worse things in their desire to obtain it, for they have been brought up to expect these lascivious refinements which one cannot have without money, and they cannot resist such things . . .

In the city of Venice there were so many decrees, laws and ordinances for the punishment of this execrable perversion that the books were full of them, and they imposed the penalty of burning on persons who committed such crimes. But these laws, ordinances and decrees were neither respected nor enforced, and that was because the persons responsible for their execution were themselves involved in these offences and had no heart to carry out the punishment, for they feared that the same penalty might fall upon themselves or their own children. For these reasons the thing was suppressed, and the fire which these criminals deserved was quenched and doused with water . . . the vice had now become so much a habit and so familiar to everyone, and it was so openly discussed throughout the city, that there came a time when it was so commonplace that no one said anything about it any more, and it neither deserved nor received any punishment – except for some poor wretch who had no money, no favours, no friends and no relations: justice was done on people like that, and not on those who had power and money and reputation, and yet committed far worse crimes.

from the diary of a Venetian, Girolamo Priuli, 1509

Michelangelo

Michelangelo was of course homosexual. That obvious fact still needs restating simply because generations of art historians have been embarrassed by it . . . The evidence for his homosexual love is too strong to be denied, particularly in the letters to and about one of his models, Febo di Poggo, and those about the fifteen-year-old Cecchino del Bracci. And it is immediately obvious in his art . . . He met the great love of his life, the Roman aristocrat Tommaso Cavalieri, when he was nearly sixty . . . Whenever he met someone with outstanding looks and talents, he once wrote, 'I am constrained to fall in love with him, and to give myself to him as prey, so that I am no longer mine but his' . . . Michelangelo certainly tried to deny his homosexuality, partly because he feared scandal and partly because as he grew more intensely religious in his old age he strove desperately to sublimate all love of worldly things into the love of God . . . the fact remains that Michelangelo's art concentrates on one kind of beauty, and one only . . . beautiful young men are everywhere, depicted with warmth and loving pleasure.

from Margaret Walters, The Nude Male *(1978)*

Divine Purposes

For if every one of our affections displeases heaven,
To what purpose would God have made the world?

from a sonnet by Michelangelo written in 1546

A Marvellous Matter

After Cellini had suggested completing the antique fragment as a Ganymede, the sculptor Baccio Bandinelli entered the room and began criticizing the torso. Always ready to quarrel with his detested rival, Cellini defended the marble and in turn excoriated Bandinelli's own *Hercules and Cacus*. Outraged, Bandinelli erupted, 'Oh keep quiet, you dirty sodomite.' The courtiers, who had hitherto been laughing at the exchange, suddenly became silent and glared at Bandinelli. Cellini, 'choked with fury,' immediately denied the slur. His reply shows that he was aware both of the connection between Ganymede and homosexuality and of the existence of such practices in his social milieu: 'You madman, you're going too far. But I wish to God I did know how to indulge in such a noble practice; after all we read that Jove enjoyed it with Ganymede in paradise, and here on earth it is the practice of the greatest emperors and the greatest kings of the world. I'm an insignificant humble man, I haven't the means to meddle in such a marvellous matter.'

from James Saslow, Ganymede in the Renaissance *(1986)*

A Humiliating End

Filthy fortune, thou didst first discover that Ganymede still pleased me. I am now degraded, as everyone can see. Thou hast stripped me of rich spoils.

Cellini, 1556, having been placed under house arrest after his third conviction for sodomy

Sodoma

His manner of life was licentious and dishonourable, and as he always had boys and beardless youths about him of whom he was inordinately fond, this earned him the name of Sodoma; but instead of feeling shame he gloried in it, writing stanzas and verses on it, and singing them to the accompaniment of the lute.

> Vasari's account of how the Italian artist Giovannantonio da Verzelli (1477–1549) acquired his nickname

The Headmaster

Nicholas Udall, author of *Ralph Roister Doister*, a work generally regarded as the first comedy in the English language, was an invert and even a pervert. As headmaster of Eton, he was noted for his love of inflicting corporal punishment on the boys, which no doubt implied a sadistic sexual impulse. In 1541, the year in which *Ralph Roister Doister* was first publicly performed, Udall was charged with unnatural crime and confessed his guilt before the Privy Council. He was dismissed from his headmastership and imprisoned, but his reputation does not appear to have been greatly injured, for he subsequently enjoyed a number of lucrative ecclesiastical livings and Queen Mary appointed him headmaster of Westminster School in 1553.

> from H. Montgomery Hyde, The Other Love (1970)

The King's Pleasure

GAVESTON: I must have wanton poets, pleasant wits,
    Musicians, that with touching of a string
    May draw the pliant king which way I please;
    Music and poetry is his delight,
    Therefore I'll have Italian masques by night,
    Sweet speeches, comedies, and pleasing shows,
    And in the day when he shall walk abroad,
    Like sylvan nymphs my pages shall be clad;
    My men, like satyrs grazing on the lawns,
    Shall with their goat-feet dance an antic hay;
    Sometimes a lovely boy, in Dian's shape,
    With hair that gilds the water as it glides,
    Crownets of pearl about his naked arms,
    And in his sportful hands an olive-tree,
    To hide those parts which men delight to see,
    Shall bathe him in a spring; and there, hard by,
    One like Actæon peeping through the grove,
    Shall by the angry goddess be transform'd,
    And running in the likeness of an hart,

By yelping hounds pull'd down, and seem to die:
Such things as these best please his majesty,
My lord . . .

Edward II, by Christopher Marlowe (1564–93), lines 51–72

The Taming of the Shrew

Here the curtains draw; there is discovered JUPITER *dandling* GANYMEDE *upon his knee, and* HERMES *lying asleep.*

JUPITER: Come, gentle Ganymede, and play with me;
   I love thee well, say Juno what she will.
GANYMEDE: I am much better for your worthless love,
   That will not shield me from her shrewish blows!
   Today, whenas I fill'd into your cups,
   And held the cloth of pleasance whiles you drank,
   She reach'd me such a rap for that I spill'd,
   As made the blood run down about mine ears.
JUPITER: What, dares she strike the darling of my thoughts?
   By Saturn's soul, and this earth-threatening hair,
   That, shaken thrice, makes nature's buildings quake,
   I vow, if she but once frown on thee more,
   To hang her, meteor-like, 'twixt heaven and earth,
   And bind her, hand and foot, with golden cords,
   As once I did for harming Hercules!
GANYMEDE: Might I but see that pretty sport a-foot,
   Oh, how would I with Helen's brother laugh,
   And bring the gods to wonder at the game!
   Sweet Jupiter, if e'er I pleas'd thine eye,
   Or seemed fair, wall'd in with eagle's wings,
   Grace my immortal beauty with this boon,
   And I will spend my time in thy bright arms.
JUPITER: What is't, sweet wag, I should deny thy youth?
   Whose face reflects such pleasure to mine eyes,
   As I, exhal'd with thy fire-darting beams,
   Have oft driven back the horses of the Night,
   Whenas they would have hal'd thee from my sight.
   Sit on my knee, and call for thy content,
   Control proud Fate, and cut the thread of Time:
   Why, are not all the gods at thy command,
   And heaven and earth the bounds of thy delight?
   Vulcan shall dance to make thee laughing sport,
   And my nine daughters sing when thou art sad;
   From Juno's bird I'll pluck her spotted pride,
   To make thee fans wherewith to cool thy face;
   And Venus' swans shall shed their silver down,

To sweeten out the slumbers of thy bed;
Hermes no more shall show the world his wings,
If that thy fancy in his feathers dwell,
But, as this one, I'll tear them all from him,
    (*Plucks a feather from* HERMES' *wings.*)
Do thou but say, 'their colour pleaseth me.'
Hold here, my little love, these linked gems,
    (*Gives jewels*)
My Juno ware upon her marriage-day,
Put thou about thy neck, my own sweet-heart,
And trick thy arms and shoulders with my theft.
GANYMEDE: I would have a jewel for mine ear,
And a fine brooch to put in my hat,
And then I'll hug with you an hundred times.
JUPITER: And shalt have, Ganymede, if thou wilt be my love.
    (*Enter* VENUS.)
VENUS: Ay, this is it: you can sit toying there,
And playing with that female wanton boy,
While my Æneas wanders on the seas,
And rests a prey to every billow's pride.
Christopher Marlowe, Dido, Queen of Carthage, *l.i. 1–53*

Kit

That the Indians and many Authors of antiquity have assuredly written of above sixteen thousand years agoe whereas Adam is proved to have lived within six thousand years. He [Marlowe] affirmed that Moses was but a Juggler and that one Heriots being Sir Walter Raleigh's man can do more than he . . . That the first beginning of Religion was only to keep men in awe . . . That Christ was a bastard and his mother dishonest . . . That St. John the Evangelist was bedfellow to Christ and leaned always in his bosome, that he used him as the sinners of Sodom. That all that love not Tobacco and Boys were fools.

    from a late-sixteenth-century manuscript

Giving In

If it be sin to love a lovely lad
Oh there sin I.

    from The Affectionate Shepherd, *by Richard Barnfield (1574–1627)*

Every Picture Tells a Story

Whether Caravaggio was essentially or exclusively homosexual is far from certain. Minnitti, with whom he supposedly lived for years, and who may have been the model for the lutenist in the *Concert*, eventually tired of Caravaggio and married . . . the sex lives of Renaissance artists were probably often much like that of Benvenuto Cellini – a bit of both sexes, as was convenient. Although we do not need to presume that Caravaggio's pictures with homoerotic content are necessarily more confessional than others, there is a notable absence of the traditional erotic females . . . In his entire career he did not paint a single female nude.

from Howard Hibbard, Caravaggio *(1983)*

The Favourite Soldier

I do marvel also what became of Piers Edmonds, called Captain Piers or Captain Edmonds, the Earl of Essex man, born in the Strand near me, one which has had many rewards and preferments by the Earl [of] Essex. His villainy I have often complained of.

He dwells in London. He was corporal general of the horse in Ireland under the Earl of Southampton. He ate and drank at his table and lay in his tent. The Earl of Southampton gave him a horse which Edmonds refused a hundred marks for him. The Earl of Southampton would coll [embrace] and hug him and play wantonly with him.

This Piers began to fawn and flatter me in Ireland, offering me great courtesy, telling me what pay, graces and gifts the earls bestowed upon him, thereby seeming to move and animate me to desire and look for the like favour. But I could never love and affect them to make them my friends, especially Essex, whose mind I mistrusted.

testimony of William Reynolds, who told the story of a soldier, Piers Edmonds, who had boasted of his connection with the Earl of Southampton, who is famous as having been William Shakespeare's patron, and possibly lover

The Bashful Lover

Even as the sun with purple-colour'd face
Had ta'en his last leave of the weeping morn,
Rose-cheek'd Adonis hied him to the chase;
Hunting he lov'd, but love he laughed to scorn;
  Sick-thoughted Venus makes amain unto him,
  And like a bold-fac'd suitor 'gins to woo him.

'Thrice fairer than myself,' thus she began,
'The field's chief flower, sweet above compare,
Stain to all nymphs, more lovely than a man,
More white and red than doves or roses are;
  Nature that made thee, with herself at strife,
  Saith that the world hath ending with thy life.

'Vouchsafe, thou wonder, to alight thy steed,
And rein his proud head to the saddle-bow;
If thou wilt deign this favour, for thy meed
A thousand honey secrets shalt thou know:
　　Here come and sit, where never serpent hisses;
　　And being set, I'll smother thee with kisses:

'And yet not cloy thy lips with loath'd satiety,
But rather famish them amid their plenty,
Making them red and pale with fresh variety;
Ten kisses short as one, one long as twenty:
　　A summer's day will seem an hour but short,
　　Being wasted in such time-beguiling sport.'

With this she seizeth on his sweating palm,
The precedent of pith and livelihood,
And trembling in her passion, calls it balm,
Earth's sovereign salve to do a goddess good:
　　Being so enrag'd, desire doth lend her force
　　Courageously to pluck him from his horse.

Over one arm the lusty courser's rein,
Under her other was the tender boy,
Who blush'd and pouted in a dull disdain,
With leaden appetite, unapt to toy;
　　She red and hot as coals of glowing fire,
　　He red for shame, but frosty in desire.

　　·　　·　　·　　·　　·　　·　　·

　　Backward she push'd him, as she would be thrust,
　　And govern'd him in strength, though not in lust.

So soon was she along, as he was down,
Each leaning on their elbows and their hips:
Now doth she stroke his cheek, now doth he frown,
And 'gins to chide, but soon she stops his lips;
　　And kissing speaks, with lustful language broken,
　　'If thou wilt chide, thy lips shall never open.'

He burns with bashful shame; she with her tears
Doth quench the maiden burning of his cheeks;

　　·　　·　　·　　·　　·　　·　　·

　　Even so she kiss'd his brow, his cheek, his chin,
　　And where she ends she doth anew begin.

Forced to content, but never to obey,
Panting he lies, and breatheth in her face;

　　·　　·　　·　　·　　·　　·　　·

Look! how a bird lies tangled in a net,
So fasten'd in her arms Adonis lies;
Pure shame and aw'd resistance made him fret,
Which bred more beauty in his angry eyes:

   .   .   .   .

  'O! pity,' 'gan she cry, 'flint-hearted boy:
  'Tis but a kiss I beg; why art thou coy?

   .   .   .   .

'Thou canst not see one wrinkle in my brow;
Mine eyes are grey and bright, and quick in turning;
My beauty as the spring doth yearly grow;
My flesh is soft and plump, my marrow burning;
  My smooth moist hand, were it with thy hand felt,
  Would in thy palm dissolve, or seem to melt.'

   .   .   .   .

And now Adonis with a lazy spright,
And with a heavy, dark, disliking eye,
His louring brows o'erwhelming his fair sight,
Like misty vapours when they blot the sky,
  Souring his cheeks, cries, 'Fie! no more of love:
  The sun doth burn my face; I must remove.'

'Ay me,' quoth Venus, 'young, and so unkind?
What bare excuses mak'st thou to be gone; . . .

   .   .   .   .

  Thou art no man, though of a man's complexion,
  For men will kiss even by their own direction.'

from Venus and Adonis, *by William Shakespeare (1564–1616), a poem dedicated to the* Earl of Southampton

Homage

Lord of my love, to whom in vassalage
Thy merit hath my duty strongly knit,
To thee I send this written ambassage,
To witness duty, not to show my wit:
Duty so great, which wit so poor as mine
May make seem bare, in wanting words to show it,
But that I hope some good conceit of thine
In thy soul's thought, all naked, will bestow it;
Till whatsoever star that guides my moving
Points on me graciously with fair aspect,

And puts apparel on my tatter'd loving,
To show me worthy of thy sweet respect:
   Then may I dare to boast how I do love thee;
   Till then not show my head where thou mayst prove me.
     William Shakespeare, Sonnet XXVI

A Memorial to Beauty

Against my love shall be, as I am now,
With Time's injurious hand crush'd and o'erworn;
When hours have drain'd his blood and fill'd his brow
With lines and wrinkles; when his youthful morn
Hath travell'd on to age's steepy night;
And all those beauties whereof now he's king
Are vanishing or vanish'd out of sight,
Stealing away the treasure of his spring;
For such a time do I now fortify
Against confounding age's cruel knife,
That he shall never cut from memory
My sweet love's beauty, though my lover's life:
His beauty shall in these black lines be seen,
And they shall live, and he in them still green.
     William Shakespeare, Sonnet LXIII

Fickle Lads

FOOL: He's mad that trusts in the tameness of a wolf, a horse's health, a boy's love, or a whore's oath.
     from William Shakespeare, King Lear, III.vi. 21–3

Dreaming

AUFIDIUS (*to Coriolanus*): O Marcius, Marcius!
Each word thou hast spoke hath weeded from my heart
A root of ancient envy. If Jupiter
Should from yond cloud speak divine things,
And say, ''Tis true,' I'd not believe them more
Than thee, all noble Marcius. Let me twine
Mine arms about that body, where against
My grained ash a hundred times hath broke,
And scarr'd the moon with splinters: here I clip
The anvil of my sword, and do contest
As hotly and as nobly with thy love
As ever in ambitious strength I did
Contend against thy valour. Know thou first,

I lov'd the maid I married; never man
Sigh'd truer breath; but that I see thee here,
Thou noble thing! more dances my rapt heart
Than when I first my wedded mistress saw
Bestride my threshold. Why, thou Mars! I tell thee,
We have a power on foot; and I had purpose
Once more to hew thy target from thy brawn,
Or lose mine arm for't. Thou hast beat me out
Twelve several times, and I have nightly since
Dreamt of encounters 'twixt thyself and me;
We have been down together in my sleep,
Unbuckling helms, fisting each other's throat,
And wak'd half dead with nothing . . .

      from William Shakespeare, Coriolanus, IV. v. 107–32

CHAPTER FOUR

The Seventeenth and Eighteenth Centuries

Over the centuries European monarchies have produced many men and women whose sexual behaviour has become a familiar item of popular history. There has always been a market for scandal, and before the arrival of the twentieth-century star this market was supplied with tales from the courts of the European kings and queens. The position of privilege occupied by monarchs and their courtiers often created opportunities to indulge and develop a variety of sexual interests and tastes. The court has often been a centre of licence, generating for the future magnificent tales that quickly enter the national folklore.

Two British kings in the seventeenth century appear to have had predominantly homosexual interests, James I (r.1603–25) and his great-grandson William III (r.1689–1702).[1] Both were foreigners: James was Scottish while William was Dutch. Neither was particularly promiscuous, both men practising serial monogamy. They were certainly more discriminating in their choice and numbers of partners than Charles II, a sexual athlete of considerable prowess with an almost insatiable appetite for the pleasures of the bedchamber, a veritable seventeenth-century Tiberius, though his interests were strictly heterosexual.

James wrote a treatise condemning sodomy while flaunting his affection for a succession of favourites, culminating in his association with George Villiers, Duke of Buckingham. William preferred to lead a more private life and lived most of his time as king in the relative privacy of Hampton Court rather than the large public palace at Whitehall, which would have placed many restrictions on his domestic interests. Appropriately enough William did not replace Whitehall when it burned down, though it had been the principal residence of all Tudor and Stuart monarchs. He was less discreet when it came to the decoration of his bedchamber, the ceiling of which depicted that perennial favourite of the homosexual, Jupiter's abduction of Ganymede. The young Trojan shepherd in that portrayal was long past his adolescence, reflecting William's own passion for the more mature male. Neither monarch escaped some measure of public censure, William having to face the satirical pen of the playwright John Vanbrugh, who alluded to the King's interests in his 1696 success *The Relapse*.

One other play written and performed in seventeenth-century England took as its theme a monarch so addicted to homosexuality that he made it compulsory in his realm. Entitled *Sodom, or the Quintessence of Debauchery*, it was written by one of the most notorious rakes at the court of Charles II, John Wilmot, second Earl of Rochester.[2]

Performed once at court, it partly pre-empts the English 'Carry On' tradition, with characters such as Barastus, 'the Bugger-master General', and Buggeranthos. Rochester was bisexual – a fact he celebrates in his poetry.

Charles II's monarchy was almost brought down by one of the most notorious homosexuals of the age, the infamous liar Titus Oates, whose fabrication of a popish plot created a major political crisis. Professor John Kenyon suggests that Oates was able to give credibility to his tales because his homosexual interests had given him an entrée to a highly-placed circle of English and Continental homosexuals who provided him with the seeds from which he cultivated his tall tales.[3] Kenyon's study allows us to examine the homosexual underworld of Stuart London, a complex scene erected around a series of notorious inns.

Historians are beginning to reconstruct the homosexual subcultures of the northern capital cities of London, Paris and Amsterdam during the seventeenth and eighteenth centuries, and are revealing patterns similar to those already found in Renaissance Italy.[4] Such scholarship is possible largely because of the emergence of one of the greatest enemies of the homosexual, the policeman. Moralists found in these full-time upholders of law and order the almost perfect instruments for the exposure of vice. Policemen, then as now, quickly discovered that hunting criminals was never easy, and not particularly rewarding, and they preferred to turn their attention to easier prey. Parisian policemen of the *ancien régime* used the same bag of tricks as their modern counterparts. A new and terrifying hazard was added to the game; cruising could turn into a very dangerous sport indeed.

The police had many triumphs in eighteenth-century London – most memorably in the raid on a London brothel in 1726 that found between forty and fifty men on the premises in a variety of compromising positions. [5] Mother Clop, the woman who ran the house, was imprisoned and also, like many of her clients, spent some time in the stocks. The Age of Reason was a particularly barbaric era in its treatment of those who broke its savage laws.

Such events were usually passed down to future generations by another new menace to the homosexual: the journalist. Increased literacy and improvements in print technology created a market for news and produced a popular press for the first time in the history of civilisation. A development much praised by historians, who are always tempted to jump on to the bandwagon of progress, for the homosexually inclined this might be viewed as an even more pernicious 'improvement' than the emergence of the police. Eighteenth-century journalists soon discovered that sensational sexual tales at whatever level in society sold newspapers and magazines. Such stories consolidated stereotypes and established popular fears that remain a feature of some Western cultures to the present day. Pornographers also exploited the possibilities offered by a mass market, and the eighteenth century has left behind a rich and interesting literature on the erotic that is still waiting for its historian.

In the age in which many powerful stereotypes became fixed and in which many of our modern myths about differences in gender were first established, several examples of rather rugged homosexuals also appeared.[6] William III was a fine general who played a major role in defeating Louis XIV's plans for European hegemony, and his contemporary Prince Eugène of Savoy (1663–1730), one of the leading generals of the period, also devoted his erotic efforts to his own sex. So too did the French soldier

Louis, Prince de Condé. All these, however, were overshadowed by the military genius and enlightened despot Frederick the Great (1712–86). As Crown Prince he had established a close friendship with another young cadet at the military academy to which he had been sent by his father. The closeness of this link so alarmed his father that he ordered the public execution of the friend (and lover?), which he insisted Frederick witness. It is hardly surprising that Frederick should have become a cold, remote and unemotional figure when he became King of Prussia in 1740. His younger brother, Henry, however, created a homosexual court in Berlin and had many male lovers. After the American Revolution he was briefly a candidate for the throne of the new nation before the revolutionary leaders plumped for a republican government.

Bad Habits

. . . for beastly Sodomy, it is rife here [Padua] as in Rome, Naples, Florence, Bologna, Venice, Ferrara, Genoa, Parma not being exempted, nor yet the smallest village of Italy: A monstrous filthinesse, and yet to them a pleasant pastime, making songs and singing sonnets of the beauty of their Bardassi, or buggered boyes . . . They [the Turks] are extremely inclined to all sorts of lascivious luxury; and generally addicted, beside all their sensuall and incestuous lusts, unto Sodomy, which they account as a daynty to digest all their other libidinous pleasure.

> *Sir William Lithgow*, Rare Adventures & Painefull Peregrinations of long nineteene yeares travayles from Scotland *(1609)*

Boy George

[George Villiers, Duke of] Buckingham made a very favourable impression upon everyone he met, for his attractive appearance and ease of manner were combined with a genuine humility (as though he was awed by his own good fortune) and a desire to please. A portrait of Buckingham, painted in 1616, shows a tall, slender young man, delicate-featured, with long tapering fingers and finely shaped legs. This impression is confirmed by the account of the antiquarian Simonds D'Ewes, who watched Buckingham talking to a group of French lords in 1621, and found 'everything in him full of delicacy and handsome features; yea, his hands and face seemed to me especially effeminate and curious'. Another eye-witness, Bishop Goodman, described Buckingham as 'the handsomest-bodied man of England; his limbs so well compacted and his conversation so pleasing and of so sweet a disposition' . . .

Somerset [the royal favourite, Robert Carr, Earl of Somerset] was still behaving in a manner calculated to anger rather than conciliate the King. Driven by suspicions, many of which were justified, Carr sought constant reassurance as he struggled to break the hold of Villiers upon the King's heart. But James, whose love for his old favourite was now clearly fading, insisted that Somerset must acknowledge his faults and return to a more respectful manner of behaviour. As far as James was concerned the situation was quite clear. He would not abandon Villiers, and if Somerset wished to retain his influence he must accept this fact . . . the King was on his summer progress, visiting one great country house after another. On its return to London the royal procession passed through Hampshire, and at the end of August 1615 the King paused for a few days at Farnham Castle. It was there that Buckingham played the trump card which ensured his victory over Somerset. The King – who celebrated his forty-ninth birthday in June 1615 – had long been starved of physical affection. His relations with his wife were those of a friend, not a lover; and as for Somerset, one of the faults which the King laid to his charge was 'your long creeping back and withdrawing yourself from lying in my chamber, notwithstanding my many hundred times earnestly soliciting you to the contrary'. The King's desires now centred on the young man who had everything to gain from gratifying him, and as Sir Anthony Weldon recorded in the gossipy memoirs that he left to posterity, 'in his passion of love to his new favourite . . . the King was more impatient than any woman to enjoy her love.' Where the details of private relationships are concerned, nothing, of course, can be known for certain, but Buckingham himself provides the evidence that at Farnham he at last gave in to the King's importunity: writing to James many years later to thank him for a particularly enjoyable visit to Court he told him how he had spent the return journey pondering the question 'whether you loved me now . . . better than at the time which I shall never forget at Farnham, where the bed's head could not be found between the master and his dog'. By giving himself to James, Buckingham confirmed his supremacy, for what he had to offer was a combination of qualities which the King could find nowhere else – youth, beauty, high spirits, sensuality, sweetness of character, and devotion . . .

The King was never ashamed about giving public expression to his love for his favourite. On the day after his creation as marquis, Buckingham held a great feast in the Cockpit at Whitehall for the King, the Prince and the leading members of the Court. The food was rich and abundant, and the wine plentiful. James was in a warm good humour, and halfway through supper rose from his place, took the Prince by the hand, and walking to the table where the other guests were seated, publicly toasted Buckingham. 'My lords,' he told them, 'I drink to you all and I know we are all welcome to my George. And he that doth not pledge it with all his heart, I would the Devil had him for my part.' Having delivered himself of this resounding declaration he returned to his seat.

from Roger Lockyer, Buckingham: The Life and Political Career of George Villiers, First Duke of Buckingham 1592–1628 *(1981)*

Hopelessly Devoted to You

My only sweet and dear child,
Notwithstanding of your desiring me not to write yesterday, yet had I written in the evening if, at my coming out of the park, such drowsiness had not come upon me as I was forced to sit and sleep in my chair half an hour. And yet I cannot content myself without sending you this present, praying God that I may have a joyful and comfortable meeting with you and that we may make at this Christmas a new marriage ever to be kept hereafter; for, God so love me, as I desire only to live in this world for your sake, and that I had rather live banished in any part of the earth with you than I live a sorrowful widow's life without you. And so God bless you, my sweet child and wife, and grant that ye may ever be a comfort to your dear dad and husband. James R.

a letter from James I to the Duke of Buckingham, December 1623

Fraternal Sermon

Andrewes and Neile [both bishops] were two other close confidants of the king. Andrewes won favour for his engaging company and ribald humour. There seems to be some truth in the old story that Neile distracted James's attention with entertaining stories whenever a godly preacher mounted the pulpit in the Chapel Royal, and on one occasion himself preached before the King on the text, 'And what are women to you and me?' No doubt this amused James.

from Kenneth Fincham, Prelate as Pastor: The Episcopate of James I (1990)

Renaissance Man

For whereas presently upon his censure at this time his ambition was moderated, his pride was humbled, and the means of his former injustice and corruption removed; yet would he not relinquish the practice of his most horrible and secret sin of sodomy, keeping one Goodrick a very effeminate faced youth to be his catamite and bedfellow, although he had discharged the most of his other household servants: which was the more to be admired because men generally after his fall began to discourse of that unnatural crime which he had practised many years: deserting the bed of his lady, which he accounted as the Italians and Turks do, a poor man's pleasure in respect of the other; and it was thought by some that he should be tried at the bar of justice for it, and have satisfied the law most severe against that horrible villainy with the price of his blood; which caused some bold and forward men to write these verses following in a whole sheet of paper, and to cast it down in some part of York House in the Strand, where Viscount St Alban yet lay.

> Within this sty a hog doth lie
> that must be hanged for sodomy.

But he never came to public trial for this crime; nor did ever that I could hear forbear his old custom of making his servants his bedfellows so to avoid the scandal was raised of him, though he lived many years after his fall in his lodgings in Gray's Inn in Holborn, in great want and penury.

Sir Simonds D'Ewes's account of Francis Bacon (1561–1626), writer and lawyer, an early modern polymath

Rich Folks

. . . pride, excess of diet, idleness and contempt of the poor . . .

a comment by Sir Edward Coke (1552–1634), Lord Chief Justice, on the causes of sodomy

Clerical Fantasies I

That night in a dream the Duke of Buckingham seemed to me to ascend into my bed, where he carried himself with much love towards me, after such rest wherein wearied men are wont exceedingly to rejoice; and likewise many seemed to me to enter the chamber who did see this.

an entry from the diary of William Laud, Archbishop of Canterbury (1633–45), for August 1625

Clerical Fantasies II

. . . thy heart is a foul sink of all atheism, sodomy, blasphemy, murder, whoredom, adultery, witchcraft, buggery; so that, if thou hast any good thing in thee, it is but as a drop of rosewater in a bowl of poison; where fallen it is all corrupted.

It is true thou feelest not all these things stirring in thee at one time . . . but they are in thee like a nest of snakes in an old hedge. Although they break not out into thy life, they lie lurking in thy heart.

from a 1640 sermon by a New England minister, Thomas Shepard

Ignorance

Sir J. Mennes and Mr. Batten both say that buggery is now almost grown as common among our gallants as in Italy, and that the very pages of the town begin to complain of their masters for it. But blessed be God, I do not know what is the meaning of this sin, nor which is the agent nor which the patient.

from Samuel Pepys's diary for 1 July 1663

Restoration Rake

George Villiers, second Duke of Buckingham, according to the title conferred on his father by King James, of whom he was the favourite, is a man full of vices and virtues . . . The Duke is still very young and extremely handsome. He lives in the grand manner, dresses and dines luxuriously, plays every game very well, and is marvellously good at riding . . . Courteous, affable, generous, magnanimous, he is liberal to the point of prodigality about making gifts . . . he is adored by the people and liked and applauded by the nobility.

On the other hand he is an atheist, a blasphemer, violent, cruel, and infamous for his licentiousness, in which he is so wrapped up that there is no sex, nor age, nor condition of persons who are spared from it . . .

Nature, who perhaps foresaw that this lord would abandon himself to the most unbridled sensuality, sought to render him unable to have intercourse with males so cleverly as to make him as much more proper and agreeable to the ladies. But it is clear that this did not serve, for without any decent consideration he allowed himself to think of other men, as is well known to a male dancer who was finally prevented from the exercising his art for some time, and a poor French lackey who, reduced to a state of poverty so that he had to be put in the public hospitals, was found one morning in a London street with his throat cut.

They say that at present the Duke is doing no more than taking his revenge for what was done him when he was very young, but with this difference, that nobody ever did anything to him that he did not want, while he often does to others what they do not wish for.

an account by Lorenzo Magalotti, a Venetian visitor at the Court of Charles II during 1667–8

A Restoration Scandal

I shall say a word about the Bishop of Rochester, who became famous a short time ago because of a lively attempt that he made to put his hand into the opening in the front of the hose of Lord Mohun, a boy on account of his age, but not on account of the beauty of his face, who is apt to confirm the evil interpretation given to the intentions of this prelate. The result is that the poor man is in a very miserable state because of the universal scandal that the indiscreet gossip of this young man has sown among that Presbyterian rabble, who have . . . acted to have him dismissed from the office that he had, of being one of the attending bishops at the chair of the King in chapel . . . In this connection, a ridiculous answer was given by a solemn Presbyterian in Parliament to a brother of this bishop. The Act of Comprehension was being discussed, and the Presbyterian protested that the Catholics ought not to be excluded, maintaining this with effective reasons. When he had finished the Protestant said to the man beside him, but in such a way that it could be overheard, 'It seems that this man has the pope in his body.' The Presbyterian rose. 'Certainly,' he replied, 'I'd much rather have the pope in my body than the bishop in my backside.'

from Lorenzo Magalotti's account

They do now all they can to vilify the Clergy, and do accuse Rochester, of his being given to boys and his putting his hand into a gentleman (who now comes to bear evidence against him) his codpiece while they were at table together.

from Samuel Pepys's diary for 30 December 1667. The Bishop (Dolben) survived the scandal and went on to become Archbishop of York.

Women

Love a *Woman*! y'are an *Ass*,
   'Tis a most insipid Passion,
To choose out for your happiness
   The idlest part of *Gods Creation*!

Let the *Porter*, and the *Groome*,
  Things design'd for dirty *Slaves*,
Drudge in *Aurelias Womb*,
  To get supplies for Age, and Graves.

Farewel *Woman*, I intend,
  Henceforth, ev'ry *Night* to sit,
With my lewd, well-natur'd *Friend*,
  Drinking, to engender *Wit*.

Then give me *Health, Wealth, Mirth* and *Wine*,
  And if busie *Love*, intrenches,
There's a sweet soft *Page*, of mine,
  Does the trick worth *Forty Wenches*.
       a poem by John Wilmot, Earl of Rochester (1647–80)

Valencia during the Seventeenth Century

Despite repression, sodomites were not rare. Abundant documentation from Valencia enables us to classify the cases. We note that almost all sodomites were single men, and that many were foreigners, prisoners and friars . . . There were slaves, often Turks or moriscos, like one Hassan Dandolia . . . a coachman . . . who in the 1620s organized parties with adolescents, mostly other slaves, whom he brought together for the purposes of eating, drinking, and gambling, and whom he enticed with money. Alternation of partners was the rule. Hassan clearly preferred young men of good looks and rejoiced unashamedly at his good fortune . . . There were the sailors and soldiers. The case of Pedro Antonio Santandreu, a native of Palma in Majorca, initiated by a Frenchman at Marseilles at the age of sixteen, who confessed his offense with sincere repentance, then began again and from 'passive' turned into 'active' . . . In the case of adolescents, there was always an initiator like that apprentice of sixteen who, at San Felice, near Jativa, had several children (two of fourteen, one of twelve, and one of ten) come into his bedroom, undress and 'touch' each other. Then at a second meeting, he had them lie on their stomachs and penetrated them one after another without ejaculating, after which he invited them to follow his example . . . One must say, for the rest, that whatever one may think of homosexuality, reading the records of these trials is a sickening experience. The cruel realism of the Inquisitorial proceedings does not spare the reader any of the medical reports . . . [Such cases even included the clergy, and in the late seventeenth century there were] two great trials [that] throw a merciless light on the Mercederian [friars] of Valencia . . . Fray Manuel is revealed as a friar who has lost his faith; he does not say or hear mass every day; it appears that he had never confessed during the five years of his stay in the convent. He does not hesitate to say mass immediately after having lascivious contacts with novices in the sacristy, after he has already donned the alb. What is most remarkable is the fascination that he exercises over the novices, a fascination that explains his success as seducer; at least eight had yielded to his advances, and perhaps all save three of the religious of the convent. 'The boys say that he must have bewitched them, for they doted and swarmed about him like dragon-flies; then he seemed like an angel to them, whereas now he appears to be a demon.' A letter from the general of the order confirms that Fray Manuel had caused scandal in the convents in which he had previously resided . . . with activities of the same kind. But the man was so intelligent, his dialectic so subtle, his defense so able, that he escaped the worst [the death penalty]; the penalty was one year seclusion, two years of exile from the kingdom of Valencia; that was all. However, the case of Fray Manuel had repercussions. The trial of 1687 [was against Fray Juan, who had been one of the accusers in the earlier trial] . . . He had seduced at least four novices, and in order to avoid detection had compelled them to confess their sins to him rather than to another priest. The affair led to a total reorganization of the Valencian order and the dispatch of the novices to other houses.

from Bartolomé Bennassar, The Spanish Character (1975)

Discretion

He had no vice except but one sort, in which he was very cautious and secret.

Bishop Gilbert Burnet (1643–1715), historian, writing about King William III

Rough Times

Where in the world does one find a husband who loves only his spouse and does not have someone, be it mistresses or boys, on the side? . . . [You] would not believe how coarse and unmannerly French men have become in the last twelve or thirteen years. One would be hard put to find two young men of quality who know how to behave properly either in what they say or what they do. There are two very different causes for this: namely, all the piety at court and the debauchery among men. Because of the first, men and women are not allowed to speak to each other in public, which used to be a way to give young gentlemen polish. And secondly, because they love boys, they no longer want to please anyone but one another, and the most popular among them is the one who knows how to be debauched, coarse, and insolent. This habit has become so ingrained that no one knows how to live properly any longer, and they are worse than the peasants behind the plough.

from the letters of Charlotte-Élisabeth, Duchess of Orleans (1652–1722)

Finding Sex in Eighteenth-Century Paris

The people arrested in the Tuileries, Luxembourg, or Palais-Royal gardens, or the Champs-Elysées, were thus mostly of the nobility or middle class, but included some master craftsmen, schoolboys, students, and household servants. These same groups frequented the streets, public squares, and river embankments; but there they could lose themselves in the mass of small shopkeepers, workers and young tradesmen.

Like numerous heterosexual couples, or like prostitutes, homosexuals did not hesitate to engage in sexual relations in any places which were somewhat sheltered from view – and scarcely that at times – behind ramparts, in thickets or ditches, in alleys. In any case, dwellings offered little more privacy: walls were thin and doors could be opened quickly. Few people had the means or inclination to obtain real privacy. In fact, all busy places (such as the Pont-Neuf or the fair of St Germain) attracted those in pursuit of *la bonnaventure*.

Rendezvous sites were kept under surveillance almost daily, with, so far as surviving archives can substantiate, increased intensity in spring and summer, on Sundays and holidays, and at certain times of day: a certain Renard 'did not fail to come to the Luxembourg gardens looking for a pick-up (*pour y rac-crocher*) from around ten in the morning until noon, and the same in the evening from seven to nine.' Most people seemed to circulate between 10 a.m. and 2 p.m. and from 8 to 10 p.m.

Making a pick-up was a trade (*métier*) whose techniques had to be mastered if one was to escape being considered a novice. In the eyes of certain practitioners, cruising distinguished homosexuals as a group similar to an important social configuration of the period: *la corporation*.

Methods of operation differed depending on sites, time of day, and conditions. During the day, at the Tuileries or the Luxembourg and in public walkways, the pick-up was carried out mostly by dialogue. 'He asked what time it was'; he walked up 'while asking me for a pinch of tobacco'. The conversation might continue for some time, touching first on mere pleasantries, then slipping into the topic of pleasures in general, before broaching any more specific pleasurable possibility. On the river embankments, on the streets or walkways at nightfall, or in pissoirs, the approach could be more direct. Certain people called attention to themselves by protracted circulating 'in places where the infamous ordinarily hung out'. The police were familiar with the codes governing these encounters: 'having come up to me, making all the signals to me which these infamous types are accustomed to, in order to speak to me', or 'having approached me, staring me in the face several times', or staring 'with affection', or 'having pissed . . . in front of me several times – being one of the signals which all these sordid types have at their disposal'. One might indicate his interest and attempt to create excitement by showing his penis: 'I'm sure you prefer that to a pinch of tobacco.' The mouche himself sometimes elicited a conversation: 'As I was about to let flow, [he] asked me what time it was according to my cock (*vit*) and said that according to his it was high noon.' On the quais, one could relieve oneself (*faire ses nécessités*) and 'expose oneself from the front and rear'. These gestures in themselves were not unusual: only the ostentation which accompanied them identified homosexuals, and they were quickly followed by a question – 'Do you have an erection?' – and a rapid reach to find out.

from M. Rey, 'Parisian Homosexuals Create a Lifestyle, 1700–1750: The Police Archives' in 'Tis Nature's Fault: Unauthorized Sexuality during the Enlightenment, ed. R.P. Maccubbin (1987)

Oxford

Young Mr. Powell came to see me with Cousin Joseph Billio. He gave us some account of the vices that are most prevalent in Oxford. They are drinking and swearing, which are very common and so are not scandalous, but as for whoring, this is not so common, at least not so public. But he has been told that among the chief men in some of the colleges sodomy is very usual and the master of one college has ruined several young handsome men that way, that it is dangerous sending a young man that is beautiful to Oxford.

from the lawyer Dudley Ryder's diary for 1 December 1715

Busybody

Charles Hitchen, Deputy City Marshal, a very busy and active Fellow for promoting the Reformation of Manners, was try'd for Sodomy; but through a nice Punctilio it could not sufficiently be prov'd therefore he was again indicted for an Attempt to commit the detestable Crime, and fully convicted thereof.

from a London newspaper, 15 April 1727

The Scene

They also have their Walks and Appointments, to meet and pick up one another, and their particular Houses of Resort to go to, because they dare not trust themselves in an open Tavern. About twenty of these sorts of Houses have been discovered, beside the Nocturnal Assemblies of great numbers of the like vile Persons, what they call the Markets, which are the Royal Exchange, Lincoln's Inn Bog Houses, the south side of St James's Park, the Piazzas in Covent Garden, St. Clement's Churchyard, etc. It would be a pretty scene to behold them in their clubs and cabals, how they assume the Air and affect the name of Madam or Miss, Betty or Molly, with a chuck under the chin, and 'Oh, you bold pullet, I'll break your eggs,' and then frisk and walk away.

from an anonymous pamphlet, Hell upon Earth: or the Town in Uproar (1727)

Unnamed

I will not act so disagreeably a part to my readers as well as myself . . . to dwell any longer on a subject the very nature of which is a disgrace to human nature, a crime not fit to be named.

from William Blackstone, Commentaries (1765)

Herveys

'This world', Lady Mary Wortley Montagu once observed, 'consists of men, women and Herveys.' In time Lady Mary's *jeu d'esprit* became the classic statement on her very close friend, John, Lord Hervey [1696–1743], courtier, politician and author. It anticipated the thrust of Hervey commentators and critics for the rest of the eighteenth century and beyond. Horace Walpole, quoting Lady Mary's witticism, suggested many years later that 'there were *three sexes*: men, women and Herveys.' For by the time of Walpole's paraphrase of Lady Mary's witty joke, Hervey's persona, of which his unique sexuality was a major part, had been firmly established. It was the product of over twenty years of mythologizing of Lord Hervey's appearance and sexual orientation in the works of William Pulteney, Alexander Pope, Henry Fielding, and a host of pamphleteers, playwrights, and novelists. The mythical Lord Hervey, the creature of the third sex humorously presented by Lady Mary, had become the reality even before Hervey's death in 1743.

from J. R. Dubro, 'The Third Sex: Lord Hervey and his Coterie' in Eighteenth-Century Life (1976)

Nursing the Bruises

By the time Hervey returned to London, Stephen had left for Bath, where he planned to join him. 'I must see you soon,' he impatiently writes (on 15 November); 'I can't live without You; Choice, taste, Habit, prejudice, Inclination, Reason & every thing that either does or ought to influence one's thoughts or one's actions make mine center in & depend on You' . . . His love for Stephen was so penetrating and pervasive that at a dinner and concert given by the Duke of Richmond, when he requested Bernacchi to sing an aria that they together had heard him sing in Naples, 'Before it was half over, I felt my Heart thump, my Throat swell, & my Eyes fill.' Everything he experienced he had to tell his friend: 'My Mind requires You constantly as my Constitution does the Sun,' he writes only the next day, and then confesses – as he had before – his fear that he loves more than he is loved in return: 'I wish you felt just so to me; we should pass many fewer Hours than I fear we are now like to do, asunder.' . . . Hervey's friendship for Stephen Fox was so peculiarly intense that the question must be asked and an answer attempted· was he expressing an affectionate camaraderie or a homosexual passion? It is easy to misread the witty sentiments written in the tradition of French gallantry; and in English court circles such effusive letters passed between ladies and gentlemen who had long since given up sexual intercourse, and also between persons of the same sex whose tastes were exclusively for persons of the opposite . . . [yet] it would be difficult to cite a series of letters from one man to another that exposes such a profound, unequivocal love as that in Hervey's letters to Stephen . . .

One of his letters to Stephen (on 1 June 1727, five months after they met) contains a paragraph that may imply a physical relationship between them. 'You left some such remembrancers behind you,' he writes, 'that I do assure you (if 'tis any satisfaction to you to know) you are not in the least Danger of being forgotten. The favours I have received at Your Honour's Hands are such a Nature that tho' the impression might wear out my Mind, yet they are written in such lasting characters upon every Limb, that 'tis impossible for me to look on a Leg or an Arm without having my Memory refresh'd. I have some thoughts of exposing the marks of your polissonerie [lewdness] to move Compassion, as the

Beggars that have been Slaves at Jerusalem doe the burnt Crucifix upon their Arms; they have remain'd so long that I begin to think they are equally indelible.'

from Robert Halsband, Lord Hervey: Eighteenth-Century Courtier *(1973)*

Bad Luck

Today Monday the 6th [July 1750], two workmen were publicly burnt at the Stake in the Place de la Grève at 5 o'clock in the evening. They were a young carpenter and a pork butcher, aged 18 and 25, whom the watch had caught in the act of committing sodomy. It was felt that the judge had been a bit heavy-handed. Apparently a drop too much of wine had led them to this degree of shamelessness.

from the journal of Edmond-Jean-François Barbier (1689–1771)

Origins

MLLE DE L'ESPINASSE: 'Where do these abominable creatures come from?'
BORDEAU: 'Everywhere, from the abnormal nervous systems in young men and from decaying of the brains of old men. From the lure of beauty in Athens, the scarcity of women in Rome, the fear of the pox in Paris.'

from Suite de l'entretien *by Denis Diderot (1713–84)*

Vile Thought

One would perhaps accuse oneself more easily of planning a major crime than of some obscure feeling that was vile and base. It would be perhaps less painful to write in one's account book: 'I have desired the throne at the expense of its present occupant's life', than to write: 'one day while I was at the bath with a large number of young men, I noticed one of surprising beauty and was not able to keep myself from approaching him.' This sort of examination would not be useless for oneself either.

from a letter of Diderot to Sophie Volland, 14 July 1762

Murder of an Art Historian

He died the morning of June 8, 1768, in the inn in which he had been staying in the Locanda Grande in Trieste, a noose round his neck, stabbed to death by a man who was then going by the name of Francesco Angelis, whose actual name was Arcangeli. Winckelmann had been born in Stendal on December 9, 1717, so was fifty when he died. A world-famous man lost his life . . . he had been the acknowledged master of his craft worthy of emulation: for his artist friends in London, the cardinals in the Vatican who lost the best man of the art collections with him, and for members of the future *Sturm und Drang* movement in Germany, from Goethe to Herder . . .

The court records of Arcangeli's murder trial . . . report in ample detail Winckelmann's slow hemorrhaging from the puncture wounds, the vigorous man's struggle with his murderer, the ugly death in a public inn surrounded by stupid and indifferent waiters and cleaning girls . . .

That Winckelmann, as his murderer apprises us, sought out his company, appears to correspond to the facts. On the other hand, there was no erotic relationship. That was something Arcangeli had asserted because it might have saved him had he been able to sustain a plea of 'self-defense'. Arcangeli was a man over thirty, and pockmarked besides, something detestable to Winckelmann, who praised the Greeks, happy because they were apparently unacquainted with that particular disfigurement. Winckelmann had been traveling incognito, a simple Signor Giovanni, and had stimulated the imagination of a fellow lodger in his hotel, Arcangeli. He had told him of a visit to the empress in Vienna, had mentioned mysterious missions that had some connection with the silver and gold medallions he showed him. Arcangeli was a professional criminal of unsteady fantasy. He began to despise this apparent wellwisher, thinking him a Jew or a Lutheran and seeking a religious opinion before buying the knife and rope he would employ as the murder instruments. Winckelmann was unsuspecting and trustful.

from Hans Mayer, Outsiders (1982)

Powderham Scandal

In March 1784 the married couple were installed in Splendens . . . [they] were presented at court. The twenty-three-year-old husband procured his parliamentary election for Wells . . . and was already jockeying for a peerage . . . [His mother] was smiles all over at the apparent fulfilment of her ambition . . . In October Beckford's name was gazetted among others about to be made peers. The title of Lord Beckford of Fonthill was actually inscribed on the patent. Both Beckfords were staying at Powderham. Ill-omened visit. The Loughboroughs were staying there too. Within a fortnight Beckford was discovered very early one morning in Kitty's bedroom by the boy's tutor. This gentleman heard 'a creaking and bustle, which raised his curiosity, & thro' the key hole he saw the operation, which it seems he did not interrupt, but informed Lord C[ourtenay] & the whole was blown up,' Charles Grenville wrote to Sir William Hamilton. Beckford was accused by Loughborough and resolutely refused to admit culpability. He had, he asseverated, been thrashing Courtenay. Kitty was forced to confess and surrender letters. Sodomy at the time was a capital offence. By November the newspapers had resorted to every indecent allegation . . . [His mother and his wife] kept their heads and staunchly maintained Beckford's innocence. Mrs Beckford made the sensible suggestion that her son should pick up half a dozen harlots in Covent Garden and parade them in Mayfair. Lady Margaret counselled flight. Unfortunately she could not accompany him because she was pregnant. On 29th October Beckford set forth, but at Dover his self-pride and courage overcame his apprehensions and he returned to Fonthill. The long and short of this distressing business was twofold. No prosecution took place, which points to the fact that the totally unscrupulous Loughborough could rake up no proof of crime having been committed. But Beckford's good name was gone. He was ostracized from English society and subjected to snubs and hostility for the remaining sixty years of his life. His character in consequence was gravely affected. A naturally high-strung, acutely sensitive man with few illusions about the nature of his fellow-men, he grew increasingly embittered, ruthless and cruel. He became solitary, introspective and . . . more and more deeply immersed in his multifarious intellectual and artistic interests.

The break with Kitty was complete. Henceforth Beckford barely suffered his name to pass his lips. In the Portuguese journal of 1787 he reviled him for allowing 'the most obnoxious papers . . . to remain in old Beelzebub's [Loughborough's] clutches', and called him 'that cowardly and effeminate fool, Wm. Courtenay'. Indeed Courtenay's character and conduct deteriorated with age. In 1811 he was forced to flee the country to avoid a charge of sodomy, and never returned. In 1785 the Beckfords retired to Switzerland where the following year Lady Margaret, after giving birth to a second daughter, died of puerperal fever.

Beckford was heartbroken . . . The effect was to drive [him] more and more into a state of defiance and bravado. He bought an additional 1,700 acres to augment the Fonthill estate. He planted a million trees. He decided once and for all to raise himself a building of a size, style and magnificence that no one in England had ever seen and what is more that few people in England should see. He would keep the world at bay. Only a handful of the choicest, most intimate friends, who still acknowledged his position in society, would be welcomed . . . 'Some people drink to forget unhappiness,' he said. 'I do not drink, I build.'

from James Lees-Milne, William Beckford (1976)

CHAPTER FIVE

The Nineteenth Century

Western society was transformed by industrialisation. Beginning in Britain during the eighteenth century and gradually spreading to France, Germany, the Low Countries and America, industrialisation made it possible for cities to expand on a particularly dramatic scale. It was soon the case that by at least 1900 over half the population of an industrial state could live in an urban environment. People's relationship with nature and their environment was radically changed. Yet the essential elements of pre-industrial society persisted. The creation of the bourgeois family made the patriarchy more powerful and more difficult to challenge.

Many new mental skills and techniques were discovered which allowed society and the environment to be examined more critically. Such methods could be applied to the evidence of the past, and in this way people might liberate themselves from the many myths and legends that had bewitched their ancestors. It was possible for scholars to begin to test the authenticity of the Bible and treat it as a historical document. Charles Darwin's challenge of the creation myth in Genesis and the acceptance of his ideas on evolution further eroded the spell of the past.

However, the nineteenth century was also a great age of faith. There was a succession of religious revivals. For all the old myths that were destroyed, many more new ones were put in their place. In many ways such myths were even more powerful than those they had replaced, because they could be spread more widely and they carried the sanction of Science, the hero of the age. Nineteenth-century European culture was like a vast myth-making factory. We have been living in its shadow ever since.

It now became possible to construct a homosexual past. Leading the way was an Englishman, John Addington Symonds. He produced a homosexual pedigree which began with the Greeks, passed through the Renaissance and culminated in Walt Whitman, the American poet. He produced an excellent translation of the poetry of Michelangelo[1] and proved the homosexuality of Michelangelo to his own satisfaction. Prim, self-righteous and energetic, he might justifiably be regarded as the father of homosexual history. His contemporary Frederick Rolfe celebrated another tradition which has continually attracted a regular succession of followers. Rolfe was a fantasist. He had aristocratic ambitions and liked to call himself Baron Corvo. A jack of all trades, he converted to the Roman Catholic Church, and his colourful writings[2] frequently feature the camp possibilities offered by Mother Church. His favourite fantasy was that he would be elected Pope. He also wrote pornography and made good use of the camera. On one Sicilian excursion he met up with the most famous homosexual lensman of all time, Baron Wilhelm von Gloeden, who had much fun arranging the local shepherds in various states of undress. Rolfe has had many imitators. The Apostle of Catholic Camp?

The expansion of education provided many opportunities for those with homosexual interests. The classics were the chief medium of instruction, and many teachers dedicated themselves to the Socratic ideal. A few stepped over the line and were tempted by some latter-day Alcibiades into sins of the flesh. One who strayed often was Oscar Browning, an Eton master sacked for intimacy with a pupil. Browning graduated to King's College Cambridge, where he became a Fellow. There he was one of the architects of possibly the most remarkably homosexual society since fifth-century Athens. Today King's can count among its distinguished old boys E. M. Forster, J. M. Keynes, Rupert Brooke, Hugh Dalton, Patrick White, Alan Turing and Simon Raven. Browning helped nurture an atmosphere sympathetic to homosexuality in a college which has exercised an important influence on modern culture and society.

Sublimation reached heights never previously attained in the march of mankind. Homosexual interest was even harnessed in the expansion of the European states across the globe: there was, as Ronald Hyam has recently shown,[3] an intimate link between Empire and homosexuality. It was, however, by Roger Casement, a British consul, most famous for his Black Diaries, that the foundations were laid for the attack on imperialism with his exposures of the dark underside of Belgian colonialism in the Congo.[4] His contemporary Baden-Powell, a soldier who defended the British Empire, must take the prize as the greatest sublimater of the age. He established his own youth movement, the Boy Scouts, which offered him many voyeuristic delights in his old age.

Exchanging Gifts

Byron had first met John Edlestone in October 1805. At that time, Edlestone was fifteen and Byron, who had just arrived at Cambridge, seventeen. Byron had become interested in Edlestone through hearing him sing in the Trinity College choir. The boy's background was humble, and Byron assumed the role of aristocratic patron to a youngster of talent, calling him his protégé . . . Edlestone was fair and thin, with dark eyes. One imagines him as rather diffident, perhaps somewhat feminine: frailness in younger males brought out the chivalric side of Byron's character . . . [Byron] tells us that he was first attracted to Edlestone by his voice, then by his looks and personality, finally an inadvertent revelation of the boy's feeling crystallised his own into love. Byron, with his typical generosity, had probably made substantial presents of money to Edlestone. When the latter wished to reciprocate, he gave Byron an inexpensive stone, a cornelian. But fearing that Byron would despise his gift, he burst into tears. This in turn melted Byron, who shed tears of his own. Byron commemorated the occasion in two poems [one entitled 'The Cornelian'] . . .

Edlestone [left Cambridge and took] a post in a 'mercantile home' in London. For whatever reason, they planned a separation of a year and a half . . . [Byron commented,] 'We shall probably not meet till the extirpation of my minority, when I shall leave to his decision, either entering as a Partner through my Interest, or residing with me altogether. Of course he would in his present frame of mind prefer the latter, but he may alter his opinion previous to that period, however he shall have his chance, I certainly love him more than any human being and neither time or Distance have had the least effect on my (in general) changeable Disposition . . . He is certainly perhaps more attached to me, than even I am in return. During the whole of my residence in Cambridge, we met every summer and winter, without passing one tiresome moment and separated each time with increasing reluctance. I hope you will one day see us together. He is the only being I esteem, though I like many.'

from Louis Crompton, Byron and Greek Love *(1985)*

Lord Londonderry's Suicide

Ah, what a frightful tragedy – I am shaking from head to foot – Londonderry! What an end! You will hear the news – accompanied by what details I do not know. Here is the information I have just gathered from Lady Conyningham. Last Friday, the 9th, Londonderry went to see the King at Carlton House. He came from North Cray with his wife, and she put him down at the door of the Palace. When he got into the King's study, he seized him by the arm and said: 'Have you heard the news, the terrible news? I am a fugitive from justice, I am accused of the same crime as the Bishop of Clogher [who had been surprised while performing fellatio on a guardsman]. I have ordered my saddle horses; I am going to fly to Portsmouth, and from there to the ends of the earth.' The King took him by both hands and begged him to compose himself, to be calm. They

were alone: he accused himself of every crime . . . [He retired to his country
home where he committed suicide a few days later.]

> Princess Lieven to Prince Metternich, 12 August 1822

On 14 August she wrote with more information, particularly of Londonderry's last
interview with George IV:

He showed the King two anonymous letters which he had received the day
before, Thursday. One of them threatened to reveal his irregular conduct to his
wife; the other concerned a more terrible subject. This letter sent him off his
head.

Fairy Tales

It would seem appropriate that the most famous writer of fairy stories should have had
homosexual inclinations, but there has been a lively debate on the subject. Dr Alfred
Kinsey, touring Europe after the successful publication of his reports on human sexual
behaviour had made him an international celebrity, examined the evidence.

Dr Kinsey Pronounces

While he was in Copenhagen, Kinsey tracked down a scholar who had amassed
an immense pile of data and papers on Hans Christian Andersen . . . [whom
Kinsey suspected of homosexuality]. In Andersen's case there had always been
hints about his homosexuality and some knowledgeable scholars had been able
to discern it by reading between the lines. But seeing the original manuscripts
which the scholar possessed, Kinsey could say unequivocally that they were
'straight-out homosexual stories'. Of the famed Little Mermaid, Kinsey observed
that she was 'a mute nymph' who 'cannot tell the world how she feels about
anything' and, similarly, 'Andersen could not tell the world of his own homosexual love for the people of the world, but the original manuscripts showed his
feelings clearly.'

> W. B. Pomeroy, Dr. Kinsey (1972)

A Danish Biographer Replies

Andersen according to one writer was 'an incurable masturbator' . . . but it is
almost certain that he never had a sexual relationship with another person, male
or female . . . he really felt that he was the 'Ugly Duckling'.

> from Elias Bredsdorff, Hans Christian Andersen: the Story of his Life and Work 1805–75
> (1975)

The Little Mermaid

This son of a mentally disabled shoemaker and an uneducated washer-woman
seems all too willing to bare his insides. As the portraitist of his poverty and
ugliness and the playstuff of his dreams, Andersen takes pleasure in portraying
his defeats . . . When [Edward] Collin [to whom Andersen was devoted] decided

to marry, Andersen wrote his famous fairytale, 'The Story of the Little Mermaid'. Nothing had ever moved him more in writing, he confessed later. Here he had not only dared to portray himself as an outsider, but as a sexual outsider . . . the little mermaid was himself – in her attempt to win the distant beloved, mortal prince, though she was handicapped in every way: a foundling, a slave, an outsider . . . She lost her prince, saw him wed another.

from Hans Mayer, Outsiders (1982)

Scot-Free

In 1866 the Reverend Horatio Alger (1832–99), a Unitarian minister near Boston, was accused of indecent assault of two boys. He ran off and made his fortune as the Jeffrey Archer of nineteenth-century American fiction, churning out a succession of lucrative bestsellers. He was also a great visitor of boys' homes and helped many lads make their way in the world. One of his most famous works was the novel *Ragged Dick*, the story of a boy who gets lucky.

An able committee of the church and society . . . now verbally report, that on the examination of two boys (and they have good reason to think there were others) they were entirely confirmed and unanimous in the opinion of his being guilty to the full extent of the above specified charges. Whereupon the committee sent for Alger and to him specified the charges and evidence of his guilt, which he neither denied or attempted to extenuate but received with the apparent calmness of an old offender – and hastily left town on the next train for parts unknown – probably Boston. Had he remained any longer an arrest or something worse might have occurred. We should scarcely have felt responsible for the consequences in an outraged community, and that outrage committed by a pretended Christian teacher.

from Gary Scharnhorst, Horatio Alger, Jr (1980)

Revolutionary Moment

The pederasts start counting their numbers and discover they are a powerful group in our state. The only thing missing is an organisation, but it seems to exist already, though it is hidden. And since they can count on important personalities, in all old and even new parties, their victory is assured. Now the motto will be 'war against the frontal orifices, peace to those behind'. How lucky we are that we are both too old – otherwise we might have to submit personally to the victors. But the younger generation! Really it can only happen in Germany, that such a no-good can transform lechery into a theory and invite us to 'enter'. Unfortunately, he [Karl Friedrich Ulrichs, whose book had provoked this letter] hasn't the courage to openly confess what he is and is forced to operate in full view of the public, though not 'frontally' as he once called it by mistake. But just you wait until the North German legislature has recognised the 'rights of the behind', then he'll sing another tune. We poor frontal fellows, with our childish passion for women, will have a bad time.

from a letter from Friedrich Engels to Karl Marx, 22 June 1868

Sodom Afloat

Like pears closely packed, the crowded crew mutually decay through close contact, and every plague spot is contagious. Still more, from this close confinement – so far as it affects the common sailors – arise other evils, so direful that they will hardly bear even so much allusion. What too many seamen are when ashore is very well known: but what some of them become when completely cut off from shore indulgences can hardly be imagined by landsmen. The sin for which the cities of the plain were overthrown still lingers in some of these wooden-walled Gomorrahs of the deep. More than once complaints were made on the *Neversink*, from which the deck officer would turn away with loathing, refuse to hear them, and command the complainant out of his sight. There are evils in men-of-war, which, like the suppressed domestic drama of Horace Walpole, will neither bear representing nor reading, and will hardly bear thinking of. The landsman who has neither read Walpole's *Mysterious Mother*, nor Sophocles' *Oedipus Tyrannus*, nor the Roman story of Count Cenci, dramatized by Shelley, let that landsman guardedly remain in his ignorance of even worse horrors than these, and forever abstain from seeking to draw aside this veil.

from Herman Melville, White Jacket *(1850)*

A Grand Passion

When Rimbaud arrived in Paris, he had been 'in a state of feverish mental exaltation, with his sexual curiosity aroused and his senses stimulated but not yet satisfied'. He was, writes his biographer, ready to be initiated, and it was chance which made him meet Verlaine at this crisis in his development. Rimbaud does not seem to have been a natural homosexual, 'and he could never overcome his sense of guilt or inferiority in this relationship. Nevertheless, there is no doubt that, with Verlaine, Rimbaud, for a time, experienced complete physical and spiritual ecstasy and complete freedom from all inhibitions.'

According to sober-minded witnesses, wrote Charles Maurras, Rimbaud had 'a rather ugly face: a flat nose, a full mouth, and pale, vague eyes. But he was big and vigorous, and a passionate sensuality emanated from all his features.' Verlaine, who had been living with a dull and pregnant wife, was stirred to the depths of his being by this sensuality, which matched his own. Years later he still talked about 'that perfect oval face, the face of an exiled angel'. His relationship with Rimbaud was, without question, the paramount experience of his life. If Rimbaud was an exiled angel, Verlaine was prepared to sacrifice his family and sell his soul to go into exile with him.

Possibly Rimbaud knew something of homosexuality. Verlaine was ten years older than Rimbaud; he now initiated him into a life of depravity. Rimbaud soon 'plunged his teacher into depths of vice he would not have explored alone'. Verlaine had found a friend to persuade him that all his appetites were legitimate; it seemed to him that the prison gates were open. He himself satisfied his appetites as a hedonist; Rimbaud did so as an explorer. But in the early months of their relationship they found perfect fulfilment in one another.

Verlaine had always had a streak of violence in his nature, and it had always been intensified by drink. Rimbaud, too, was violent; at a literary dinner, le Dîner des Vilains Bonshommes, he had seized Verlaine's swordstick, and rushed at Étienne Carjat, the photographer. He would have done him bodily harm if some of the other guests had not restrained him.

Valade told Blémont that Rimbaud's imagination, 'full of unheard-of power and corruption, fascinated or terrified all our friends'. Lepelletier thought him 'strange, fantastic and disturbing'. Maurice Rollinat, the poet, told Goncourt that Rimbaud was the very genius of perversity. 'Yes, the genius of perversity . . . He had a malevolent imagination . . . and he spent his life inventing acts of ruthless malice.'

Verlaine was not exempt from them. The two of them fought with knives. On one occasion Rimbaud asked him to put his hands, palm upwards, on the table; then he stabbed them. It was not merely to prove to himself his unbreakable hold on Verlaine; it was not simple indulgence in wrongdoing. It was part of his creed, 'le long, immense et raisonné *dérèglement* de tous les sens'.

The quickest way to achieve degradation was to get drunk on absinthe; and early in 1872, when he and Verlaine began to be shunned even by Bohemian friends, they spent much of the day in the cafés of the Boul' Mich', spending Verlaine's inheritance on absinthe, and living in a more or less continual state of intoxication. When the cafés finally closed, they used to go to the rue Campagne-Première.

It cannot be proved that they practised sodomy. In the medical report on Verlaine in 1873, it was said that his body showed signs of recent active and passive sodomy; but some doctors now consider that the facts revealed by such an examination are not reliable evidence. However, it is impossible to believe that Verlaine and Rimbaud contented themselves with a romantic friendship; there is no doubt that both men felt physical rapture, and, repeatedly, in his poems, Verlaine proclaims his passion.

from Enid Starkie, Arthur Rimbaud *(1938)*

Flaubert in Egypt

I was indignant and very sad that you weren't here. Three or four musicians playing curious instruments took up their positions at the end of the hotel dining-room while one gentleman was still eating his lunch and the rest of us were sitting on the divan smoking our pipes. As dancers, imagine two rascals, quite ugly, but charming in their corruption, in their obscene leerings and effeminacy of their movements, dressed as women, their eyes painted with antimony. For costume, they have wide trousers and an embroidered jacket. The latter comes down to the epigastrium, whereas the trousers, held up by an enormous cashmere girdle folded double several times, begin only about at the pubis, so that the entire stomach, the loins, and the beginning of the buttocks are naked, seen through a black gauze held tight against the skin by the upper and lower garments. This ripples on the hips like a dark, transparent wave with every movement they make. The music is always the same, and goes on for two hours without stopping. The flute is shrill, the drumbeats throb in your breast, the singer dominates all. The dancers advance and retreat, shaking the pelvis with a short convulsive movement. A quivering of the muscles is the only way to describe it; when the pelvis moves, the rest of the body is motionless; when the breast shakes, nothing else moves. In this manner they advance toward you, their arms extended, rattling brass castanets, and their faces, under the rouge and the sweat, remain more expressionless than a statue's. By that I mean they never smile. The effect is produced by the gravity of the face in contrast to the lascivious movements of the body. Sometimes they lie down flat on their backs, like a woman ready to be fucked, then rise up with a movement of the loins similar to that of a tree swinging back into place after the wind has stopped. In their bowings and salutations their great red trousers suddenly inflate like oval balloons, then seem to melt away, expelling the air that swells them. From time to time, during the dance, the impresario, or pimp, who brought them plays around them, kissing them on the belly, the arse, and the small of the back, and making obscene remarks in an effort to put additional spice into a thing that is already quite self-evident. It is too beautiful to be exciting. I doubt whether we shall find the women as good as the men; the ugliness of the latter adds greatly to the thing as art. I had a headache for the rest of the day . . . Speaking of bardashes, this is what I know about them. Here it is quite accepted. One admits one's sodomy, and it is spoken of at table in the hotel. Sometimes you do a bit of denying, and then everybody teases you and you end up confessing. Travelling as we are for educational purposes, and charged with a mission by the government, we have considered it our duty to indulge in this form of ejaculation.

from a letter from Gustave Flaubert to Louis Bouilhet, 15 January 1850

A Double Life

In February 1877 an old acquaintance took him [John Addington Symonds] to a male brothel near the military barracks in Regent's Park. Here he met a strapping young soldier with whom he made an assignation for the following day. For the first time he had a profound sexual experience with someone of a lower social rank and this aspect of the encounter intrigued him as much as the delight of gazing on the beauty of the trooper's body. When his desire had been satisfied, they dressed and sat smoking and talking on the side of the bed. This part of the afternoon was idealized by Symonds as a revelation of the superb comradeship which might exist between men, even two men from entirely different social classes of society, and yet when he left the house, he hurried away in horror and disgust.

At this time he was delivering three lectures on 'Florence and the Medicis' at the Royal Institute. The first was given on the day that he had arranged to meet the soldier. All the time he stood there addressing his cultured audience, he despised their self-righteous, middle-class faces gazing earnestly up at him, while he chafed with longing for the time to pass so that he could rush to his soldier.

from Phyllis Grosskurth, John Addington Symonds: A Biography *(1964)*

The Dilemma

The accomplished languages of Europe in the nineteenth century supply no terms for this persistent feature of human psychology, without imparting some implication of disgust, disgrace, vituperation.

from John Addington Symonds, A Problem in Modern Ethics *(1891)*

Snaps

Symonds was in the habit of sending his friends photographs of himself. There was nothing very unusual about that. The Victorians were always sending each other photographs of themselves . . . What was more unusual was that Symonds sent his friends, as well as photographs of himself, photos of Angelo, his favourite gondolier, and of other young men he knew. There was an excellent amateur photographer in Davos; Symonds often mentioned him in his letters. Symonds sent photographs not only to men, but also to his great friends Mary Robinson and Janet Ross. There is no suggestion, even in relation to one photograph he sent Miss Robinson of a naked young man with a sword between his legs, that anyone might consider them obscene or offensive. Symonds was working on his biography of Michelangelo and would encourage models to pose in 'the imposs- ible positions discovered by Michelangelo'.

from Ann Thwaite, Edmund Gosse: A Literary Landscape 1849–1928 *(1984)*

Man of Principle

When I was your age and for a long time after, I contented myself . . . with seeing and admiring people, entering by imagination into sympathy with their lives. I now want to love immensely. And I love beauty with a passion that burns the more I grow old. I love beauty above virtue, and think that nowhere is beauty more eminent than in young men. This love is what people call aesthetic with me. It has to do with my perceptions through the senses, and does not affect my regard for duty, principle, right conduct. I know well enough that there are more important things in the Universe than beauty. But there is nothing I was born to love more.

With my soul and heart I love you more than the world. With my aesthetic perceptions I love physical perfection.

from a letter from John Addington Symonds to his daughter Madge

The Gondolier

Sitting together one May afternoon in 1881 in the garden of an osteria, [Horatio] Brown pointed out a striking young gondolier, the servant of the General de Horsey. Symonds was immediately entranced by an electric quality that seemed to run through the young man. For the next few days he was haunted by the memory of a hoarse voice, a mass of dark hair, and dazzling teeth under a short blonde moustache. In his waking dreams he imagined himself as a different being, even a woman who was loved by the vibrant gondolier.

A few nights later, in a state of trembling agitation, he stood waiting in front of the Church of the Gesuati, while the young man strode nonchalantly toward him. Symonds had no difficulty in persuading him to go back to his room in the Casa Alberti where he was staying. Here he questioned him about his life and learned that his name was Angelo Fusato, he was twenty-four years old, and had just completed three years' service in the Genio. Angelo assumed that Symonds was just another English gentleman of perverted tastes which he was willing to satisfy for a stipulated number of lire. The indignity of the situation appalled Symonds and he could not bring himself to touch him. In a turmoil of emotion, the next day he left abruptly for Monte Generoso. Here he wrote the series of sonnets called 'The Sea Calls', expressing his longing to return to Venice . . . By September he realized that 'Sonnet writing will not suffice for the human soul,' and he returned to Venice, determined to establish some sort of permanent relationship with Angelo. This time he took rooms in the Casa Barbier, where the gondolier began to visit him at night. Symonds was completely infatuated and showered Angelo with presents and money, but the reckless way the young man squandered it made Symonds understand why his friends called him *il matto* (the madcap). However, he seemed to have formed a serious attachment for a girl who had borne him two sons and he would have married her, he claimed, if he had enough money. For two months Symonds tried desperately to convince Angelo that his interest in him extended beyond a passing amour. To his great joy he finally persuaded him to leave General de Horsey's service and become his own gondolier at a fixed wage so that he would be able to marry his mistress . . . Gradually Angelo responded to Symonds's fervent sincerity, and in time the relationship almost developed into his ideal of 'comradeship' . . . Angelo grew to trust him so completely that he concealed nothing from him and he continued to serve him until Symonds's death in 1893. Sometimes he gave vent to outbursts of

Italian passion but his disposition was, on the whole, sunny and kindly, and in his company Symonds could relax without the constant strain of being amusing or profound as he had to be with his more cultivated friends.

from Phyllis Grosskurth, John Addington Symonds: A Biography (1964)

The Impact of Semen

I have no doubt myself the absorption of semen implies a real modification of the person who absorbs it, and that, in these homosexual relations, this constitutes an important basis for subsequent conditions – both spiritual and corporeal.

from a letter from John Addington Symonds to Edward Carpenter, 29 December 1892

Classlessness

The blending of Social Strata in masculine love seems to me one of its most pronounced, and socially hopeful, features. Where it appears, it abolishes class distinctions, and opens by a single operation the cataract-blinded eye to their futilities. In removing the film of prejudice and education, it acts like the oculist and knife. If it could be acknowledged and extended, it would do very much to further the advent of the right sort of Socialism.

from a letter from John Addington Symonds to Edward Carpenter, 21 January 1893

A Career Open to Talent

What the guardsman said to your friend accords with what I know about military prostitution. I made an acquaintance last autumn in Venice with a Corporal of the 2nd Life Guard who was travelling with a man I knew. He gave me a great deal of information. But it all pointed to the mercantile aspect of the matter. However, he said that some men 'listed on purpose to indulge their propensities'. An Italian Colonel told me the same thing – i.e. that young men of the best families, after serving as volunteers, or in the natural course of conscription, would sometimes remain on in the ranks with a view to the opportunities afforded by barracks.

from a letter from John Addington Symonds to Edward Carpenter, 5 February 1893

Taming the Wild Beast

One man with whom he did achieve complete sympathy was Edmund Gosse. Symonds's resolute determination to continue his investigations elicited Gosse's admiration and moved him – after fifteen long years of friendship – to admit at least the truth of Symonds's suspicions. 'I know of all you speak of,' Gosse wrote,

'— the solitude, the rebellion, the despair. Yet I have been happy, too; I hope you also have been happy, — that all you has not been disappointment & revulsion of hope? Either way, I entirely & deeply sympathise with you. Years ago I wanted to write to you about all this, and withdrew threw cowardice. I have had a very fortunate life, but there has been this obstinate twist in it! I have reached a quieter time — some beginning of that Sophoclean period when the wild beast dies. He is not dead, but tamer; I understand him & the trick of his claws.'

from Phyllis Grosskurth, John Addington Symonds: A Biography *(1964)*

Gladstonian

If he [Symonds] has, or gathers, a band of the emulous, we may look for some capital sport. But I don't wonder that some of his friends and relations are haunted with a vague malaise. I think one ought to wish him more humour, it is really the saving salt. But the great reformers never have it — & he is the Gladstone of the affair.

from a letter from Henry James to Edmund Gosse, 1893

Unnecessary Enquiry

Ever since Symonds wrote to him [Walt Whitman] in 1871, enclosing a poem inspired by 'Calamus', he continued to drop hints as to how much he longed to know its real meaning. The meaning was clear enough to him, but he wanted Whitman to spell it out explicitly and uncompromisingly. Whitman answered his letters courteously; sent him photographs; but for twenty years he turned a deaf ear to his pleas. After receiving from Whitman a complete edition of the poems — albeit with the omission of 'Long I thought that knowledge alone would suffice me', which had been left out of all editions since 1860 — Symonds was emboldened to put the question once more. On 3 August 1890, he wrote more urgently than he had ever done before, asking specifically if 'adhesiveness' included sexual relations between men; he justified the persistence of his demands with the explanation that he could not write the study of the poet which he had long been contemplating unless Whitman's intention was absolutely clear to him. The letter is a very ingenious piece of subtilizing — and Whitman would have been a fool to have fallen into the trap so skilfully — and so obviously — laid for him. Symonds in effect challenged him to state his position because he, Symonds, and Whitman's other disciples, often found themselves defending him against the charge that his doctrines led to degradation — even though they weren't quite sure what his doctrines were! Ingenuously Symonds went on to say that he agreed with Whitman's detractors that, since some men *did* have a bias towards their own sex, 'Calamus' might encourage them in sexual intimacies; yet, for his part, he could see nothing anti-social in such behaviour. Did Whitman leave the physical nature of a relationship to the individual conscience? There follows a passionate exclamation that he is sure Whitman would speak candidly to him if they met in the flesh! Then, in a final careless aside, as if to reassure Whitman, he concludes with the casual remark that he is really not interested in the subject at all, but enquires only because it is a necessary part of Whitman's philosophy which he hopes to disseminate to the world.

Whitman had had enough. The anger fairly burns from his scalding reply of 19 August; yet he was concerned enough about the interpretation Symonds might make of his words, to work them out carefully in a pencilled draft before the final answer went off. He first admits to having six illegitimate children (scattered far and wide!), the implication apparently being that he was a perfectly normal man. Then the voice roars out in righteous indignation: 'About the questions on "Calamus", etc, they quite daze me. *Leaves of Grass* is only to be rightly construed by and within its own atmosphere and essential character – all its pages and pieces so strictly coming under. That the Calamus part has ever allowed the possibility of such construction as mentioned is terrible. I am fain to hope that the pages themselves are not to be even mentioned for such gratuitous and quite at the time undreamed and unwished possibility of morbid inferences – which are disavowed by me and seem damnable.' After twenty years Symonds finally had his answer.

His reaction was bitter disappointment . . . It was the end of a long idyll. His 'Master' had not only failed him lamentably, but, unkindest cut of all, had turned viciously upon him.

from Phyllis Grosskurth, John Addington Symonds: A Biography *(1964)*

Comrades

To tell the secrets of my nights and days,
To celebrate the needs of comrades . . .

from Walt Whitman, Calamus *(1860)*

A Straight Friend

John Burroughs, who was unquestionably 'straight', writes as follows in 1863–4. 'I have been much with Walt. Have even slept with him. I love him very much . . . He loves everything and everybody. I saw a soldier the other day stop on the street and kiss him. He kisses me as if I were a girl . . . He bathed today while I was there – such a handsome body, and such delicate, rosy flesh I never saw before. I told him he looked good enough to eat.'

from Justin Kaplan, Walt Whitman: A Life *(1980)*

An Innocent Abroad

Dan'l Spencer . . . told me he had never been in a fight and did not drink at all, gone in 2d NY Lt Artillery deserted, returned to it slept with me Sept 3d

+Theodore M Carr – Deserted Capt. Dawson's Co . . . met Fort Green forenoon Aug. 28 – and came to the house with me . . . left Sept 11th

Peter Calhoun, Oct. 10 '62 aged 23, born in Rome, N.Y. worked on canal 3 years . . . my ride with him a trip or more at night . . .

David Wilson night of Oct. 11, '62 walking up from Middagh – slept with me – works in a blacksmith shop in Navy Yard – lives in Hampden st. – walks together Sunday afternoon & night – is about 19.

Horace Ostrander Oct 22 '62 . . . his experiences as a green hand slept with him Dec 4 '62 . . .

Jerry Taylor . . . slept with me last night
    from Walt Whitman's diary

Washington 1865

Whitman spent much of the Civil War in Washington nursing wounded soldiers, an experience which had a profound effect on him. He wrote many accounts for the newspapers telling of his experiences in the capital.

The streets, the public buildings and grounds of Washington still swarm with soldiers from Illinois, Indiana, Ohio, Missouri, Iowa, and all the Western States. I am continually meeting and talking with them. They often speak to me first, and always show great sociability, and glad to have a good interchange of chat. These Western soldiers are more slow in their movements, and in their intellectual quality also; have no extreme alertness. They are larger in size, have a more serious physiognomy, are continually looking at you as they pass in the street. They are largely animal, and handsomely so. During the war I have been at times with the Fourteenth, Fifteenth, Seventeenth, and Twentieth Corps. I always feel drawn towards the men, and like the personal contact when we are crowded together, as frequently these days in the street cars.

The Coming of his Friend

When I heard at the close of the day how I had been praised in the Capitol,
    still it was not a happy night that followed;
Nor when I caroused – Nor when my favourite plans were accomplished – was
    I really happy,
But that day I rose at dawn from the bed of perfect health, electric, inhaling
    sweet breath,
When I saw the full moon in the west grow pale and disappear in the morning
    light,
When I wandered alone over the beach, and undressing, bathed, laughing
    with the waters, and saw the sun rise,

And when I thought how my friend, my lover, was coming, then O I was
    happy;
Each breath tasted sweeter — and all that day my food nourished me more —
    And the beautiful day passed well,
And the next came with equal joy — And with the next, at the evening, came
    my friend.

And that night, while all was still, I heard the waters roll slowly continually up
    the shores
I heard the hissing rustle of the liquid and sands, as directed to me,
    whispering, to congratulate me, — For the friend I love lay sleeping by my
    side,
In the stillness his face was inclined toward me, while the moon's clear beams
    shone,
And his arm lay lightly over my breast — And that night I was happy.
from Walt Whitman, Calamus *(1860)*

Candid Camera

Photography was a serviceable amusement for Rolfe and his friends. Through it
they were never far from the absorbing matter of boys since picture-taking
gave him an excuse to approach boys and to be in their company, he rarely went
into the streets without a camera. At the same time, he was extremely careful
with his friends, taking pains to get the Gleeson Whites' permission to make
camera studies of their thirteen-year-old son Eric, and Kains Jackson's, to
photograph Cecil Castle. Because Rolfe was a 'perfectly loyal friend over boys'
and never attempted to intrude between lovers, Kains Jackson liked having the
boy pose for Rolfe. Thirty years afterwards, Kains Jackson recalled how the
young man, nude except for a knit cap, assisted Rolfe in getting a 'spontaneous'
pose. 'I can recall as though it was yesterday,' Kains Jackson said, 'my enjoyment
of the . . . all but realised anticipation of Cecil in his eagerness to run from the
sea not stopping in time but upsetting Corvo and his camera. But Cecil was
wonderful in those things and stopped dead on the towel laid down as his
objective.'
from Miriam J. Benkovitz, Frederick Rolfe: Baron Corvo — a Biography *(1977)*

Uncorrupted

Rolfe's ideal was a large boy of sixteen to eighteen years clothed with 'most lovely
pads of muscular sweet flesh', whose skin was of a 'rosy satin fineness and
softness'. Such a boy was at his prime before 'some great fat slow cow of a girl'
had an opportunity to 'open herself wide and lie quite still & drain him dry',
before he had got 'hard and hairy' with a moustache, 'brushes in his milky
armpits' and 'brooms on his splendid young thighs'.
    Thus the divine friend much desired must be male, preferably young, and,
according to Rolfe's demands, he must exhibit those qualities of which Rolfe

believed himself capable, self-sacrifice, honour, and unflinching fidelity. Of course, Rolfe was doomed to disappointment. No friend proved to be quite what he seemed and even at his most devoted, if he failed in judgement or achievement, Rolfe suspected him of malice.

from Miriam J. Benkovitz, Frederick Rolfe: Baron Corvo – a Biography (1977)

Inspecting Flesh

I make a point of being up during Eights Weeks, because (as a physical epicure) I like to see how England's most recent flesh is coming on.

Frederick Rolfe's explanation for his annual pilgrimage to Oxford

Posing

On leaving the University of Rostock, Wilhelm [von Gloeden] showed scant interest in the social life open to him in Berlin through his rank and his stepfather's friendship with the Kaiser. With the financial independence of a fortune . . . he was free to follow his own passions for the arts, particularly Greek classicism and the growing cult of aestheticism . . . Sometime about 1880, Wilhelm arrived in Taormina and rented a villa . . . He entertained lavishly, supplying his guests with a cortège of local boys dressed, when at all, like Greek acolytes . . . von Gloeden made no secret of his homosexuality . . . [soon after coming to Taormina, he took up photography] . . . His cards sold by the thousand . . . he made almost daily treks up the rough mountain paths to pose his models in magnificent settings, steep crags or sunny glades, with Mount Etna as an ever-splendid backcloth. Sun worship was a constantly recurring theme, and shots of young bodies, glistening from a mixture of milk and olive oil, basking on rocks or fondly embracing on sunny beaches, had an inevitable appeal to sun-starved Northerners . . . Whilst never pornographic, his technique of posing two boys together, often an older with a younger one, evoked a subtle suggestion of eroticism and sexuality which is impossible to ignore . . . von Gloeden seems to have had no difficulty in finding young lads, farm boys and rugged young fishermen, willing to drop their clothes. Exactly how von Gloeden marketed his nude photographs is not clear. A large selection was sent to King Edward VII's private secretary under the cover of the diplomatic bag.

from Gay News, March 1981

Apologia

His [Edward Carpenter's] *Intermediate Sex*, however, was a quiet success: it went through three impressions in four years. He was thus encouraged to write, not merely in defence of homosexuality, but also in praise of its unique virtues. He somehow believed that 'there is an organic connection between the homosexual temperament and unusual psychic or divinatory powers', and sought to prove this contention in an article in a French periodical. The Jews and the

Christians both persecuted homosexuals as heretics and sorcerers, and these circumstances, together with their peculiarities as the feminine man and the masculine woman, or the non-warlike man and the non-domestic woman, he maintained, led to their adopting extraordinary or even uncanny activities and vocations by becoming seers, healers, or teachers of esoteric arts, and thus 'laid the foundation of the priesthood, and of science, literature and art'. His conclusion sounds somewhat sweeping, but he went ahead with a eulogy of homosexuality which, he now declared, was 'a forward force in human evolution'.

from Chushichi Tsuzuki, Edward Carpenter 1844–1929: A Prophet of Human Fellowship (1980)

A Comrade

I made a few special friends and at last it came to me occasionally to sleep with them and to satisfy my imperious need by mutual embraces and emissions. Before this happened, however, I was once or twice on the brink of despair and madness with repressed passion and torment. Meanwhile from the first, my feeling physically towards the female sex was one of indifference, and later on, with the more special development of sex desires, one of positive repulsion. Though having several female friends, whose society I liked and to whom I am sincerely attached, the thought of marriage or cohabitation with any such has always been odious to me . . . Now – at the age of 37 – my ideal of love is a powerful, strongly built man, of my own age or rather younger – preferably of the working class. Though having solid sense and character, he need not be specially intellectual. If endowed in the latter way, he must not be too glib or refined. Anything effeminate in a man, or anything of the cheap intellectual style, repels me very decisively. I had never had to do with actual paederasty, so called. My chief desire in love is bodily nearness or contact, as to sleep naked with a naked friend; the special sexual, though urgent enough, seems a secondary matter . . . I am an artist by temperament and choice, fond of all beautiful things especially the male human form; of active, slight, muscular build; and sympathetic, but somewhat indecisive, character, though possessing self-control.

Edward Carpenter in 1881

Footballers

I have an inborn admiration for beauty, of form and figure. It amounts almost to a passion, and in most football teams I can find one Antinous . . . some folk would say it was . . . sentimentalism to admire any but feminine flesh. But that only proves how base is the carnality, which is now reckoned the only legitimate form. The other is far nobler . . . Platonic passion in any relationship is better than animalism.

a comment by Edward Lefroy, a Victorian clergyman and poet who devoted most of his output to the celebration of boys

Schoolfriends

At school, friendship is a passion . . . All loves of after-life can never bring its rapture, or its wretchedness; no bliss so absorbing, no pangs of jealousy . . . so keen! . . . what bitter estrangements and what melting reconciliations; what scenes of wild recrimination, agitating explanations, passionate correspondence . . . what earthquakes of the heart . . . are confirmed in that simple phrase, a schoolboy's friendship!

from Benjamin Disraeli, Coningsby *(1844)*

Schooldays

One thing at Harrow soon arrested my attention. It was the moral state of the school. Every boy of good looks had a female name, and was recognized either as a public prostitute or as some bigger fellow's 'bitch'. Bitch was the word in common usage to indicate a boy who yielded his person to a lover. The talk in the dormitories and the studies was incredibly obscene. Here and there one could not avoid seeing acts of onanism, mutual masturbation, the sports of naked boys in bed together. There was no refinement, no sentiment, no passion; nothing but animal lust in these occurrences.

from the memoirs of John Addington Symonds

Protector

'Good night, young Copperfield,' said Steerforth. 'I'll take care of you.'

'You're very kind,' I gratefully returned. 'I am very much obliged to you.'

'You haven't got a sister have you ?' said Steerforth yawning.

'No,' I answered.

'That's a pity,' said Steerforth. 'If you had one, I should think she would have been a pretty, timid, little bright-eyed girl. Good night, young Copperfield.'

'Good night, sir,' I replied.

I thought of him very much after I went to bed, and raised myself, I recollect, to look at him where he lay in the moonlight, with his handsome face turned up.

from Charles Dickens, David Copperfield *(1850)*

The School Story

Find a school novel and, unfailing, you'll find a faggot or three. Even David Blaize, E. F. Benson's turn-of-the-century hero in the book of the same name – a rosy-cheeked, clean-living, young chap who, like Pollyanna, spreads sunshine wherever he goes – gets a strong dose of hero worship for the 'demi-god' Frank Madox, a prefect two years his senior. But our little chap still has an 'utter want of curiosity about all that is filthy' and is totally perplexed when his headmaster hints strongly that 'there are worse things even than stealing'. It's only when a fellow-pupil is expelled for being 'a damned beast' that the truth begins to dawn on the innocent cherub. You can imagine David's horror when Frank finally tries it on him. Luckily the older boy avoids bringing disgrace on himself and 'the entire school', because David redeems him by turning his passion into brotherly love; 'the door is triumphantly slammed on it' and Frank loudly declaims his gratitude ('You and your innocence made me suddenly see what a beast I was . . . You've been an absolute brick to me.') All is well again, thank God. Or is it ? At the close of the book we find David in a coma, the result of stopping a galloping horse from mowing down some 'townsfolk'. He awakens to find Frank keeping vigil at his bedside. 'I say,' whispers our little angel, 'would it bore you awfully to hold my hand?'

from Him, *December 1983*

False Teacher

I am aware, sir, that Plato, in his symposium, discourseth very eloquently touching the Uranian and Pandernian Venus: but you must remember that in our Universities, Plato is held to be little better than a misleader of youth; and they have shown their contempt for him, not only by never reading him . . . but by never printing a complete edition of him.

Dr Folliott, a character in Thomas Love Peacock, Crotchet Castle *(1831)*

The Other Oscar

His [Oscar Browning's] vivacity, his contempt for dignity, his love of youth, and his frank devotion to the world delighted all undergraduates who were not prigs, and all dons who were not pedants . . . [he] made himself acquainted with a number of boys in the town and the neighbouring villages, and started them in their careers . . . [after 1908 he moved to Italy where he] resumed the classes on Dante which had been a feature of his life in Cambridge, and assisted young Italians, as he had done young Englishmen, towards the openings they desired.

from Oscar Browning's entry in the Dictionary of National Biography, *written by his former pupil G. Lowes Dickinson*

Purpose

. . . the realization of oneself is the prime aim of life, and to realize oneself through pleasure is finer than to do so through pain . . . It is a pagan idea.

Oscar Wilde

Understanding

He [Lord Alfred Douglas] understands me and my art, and loves both. I hope
never to be separated from him.

Oscar Wilde to Leonard Smithers, 1 October 1897

Friends and Favours

Sidney Arthur Mavor, examined by Mr. Gill – I live at 66 St. Helen's Gardens,
North Kensington. I am in partnership with a friend in business in the city. I first
met Taylor at the Gaiety Theatre in 1892. Taylor introduced himself and was
very friendly and civil. Afterwards Taylor asked me to go to Little College Street,
and I went to afternoon tea. I went to tea there a dozen times perhaps, and I have
slept there with Taylor. I was introduced by Taylor to different people. At that
time I did not think that he had any ulterior designs. One day, however, Taylor
said to me, 'I know a man in an influential position who could be of great use to
you, Mavor. He likes young men when they're modest and nice in appearance, I'll
introduce you.' It was arranged that we should dine at Kettner's Restaurant the
next evening. I called for Taylor, who said, 'I'm glad you've made yourself pretty.
Mr. Wilde likes nice clean boys.' That was the first time Wilde's name was
mentioned. On our arrival at the restaurant we were shown into a private room.
A man named Schwabe and Wilde and another gentleman came in. I believe the
other gentleman was Lord Alfred Douglas. I thought the conversation at dinner
peculiar, but I knew Wilde was a Bohemian and the talk therefore did not seem
strange. I was placed next to Wilde, who used occasionally to pull my ear or
chuck me under the chin, but he did nothing that was actually objectionable.
Wilde said to Taylor, 'Our little lad has pleasing manners. We must see more of
him.' Wilde took my address and soon afterwards I received a silver cigarette
case with my Christian name scratched inside it. It was inscribed 'Sidney from
O. W., October, 1892'. It was quite a surprise to me ! . . . In the same month I
received a letter from Mr. Wilde making an appointment to see him at the
Albemarle Hotel. In the meantime I had met Mr. Wilde several times at tea in
Little College Street. I arrived at the hotel soon after eight, and we had supper in
a private sitting room . . .

from the transcripts of Oscar Wilde's second trial, 1895

The Love that Dare not Speak its Name

The 'Love that dare not speak its name' in this century is such a great affection of
an elder for a younger man as there was between David and Jonathan, such as
Plato made the very basis of his philosophy, and such as you find in the sonnets
of Michelangelo and Shakespeare. It is that deep, spiritual affection that is as
pure as it is perfect. It dictates and pervades great works of art like those of
Shakespeare and Michelangelo, and those two letters of mine, such as they are. It

is in this century misunderstood, so much misunderstood that it may be described as the 'Love that dare not speak its name', and on account of it I am placed where I am now. It is beautiful, it is fine, it is the noblest form of affection. There is nothing unnatural about it. It is intellectual, and it repeatedly exists between an elder and a younger man, when the elder man has intellect, and the younger man has all the joy, hope and glamour of life before him. That it should be so the world does not understand. The world mocks at it and sometimes puts one in the pillory for it.

At this point, Wilde was applauded by one section of the court while other listeners hissed. The Judge reacted angrily at this disturbance.

MR JUSTICE CHARLES: If there is the slightest manifestation of feeling I shall have the court cleared. There must be complete silence preserved.

Oscar Wilde, at his first trial, 1895

Applause

Oscar has been quite superb. His speech about the Love that dares not tell his name was simply wonderful and carried the whole court right away, quite a tremendous burst of applause. Here was this man, who had been for a month in prison and loaded with insults and crushed and buffeted, perfectly self-possessed, dominating the Old Bailey with his fine presence and musical voice. He has never had so great a triumph, I am sure, as when the gallery burst into applause – I am sure it affected the jury.

from a letter from Max Beerbohm to Reggie Turner, 1895

The Judgement

Oscar Wilde and Alfred Taylor, the crime of which you have been convicted is so bad that one has to put stern restraint upon one's self to prevent one's self from describing, in language which I would rather not use, the sentiments which must rise to the breast of every man of honour who has heard details of these two terrible trials. That the jury have arrived at a correct verdict in this case, I cannot persuade myself to entertain the shadow of doubt; and I hope, at all events, that those who sometimes imagine that a judge is half-hearted in the cause of decency and morality, because he takes care no prejudice shall enter into the case, may see that that is consistent at least with the common sense of indignation at the horrible charges brought home to both of you.

It is no use for me to address you. People who can do these things must be dead to all sense of shame, and one cannot hope to produce any effect upon them. It is the worst case I have ever tried. That you, Taylor, kept a kind of male brothel it is impossible to doubt. And that you, Wilde, have been the centre of a circle of extensive corruption of the most hideous kind among young men, it is equally impossible to doubt.

I shall, under such circumstances, be expected to pass the severest sentence that the law allows. In my judgement it is totally inadequate for such a case as this. The sentence of the Court is that each of you be imprisoned and kept to hard labour for two years.

Mr Justice Wills passing sentence in the third trial of Oscar Wilde, 25 May 1895

Cleopatra's Nose

I read for the first time the (almost) complete account of Oscar's trials . . . It is very interesting and depressing. One of the surprising features is that he very nearly got off. If he had, what would have happened I wonder? I fancy the history of English culture might have been quite different, if a juryman's stupidity had chanced to take another turn.

from a letter from Lytton Strachey to Dora Carrington, September 1921

Sermonising

Never has the lesson of a wasted life come home to us more dramatically and opportunely. England has tolerated the man Wilde and others of his kind too long. Before he broke the law of his country and outraged human decency he was a social pest, a centre of intellectual corruption. He was one of the high priests of a school which attacks all the wholesome, manly, simple ideals of English life, and sets up false gods of decadent culture and intellectual debauchery. The man himself was a perfect type of that class, a gross sensualist veneered with the affectation of artistic feeling too delicate for the appreciation of common clay. To him and such as him we owe the spread of moral degeneration amongst young men with abilities sufficient to make them a credit to their country. At the feet of Wilde they have learned to gain notoriety by blatant conceit, by despising the emotions of healthy humanity and the achievements of wholesome talent. Such people find their fitting environment in the artificial light and the incense-laden air of secret chambers curtained from the light of day. Their pretences fall from them in fresh air and honest sunshine. Light has been let in upon them now in a very decisive fashion, and we venture to hope that the conviction of Wilde for these abominable vices, which were the natural outcome of his diseased intellectual condition, will be a salutary warning to the unhealthy boys who posed as sharers of his culture. Wilde's fate will teach them that brilliance does not justify disdain of all moral restraints . . . a delusion common to them, and by no means unknown amongst more honest folk. It has been the fashion to concede a certain amount of immoral licence to men of genius, and it is time that public opinion should correct it . . . all the more when we find a counsel as distinguished as Sir Edward Clarke gravely submitting to a jury that his client should not be judged as an ordinary man in the matter of decent language and manly feeling because forsooth he had intellectual powers above the average.

the London Evening News editorial on the day of Wilde's conviction

Feasting with Panthers

It was like feasting with panthers; the danger was half the excitement. I used to feel as a snake-charmer must feel when he lures the cobra to stir from the painted cloth or reed basket that holds it and makes it spread its hood at his bidding and sway to and fro in the air as a plant swaying restfully in a stream. They were to me the brightest of gilded snakes, their poison was part of their perfection. I did not know that when they were to strike at me it was to be at another's piping and at another's pay. I don't feel at all ashamed at having known them.

Oscar Wilde after his conviction

Remembering

. . . the memory of our friendship is the shadow that walks with me here: that seems never to leave me: that wakes me up at night to tell me the same story over and over till its wearisome iteration makes all sleep abandon me till dawn: at dawn it begins again: it follows me into the prison-yard and makes me talk to myself as I tramp round: each detail that accompanied each dreadful moment I am forced to recall: there is nothing that happened in those ill-starred years that I cannot recreate in that chamber of the brain which is set apart for grief or for despair: every strained note of your voice, every twitch and gesture of your nervous hands, every bitter word, every poisonous phrase comes back to me: I remember the street or river down which we passed, the wall or woodland that surrounded us, at what figure on the dial stood the hands of the clock, which way went the wings of the wind, the shape and colour of the moon.

from Oscar Wilde, De Profundis (1905)

The Great Purge

If all persons guilty of Oscar Wilde's offences were to be clapped into gaol, there would be a very surprising exodus from Eton and Harrow, Rugby and Winchester, to Pentonville and Holloway. It is to be hoped that our headmasters will pluck up a little courage from the result of the Wilde trial, and endeavour to rid our Protestant schools of a foul and unnatural vice which is not found in Catholic establishments, at all events in this country. But meanwhile public school boys are allowed to indulge with impunity in practices which, when they leave school, would consign them to hard labour.

W. T. Stead in the Pall Mall Gazette, 1895

Prison

I . . . wish we could talk over the many prisons of life – prisons of stone, prisons of passion, prisons of intellect, prisons of morality and the rest – all limitations, external or internal, all prisons, really. All life is a limitation.

Oscar Wilde

Dedicated Servants of the State

Many were the men who, blue of eye, bristling of moustache, and deeply serious of intent, created an empire out of the wilderness beyond, and one suspects, the wilderness within. They were brilliant organisers, good generals; they were especially good at inspiring and sorting out their young officers. They were often also rumoured to be 'women-haters'; there were whispers about their special attachment to this or that junior officer . . . [from the recent past he cites as examples Lord Kitchener, Cecil Rhodes, Marshal Lyautey, General Gordon, Lord Mountbatten and Maurice Oldfield; from earlier times he lists Richard the Lionheart, the Knights Templar and Frederick the Great] . . . That there is an extremely strong link between homosexuality and the service of the state is, I think, one of the more obvious themes of European history . . . In all this, only one thing is certain: that a particular type of entrenched homosexual, whose emotional life consists of Cuthberts and Trevors who are either not there or are very unpleasant when they are there, learns at an early age a kind of iron self-discipline that gets him going, day after day, and makes him emotionally dependent on his job in a way that married men would seldom know. In many senses this is rather miserable, even heroic.

Norman Stone in the Sunday Times, *26 April 1987*

A Matter of Honour

[Major-General Sir Hector Macdonald of the Gordon Highlanders, Officer Commanding Troops, Ceylon] was unfortunately discovered with four native boys in a railway carriage in Kandy. He was surprised by an English tea-planter who immediately recognized him, although he was in civilian clothes . . . the planter went home and described what he saw. It was then only a matter of time before rumours and gossip were circulating around the verandas and tea tables and clubs, and it did not take long for [Sir Joseph] West-Ridgeway [Governor of Ceylon] to send for Macdonald and advise him to go on leave to London where he could no doubt obtain another appointment, after which the affair would soon be forgotten. There is no doubt that Macdonald did not deny the charges. He was an honest soldier and had fought his way up from being a boy recruit, a rare event in those days . . . The Governor was embarrassed by the situation and felt unable to deal with a popular national hero, a Knight Commander of the Bath, a holder of the DSO for gallantry, and the hero of Omdurman and the Boer War . . . [Macdonald arrived in London.] The King, though, in an interview with him advised him to behave 'honourably'; he went at once to Paris where one morning he saw his picture on the front of the European edition of the *New York Herald* of 24 March 1903 and went upstairs to his bedroom and shot himself with the revolver he had carried into battle.

from Gay News, *October 1978*

Sublimation

In recent years two authors have suggested that Baden-Powell may have been homosexual. Neither offered any evidence, and both based their supposition entirely upon a shared suspicion that his relationship with Kenneth McLaren might have been a physical one. Yet by confining their attention to one friendship, and by making physical relations the acid test of a homosexual orientation, they missed a more important point. Whether a man acts upon a homosexual inclination or not (or even acknowledges his tendency) is less significant than the effects such a tendency will have upon his life if it is denied. Indeed, a repressed instinct may well affect behaviour and thoughts more dramatically than a proclivity actively pursued . . . his years of advice-giving to soldiers, followed by the invention of the world's greatest youth movement, offered Baden-Powell scope for sublimation which Freud himself would have marvelled at.

from Tim Jeal, Baden-Powell *(1989)*

Agony Aunt

[Baden-Powell] was still carrying on a vast correspondence with Boy Scouts, principally about their struggles not to masturbate. He was still doing so in 1937, when aged 80. 'My correspondence is largely a confidential one with Rovers and young men in this stage [late adolescence] anxiously seeking advice or comfort in the chaotic state of their minds.'

from Tim Jeal, Baden-Powell *(1989)*

Popular Album

Whereas female nudity, even in the sanitized context of art, smacked of 'dirtiness', male nudity was quite different. During the Great War . . . [Baden-Powell] watched the men 'trooping in to be washed in nature's garb, with their strong well-built naked wonderfully made bodies' and took his pleasure in this 'happy brave family laughing together' . . . At Gilwell Park, the Scouts' camping ground in Epping Forest, he always enjoyed watching the boys swimming naked, and would sometimes chat with them after they 'had just stripped off' . . . Another incident illustrative of Baden-Powell's appreciation of naked boys occurred at Charterhouse, when he was staying overnight with his old friend A. H. Tod, who had been in the Rifle Corps and in the football XI with him. In November 1919 Tod was over the retirement age but still teaching because it was wartime and all the younger staff had joined up. 'Stayed with Tod,' Stephe [Kenneth McLaren] wrote in his diary. 'Tod's photos of naked boys and trees etc. Excellent.' That a bachelor housemaster should have taken large numbers of nude photographs of his boys evidently did not strike Baden-Powell as undesirable. A few days later he wrote to Tod about starting a scout troop at the school and added that he would soon be visiting Charterhouse again, 'which will give me the opportunity of seeing the football; and possibly I might get a further look at those wonderful photographs of yours?'

This album of 'figure studies', as Tod described it, was still at Charterhouse in the mid-1960s, but by the end of that permissive decade had been destroyed. This appalling act was undertaken 'to protect Tod's reputation' and out of deference to the feelings of the sons and grandsons of the boys depicted.

from Tim Jeal, Baden-Powell *(1989)*

A Different World

The Victorians and Edwardians were more sophisticated than we are today in understanding and accepting that a man can love and physically worship one of his own sex without seeking any closer contact than an embrace or, at most, a kiss. Homosexuality was rife and, if discovered, was treated as a criminal act to be punished with imprisonment and social ostracism, but it is important to remember that there was an immense chasm between the sexual appetites of men like Wilde and the near non-existent ones of men in [Henry] James's mould whose loves were of a romantic nature, with the yearning more passionately expressed in words and looks than in actions. This was the era of lad-love when the schoolmasters, clergymen and scholars of the Uranian group were circulating pamphlets and poems which, at their most idealistic, proposed adoration of the young male body without sex as the noblest form of love, along the lines of Walter Pater's magnificent essay on Winckelmann in which he argues that Winckelmann's pure love of beautiful young men 'perfected his reconciliation to the spirit of Greek culture' . . . Male love, in the 1890s and the early part of this century, was frequently experienced in the spirit of Winckelmann. Looking at James's circle of friends, it is apparent that, while a few were actively homo- or bisexual . . . the majority were like James himself, lovers in the Pater mould . . . They could, and did, discuss each other's grand passions with a frank and avid interest which had much to do with the possessive adulation of the older men for the younger members of their circle, but which it would be rash to interpret as the gossip of a group of promiscuous homosexuals. The concern was, rather, with the suitability of the chosen love.

from Miranda Seymour, A Ring of Conspirators: Henry James and his Literary Circle *1895–1915 (1988)*

Friends and Sex

There is no friendship between men that has not an element of sexuality in it, however little accentuated it may be in the nature of the friendship, and however painful the idea of the sexual element would be. But it is enough to remember that there can be no friendship unless there has been some attraction to draw the men together. Much of the affection, protection, and nepotism between men is due to the presence of unsuspected sexual compatibility.

from Otto Weininger, Sex and Character *(1903)*

CHAPTER SIX

Freud and the Doctors

Science discovered homosexuality in the middle of the nineteenth century. It was first made a respectable subject by the practitioners of forensic medicine working within the legal system. They were searching for physical differences that would allow scientists to identify deviants, making the job of the policeman much easier. By the late nineteenth century homosexuality had become the province of the psychologists, as it became clear that it was difficult to support theories based on physical difference.

It was Sigmund Freud who created most of the modern mythology that surrounds homosexuality. In his writings, the Viennese psychologist devoted much attention to this problem. Freud suggested that all people were bisexual but that heterosexuality was the normal or natural goal for all healthy men and women. In the course of a man's development towards full-blooded heterosexuality there were a number of obstacles which had to be negotiated before he made the grade. Failure to cross any of these hurdles successfully would lead to a descent into homosexuality. Such theories might have been calculated to promote guilt among all parents: one mistake and everything could be ruined. Freud, the Jewish patriarch, placed most of the burden on the shoulders of Mother, for much of his doctrine was deeply misogynistic. Adults might appear to have cleared all the hurdles but then regress just as they seemed to be in the final straight, displaying what Freud called 'latent homosexuality'.

Freud was possibly the greatest intellectual charlatan of the century (though there is much competition for that particular accolade). We now appreciate that most of his theories were the product of his overheated imagination, as his casebook has been exposed as extremely thin.[1] He was an immensely clever communicator, he wrote beautifully and mesmerised audiences as he advanced theories that seemed to explain the secrets of the human personality. He attracted a loyal band of disciples who turned him into an idol and popularised his ideas throughout the world. Freud's ideas became a staple item for newspapers and magazines and quickly won wide acceptance. He became one of the century's greatest prophets.

The dissemination of his ideas was enormously enhanced by the mass exodus of Jewish intellectuals from Germany and central Europe in the 1930s. The triumph of Nazism sent most psychologists and psychiatrists across the ocean to America. Here they found a receptive audience for their ideas and became a powerful force in American society. The therapists peddled explanations that won them many clients and made them immensely rich in the process.

One of the most extraordinary figures in this movement was Dr Edmund Bergler, whose books became bestsellers during the 1940s and 1950s. He advanced the notion that homosexuality was the 'counterfeit sex', and he, like so many of his colleagues, offered a cure to those troubled by this malady. Aversion therapy enjoyed a considerable vogue at this time, and all practitioners claimed a high rate of success.

In the 1970s many psychiatrists and psychologists tried to atone for their professions' follies in the past, most notably by abandoning the classification of homosexuality as a mental illness. An important minority of doctors resisted that move, however, and it is still possible to meet practitioners who see homosexuality in this way.

In the course of the century the greatest legacy of psychoanalysis has been for the social historian, the case histories often providing an important insight into the lives of many people unlucky enough to fall into the hands of the doctors.

Tricks of the Trade

I shall now endeavour (and I think the attempt is neither unnecessary nor unjustifiable) to show that the knowledge of psychological processes, which, thanks to psychoanalysis, we now possess, already enables us to understand the part played by a homosexual wish in the development of paranoia. Recent investigations [a footnote at this point to an earlier essay by Freud, and to another by a pupil] have directed our attention to a stage in the development of paranoia. Recent investigations have directed our attention to a stage in the development of the libido which it passes through on the way from auto-erotism to object-love [a further footnote here to another essay by Freud]. This stage has been given the name of narcissism [by Freud of course: another essay of his own is cited at this point]. What happens is this. There comes a time in the development of the individual at which he unifies his sexual instincts (which have hitherto been engaged in auto-erotic activities) in order to obtain a love-object; and he begins by taking himself, his own body, as his love-object, and only subsequently proceeds from this to the choice of some person other than himself as his object. This half-way phase between auto-erotism and object-love may perhaps be indispensable normally; but it appears that many people linger unusually long in this condition, and that many of its features are carried over by them into the later stages of their development. What is of chief importance in the subject's self thus chosen as a love object may already be the genitals. The line of development then leads on to the choice of an external object with similar genitals – that is, to homosexual object-choice – and thence to heterosexuality. People who are manifest homosexuals in later life have, it may be presumed, never emancipated themselves from the binding condition that the object of their choice must possess genitals like their own; and in this connection the infantile sexual theories which attribute the same kind of genitals to both sexes exert much influence. [Another Freud essay cited in support here.]

After the stage of heterosexual object-choice has been reached, the homosexual tendencies are not, as might be supposed, done away with or brought to a stop; they are merely deflected from their sexual aim and applied to fresh uses. They now combine with portions of the ego instincts and, as 'attached' components, help to constitute the social instincts, thus contributing an erotic factor to friendship and comradeship, to *esprit de corps* and to the love of mankind in general. How large a contribution is in fact derived from erotic sources (with the sexual aim inhibited) could scarcely be guessed from the normal social relations of mankind. But it is not irrelevant to note that it is precisely manifest homosexuals, and among them again precisely those that set themselves against an indulgence in sensual acts, who are distinguished by taking a particularly active share in the general interests of humanity – interests which have themselves sprung from the sublimation of erotic instincts.

In my *Three Essays on the Theory of Sexuality* I have expressed the opinion that each stage in the development of psychosexuality affords a possibility of 'fixation' and thus of a dispositional point. People who have not freed themselves completely from the stage of narcissism – who, that is to say, have at that point a fixation which may operate as a disposition to a later illness – are exposed to the danger that some unusually intense wave of libido, finding no other outlet, may lead to a sexualization of their social instincts and so undo the sublimations which they had achieved in the course of their development. This result may be produced by anything that causes the libido to flow backwards (i.e. that causes a 'regression'): whether, on the one hand, the libido becomes collaterally reinforced owing to some disappointment over a woman, or is directly dammed up owing to a mishap in social relations with other men – both of these being instances of 'frustration'; or whether, on the other hand, there is a general intensification of the libido, so that it becomes too powerful to find an outlet along the channels which are already open to it, and consequently bursts through its banks at the weakest spot. Since our analyses show that paranoics *endeavour to protect themselves against any such sexualization of their social instinctual cathexes*, we are driven to suppose that the weak spot in their development is to be looked for somewhere between the stages of auto-erotism, narcissism and homosexuality, and that their disposition to illness (which may perhaps be susceptible of more precise definition) must be located in that region. A similar disposition would have to be assigned to patients suffering from Kraepelin's dementia praecox or (as Bleuler has named it) *schizophrenia*; and we shall hope later on to find clues which will enable us to trace back the difference between the two disorders (as regards both the form they take and the course they run) to corresponding differences in the patients' dispositional fixations.

from Sigmund Freud, Psychoanalytic Notes on an Autobiographical Account of a Case of Paranoia (Dementia Paranoides) *(1911)*

For the Record

There are plenty of people who are ready to call any unusual behaviour neurotic,' I [Wortis] said, 'like the students at my college who thought there must be something wrong with anybody who read poetry.'

'Unusual conduct isn't necessarily neurotic,' said Freud.

'Many people take it for granted too,' I said, 'that homosexuals are neurotic, though they might be perfectly capable of leading happy and quiet lives if society would tolerate them.'

'No psychoanalyst has ever claimed that homosexuals cannot be perfectly decent people,' said Freud. 'Psychoanalysis does not undertake to judge people in any case.'

'Still,' I said, 'it makes a difference to homosexuals whether they are considered neurotic or not.'

'Naturally homosexuality is something pathological,' said Freud. 'It is arrested development [*eine Entwicklungshemmung*].'

'But plenty of valuable qualities could be called the same: you might call the simplicity of genius a kind of childishness or arrested development too,' I said.

Advice

He told me to pull my socks up, find a nice girl and get married.

I told my doctor I wanted to see a psychiatrist. He said I was a namby-pamby. He told me to get a piece of paper and draw pictures of nude women. I think he was off his rocker.

from Michael Schofield, A Minority (1960)

Crackers

I've had patients come in and resign from the process of happy living . . . A patient, a new one I got recently, said, 'All through World War II I was an overt homosexual. I re-enlisted two years over in Italy so that I could remain in Italy where the kids are so numerous and would do anything for you.' He said, 'My last homosexual experience with a kid was two years ago. I haven't been tempted. I have often gone hunting with a 16-year-old. I'm a welcome visitor to his home. But the other day I thought to myself, what the hell, so I went down on him, got him to go down on me. Then I went down to South Phoenix; I picked up some more, knowing all the time I wouldn't go back to my wife, my mother, my brother, or anybody. I'm going down to skid row.' That's what he's doing. 'How can I go down to skid row', was the question he put to me, 'more safely?' What does he mean by that? So that he can get a long sentence on a relatively minor crime.

I think that if you make a searching enough inquiry in a lot of patients, you'll find a long period of adjustment, and then some screw comes loose. They go haywire. You see these people who are perfectly wonderful people, and friends; and they hit the age of 25, and they cease to be nice, likeable, friendly people that you want to associate with. Each half decade wipes out some people; even though their bodies remain alive, their personalities have died

from Conversations with Milton D. Erickson, ed. Jay Haley (1985)

Old Boar

Patient is an adolescent boy whose fantasies, masturbatory and otherwise, are exclusively directed toward his being loved by a handsome athlete. He has never had any overt sexual relations, although he is exclusively (consciously) directed toward a homosexual object. He shows no overtly effeminate behaviour. He feels himself to be weak, however, in constant danger of breakthrough of unmanly emotion, and consciously desires only to make a powerful man happy. He reported the following dream: 'I am watching without feeling a car driving down the street near where I lived when I was little. The car is being chased by a boar.' In the patient's associations, the car was a little car; the boar was a large wild animal with tusks with which it was trying to attack the car from the rear; a boar was related to a pig, which is a milder domesticated version of this wilder animal;

and the patient's last name (which he has received from his father) is also that of a wild animal that is related to a domesticated animal. He continued that his father is a cold and unfeeling man interested only in his work, to which he attends all day at his office and throughout the evening at home. The therapist said, 'He is a bore,' and the patient responded, 'That's exactly what I was thinking last night,' before recognizing the pun in surprise. He then added that his father is not only a bore but also persistently questions him, goads him, criticizes him, and bores into him. The associations in the hour ended with the patient revealing for the first time that in his homosexual fantasies he pictures the intercourse being performed on him. At that moment, he recalled that the little car had a tail pipe at which the boar's tusks were aimed in the dream.

from Sexual Inversion, *ed. Judd Marmor (1965)*

Bisexual I

. . . your definition of a bisexual is wrong. It is not a person who can do it 'both ways'. Such a person is a real homosexual, with a few heterosexual defences left. His emotions are tied up with men.

from Edmund Bergler, The Counterfeit Sex *(1958)*

Fugitives

Male homosexuals are neither the 'higher class' of person they claim to be, offering as proof the names of renowned perverts, nor the mysterious 'third sex' nor 'something special'. They are unconsciously simply the frightened fugitives from women, fleeing in their panic to 'another continent'. Since they are unaware of all this, since all this happened in early childhood, and under exclusion of consciousness, they use the old but effective technique of 'pride' in their 'difference' − an inner hoax which, unfortunately for them, only works consciously.

from Edmund Bergler, The Counterfeit Sex *(1958)*

Trapped

. . . at fifty the homosexual has not progressed beyond his teens emotionally . . .

from Edmund Bergler, The Counterfeit Sex *(1958)*

The Disappointed

Sometimes homosexuals assert that they are completely 'happy', the only thing bothering them being 'the unreasonable approach' of the environment. That is a convenient blind. There are no happy homosexuals; and there would not be, even if the outer world left them in peace. The reason is an internal one.

Unconsciously they want to be disappointed, as does every adherent of 'the mechanism of cruelty'. A man who unconsciously runs after disappointment cannot be consciously happy. The amount of conflict, of jealousy for instance, between homosexuals surpasses everything known even in bad heterosexual relationships.

from Edmund Bergler, The Counterfeit Sex *(1958)*

A Mix-Up

All boys identify penis with breast, urine with milk. But the normal male eventually completes this process of active reversal by applying this identification in intercourse unconsciously acting the giving mother with the woman whom he unconsciously sees as the nursing baby. The early identification of penis with breast and urine with milk is extended to an identification of the mouth with the vagina, of milk with sperm.

The homosexual does not take this second and decisive unconscious step. Because of his exaggerated narcissism, he cannot accept the partial victory of active reversal, but must instead reject the whole disappointing sex. His narcissism allows him only a 'reduplication of his own defense mechanism'. He negates the trauma of weaning through his identification of breast with penis, and the identification remains his decisive defense, finding the affirmation in the penis of the other man. Naive observers assume that the homosexual is 'attracted' to other men; actually, men merely represent defensive allies in his continuing unconscious battle to establish the pre-eminence of the penis and to negate his masochistic attachment to mother. As a result, the homosexual conceals his unconscious fear of women by finding them either 'repellent' or 'sexually uninteresting'. Sometimes remnants of heterosexual tendencies make him – as he believes – 'bisexual'. He may even construct an alibi marriage. The bisexual is a homosexual with an easily shaken alibi.

from Edmund Bergler, Principles of Self-Damage *(1959)*

Dad

. . . one might wonder whether homosexuality is also due to an oedipal situation inverted in the sense that it is the father who is jealous of his little son, so that the latter cannot afford a relationship with a woman as the very idea of it would for the rest of his life engender in him fears of the displeasure of his father.

E. Bene, 1965

Mom

. . . the homosexuals more often described themselves as frail or clumsy as children and less often as athletic. More of them were fearful of physical injury, avoided physical fights, played with girls, and were loners who seldom played baseball and other competitive games. Their mothers more often were considered puritanical, cold towards men, insisted on being the center of the son's attention, made him her confidant, were 'seductive' towards him, allied with him against the father, interfered with his heterosexual activities during adolescence, discouraged masculine attitudes and encouraged feminine ones.

Evans study, 1969

Taboos

'Anything that discourages heterosexuality encourages homosexuality,' says Paul Gebhard, executive director of the Kinsey Institute for Sex Research. Is the opposite true? Some psychiatrists speculate that the new sexual freedoms enjoyed by teen-agers may lead to a decrease in homosexuality. 'Because there are fewer sexual taboos in our society today, the adolescent is more likely to find a heterosexual pathway,' says Dr. Judd Marmor of Los Angeles.

from Time, *21 August 1972*

Bisexual II

Bisexual is used only to indicate someone whose attractions are not *currently* confined to one sex.

from J. C. Gonsiorek and J. D. Weinrich, Homosexuality: Research Implications for Public Policy *(1991)*

Redefinition

People can be defined as 'homosexual' even if they do not perform any homosexual acts, or even if they despise the gay world or their homosexual feelings. People are homosexual if they experience romantic and/or sexual arousal repeatedly and consistently in the presence of some members of their own sex, but not with members of the other sex. A homosexual person can exist in a society that has no name for the trait. In a society that does not categorize individuals according to their sexual preferences inclined persons are unlikely to set themselves apart by choosing distinctive social arrangements or by calling themselves distinctive names. But the more perceptive people in such a society will, if the occasion arises, be able to discern the existence of these different patterns and comment upon them.

from J. C. Gonsiorek and J. D. Weinrich, Homosexuality: Research Implications for Public Policy *(1991)*

The Future

[In Florida] social scientist Henry Winthrop has prophesied that copulation for extended periods will become possible through biochemical developments enabling people to stimulate fluid regeneration and sex hormones while coping with fatigue. In the computer-operated world of the future, he says, it will be of invaluable aid to people with time on their hands.

from Gay News, July 1973

The New Inquisitors

Psychiatrists are the true inheritors of the mantle of the Holy Inquisition and the Witch Hunters – the Inquisitors defined a minority opinion as heresy, and having defined it, went on to 'treat' it by torture and imprisonment, until the 'heretic' repented of those opinions and satisfied the Inquisition that he had accepted the Inquisitors' outlook on the matter involved . . . in our society it is the role of the homosexual to be subjected to 'treatment', i.e. torture, to make him conform to the Inquisitors' moral viewpoint. And it is only by making clear the psychiatrist's relationship to his predecessor of the Holy Office – and the relationship between their methods – that we can hope to have their brainwashing and torturing stopped.

Peter Maxwell Davies in Gay News, June 1973

Intervention

Homosexual behavior through adolescence in the absence of anxiety, guilt or conflict together with perverted fantasies is an alarming sign. It is imperative to initiate therapy in order to create a conflict for the patient.

Charles W. Socarides, American psychiatrist, 1978

Catholic Psychiatry

Not all homosexuality is the effect of mental illness, and a large number of homosexuals are morally responsible for their actions. For these, the severe judgement of St. Paul holds (Romans 1:24, 26–27), according to which they should be punished for their transgressions. If and when it is established that homosexuality is caused by or associated with mental illness, the patient should be confined to a mental hospital.

from J. H. Van der Veldt and R. P. Odenwald, Psychiatry and Catholicism *(1957)*

Vegetables

The 'evidence' often cited for the 'vegetarian' view of homosexuality (some like meat, some like vegetables), as it has been called, is grossly inadequate and in a number of cases outright nonsense . . . wherever it has been investigated, an exclusive homosexual orientation has been found to result from deep-seated heterosexual frustration. This commonsense notion has been amply confirmed by analytic theory and analytic experience . . . the topic of homosexuality has become a political football. The intellectual arguments in its favor are not to be taken seriously. No one brought up with free sexual expression would ever prefer homosexuality, although in adolescence or later he may occasionally experiment with it . . . the very violence sometimes displayed by groups of overt homosexuals is an indication that they are sometimes more interested in violence than in sex.

from Reuben Fine, The Psychoanalytic Vision (1981)

Telling the Difference

The nature of the homosexual act among adolescent boys indicates whether this is associated with a transient stage of sexual experimentation or whether an ultimate homosexual orientation is likely . . . In adolescence, mutual masturbation is commonly associated with a general sense of loneliness and insecurity, sexual curiosity, intense sexual frustration, and social acceptability within a group. Fellatio among boys is more likely to indicate a homosexual orientation in Britain, where it is a less generally acceptable form of normative sexual activity, than in the United States. The enjoyment of anal intercourse almost always implies an active homosexual involvement, as initially this is not comfortable and requires an ability to be relaxed with another male. Boys who report feeling 'good' after such an episode always have a basic homosexual inclination.

from Derek Miller, The Age Between: Adolescence and Therapy (1983)

Colluding Mother

Paul was hospitalized because of drug dependence. He was fifteen, and he had become very dependent on marijuana in association with an active homosexual relationship with a man of twenty-three. Paul's physician thought that communication with this homosexual partner was disturbing to him and recommended that his patient not communicate with his lover. The patient did not openly defy his physician, but arranged for his mother to smuggle letters from the lover to her son in her own letters.

a case history from Derek Miller, The Age Between: Adolescence and Therapy (1983)

Latent Homosexuals

Most adolescents ruminated about their homosexuality, usually the fear of being discovered and methods to avoid this. More than a few said that they thought about it every minute of every day, a fact that is not surprising when one considers how often the average adolescent has thoughts relating to sexual or sociosexual activities. Exhibitionistic efforts to appear before their families and peers undoubtedly heterosexual were made and included: heterosexual dating, involvement in contact sports, or rowdy or mildly antisocial activities. Other endeavors for which the individual may have had considerable interest or talent were sometimes purposefully avoided, such as dramatics, singing, dance, or the creative arts. Especially for the boys, the self-conscious dialogue that accompanies the aforementioned behaviors may have marked deleterious effects on interpersonal relationships, particularly on the development of intimacy and friendship with other boys. Gay adolescents are forever monitoring themselves: 'Am I standing too close?' 'Is my voice too high?' 'Do I appear too happy to see him (her)?' What should be spontaneous expressions of affection or happiness become moments of agonizing fear and uncertainty. Some of the more painful moments occur when homophobic sentiments are expressed in a social setting, such as when an antigay joke is told, or when another individual, perhaps a boy with some traditionally feminine characteristics, is harassed or ridiculed or called some epithet that is commonly applied to gay persons. It is not unusual for a gay adolescent to join in these homophobic activities in order to maintain his or her own 'cover'. For similar reasons, gay boys and lesbian girls, often because of a fear of drawing attention to themselves, will not associate in their schools with other students whom they believe to be gay.

from an article by D. Anderson in Adolescent Psychiatry, *vol. 14 (1987)*

Homosexual Panic

Homosexual panic refers to a feeling of intense anxiety that occurs when an individual with strong latent homosexual desire is placed in a situation where there is a possibility to act out his desire. Dormitories and barracks, with their associated horseplay, are situations which provide stimulation of homoerotic fantasies. In addition, homosexual panic may occur when such a person is raped or seduced, discovers that the act is not entirely without pleasure, and becomes fearful and anxious. These patients may be paranoid, prone to violence, and appear as if they are having a psychotic decompensation. Such a patient may strike out at others especially if they touch him or seem to wish to 'take advantage' of him.

> A 22-year-old white, single, male football player on a college team was hitching back to his campus room one evening when he was picked up by a driver who asked if he wished to spend the night with him. He agreed and the next day appeared tearful, frightened and crying in the emergency room. He stated he wanted to 'kill all queers'. History revealed he allowed the driver, a man much smaller than himself, to have fellatio with him. The next morning after he left the man's apartment he became increasingly tearful and paranoid.

Treatment consists of reassurance and allowing the patient to ventilate his experience and fears. If he is exceptionally anxious a minor tranquilizer such as haloperidol or chlorpromazine should be given if there is evidence of psychotic thinking. If possible, a female rather than a male nurse or aide should be in attendance. Because any physical contact may be taken as a homosexual advance, a genital and rectal exam should be deferred until a more suitable time.

from A. E. Slaby, L. E. Tancredi and J. Lieb, Clinical Psychiatric Medicine *(1981)*

Spots

Critics of a psychosexual approach to homosexuality have pointed out that many homosexuals are not in distress and therefore should be considered normal. These critics however fail to acknowledge studies of Rorschach protocols [ink-blot tests] in which overt homosexuals had consistently different dynamic patterns from those of heterosexuals . . . Lack of distress may represent repression or denial, and many homosexuals utilize denial as a defense.

Herbert Stearn, American psychiatrist, in Samuel S. Turner (ed.), Adult Psychopathology and Diagnosis *(1984)*

Applied Anthropology

Contrary to the assumption that much of gay male sexuality is deficient in intimacy, the time spent during and after sex frequently results in a degree of intimacy that exceeds what is attained by many monogamous couples (gay or straight) after years of living together. It is in the après-sex milieu of a casual sexual encounter when people often open up and speak honestly and profoundly about their lives, sharing thoughts with a partner that may never be voiced in any other context . . . [it] offers the opportunity to engage in immediately significant applied anthropology, action anthropology in all senses of the term. It is in the setting of the sexual encounter that the most effective safer-sex education may take place. This alone can justify the research strategy I am advocating, a combined research/applied fieldwork that saves lives directly.

Comments by Ralph Bolton outlining his fieldwork in Flanders and California, in G. Herdt and S. Lindenbaum, The Time of AIDS *(1992)*

The Menu – a Partial List of Erotic Behaviours that May Occur during Gay Male Sexual Encounters

1. Anal intercourse, insertive, without a condom
2. Anal intercourse, insertive, with a condom
3. Anal intercourse, receptive, without a condom
4. Anal intercourse, receptive, with a condom
5. Oral sex, insertive, without a condom
6. Oral sex, insertive, with a condom
7. Oral sex, receptive, without a condom
8. Oral sex, receptive, with a condom

9. Stimulating the nipples/breasts, hard
10. Stimulating the nipples/breasts, soft
11. Having your nipples/breasts stimulated, hard
12. Having your nipples/breasts stimulated, soft
13. Using a cock ring
14. Masturbating yourself
15. Masturbating your partner
16. Being masturbated by your partner
17. Simultaneous mutual masturbation
18. Kissing on lips
19. French kissing
20. Biting/nibbling your partner in the neck area
21. Having your partner bite/nibble you in the neck area
22. Licking the testicles of your partner
23. Having your testicles licked by your partner
24. Having your testicles taken into your partner's mouth
25. Taking your partner's testicles in your mouth
26. Sucking on your partner's toes
27. Having your toes sucked
28. Being tickled in sensitive areas
29. Tickling your partner in sensitive areas
30. Having your testicles squeezed or tugged
31. Squeezing or tugging on your partner's testicles
32. Using tit clamps
33. Having your partner employ dildo/vibrator on you
34. Using a dildo/vibrator on your partner
35. Caressing your partner's back
36. Having your back caressed
37. Giving your partner a full body massage
38. Receiving a full body massage
39. Hearing your partner talk dirty
40. Talking dirty to your partner
41. Watching porno videos
42. Watching your partner masturbate
43. Having your partner watch you masturbate
44. Sucking on your partner's fingers
45. Having your fingers sucked
46. Fingering your partner's anus
47. Being fingered anally by your partner
48. Using cream or lotion for masturbation
49. Being the S in S/M activities
50. Being the M in S/M activities
51. Slapping your partner's butt/thighs
52. Having your own butt/thighs slapped
53. Hugging each other
54. Expressing appreciation verbally to your partner

55. Having your partner verbally express appreciation for your actions
56. Golden showers, active
57. Golden showers, passive
58. Dressing in leather
59. Having your partner dress in leather
60. Dressing in women's clothing
61. Having your partner dressed in women's clothing
62. Standing up during sexual activity
63. Sitting down during sexual activity
64. Kneeling during sexual activity
65. Lying down during sexual activity
66. Being lightly caressed on the entire body
67. Lightly caressing your partner's entire body
68. Heavy kneading of your partner's body/muscles
69. Putting a condom on your partner
70. Having your partner put a condom on you
71. Ejaculating
72. Having your partner ejaculate
73. Engaging in sex with multiple partners (four or more)
74. Having sex with more than one person (threeways)
75. Swallowing your partner's semen
76. Having your partner swallow your semen
77. Ejaculating inside your partner during anal sex
78. Having your partner ejaculate inside you during anal sex
79. Rimming your partner
80. Having your partner rim you
81. Fisting, top
82. Fisting, bottom
83. Frottage, body rubbing
84. Fucking your partner between the thighs
85. Getting fucked between the thighs
86. Having sex
87. Abstaining from sex
88. Engaging in scat (active)
89. Engaging in scat (passive)
90. Showering before sex
91. Showering after sex

from G. Herdt and S. Lindenbaum, The Time of AIDS *(1992)*

A Doctor Speaks

I view homosexuals with the kind of vague loathing that I view terrorists.

a comment by Dr T. Russell in The General Practitioner, *March 1988*

CHAPTER SEVEN

The German Experience

It was in Germany that the first properly organised movement for homosexual rights developed with the creation in 1897 of the Scientific Humanitarian Committee. The guiding figure of the committee was Magnus Hirschfeld, a campaigning doctor who devoted his life to the cause. Hirschfeld hoped to win support for the repeal of paragraph 175 of the Prussian penal code, which criminalised homosexual acts. Hirschfeld was a rather naïve character who tried to discover the number of homosexuals in Germany by means of questionnaires distributed to different groups. He did not understand the strength of the negative reaction that he encountered since he laboured under the illusion that he would be seen as a disinterested scientist rather than as a proselytiser. On the basis of his surveys, he calculated the number of homosexuals in Germany as around 2 per cent of the population.[1]

Despite the law, Germany had a strongly developed homosexual subculture and, as a succession of scandals during the years before the First World War revealed, homosexuality had many friends in high places.[2] Several members of the Kaiser's entourage were implicated in homosexual scandals, most of them generated by the Socialists in an effort to embarrass German conservatives.

After the war, during the period of the Weimar Republic (1918–33), Germany acquired a reputation as the homosexual Mecca of Europe. Weimar Berlin, immortalised in the novels of Christopher Isherwood, was the sex capital of the West, supporting a large sex industry that drew many foreigners. Homosexuality was practised in a largely liberal and tolerant environment, and newspapers and magazines for homosexuals were published and available in most large cities.

There was, of course, a backlash – orchestrated by right-wing moralists eager to embarrass the largely left-of-centre coalitions that ran the Republic. The permissive policy of the state was used to frighten many voters away from the left and the centre, but the Republic was eventually destroyed largely by the impact of the depression on the German economy, which turned many voters into supporters of extremist parties.

The Nazis, under Adolf Hitler, were the chief beneficiaries of this discontent. One of Hitler's chief lieutenants, Ernst Roehm, who ran the Nazi paramilitaries – the SA, or Brown-shirts – was actively homosexual. The Brown-shirts had many leaders who shared Roehm's tastes, and homosexuals enjoyed many privileges in that organisation. In the summer of 1934 Hitler felt that it was necessary to remove Roehm and destroy the Brown-shirts. He found it prudent to use Roehm's homosexuality as a way of mobilising popular support against him after the leadership of the SA had been killed during what became known as the Night of the Long Knives.

The SS, under Heinrich Himmler, replaced the Brown-shirts. Himmler was a violent enemy of homosexuality, and he used his position in the Nazi hierarchy to persecute homosexuals throughout Germany. As a result, many homosexuals found their way into the concentration camps run by Himmler and his henchmen. It is estimated[3] that around 60,000 men were killed for their sexual inclinations – easily the largest act of violence against homosexuals in the history of the West. Homosexual prisoners wore a pink triangle in the camps, and this has become a universally accepted symbol of homosexual-rights movements across the globe.

Though many German homosexuals died in the camps, the state was unable to launch the type of genocide it did against the Jews: many men could simply hide their true nature, while Jews could never escape in this way. As a consequence, many Jews feel that homosexual polemic focusing on a Homosexual Holocaust tends to detract from the nature of their plight, the mass destruction of an entire people. We need, though, to remember all victims of this hateful ideology and the vulnerability of all groups who can be labelled 'different'.

German Guards

During my time as Commissioner at Police Headquarters the regiments quartered in Berlin and Potsdam were demoralized through and through by homosexualists who made a speciality of soldiers as the object of their passion. This was particularly so in the cavalry regiments. They were being normally enticed by homosexualists who found the gala uniform attractive, and many fine young fellows from the country were physically and morally corrupted, during their period of service as military conscripts. Also among the officers, especially in the Guards regiments, there were several homosexualists.

from the memoirs of the Berlin police chief, Superintendent von Tresckow

The Krupp Scandal

In 1887, when Fritz Krupp became sole proprietor of the enterprise [the family armaments business], the firm already employed 19,000 men, occupied more than 1,000 acres of land and had an annual production in excess of 50 million marks. By April 1901 it had a managerial staff of 3,823 and a labour force of 46,077. The family residence, the Villa Hugel, linked to the national railway network by means of a special station, was itself graced by a permanent domestic staff of 150 . . . Krupp's personal annual income increased threefold between 1885 and 1902.

Krupp was also clearly identified with the aspirations of the new expansionist Germany . . . The SPD's attitude to the Krupp empire was that its material success rested entirely on the exploitation of the productive capacity of its workers. Krupp was therefore not a man on whom the SPD was likely to expend many tears or to whom it might conceivably show much sympathy.

Fritz Krupp's homosexual inclinations had been known to interested circles for some time before his personal scandal became public. It was conspicuous that whenever he and his wife visited Berlin together, they never stayed at the same hotel. The 20-mark pieces, which he used to bestow liberally on court flunkeys and hotel staff, had also become legendary, and by the turn of the century his name was already in the secret register of homosexuals kept by the Berlin police.

During the spring of 1902 the excesses and extravagances on the island of Capri, to which Krupp had become accustomed, reached a new pitch of reckless abandon. Tresckow of the Berlin police department received information that Krupp had begun exceeding even the bounds of tolerability accepted by Italian society, where homosexual practices did not *ipso facto* constitute a criminal offence, to the extent of seducing young boys and allowing himself to be featured in pictorial representations of group orgies. By this time an article had already appeared in the Rome paper of the Italian socialist movement, *Avanti*, but Tresckow's suggestion that the Kaiser should be informed was rejected by Polizeipräsident von Windheim. Such was the level of interest aroused by the affair that, even when Krupp suddenly departed from Capri at the end of May, the Neapolitan socialist paper *Propaganda* and gradually the entire Italian press simmered with disclosures of one kind or another. In the circumstances it was only a matter of time before the news began to cross national frontiers. It first reached the German public by means of a veiled article in the leading journal of the Bavarian Centre Party, the *Augsburger Postzeitung*, on 8 November. The real scandal did not come, however, until the *Vorwarts* published its celebrated article exactly a week later . . . Krupp issued a writ for libel against the *Vorwarts* . . . the whole apparatus of the state was launched against those who had unleashed the scandal.

Krupp returned to the Villa Hugel on 19 November, after three days in Kiel, and on 22 November came the announcement of his sudden death. Despite the attempts of his personal physicians, friends and a number of contemporary observers to suggest otherwise, the circumstances suggest that Fritz Krupp had taken his own life. This was borne out by the speed with which the coffin was sealed and the funeral service arranged.

The funeral was held on 26 November and the mourners were led by the Kaiser . . . the day was notable for a speech delivered by the Kaiser to the Krupp directorate and members of the labour-force. In it emerged not only Wilhelm II's personal emotion at the loss of a close friend, on whom he bestowed the accolade '*Kern-deutsche*', but a quite obvious and deliberate identification between the house of Hohenzollern and the house of Krupp.

from Alex Hall, Scandal, Sensation and Social Democracy: SPD Press and Wilhelmine Germany, 1890–1914 *(1977)*

Hirschfeld

Many diverse activities filled the years following Hirschfeld's move to Charlottenburg as a medical practitioner. He had become the guru of the homosexual underworld. His empathy with homosexuals bordered on identification, but he had his own burden to bear for his love of men. He felt he had to dissimulate his sexual orientation in order to protect his reputation as a doctor and scientist. He showed himself in appearance and dress as a well-to-do Jewish bourgeois, who could easily have been taken for a businessman or a banker.

After Hirschfeld had sent the famous petition [against antihomosexual legislation embodied in paragraph 175 of the Prussian penal code] to the Reichstag in 1897, he engaged in unceasing propaganda against Paragraph 175. He gave lectures and courses on the nature of love, always with an eye on homosexuality. Professional people as well as the 'man in the street' were bombarded with leaflets and pamphlets about the stupidity and injustice of the law, and the prejudiced attitude towards those who did not conform to the mass suggestion of heterosexuality. Hirschfeld wrote a pamphlet '*Was soll das Volk vom dritten Geschlecht wissen*' ('What the People Should Know of the Third

Sex') which was published by Max Spohr in 1901, unsigned, and issued by the S.H.C. [Scientific Humanitarian Committee]. It became a great success. In 1903 Hirschfeld lectured about it at the invitation of the Berlin Union of Masons . . .

By the beginning of the century he had already been asked many times to give evidence in court for the defence of homosexuals. In one of his autobiographical statements he wrote that it was the greatest satisfaction of his life to have prevented many *Urnings* [homosexuals – a word coined by K. H. Ulrichs] from going to prison, and some from committing suicide.

He was, of course, aware that there were far more homosexual men and women in Germany than was generally known. He realized the difficulty of getting an accurate estimate of their percentage in the population, but he was determined to establish it with all the statistical means available at that time. The method he used demonstrates his ingenuity.

In December 1903 he sent questionnaires to 3000 male students of the Charlottenburger Technische Hochschule. They were asked to answer on a postcard, without giving their identity away, whether they were attracted to women only, to both sexes, or to the same sex. The published card shows a W printed on the left-hand side, an M in the middle, and W+M on the right. There was also a column headed 'Deviates' for those who did not fit into any of the categories. In February 1904 the same inquiry was sent to 5000 metal-workers, after Hirschfeld had given a lecture on homosexuality at their invitation . . .

Hirschfeld . . . [was] surprised at the malice which followed the sending of the first questionnaire. The right-wing press called it offensive and an attempt to seduce German youth . . .

The inquiry sent to the metal-workers was, however, well received, and resulted in a high percentage of answers. In contrast to the workmen, many students had indeed resented the questionnaire, just as the conservative press had prophesied. Six of the students were enraged enough to take Hirschfeld to court. In March 1904 he received a writ accusing him of propagating obscene inquiries and pamphlets. Chief Justice Isenbiel, notorious for his hatred of homosexuals, presided over the court. The judgement went against Hirschfeld. He was sentenced to a fine of DM 200 and had to pay costs. His lawyer had asked the court not to proceed. He gave a number of weighty reasons, emphasizing the scientific importance of the investigation and pointing out that the inquiry had not been done on Hirschfeld's initiative alone, but at the request of 200 members of the S.H.C., many of whom were physicians and scientists . . .

The metal-workers wrote to Hirschfeld: 'Our circle of workers has understood the questions of your inquiry in the way it should be understood – namely, as scientific research.'

The results of these inquiries were obtained by a statistical method which would not be satisfactory today but, all the same, they are of considerable interest. The percentage of homosexuals among the students who answered the inquiry was 1.5, that of bisexuals 4.5. Of the 5000 metal-workers 1.15 per cent were homosexual, 3.19 per cent bisexual.

from Charlotte Wolff, Magnus Hirschfeld: A Portrait of a Pioneer in Sexology *(1986)*

The Work Ethic

When homosexuals have asked my advice, I have always maintained the following: regular, intensive work, whether manual or intellectual, is the most important condition for their well-being. There are several reasons for this. First, any useful activity fills the existence of a person, it is an aim in itself; then it makes him forget his problems; further, he can prove his usefulness to himself and his family. And work is an anchor; if anything detrimental should happen, it gives one the inner strength needed, the belief in one's importance.

from an article by Magnus Hirschfeld (1914)

The Secretary

Hirschfeld's emotional life had been carefully hidden from the world, although years before he became famous the secret of his homosexuality was talked about with approval by the 'converted', and with disgust by rivals and enemies. The fact that he himself broke the barrier of secrecy through the openness of his love for his secretary, Karl Giese, was as much a turning point in his life as the realization of his dream – the creation of the Institute for Sexual Science. The one might not have succeeded so well without the other.

It is not known exactly when Hirschfeld met Karl Giese, but the likely time was around 1919–20. The much younger man fell madly in love with him, and Hirschfeld requited his love. Karl Giese became the most important person in his life. In a much later photograph where the two stand arm in arm on the Mediterranean shore one can still recognize the power of their relationship.

Karl Giese seemed to supply all Hirschfeld's needs. He was his secretary, the guardian of the Archive and planner of new projects for the education of the public about homosexuality. His infinite knowledge of Hirschfeld's work and ideas made him his natural confidant. In short, Giese had the unique position of being his lover and most trusted collaborator. He had native wit and considerable intelligence. He had been a brilliant autodidact. He was also an articulate speaker, and Hirschfeld entrusted him with lecturing to the general public on questions of sexual conflict and homosexuality. He fulfilled his many tasks with enthusiasm and at the same time cared for Hirschfeld's well-being like a mother.

Hirschfeld was attracted by people much younger than himself, and this had found the desired response in Karl Giese. This very handsome, tall man looked virile, but behaved like an effeminate man.

Giese's physique was disproportionate to his make-up. Hirschfeld had always had a weakness for the 'feminine type' of homosexual. The paradox of age was in their case the right condition for an intimate attachment. Christopher Isherwood has given an evocative description of Karl Giese's looks and personality in his autobiography. He wrote that he used to visit him with Francis Tourville-Petre 'for coffee and gossip'.

Isherwood also gave something away about the circle around Karl Giese: 'Nearly all the friends who looked in on Karl in the afternoon were middle-class queens. They had a world of their own which included clubs for dancing and drinking. These clubs were governed by the code of heterosexual middle-class propriety.'

But who can ever explain the magnetic power which makes people love one another? The love between Hirschfeld and Giese seemed to be as complete as any romantic could wish for. They shared their lives; their inner worlds fitted together like two halves of one organism. The Socratic passion between teacher and pupil was probably an important part of their mutual attachment, but by no means the whole of it.

Hirschfeld not only had 'emotional' preferences for young men; he liked to be surrounded by youth. He repeatedly referred in his book to its revitalizing effect on the old. And his wish to remain young might have influenced his libidinous desire for youths, as well as his pleasure in working with them. He liked to be called 'Papa', but his detractors called him 'Tante Magnesia'.

Hirschfeld, a man of voluptuous sensuousness and highly sexed, was in his early fifties when he met Giese. Gunter Maeder, who had been much in Hirschfeld's confidence, told me that his sensuality was such that he could not keep his hands off attractive youths.

from Charlotte Wolff, Magnus Hirschfeld: A Portrait of a Pioneer in Sexology *(1986)*

A Progressive School

One of the first battle cries I heard when I arrived at Salem was 'sticky, sticky!' The expression came of course originally from the headmaster and his staff. It was sticky when one boy put his hands on another's shoulder, when two boys rode on the same bicycle, when there was not enough space between boys during the evening 'lying down' period, and so on. Any dirty word, any obscene joke, even when we were among ourselves, was avoided as a matter of course; the atmosphere required that. Hahn's most intelligent and wise collaborator, Marina Ewald, who remained a guardian spirit of the school even when she was an old lady . . . told me once in her early seventies that Kurt Hahn had thought he could get children to 'skip puberty'. A good way of putting it. He saw puberty as an unavoidable disease that one should try to ignore, to overcome by keeping busy with healthy pleasures and strenuous activity, and, if need be, cold showers. This policy brought a tinge of dishonesty to the life of the school, whose fundamental principle was supposed to be honesty. Here, without realizing it, he forced us to be dishonest toward him as well as toward each other. My brother Klaus, sexually experienced at an early age, later commented that Kurt Hahn had done me great harm with his principles. That I do not believe. I think it was the milder cases who suffered preventable damage from Hahn's sex education, or lack of it.

from Golo Mann, Reminiscences and Reflections *(1990)*

Common Sense

It appears to me to defy all laws of common sense if the state takes it upon itself to regulate the private lives of human beings or tries to redirect these lives towards other goals.

Ernst Roehm

Indifference

I have nothing against Roehm as a person. As far as I am concerned, a man can fancy elephants in Indochina and kangaroos in Australia – I couldn't care less.

Martin Bormann in a comment to Rudolf Hess

Vice Man

Edmond Heines, the group leader of the storm troopers at Breslau, was a repulsive brute who turned the Nazi headquarters of the city into a homosexual brothel. Having 300,000 storm troopers under his command, he was in a position to terrorize the neighbourhood. He extracted money right and left, from all and sundry, under physical threats and the moral threat of blackmail. One of his favourite ruses was to have members of the youth organizations indulge in unnatural practices with one another and then threaten their parents that he would denounce these youths to the police and thus expose the whole family to shame unless he received a certain consideration in the form of hush money. These blackmail messages were often delivered by members of the S.A. in uniform, to make the threat more impressive. Then Heines not only indulged in homosexual orgies himself – he was often Roehm's consort in this – but he promoted vice as a lucrative business.

from Samuel Igra, Germany's National Vice *(1945)*

An Early-Morning Call

Just before Wiessee, Hitler suddenly breaks his silence: 'Kempka,' he says, 'drive carefully when we come to the Hotel Hanselbauer. You must drive up without making any noise. If you see an SA guard in front of the hotel, don't wait for them to report to me; drive on and stop at the hotel entrance.' Then, after a moment of deathly silence: 'Roehm wants to carry out a coup.' . . .

I drive up carefully to the hotel entrance as Hitler has ordered. Hitler jumps out of the car, and after him Goebbels, Lutze and the adjutants. Right behind us another car stops with a squad of detectives which has been raised in Munich . . . [They enter the hotel.] I run quickly up the stairs to the first floor where Hitler is coming out of Roehm's bedroom. Two detectives come out of the room opposite. One of them reports to Hitler: 'My Führer . . . the Police-President of Breslau is refusing to get dressed!'

Taking no notice of me, Hitler enters the room where Obergruppenführer Heines is remaining. I hear him shout: 'Heines, if you are not dressed in five minutes I'll have you shot on the spot!'

I withdraw a few steps and a police officer whispers to me that Heines had been in bed with an 18-year-old SA Obertruppführer. At last Heines comes out of the room with an 18-year-old fair-haired boy mincing in front of him.

'Into the laundry room with them!' cries Schreck.

Meanwhile Roehm comes out of his room in a blue suit and with a cigar in the corner of his mouth . . . I stay in the corridor a little to one side and a detective tells me about Roehm's arrest.

Hitler entered Roehm's bedroom alone with a whip in his hand. Behind him were two detectives with pistols at the ready. He spat out the words: 'Roehm, you are under arrest.' Roehm looked up speedily from his pillow: 'Heil, my Führer.' 'You are under arrest,' bawled Hitler for the second time, turned on his heel and left the room.

> *Hitler's driver's account of the events of 30 June 1934 – the Night of the Long Knives. The leaders of the SA were taken to Munich and shot there. The SA was destroyed.*

American Women

If a man just looks at a girl in America, he can be forced to marry her or pay damages . . . therefore men protect themselves in the USA by turning to homosexuals . . . women in the United States are like battle-axes – they hack away at males.

> *a comment by Heinrich Himmler*

Frederick the Great

One day Dr Felix Kersten suggested to his boss Heinrich Himmler that Frederick the Great had been homosexual. He received the following reaction.

'What are you implying by that?' Himmler retorted. 'You're not trying to suggest that the great king had abnormal tendencies? I know those dirty Jews who assert things of the kind in order to take our heroes from us and drag them in the mud. Any great man who has done wonders for his people must somehow or other be abnormal, or at best demented. But with the best will in the world it's quite impossible to assert that Frederick the Great should even be suspected of homosexuality. Only mediocrity is normal and conventional because it produces no greatness and is therefore politically and economically "safe". To portray Frederick the Great as abnormal is the obvious malice of a sick mind. I know that his coldness towards his wife is brought forward as evidence. But just consider that poor-spirited creature; it's no wonder that he viewed her as a holy terror and refused to live with her. Why can't it be looked at in this way: as he could not live with his lawful wife, he gave himself up to an ascetic life as king, which fitted him for his great achievements. Instead of that mud is slung and homosexual tendencies attributed to him – for which there was, moreover, no foundation in fact. If you looked you could only find indications, no clear and indisputable proof.'

'It might be difficult, Herr Himmler, to prove such a thing,' I objected.

'Then people should keep quiet,' Himmler answered, 'and bow in silence before his greatness. I would say only one thing to them: if a dozen so-called proofs were put before me, I would brush them aside and assert that they had been made up after the event, because my feelings tell me that a man who won for Prussia her place in the sun could not have had any tendencies of these homosexual weaklings.'

from Felix Kersten, The Kersten Memoirs, 1940–1945 (1956)

Personal Picture Show

A Rumanian prince, who lived with his mother in Munich, had become a public scandal owing to his unnatural behaviour. Despite all political and social considerations, the publicity which he had brought on himself had become intolerable and he was brought to Dachau. The police thought that his excessive debaucheries had wearied him of women, and that he had taken to homosexuality as a pastime in order to get a new thrill. The Reichsführer SS believed that hard work and the strict life of a concentration camp would soon effect a cure.

The moment he arrived, it was obvious to me what was wrong with him. His roaming eyes, the way he startled at the slightest noise, his weak and dancer-like movements, all made me suspect the true homosexual at once. When the commandant harshly ordered him to go through the customary routine for new entrants, he began to weep. Then he did not want to have a bath, because he was shy. We saw the reason when he undressed. The whole of his body, from neck to wrists and ankles, was tattooed with obscene pictures. Curiously enough, these pictures not only depicted every form of perversion that the human brain could invent, but also normal intercourse between men and women. Students of sexology would certainly have obtained some new and unusual material for their researches from this living picture-book. On being interrogated, he said that he had acquired these tattooings in every sort of seaport, both in the old world and the new.

When his sexual picture-book was photographed by the police, for all tattoo marks had to be recorded for the purposes of the State Criminal Police Office, he became sexually excited, particularly when touched. I told the room senior that he was directly responsible for him and that he was never to let him out of his sight. After a few hours I went to see how this rare plant was thriving, and I was met by the room senior who begged me to release him at once from his charge. It was, he said rapidly 'getting him down'. The prince stood the whole time in front of the stove, staring before him. Whenever anyone came near him, or touched him in order to move him away, he became sexually excited and began to masturbate. I took him to the doctor. No sooner had the doctor started to ask him questions about his condition than he began to get excited again. He said that since his earliest youth he had suffered from strong sexual impulses, for which he had never been able to find any means of complete satisfaction. He was perpetually seeking new ways to satisfy these impulses.

The doctor prepared a report for the Reichsführer SS, which concluded by saying that the prisoner ought to be in a nursing-home and not in a concentration camp. Any attempt to cure him by hard work was doomed to failure from the start.

The report was sent off and while we were awaiting a reply the newcomer was given work, as had been ordered. His job was to cart sand. He could scarcely lift a shovel. He fell over while pushing an empty wheel-barrow. I had him taken back to his room, and informed the commandant. The commandant wished to see this performance with his own eyes on the following day. The man must work, for the Reichsführer SS had ordered it. On the next day he was staggering so that he could hardly get to the sandpit, although it was not far away. Work was out of the question: even Loritz realised this. He was taken back to his room and put to bed. That too was wrong, for he masturbated constantly. The doctor talked to him as a sick child. It was all quite useless. They tried tying his hands, but that was not effective for long. He was given sedatives and kept cool. All in vain. He became weaker and weaker. Nevertheless he crawled out of bed in an attempt to reach the other prisoners. He was put under arrest, pending the decision of the Reichsführer SS. Two days later he was dead. He died while masturbating. Altogether he had been five weeks in the camp. The Reichsführer SS ordered a post-mortem examination to be carried out and a detailed report sent to him. The examination, at which I was present, showed a complete physical debilitation but no abnormality. The professor at the Munich Institute of Pathology, who performed the post-mortem, had never before come across a similar case in all his experience covering a great many years.

I was present when the commandant showed the man's corpse to his mother. The mother said that his death was a blessing, both for himself and for her. His uncontrollable sex life had made him impossible to everyone. She had consulted the most famous medical specialists throughout Europe, but without success. He had run away from every sanitorium. He had spent some time in a monastery. But he could not stay there either. She had even, in her despair, suggested to him he take his own life, but he lacked the courage to do so. Now he would at least be at peace with himself. It makes me shiver even now when I remember this case.

from Rudolf Hoess, Commandant of Auschwitz *(1959)*

Saved

We were led to our block by an SS guard, and transferred there to the sergeant in charge . . . a group of eight to ten Kapos gathered round us and looked us up and down. I was already wise enough to know exactly why [they] . . . were admiring us in this way. They were on the lookout for a possible lover among the new arrivals. Because I still did not have a full beard, even though twenty-three, so looked younger than my years, and because I filled out a bit again thanks to the supplementary rations from my Sachsenhausen Kapos, I was obviously very much at the center of these Kapos' considerations. I could tell as much from their unconcealed discussions. The situation in which the five of us found ourselves seemed to me very much like a slave-boy market in ancient Rome . . . When the sergeant had departed, and the block senior had to assign us new arrivals our beds, he immediately came up to me and said: 'Hey you kid, do you want to come with me?'

'Yes certainly,' I said right away, knowing very well what he meant. My immediate acceptance somehow made an impression on him. He said: 'You're a clever kid, I like that,' and patted me on the shoulder . . . The senior whose lover I became was a professional criminal from Hamburg, very highly regarded in his milieu as a safecracker. He was much feared by the prisoners for his ruthlessness, and even by his Kapo colleagues, but he was generous and considerate to me. Only half a year later he became camp senior, and remained so until the Americans liberated the camp. Even later on, when I was no longer his lover, his eye having fallen on a young Pole, he kept a protecting hand over me. He saved my life more than ten times over, and I am still very grateful to him today, more than twenty-five years later.

from Richard Plant, The Pink Triangle *(1987)*

A Captive Audience

In February 1944 . . . a naval court convened in the northern German town of Gluckstadt to try three French-speaking Arabs. It seems that Dhu, Deb, and Beaug had satisfied each other's needs quite openly at various places, mainly in the showers. One episode in particular shocked the court. While a marine captain had delivered an illustrated lecture about the wartime duties of the true German fighting man, defendant Dhu, protected by the backs of the sailors sitting in front of him, went down on his knees and satisfied his companion Deb. Two German sailors had watched and reported the crime. Verdict: seven months in jail for Dhu, five months for Deb, and two months for the less active Beaug, who was only involved in the shower incidents.

from Richard Plant, The Pink Triangle *(1987)*

The German Vice

. . . the widespread existence of sexual perversion in Germany, not only at the time the Hitler movement rose to power but also under the Kaiser's regime, is notorious. And authorities on criminal sociology are agreed that there is a causal connection between mass sexual perversion and the kind of mass atrocities committed by the Germans in the two world wars. Furthermore, there is no doubt that this also explains why the Jews were made the chief victims of German sadistic torture, rapine and murder . . . the scourge of German militarism is only the secondary effect of a primary evil. And the evil lies in the region of personal morality, the region from which all political evil springs. The poison in Germany has penetrated from above downwards, from the leaders to the followers. This was true of Germany in the Middle Ages, where the Prussian State was first founded by the military pseudo-religious order of the Teutonic Knights, among whom the vice of homosexuality was rampant. The poison grew more virulent under Frederick the Great, who was himself a moral pervert. It broke out as a mass malady under the last Kaiser, whose court was the rendezvous of a camarilla that had made a cult of unnatural vices. This fact, and the further fact that the origin of the first world war was partly attributable to the scandals brought to light in connection with the Kaiser's court, are proved by unquestionable documentary evidence   the Hitler movement has been contaminated by these vices from the start, and its violent anti-semitic bias is to be explained by reference to the uncompromising stand which Israel has maintained throughout her long history against practices that poison the source of life itself. The Bible, both the Old Testament and the New, had persistently denounced these vices in the most solemn manner. And that is one of the main reasons why national-socialist Germany has overthrown the Bible, in self-justification.

The gangster-militarist clique in Germany were the originating source of that evil which has infected the whole body politic of the German people, breaking out like rabies among them and forcing them in a compulsive urge to spread destruction all round . . . the poison has permeated the whole body.

from Samuel Igra, Germany's National Vice *(1945)*

CHAPTER EIGHT

The American Century

During the Second World War American society experienced a massive mobilisation of manpower that did much to promote the incidence of homosexual behaviour in the United States. Young men and women were taken from their homes in their late teens and early twenties and found employment in the armed services and in the munitions factories, thus usually giving them some access to city life. The big cities offered many opportunities for sexual experiment away from parents and childhood contemporaries. Many young men were drawn into the large homosexual subcultures that existed in the largest American cities, and after the war many chose to settle in these urban centres, further strengthening already powerful communities of homosexuals.

This change went largely unnoticed by contemporaries. Homosexuality was even more of a taboo in the United States than it was in Europe, and many people were ignorant of the phenomenon. This situation was challenged in 1948 with the appearance of Alfred Kinsey's *Sexual Behavior in the Human Male* – the Kinsey Report – possibly the single most important event in the history of homosexuality. The Kinsey Report became a bestseller, and its results were widely disseminated in newspapers and magazines.

What surprised everyone was the amount of homosexuality that Kinsey detected in American society. According to his investigations, most of which were reported in an impressive series of statistical tables, 37 per cent of the American male population had experienced some homosexual activity since adolescence. He identified around 10 per cent of the male population as more or less exclusively homosexual. Homosexuality had become a social problem.

Kinsey was a scientist, a biology professor from Indiana. His main life's work had been a large-scale study of gall wasps, on which he became the leading expert. In 1938 he was asked to deliver a course of lectures to students on human sexuality, and as he prepared the course he was astonished by the absence of comprehensive surveys of the sexual life of the human, of a type that he was accustomed to in his studies of insects. It was this which launched him on the work that was to win him fame and fortune. It was Kinsey's background that gave such force to his findings. As the magazine *Life* told its readers in an editorial, 'What they have learned and will learn may have a tremendous effect on the future history of mankind. For they are presenting facts. They are revealing not what should be, but what is. For the first time data on human sex behavior is entirely separated from questions of philosophy, moral values, and social customs.'

Kinsey became a celebrity, and he toured the world. His expert status gave him the authority to interrogate individuals in every country he visited on their most intimate personal history.

The war had made many Americans incredibly affluent; the United States was the richest, most powerful nation on earth. Its inhabitants lived in what the publisher of *Life* described in 1945 as the 'American century', and Kinsey was an important prophet and guide to them.

Across the globe, Kinsey's figures became the starting-point in every discussion of sexuality. His suggestion that 10 per cent of the adult male population were homosexual became an article of faith, accepted by apologists and critics of homosexuality without question. Yet there were serious problems about Kinsey's surveys. Though he interviewed 17,000 men for his report, most of his sample was drawn from the cities of the American north-east, which was bound to weight his survey in favour of men who had access to the homosexual subculture. He restricted his survey to native-born white Americans and completely ignored blacks. His work of course relied on self-assessment, which Kinsey converted through a curious act of alchemy into raw figures. He had an obsession with measurement, and possessed an insatiable appetite for quantification, producing in one section of his report a table that classified cases of bestiality by the size and weight of the animal concerned.

The oddest feature of the survey, one criticised in a famous essay by the liberal critic Lionel Trilling,[1] was the isolation of sex from emotion. Kinsey treated sex as an outlet, and in this way did much to sanction promiscuity. Is it possible to divorce sex from love or from 'questions of philosophy, moral values, and social customs'? Is it even desirable? Kinsey was as much a myth-maker as the moralists that his surveys did so much to threaten and undermine.

Curiously, a book appeared in 1950 that supported many of Kinsey's findings without a single statistic. *The Homosexual Outsider*, by D. W. Cory, described the life of the homosexual in contemporary America in one of the most powerful front-line reports ever published. Cory relied entirely on his own impressions of living as an active homosexual in America and offered an insight into the operation of what was by then a highly sophisticated and well-organised community. But Cory's book attracted little attention and was easily eclipsed by the pseudo-scientific reports of Kinsey, which failed to place sexual behaviour in a social or even cultural context. Kinsey had only a limited understanding of how society functioned and how far sexual behaviour might be shaped by social and cultural factors. He remained the insect expert and analysed human society in similar terms.

One of the most important aspects of the Kinsey Report was the creation of a seven-point scale, from zero to six, which Kinsey suggested classified the sexual behaviour of adults. At either end were the adults who were exclusively heterosexual or homosexual, with bisexual individuals being placed along the scale according to predominance of hetero or homo elements in their make-up. This scheme, which is in some ways the most convincing part of the book, did little to damage the power of Freud's theory of universal bisexuality either at a popular or at a scientific level.

The exposure of the American homosexual came at a moment of considerable national tension, and the Republican Party, which by the end of 1948 had lost five presidential elections in succession, turned the homosexual into a scapegoat for the nation's ills. Americans had been caught in the grip of a peculiar kind of hysteria generated by the Cold War, a hysteria which did much to excite fears of a fifth column operating secretly within the state to destroy the American nation. This paranoia was of course ridiculous, as America was in fact the most powerful nation on the planet, but this did not seem to matter. It was a state of affairs that allowed the witch-hunts of Senator Joe McCarthy to take place. He was quick to single out homosexuals as an unreliable element in government, and many thousands of homosexuals lost their jobs in a major purge of the Washington bureaucracy. The witch-hunts gave many homosexuals a sense of grievance which has done much to influence the political stance of gay activists since the late 1960s, though these purges were on a relatively small scale.

McCarthy and his allies had no more effective way of identifying homosexuals than did Himmler during the Third Reich, and the majority slipped through the net. Psychiatrists called on to help were of little assistance. They had designed the screening test established at the beginning of the Second World War to weed out all homosexual servicemen.[2] The test was largely the work of a homosexual psychiatrist, Harry Stack Sullivan, who lived with his lover in Washington. McCarthy's right-hand man, the New York lawyer and political fixer Roy Cohn, was also a homosexual. Indeed it was Cohn's efforts to secure special treatment in the US Army for David Schnide, with whom he was infatuated, that led directly to McCarthy's downfall. Cohn went on to become a powerful political broker, a friend of successive presidents, even bringing his lover to a reception in the Reagan White House. He died in 1986 of Aids.

McCarthy was surrounded by men who preferred to select their sex partners from among their own sex, and some of his best friends were heavily into homosexuality. The Roman Catholic Archbishop of New York, Cardinal Francis Spellman, who arranged for the childless McCarthys to adopt a child, was a vigorous opponent of Communism. He also held homosexual parties and had a succession of male lovers. By the 1950s he had become the richest prelate in the Catholic Church.

J. Edgar Hoover, the head of the FBI, was another McCarthy buddy and a lifelong bachelor. He lived with his best friend and deputy in what one might describe as a 'homosexual marriage'. Hoover was one of the most powerful men in the American state and used some of that power to ensure that rumours of his sexual proclivities did not circulate. It was a forlorn hope. Homosexuality was so extremely well-established in American society by the 1940s that it had penetrated the highest echelons, where it operated without much interference. Some witch-hunt.

One of the few ways in which we can try to excavate that culture today is through the reports of sociologists in the 1920s and 1930s which give some evidence of the social impact of homosexuality. There is good evidence to suggest that homosexuality was well-established in the American prison system, for example. Joseph Fishman wrote an astonishingly explicit book on the subject which appeared in 1936.[3] America had had a large population of transients since the mid-nineteenth century – the so-called 'hobos'. Sociologists discovered that homosexuality flourished in these groups, and it is not difficult to imagine that such groups would attract young men in the way that theatres and travelling companies did in the Old World.

During the 1940s three major American homosexual writers appeared: Tennessee Williams, Truman Capote and Gore Vidal. In an act of considerable personal courage, Vidal, a member of an American political dynasty and a war hero, published an outstanding novel about homosexuality, *The City and the Pillar*, that appeared in the same year as the Kinsey Report. Vidal was ostracised by the literary establishment for many years but became one of the most perceptive critics of the American political and social system and has been much celebrated since the 1960s.

The McCarthy campaign had the full support of the psychiatric establishment. The American Psychiatric Association had classified homosexuality as an illness in 1942, and from that time many practitioners had claimed that they could cure homosexual feelings. This lucrative classification also led psychiatrists to produce some remarkable anti-homosexual polemic. Jewish refugees, many of them trained in Germany and central Europe, were particularly prominent in a vicious campaign of vilification. Such men brought their profession into disrepute and led to a widespread suspicion of psychiatrists among homosexuals.

The late 1940s saw the emergence of a male image that was brought to life by a number of homosexual artists and which came to dominate Western depictions of the male. Marlon Brando popularised the white T-shirt, jeans and leather jacket which have become the uniform of masculinity. Tennessee Williams provided Brando with a role that allowed him to play the confused and sensual hunk by casting him as Stanley Kowalski in *A Streetcar Named Desire* in 1947. Elia Kazan, who directed both the stage play and the film of *Streetcar*, described the character of Stanley as created by Williams as 'walking penis'. There have been many imitators.

Illustrators George Quaintance and Neel Bates ('Blade') produced an image which was to be much copied. They drew 'the idealised macho stud whose well-filled crotch, large penis, beautiful, developed muscular body and square-cut features came to define a particular stereotype of powerful, non-sissy manhood which was at the same time homosexual'.[4] They worked for the nascent American homosexual porn industry – one of the success stories of the post-war American economy. Bob Mizer created the Athletic Model Guild, and the physique magazines he and the illustrators supplied had a powerful impact on the baby-boom generation that came of age in the 1970s. Modern advertising owes much to this particular source. In 1948, the year of Kinsey, Bantam books issued its first beefcake cover with the publication in paperback of C. S. Forester's *The African Queen*. Male sexual images could sell the merchandise. With this, homoeroticism began the association with the forces of advertising and capitalism that has created an aesthetic tradition which has shaped modern masculine identity and exposed men across the globe to the full force of the homosexual tradition.

An important item in the package has been the cult of James Dean. A not particularly brilliant actor (acting talent does not always coincide with a pretty face and an appealing torso, whatever Hollywood might tell us to the contrary), Dean came to occupy a position in twentieth-century culture similar to that enjoyed by Helen of Troy in the ancient world. The most famous male erotic image of the age was the product of the American century.

While the 'American homosexual' had been discovered in 1948, it was not until the mid-1960s that the homosexual subculture was finally explored by the media. Through most of the 1940s, 1950s and 1960s the American media and academia simply ignored a sizeable element of their society. When Gay Liberation exploded on the scene after 1969 this fact of life could no longer be ignored: twenty-one years after Kinsey, the homosexual subculture finally came of age.

The Melting-Pot

I believe the main purport of America is to be found in a new ideal of manly friendship, more ardent, more general.
Walt Whitman

Macho Man I

Nature's attempt to get rid of soft boys by sterilizing them.
from F. Scott Fitzgerald's notebook

Macho Man II

Somehow they always made me angry. I know they are supposed to be amusing, and you should be tolerant, but I wanted to swing on one, any one, anything to shatter that superior, simpering composure.
from Ernest Hemingway, The Sun also Rises (1926)

If he was one he should redeem, for the tribe, the prissy exhibitionistic, aunt-like, withered old maid moral arrogance of a Gide; the lazy, conceited debauchery of a Wilde who betrayed a generation; the nasty, sentimental pawing of humanity of a Whitman and all the mincing gentry.
from Ernest Hemingway, Death in the Afternoon (1932)

Flawed Vision

No homosexual has a vision that is decent enough to make him a writer.
from the New York Times, 1967

The American Prison System

Every year large numbers of boys, adolescent youths, and young men are made homosexuals, either temporarily or permanently, in the prisons of America. This unfortunate condition is achieved not only through the negation of normal sexual habits, but because of the constant talk concerning sex, enforced idleness, the loneliness in one's cell; and finally the relentless pressure of the 'wolves' or 'top men' housed among the normal inmates in the prison, who 'spot' those among the younger prisoners whom they wish to make their 'girls', and who 'court' them with a persistence, a cunning, and a singleness of purpose which is almost incredible in its viciousness. They usually begin with a friendly offer to protect the newcomer, and to see that his life in prison is made as easy as possible for him. This offer is often gratefully accepted by the new inmate because he is not yet accustomed to prison life. The pressure of the older prisoner on the new and young arrivals can and often does make itself felt in a thousand subtle, irritating ways.

The first advance is usually followed by the giving of small presents, such as a box of cigarettes purchased from the prison commissary. Unless the new prisoner has someone to 'put him wise', assuming that he does not know the object of these advances, he gradually slips into a position of helpless dependency on his self-styled protector. When the final purpose of these attentions becomes known, and if the object of them resists, he is very often threatened with physical harm. This unfortunately is too common. It was necessary, recently, to transfer a Chinese boy to another institution because another prisoner threatened to stab him in the throat with a long pointed fingernail file if he did not permit homosexual relations . . . There can be no doubt that such things go on at all times and in every American prison. A deputy warden of one of the large prisons in the Middle West once showed me a remarkable collection of notes that he had received in one day from various inmates. Each note stated that the undersigned was a relative of a boyish-looking prisoner who had arrived the day before, and requested that for this reason he be placed in the same cell with him. There were thirty-nine notes in all. That number of prisoners had seen the boy and made up their minds that they would like to have him for their 'girl'. That there were others who did not write notes but who were bent on the same quest is of course obvious.

from Joseph Fishman, Sex in Prisons *(1936)*

Exercises in Deception

A striking practice of latent homosexuals [noted by an American sociologist in the 1930s] . . . was for two friends to go to a brothel together, each have intercourse with a different girl, and then have intercourse a second time with the girl just used by the other. In this way the 'friends' were able to indulge, without conscious admission of its existence, their homosexual attraction for one another.

There are also those males, still more obviously homosexual, who are potent only after watching another male have intercourse with a prostitute, and then quickly following after him – sometimes with the additional requirement that the first male's semen is left in the prostitute's vagina. Others wish to perform cunnilingus on the prostitute while the preceding male's semen is in her vagina – a not too thinly veiled vicarious fellatio. Such practices may also employ fetishisms . . . where the customer had to be preceded by a man or men in military uniform.

from Harry Benjamin and Robert E. L. Masters, Prostitution and Morality *(1965)*

The War

The military experience of homosexuality in World War II chipped away some of the old taboos. Servicemen living in close proximity to one another were made aware that men who chose a sexual relationship with other men were not suffering from a deadly disease, nor were they cowards or effeminates. Many thousands of homosexuals discovered a new consciousness of their collective identity in the sub-culture of bars and camaraderie which expanded to meet the wartime demand . . . World War II, by the very act of bringing so many homosexuals together, contributed to the evolution of the so-called Gay Liberation Movement in the United States twenty years after the war had ended.

from John Costello, Love, Sex and War: Changing Values 1939–1945 (1985)

The Examination

What would it be like, I wondered, as a raw recruit in the army or navy? The answer was clear: like a pasha in a harem forbidden to touch the naked girls. A well-informed pacifist friend dissuaded me from any inclination to join up, recommending Dalton Trumbo's book about the first war, *Johnny Get Your Gun*. If the draft board believed I was not suitable military material, she said, they would grant a deferral. I decide to be myself, whoever that was.

Days later in a high school gym with hundreds of other naked youths, like government-inspected hunks of meat we waited in line and watched 'short-arm' and 'brown-eye' inspection, bending over and spreading our buttocks for Uncle Sam. When the finger probed deep into the anal recesses every head turned away. The whole scene screamed Queer – but it was a case of the emperor's new clothes. The men played it with a straight face. I was afraid I'd get an erection, but to my relief found the probe painful. This proved I was a man. I had always felt like one. Our totem poles in this extended family of brothers under the foreskin were not supposed to stick out lest we show that we loved one another better than our country, which was unpatriotic.

So many conflicting emotions arose within me that I could hardly think. I was directed to a row of cubicles and, at a signal from a guard, I entered one. A bespectacled snowy owl at an oak desk motioned me to a seat opposite him. After perusing some official papers, he began questioning me.

'Do you think you could adjust quickly to the armed forces?'

'I don't know, doctor. Maybe not quickly.'

'Is there any reason why you might not adjust?'

'Well, I – I might find army routine hard to take.'

'I see.' He scribbled something as a faint cloud of suspicion crossed his features. 'Do you consider yourself normal?'

'I – well, yes, I guess so,' I stammered. He shot me a penetrating look.

'What do you most enjoy doing?'

'Writing and reading poetry.' I watched his eyebrows arch.

'Poetry?' I had blown my cover. 'Do you dream of women?'

'Oh, yes, yes!' I tried to sound enthusiastic.

'And do you' – he lowered his voice – 'also dream of men?'

'Uh – doesn't everyone?' I mumbled.

He looked stern. 'Intimate dreams, young man?'

I nodded.

'By intimate I mean of a – sexual nature.' He barely whispered.

'Sometimes,' I said softly.

The pen scratched rapidly. When he looked up his face had set. I was trapped by the machinery of government into an admission of the most personal, confidential sort. I hadn't, however, confessed to an overt act of 'perversion'. With an air of finality the shrink stamped the documents, coldly instructing me to present them at the outside desk.

As I stumbled through the gym in a daze I glanced at the nude bodies of the silent young men, so exposed, so vulnerable, such fresh, tender meat on the government rack, and I was almost swept away by a wave of brotherly lust. They were so silent, obedient, cowed, and ashamed that I felt like kissing and licking them all back to shape, saying, 'There, now doesn't it feel better?' Before reaching the desk I glimpsed the top page of the report. It bore a large red stamp: PRE-PSYCHOTIC STATE. 4–F. DEFINITELY NOT TO BE RETURNED. Beneath were scribbled F–REACTIONS. Feminine reactions? Fag, freak, funny reactions? Officially, I was a borderline case in a pre-psychotic state. But I was free.

from Harold Norse, Memoirs of a Bastard Angel *(1989)*

YMCA

On the third floor of the old West Side YMCA on Sixty-second Street I had a monkish cell over Central Park with the standard bed, chair, desk, and Bible. There was a housing shortage, which grew more acute on weekends when servicemen arrived from their bases like invading troops, their pent-up erotic needs demanding immediate attention. Greenwich Village and Times Square were the main targets; YMCAs were another. In a discreet way men surrendered to the pressures of loneliness and transience by making contact under the bright lights. With the stress of dislocation and impending doom, almost anyone in uniform was available, although some young men, mostly from farms and small towns, retained their objections, their bigotry died hard. A significant number thus became sexually liberated. Toward this end I performed my patriotic duty.

My experiences ranged from quickies in hot showers or behind park bushes to one-night stands. Straight boys, facing the threat of extinction, quickly yielded to the gods of nature, Priapus and Bacchus (who never die). Far from their home communities, unhindered by what others thought, most responded willingly to homosexual acts. With a cross-section of young men from the entire country overrunning the city, it became apparent that our sexual behavior could hardly be regarded as 'different' – if anything, it seemed very much the norm. When thrown together en masse American males indulged in same-sex acts in overwhelming numbers, indicating that, at least under wartime conditions, such behavior is natural. In the all-male atmosphere at the Y, whether in the lounge, washrooms, or showers, this was conspicuously evident. During the war one might safely assume that those who resisted homosexuality were perverts. But we were tolerant, setting out with moral zeal to convert the heathen.

from Harold Norse, Memoirs of a Bastard Angel *(1989)*

Breakfast at Tiffany's

During World War II a man of middle age entertained a Marine one Saturday night. The man enjoyed himself so much in the Marine's muscular embrace that he felt he should buy him something to show his gratitude; but since it was Sunday when they woke up, and the stores were closed, the best he could offer was breakfast. 'Where would you like to go?' he asked. 'Pick the fanciest most expensive place in town.' The Marine, who was not a native, had heard of one fancy and expensive place in New York and he said: 'Let's have breakfast at Tiffany's.'

from Gerald Clarke, Capote (1988)

Helpless Victim

During one of his Saturday night outings with Mary and me in the spring of 1944, a day after he [Chester Kallman] had received his paycheck from the Bureau of Censorship, he picked up a sailor in a bar. The sailor, named Bernie, was a lean blond macho type of about twenty with pale round blue eyes and long white lashes. Mary and I called him the Caterpillar. He went home with Chester that Saturday night. When Chester awoke on Sunday morning, the Caterpillar was gone, and so was Chester's weekly paycheck. Chester rushed crosstown to wake Mary and me, and, mad with anger and outrage, told us of his plight. We lent him enough money to tide him over the next week, hoping that Bernie was gone for good.

Bernie was gone for a week. The next weekend, the Caterpillar appeared again on payday at Chester's favourite haunt on Macdougall Street – as Mary and I looked darkly on – and again went home with Chester. Stunned by Chester's willingness to be victimized again, we were not surprised to learn that Bernie had once more taken off with Chester's paycheck. Mary convinced Chester to report his check stolen and to apply for a duplicate from the bureau. Bernie had twice forged Chester's name, it was discovered, and had twice cashed his paycheck. Deciding to find the Caterpillar and call the police, Chester agreed to prefer charges. The next weekend, Chester, Mary and I discovered the Caterpillar in another bar. However, instead of reporting him, Chester again took him home. When Chester awoke next morning, his typewriter was gone as well as his paycheck.

Bernie would eventually go off to sea, be killed, or simply disappear, but he would be replaced by another Bernie, just as unprincipled as the last . . . [Chester] was continually robbed: he was often beaten. Yet as the years went by he continued to return to the same bars where the Bernies were to be found, if not in New York then in Europe.

from D. J. Farnan, Auden in Love (1984)

California Cruising I

Most people found the war years sexually stimulating, in the sense that brief encounters were more frequent. There was an urgency about them too which appealed to some tastes, as did the blackout. Servicemen on leave would hang around the corners of Sunset Boulevard and other Hollywood streets, ready for a party that could easily become an orgy. The beaches north of Santa Monica became regular meeting-places and the scenes of nocturnal gatherings until, several years after the war, there was a big clear-up.

from Jonathan Fryer, Isherwood (1977)

California Cruising II

The American writer James Agee (1909–55), based in New York, went West for a visit in 1944.

When he was not haunting the studios, Agee roamed the nearby beaches, where he was mesmerized by the sight of the muscular young men sunning themselves and splashing in the surf. He found himself so attracted to their open, narcissistic sensuality that he suspected himself of homosexual tendencies . . . On his return to New York he discussed his attraction to muscular young men with his *Nation* colleague Clement Greenberg, who was quick to dismiss Agee's feelings as transient and baseless. In a Freudian-ridden era, he later explained, 'It was the fashion to suspect one's self of homosexuality.'

from Laurence Bergreen, James Agee: A Life (1984)

Complacent Cardinal

In 1942, for instance, [Cardinal Francis] Spellman formed a liaison with a chorus boy who appeared in the aptly named Broadway show *One Touch of Venus*. After evening performances, the archdiocesan limousine arrived at the theater's side entrance. The chorus boy entered and was driven to Spellman . . . Word of the affair spread beyond clerical circles because of the youth himself. He bragged that Archbishop Spellman was his lover. A layman who stumbled onto the affair was C. A. Tripp, who later became a sex researcher . . . A friend . . . introduced Tripp to the young man whom Spellman was seeing. The youth was so outspoken about his relationship with the churchman that Tripp was flabbergasted. He wondered why Spellman wasn't more discreet.

After listening to the youth, Tripp made a request: 'Would you ask the Archbishop a question for me?'

The chorus boy replied that he would.

'Why', Tripp wanted to know, 'isn't he afraid that this will get around and harm his reputation?'

Several days later, the young man approached Tripp with Spellman's answer. 'The archbishop says "Who would ever believe that?" '

from John Cooney, The American Pope (1984)

The Cheating Wife

'I would never have become homosexual if Joan had stayed with me,' Jack [Dunphy] said, and it is probably so. He had had homoerotic fantasies before, and he had moved in a dance and theatrical circle that was largely populated by homosexuals, but his sexual experience, starting in his mid-teens with a high-school teacher, had been entirely with women. He was not a man who could react in a moderate or measured way, and when Joan cheated on him, he turned against the entire female sex. 'Women were very distasteful to me, and I decided I wanted to go to bed with men. I had had dreamy crushes on men before, but I had never thought of doing anything about them. I knew the jars of honey were there, but I didn't know they could be opened.' Remembering the advances made to him by an Army buddy, he took a bus to Florida, where the man was living, to see if the offer was still open. It was not; his friend was now thinking civilian thoughts of marriage and children. Jack was undaunted. The jars of honey were waiting for him in New York, as they had always been, and although he fumbled and sweated, he soon learned how to open them. 'When I did turn to men, it was very difficult,' he explained. 'I really had to work at it. Men's legs were hard.' He was still working at it – he had been to bed with only two men – when Truman [Capote] came through Leo's door and showed him how easy it was.

the story of Jack Dunphy, from Gerald Clarke, Capote (1988)

Annus Mirabilis

That [1948] was the year everybody in the United States was worried about homosexuality. They were worried about other things, too, but their other anxieties were published, discussed, and ventilated while their anxieties about homosexuality remained in the dark: remained unspoken. Is he? Was he? Did they? Am I? Could I? seemed to be at the back of everyone's mind. A great emphasis, by way of defense, was put upon manliness, athletics, hunting, fishing, and conservative clothing, but the lonely wife wondered, glancingly, about her husband at his hunting camp, and the husband himself wondered with whom he shared a rude bed of pines. Was he? Had he? Did he want to? Had he ever? But what I really mean to say is that this is laughable. Guilty man may be, but only an absurdly repressed people would behave this way.

from John Cheever, The Journals (1990)

Starting-Point

Scientific explanations of the origin and development of the homosexual . . . will only be on any sound basis until we know the basis, until we know the number of people who are involved in each type of activity, the ages at which they first became involved, and the age at which they are most frequently involved. There is no other aspect of human sexual behavior about which it has been more important to have some precise knowledge of the incidences and figures.

from Alfred Kinsey, Sexual Behavior in the Human Male (1948)

The Conclusion

. . . it is difficult to maintain the view that psychosexual reactions between individuals of the same sex are rare and therefore abnormal or unnatural, or that they constitute within themselves evidence of neuroses or even psychoses.

from Alfred Kinsey, Sexual Behavior in the Human Male *(1948)*

The Lesson to be Learned

The world is not divided into sheep and goats. Not all things are black nor all things white. It is a fundamental of taxonomy that nature rarely deals with discrete categories. Only the human mind invents categories and tries to force facts into separated pigeon-holes. The living world is a continuum in each and every one of its aspects. The sooner we learn this concerning sexual behavior the sooner we shall reach a sound understanding of the realities of sex.

from Alfred Kinsey, Sexual Behavior in the Human Male *(1948)*

The First Touch

The physical basis, he [Kinsey] believed, of both homosexual and heterosexual behavior was a touch response. When an individual had a pleasurable first experience, he looked forward to a repetition of the experience, often with such anticipation that he could be aroused by the sight or mere thought of another person with whom he might make contact. Unsatisfactory experience, on the other hand, built up a prejudice against repetition. Whether one built a heterosexual or a homosexual pattern depended, therefore, partially on the satisfactory or unsatisfactory nature of one's first experience.

from W. B. Pomeroy, Dr. Kinsey *(1972)*

An Outlet

After the publication of his reports, Kinsey became something of an agony aunt. One young man who wrote to him was wracked with guilt about his homosexual inclinations and had remained celibate. The good doctor wrote back a reassuring note, managing in the process to make sex as commonplace as cooking.

The thing that is most immediately necessary is some sort of outlet for your aroused states. As a biologist, that seems to me as necessary as the tying off of an artery that has been cut, the provision of air for a suffocating man or food for a starving man. On that point I am very certain. Whether the outlet, the food, comes from one source or another may ultimately be of some social significance, but it is not the thing that is most immediate in the treatment of the starvation. Until you get something like sufficient and regular outlet, you are never going to think straight on things, not going to find the grip on yourself, the confidence which will carry you through to the things of which you are capable. Biologically there is no form of outlet which I will admit as abnormal . . . As to the desirability, socially, of one outlet or another it is not possible to secure objective data. You can decide that after you get your head cleared by sufficient sexual outlet.

from W. B. Pomeroy, Dr. Kinsey (1972)

Dribbling

Tripp met Kinsey just after the Second World War. Tripp had been in the secret service working on various private and confidential film projects which included moving the applause round on Churchill and Roosevelt's speeches for Movietone News to make various statements appear more popular than they really were. The meeting with Kinsey changed Tripp's attitude to everything. 'He was certainly the most objective, the most thoroughly trained sex researcher who ever walked the earth. He came from a very priggish background and at one point when he was a student at Harvard he and his roommate got down on their knees to pray because the roommate had gotten into masturbation. Later, of course, Kinsey would take any kind of sexual variation in his stride.'

Kinsey was interested in Tripp not for his psychological skills — he didn't begin training until the early Fifties — but for his photographic skills. 'I had degrees in sensitometry and photographic technology and I helped Kinsey set up his photographic laboratories. One day Kinsey asked me how long it would take me to get him pictures of 2,000 male orgasms. I said "I can print 'em if you deliver 'em." The orgasms arrived . . . and they proved that 73% of males don't squirt at all — they dribble.'

from Gay News, May 1977

Adjustments

Dr. Jule Eisenbud, psychiatrist and psychoanalyst, charged Dr. Kinsey with ignoring the most formally established precept of psychiatry, 'as firmly established as the data established by Dr. Kinsey and dressed up in decimal points — that the major determinants of the behavior of an individual and especially sexual behavior are largely unconscious.' He also criticized Dr. Kinsey for making inferences of a psychological, anthropological, social and moral nature, and for depending for his material on direct statements from his subjects. The survey contains no measure of the adjustment of the individual as a total personality, including social and personal as well as sexual adjustments, he said, except identifying individuals as bankers or lawyers and taking their own word for their degree of happiness.

from the New York Times, 31 March 1948

The American Dream

This is the story of a simple employee in the freight claims department of the Santa Fe Railroad, who decided one day in 1945 to set up a guild of physical culture models in Los Angeles. A kind of agency designed to supply Hollywood show business with a stream of young men, each more beautiful than the other. At this moment, when the moral climate was governed by leagues of decency and the like, the Athletic Model Guild was wrongly suspected of being a network of call-boys, or something of the kind. Clearly it wasn't that at all, and Robert Mizer, not upset by this initial setback, decided to transform his operation into a photo agency. To start with, he hardly even knew how to use a camera, but he very quickly learned the technique of his 4 x 5, as he journeyed from the gyms at the beach clubs through to the Greyhound bus stations where fresh-faced young men would disembark, set on his quest for fame and success. A patient work inspired by a passion which, without his knowing, was to create the most impressive photo collection of young guys imaginable. A unique work, that of a real artist. In the shadow of Hollywood, an adventure as brilliant and generous as a Californian dream. A truly American story.

Some forty years later, AMG has in its files over 6,000 models, from athletes to cowboys, by way of young GIs, leather boys straight out of a motorbike gang, angel-faced hoodlums, street kids or simple 'boys next door'. The aesthetic quality of this work may sometimes be debatable, as it does have its kitsch side, but given the evident sociological richness of the material, even this can't detract from its value . . . These photos have done more than make their contribution to the various physical culture magazines, they have offered a dream, sharing the myth of California . . .

Everything started by the side of his pool in his villa at 1834 West 11th Street . . . Due to social conditions the Eisenhower years were not easy. Mizer was the constant target of various criticisms, both moral and political, but this forced him to use various subterfuges and artifices to achieve his ends . . . Bob Mizer is now 65 and still keeps the extreme modesty of those whose work is inspired by sincerity.

from The Athletic Model Guild *(1987)*

Witch-Hunt

The Senate Investigations Subcommittee on Expenditures in the Executive Departments was directed . . . to make an investigation into the employment by the Government of homosexuals and other sex perverts . . . The primary objective of the subcommittee in this inquiry was to determine the extent of the employment of homosexuals and other sex perverts in Government; and to examine into the efficacy of the methods used in dealing with the problem . . . A number of eminent physicians and psychiatrists, who are recognized authorities on this subject, were consulted and some of these authorities testified before the subcommittee . . . In addition, numerous medical and sociological studies were reviewed. Information was also sought and obtained from law enforcement officers, prosecutors, and other persons dealing with the legal and sociological aspects of the problem in 10 of the larger cities in the country . . .

Psychiatric physicians generally agree that indulgence in sexually perverted practices indicates a personality which has failed to reach sexual maturity. The authorities agree that most sex deviates respond to psychiatric treatment and can be cured if they have a genuine desire to be cured. However, many overt homosexuals have no real desire to abandon their way of life, and in such cases cures are difficult, if not impossible . . .

Those charged with the responsibility of operating the agencies of Government must insist that Government employees meet acceptable standards of personal conduct. In the opinion of this subcommittee homosexuals and other sex perverts are not the proper persons to be employed in Government for two reasons: first, they are generally unsuitable, and second, they constitute security risks . . .

Aside from the criminality and immorality involved in sex perversion, such behavior is contrary to the normal accepted standards of social behavior that persons who engage in such activity are looked upon as outcasts by society generally . .

In further considering the general suitability of perverts as Government employees, it is generally believed that those who engage in overt acts of perversion lack the emotional stability of normal persons. In addition there is an abundance of evidence to sustain the conclusion that indulgence in acts of sex perversion weakens the moral fiber of an individual to a degree that he is not suitable for a position of responsibility.

Most of the authorities agree and our investigation has shown that the presence of a sex pervert in a Government agency tends to have a corrosive influence upon his fellow employees. These perverts will frequently attempt to entice normal individuals to engage in perverted practices. This is particularly true in the case of young and impressionable people who might come under the influence of a pervert. Government officials have the responsibility of keeping this type of corrosive influence out of the agencies under their control . . .

Another point to be considered in determining whether a sex pervert is suitable for Government employment is his tendency to gather other perverts about him . . . if a homosexual attains a position in Government where he can influence the hiring of personnel, it is almost inevitable that he will attempt to place other homosexuals in Government jobs . . .

The Federal Bureau of Investigation, the Central Intelligence Agency, and the intelligence services of the Army, Navy and Air Force . . . are in complete agreement that sex perverts in Government constitute security risks.

The lack of emotional stability which is found in most sex perverts, and the weakness of their moral fiber, makes them susceptible to the blandishments of the foreign espionage agent. It is the experience of intelligence experts that perverts are vulnerable to interrogation by a skilled questioner and they seldom refuse to talk about themselves . . .

A classic case of this type involved one Captain Redl who became chief of the Austrian counterintelligence service in 1912 [and betrayed his country to Russia after the Russians trapped him in a homosexual liaison] . . . Other cases have been brought to the attention of the subcommittee where Nazi and Communist agents have attempted to obtain information from employees of our Government by threatening to expose their abnormal sex activities . . .

The present danger of this security problem is well illustrated by the following excerpt from the testimony of D. Milton Ladd, assistant to the Director of the Federal Bureau of Investigation, who appeared before this subcommittee in executive session:

> The Communists, without principle or scruples, have a program of seeking out weaknesses of leaders in Government and industry. In fact, the FBI has in its possession information of an unquestionable reliability that orders have been issued by high Russian intelligence officials to their agents to secure details of the private lives of Government officials, their weaknesses, their associates, and in fact every bit of information regarding them, hoping to find a chink in their armor and a weakness upon which they might capitalize at the appropriate time.

. . . There is no place in the United States Government for persons who violate the laws or accepted standards of morality, or who otherwise bring disrepute to the Federal service by infamous or scandalous personal conduct. Such persons are not suitable for Government positions and in the case of doubt the American people are entitled to have errors of judgement on the part of their officials, if there must be errors, resolved on the side of caution. It is the opinion of this subcommittee that those who engage in acts of homosexuality and other perverted sex activities are unsuitable for employment in the Federal Government.

from an American congressional report, 1950

Gay's the Word

The language of homosexual life has in it an element of cant – the keeping in secrecy from the out-group that which is clear to the in-group; it has the argot that is characteristic of any trade or profession; the slang that is on the fringe of society; the euphemisms and their counterpart from which they grew, the hostile words and expressions. For many years, homosexuals found a burning need for a language that would not have unpleasant connotations. The words must be free of the stereotype concepts, free likewise of hostility, and less cumbersome and heavy than such a word as *homosexual* itself. The language must be utilizable to describe all those sexually directed in their passions towards their own sex, regardless of virility or lack of it, regardless of the type or age of the person coveted, or of the character of the physical relationship entered into. It was in this spirit that Ulrichs, a German writer and civil servant, proposed that homosexuality be called Uranism, and the individual a Uranian or urning.

Ulrichs found inspiration for his etymology in the planet Uranus, which of all the planets visible to the naked eye is furthest from the sun and therefore nearest to heaven . . . the word has a particularly foreign flavour and never seems to have become popular in our tongue . . . the scientific terminology was rather obscure. Somehow the word *invert*, although quite acceptable, never became widely used . . . on the other hand, . . . pervert . . . brings forth the ugly picture of an elderly man accosting a child . . .

Needed for years was an ordinary, everyday, matter-of-fact word that could express the concept of homosexuality without glorification or condemnation. It must have no odium of the effeminate stereotype about it. Such a word has long been in existence, and in recent years has grown in popularity. The word is gay.

How, when, and where this word originated I am unable to say. I have been told by experts that it came from the French, and that in France as early as the sixteenth century the homosexual was called *gaie*; significantly enough, the feminine form was used to describe the male. The word made its way to England and America, and was used in print in some of the more pornographic literature soon after the First World War. Psychoanalysts have told that their homosexual patients were calling themselves gay in the nineteen-twenties, and certainly by the nineteen-thirties it was the most common word in use among homosexuals themselves. It was not until after Pearl Harbor that it became a magic by-word in practically every corner of the United States where homosexuals might gather . . . Within homosexual circles, the use of the word is almost universal, but its acceptance is often with reluctance. Some object to its ambiguous meaning, which is precisely what the group has found most advantageous about it . . . Some of the usefulness of gay diminishes as its meaning becomes more widely understood. New and wider circles are constantly becoming familiar with the word, although the public at large, except for theatrical and artistic people, literary groups, bohemians, underworld characters and police officers, are unaware of its slang meaning. However, as it becomes better known, its secret character and the advantages derived therefrom are to a certain extent vitiated.

from D. W. Cory, The Homosexual Outlook (1953)

The Absence of Women

The key to the puzzle and problem of homosexual promiscuity is therefore quite simple: the promiscuous (heterosexual) male meets the discriminating (heterosexual) female. She acts as the restraining factor. He cannot indulge indiscriminately without her, but she will not permit him to do so with her. But, the promiscuous (homosexual) male meets the promiscuous (homosexual) male and the restraints are entirely removed . . . [a view] which corresponds to the facts as seen by any astute observer in homosexual circles; namely, that the females do not follow the promiscuous patterns so common among the males.

The importance of this observation is that homosexuals (and others) must realize that there is nothing in the nature of homosexuality that prevents a stable relationship. It is not heterosexuality that produces stability, but the presence of a female.

from D. W. Cory, The Homosexual Outlook *(1953)*

Homosexual Language

. . . the geographical variations in the homosexual language are probably more severe than are to be found in most of the analogous slang, because of the lack of any volume of printed literature. The words cannot be used on the radio, and are seldom found in print. Visitors travelling from one part of the country to another find it impossible to introduce the slang of their native region, and soon begin to use the terms that are understood in their new surroundings.

from D. W. Cory, The Homosexual Outlook *(1953)*

American Underworld Lingo

MR BROWN: (or 'one of the Brown family') A passive pederast.

PEG-HOUSE: 1. A house of prostitution which includes or specializes in the services of passive pederasts. 2. Any prisons where pederastic degeneracy is common.

BENDER: A passive pederast.

KEISTER BANDIT: 1. An active homosexual, especially one who uses threats or force. 2. (By extension) A seducer or rapist.

FRUIT FOR THE MONKEYS: (Very contemptuous when not uttered in callous bantering.) So loose morally as to be the eager passive subject of anyone's advances.

SIXTY-NINE: A form of degeneracy in which two parties exchange oral service simultaneously.

HAND-JOB: Masturbation practised upon another.

definitions from The Dictionary of American Underworld Lingo, *ed. Hyman E. Goldin (1950)*

Guestimate

A Washington police vice officer said it was his 'own judgment' that 3,500 perverts were employed in Government agencies. The officer, Lieut. Roy E. Blick, testified . . . that he thought 300 to 400 of these persons were in the State Department. This, he said at one point, was a 'quick guess' in the sense that it was based upon his experience that arrested persons not connected with the State Department sometimes would say: 'Why don't you go get so-and-so?' They all belong to the same clique. 'By doing that,' Lieutenant Blick added, 'their names were put on a list and they were cataloged as such, as a suspect of being such.'

from the New York Times, *20 May 1950*

Denial

Rumors that he was a homosexual especially piqued his interest. Because these allegations impugned his integrity and thereby detracted from his lofty reputation, he demanded that his aides run any such rumor down and then intimidate his detractors. Having successfully turned the FBI into his own personal instrument, by the 1940s Hoover unhesitatingly employed its resources for personal reasons . . .

Because rumors of Hoover's homosexuality circulated widely, all FBI personnel were required to be alert to them — regardless of the context . . . when Cleveland SAC [Special Agent in Charge] L. V. Boardman learned that a woman attending a bridge party held by the aunt of an FBI agent had stated that 'the Director was a homosexual and kept a large group of boys around him,' he summoned the woman to his office and severely chastised her, pointing out that 'he personally resented such a malicious and unfounded statement.' The terrified woman claimed not to have repeated the story at any time except on this one occasion and promised to advise her friends at a future meeting of the bridge club that her allegation 'was not founded on fact and that she was deeply sorry that she had made it and it should not have been made at all.' She also promised to tell Boardman 'when this had been done'. Concluding his report to Hoover on this matter, Boardman repeated that he had 'chastised her most vigorously' and ensured that she 'understood the untruth of her statements and the serious nature of her action in having made them.'

Learning of another incident in which a Washington beauty parlor operator and one of her beauticians had claimed that 'all of the bookies in Washington turned in money to the Director and paid him off' and that 'the Director was a sissy, liked men and was a queer,' Hoover immediately dispatched two agents 'to take this scandal monger & liar on'.

Hoover's agents aggressively confronted his detractor, warning her and the beautician that 'such statements' would not be 'countenanced' and threatening to have both called before a grand jury where they and their accuser (an FBI clerk who heard the remark while having her hair done in the shop) 'will be given an opportunity to testify . . . as to exactly what they did or didn't say.' This intimidation succeeded, and Hoover was subsequently assured that both women fully realized the seriousness of their accusations and would never 'be guilty of such statements again.' For that reason no 'further action' was taken, since 'nothing will be gained by further pursuit of the matter.' Hoover commended the FBI clerk 'for her loyalty to the Director and the Bureau'.

from Athan Theoharis and John Stuart Cox, The Boss: J. Edgar Hoover and the Great American Inquisition *(1988)*

The Loving Eye

Whether the Hoover–Tolson relationship did include a sexual union is simply not known. An indication of the intimacy of the relationship is the collection of hundreds of candid photographs Hoover took of Tolson (who was strikingly handsome as a young man, as was Baughman) during their forty-two years together. Hoover did not expect these albums to survive his death, but they escaped the notice of Tolson and Hoover's secretary when they destroyed Hoover's personal effects in accordance with his wishes. These albums consist almost exclusively of photographs of Tolson in front of the varied backdrops of their vacation resorts. Although the photos convey a feeling of affection, when the two men appear together in a photo they are never seen touching one another, except in two group photos in which all present had their arms around each other's shoulders. On the other hand, Hoover took several photos of Tolson while he was sleeping, a situation in which most men might find it embarrassing to be photographed. Other photos show the two men in bathrobes or bare-chested at the beach. The photos convey the sense of a caring, emotionally involved eye behind the lens, and whether it was a lover's eye or a close friend's, it was still qualitatively different from a business associate's.

Given Hoover's straitlaced Presbyterian upbringing and his almost fanatical conventionality, it is not inconceivable that Hoover's relationship with Tolson excluded the physically sexual dimension. Yet, human drives being what they are, it is also possible that it was a fully sexual relationship. There is no compelling evidence for a definitive judgement in either direction. Weighing all known information, such a term as 'spousal relationship' describes most fairly what is known about the bonds between the two men, bonds that grew stronger and more exclusive with the passing years . . . Hoover was never abashed by his relationship with Tolson, and always insisted that if he was expected to attend a social affair, Tolson should also be invited. Throughout Hoover's life, official Washington simply accepted the situation at Hoover's own valuation: that he and Tolson were associates and friends. The prevailing attitude was that the actual nature of the relationship was no one else's business.

from R. G. Powers, Secrecy and Power: The Life of J. Edgar Hoover *(1987)*

Defending American Values

'I can remember', said one of the people who worked for Roy [Cohn], 'driving him to some outfit, oh, along the lines of The American Society for the Preservation of the Family, quote and unquote, and I drove Roy and his male date to the affair and Roy delivered his address attacking gay rights and then they came out and I drove them off to dinner.'

from Nicholas von Hoffman, Citizen Cohn *(1988)*

The Tormentor

Richard Dupont was a client cheated by Roy Cohn who took his revenge on an elaborate scale. He would impersonate Cohn and cancel plane reservations and make embarrassing phone calls to associates.

At one time right outside Saxe, Bacon [Cohn's law firm] on Sixty-eighth Street, Richard wrote on the sidewalk all up and down Sixty-eighth Street, 'Roy Cohn is a fag.' . . . Richard scared the hell out of Roy and everybody else by dressing up in whites and inserting himself into Roy's hospital room after Roy had been given one of his surgical facials . . . When Bob Guccione, the owner of *Penthouse*, had a party marking Peter Manso's interview with Roy in the magazine, Richard papered the block with sheets advertising Roy's homosexuality . . . Ultimately Roy's power was too much for Richard, who was tried and convicted for harassment and sent to jail for eighteen months.

from Nicholas von Hoffman, Citizen Cohn *(1988)*

Lubrication

Roy Cohn usually travelled light.

Jack Martin remembered the time George Barry, the top man at Fabergé, got married and Roy and friends flew to Las Vegas to help the happy couple celebrate. After the nuptials and the merrymaking, the newlyweds and their well-wishing friends spent the night at Caesar's Palace, Roy sharing a room with a handsome young fellow. 'They were all to rejoin in the lobby of Caesar's Palace the following morning,' Jack related. 'I was there first. Then Mr. and Mrs. Barry came down, and Roy and the boyfriend on the elevator were the last to arrive. The elevator opened and Roy was carrying a paper shopping bag, which was his luggage, off of which, the minute the elevator door opened and he started to cross the lobby, tumbled what can only be described as an industrial-sized jar of Vaseline. It rolled, took on a life of its own, and made its way to the feet of the bride. Roy did not acknowledge this at all. He looked skyward and wistful or something, and I scooped up the Vaseline and put it in my flight bag. I didn't know such a size existed.

'Subsequently, on the Fabergé jet, I extricated this jar from my luggage. I noticed that it was down to the last drop. I said, "Roy you dropped this," and this man, the enormously generous Roy, said, "Oh you can keep it." '

from Nicholas von Hoffman, Citizen Cohn *(1988)*

Yale Swimmers

I suppose I reached puberty officially at age fourteen, when I had my first wide-awake orgasm while staring at a magazine photograph of the Yale swimming team.

from an interview with novelist Richard Amory in Gay News, *June 1976*

Uncle Tom

The black homosexual, when his twist has a racial nexus, is an extreme embodiment of this contradiction. The white man has deprived him of his masculinity, castrated him in the center of his burning skull, and when he submits to this change and takes the white man for his lover as well as Big Daddy, he focuses on 'whiteness' all the love in his pent up soul and turns the razor edge of hatred against 'blackness' – upon himself, what he is, and all those who look like him, remind him of himself. He may even hate the darkness of night.

The racial death-wish is manifested as the driving force in James Baldwin . . . Homosexuality is a sickness, just as are baby-rape or wanting to become the head of General Motors.

Eldridge Cleaver, black Muslim, from an essay 'Notes on a Native Son' in Soul on Ice *(1969)*

Uneconomic Activity

It is interesting to note that the male prostitute, far more often and to a much greater extent than the female, is interested in the age and appearance of the customer – and may adjust his prices accordingly, with an older or physically unattractive male having to pay a higher fee than a young, attractive one . . .

Most of these youths, since they are not homosexual or do not consider themselves to be such, also adjust their fees in terms of the nature of the act demanded by the customer – some sexual acts being considered 'more homosexual' than others. The lower fees are charged when only the hustler's penis is used in the commission of the act – that is, when the prostitute is fellated or masturbated, or when he has anal intercourse with the passive 'John'. Many youths will not perform fellatio on a customer or permit the customer to penetrate them anally; when they do take the passive or 'female' role, the price is raised, usually doubled. (The hustler will usually masturbate the customer without any increase in fee.)

It is worth noting here that these conditions make no sense economically. After all, the hustler whose penis is used by the customer is 'put out of action' for a number of hours; but if he performs in such a manner that he does not have to ejaculate, while giving an ejaculation to the 'John', he can continue to function over and over again, like his female prostitute counterparts.

from Harry Benjamin and Robert E. L. Masters, Prostitution and Morality *(1965)*

Bad Boys

Danny S., leader of the Black Aces, tells of his gang's group experiences with queers:

There's this one gay who takes us to the Colonial Motel out on Dickerson Pike . . . usually it's a bunch of us boys and we all get drunk and get blowed by this queer . . . we do not get any money then . . . it's more a drinking party.

The Black Aces are a fighting gang and place great stress on physical prowess, particularly boxing. All of its members have done time more than once at the State Training School. During one of these periods, the school employed a boxing instructor whom the boys identified as 'a queer', but the boys had great respect for him since he taught them how to box and was a game fighter. Danny refers to him in accepting terms:

He's a real good guy. He's fought with us once or twice and we drink with him when we run into him . . . He's taken us up to Miter Dam a coupla times; he's got a cabin up there on the creek and he blows us . . . But mostly we just drink and have a real good time.

from John H. Gagnon and William Simon, Sexual Deviance *(1967)*

Dancing

Dancing was in those days [the late 1950s and early 1960s] an important symbol of the hampering of homosexual freedom. Forbidden by law to dance as male couples in public, they had devised a form of group dancing – perhaps originally an adaptation of folk dance – in which they lined up side by side, ten or fifteen abreast, and executed in unison a rather elaborate pattern of steps. (By the late 60s, when people on dance floors danced by themselves only in some rough proximity to their partners, did they know that they were engaged in a borrowing from the homosexuals?) This dance, known first as the 'hully-gully' and later much elaborated upon, they rehearsed assiduously, instructing all newcomers, at the edge of the surf [at Fire Island]. On any afternoon, groups of them could be seen up and down the beach, going through their paces: step–kick–back–turn. Here at least they could spend their days without concern for the impression they were making. If we, arrayed on the beach with our toddlers, bottles, toys, sand pails, bags of fruit, were inclined to laugh at the deadly earnestness of those rehearsals, it mattered not the tiniest bit to them.

from M. Decter, 'The Boys on the Beach', in Commentary, *September 1980*

Restraint

I was meeting all these really wonderful people, boys, who were my friends. And it was sufficient to have them as friends. Some of them I was really sexually attracted to . . . One friend, who was on my rowing team, I got a huge crush on the first night when we became pals. I met him over at the high-school yard and there was a whole gang of us, and he wanted to change his pants – we were going swimming – so he was going over to this other guy's house to get his cutoffs and he came over to me and said come on over, and the two of us went to this guy's place and we got to know each other, and I also got to sit on this guy's bed while my friend took off all his clothes and put on his cutoffs. It's a great way to meet somebody, I remember that. Very hot as he undressed. Anyhow, we became very close friends.

It was very seductive, but at this point I was kind of determined I wasn't going to fall for anybody and go through all that shit. He ended up inviting me to stay over at his place one night, which I thought was nice, and we were lying on our stomachs, watching TV, and he had this trick where he would just put his leg over my side and his arm 'round me while we watched TV; meanwhile, I would try and remain conscious . . . I know the first time he did it I was surprised because the gesture was such an obvious 'let's-have-sex' gesture. It was the sort of thing that [before] I would automatically have had sex. But that's what I'd just been through, so when he did it I kind of froze up. We didn't have sex. We always ended up getting in a knot. Whenever he came to my place we slept entwined together in various positions, but we just didn't have sex. I had a lot of friendships in high school very similar to that. We always seemed to end up in each other's beds, sleeping together. But I wasn't having sex, because I was afraid to; I thought I had a lot to lose by having sex with these guys.

from Brian Pronger, The Arena of Masculinity *(1990)*

Modern Slang

AUNTIE: Aging male homosexual who serves as confidant to younger males, occasionally giving financial assistance.

BENNY-HOUSE: A brothel which caters principally to heterosexual clients, but which will procure boys or men for homosexuals on special order.

DINGE QUEEN: Male homosexual who prefers Negroes.

FISH: Woman (used only by males and with strongly pejorative connotations).

KLEENEX: Pick it up, throw it away.

MARY!: Exclamation. An expression of mock amazement from Elizabethan Marry! euphemization of Mary (i.e. the Virgin Mary).

MEAT MARKET: Street on which homosexuals gather, cruise and pick up tricks.

RENT: 'I don't sell it, I just rent it.'

SEAFOOD: Sailors as an object of sexual interest.

SIXTY-EIGHT: You suck me and I'll owe you one.

WATCH QUEEN: Voyeur.

from J. Stanley, 'Homosexual Slang', in American Speech *(1970)*

CHAPTER NINE

British Aberrations

What has made Britain different? It followed neither the more liberal and tolerant path of most Continental nations (such as France or Italy), where the nineteenth century saw the slow erosion of the laws concerning homosexuality; nor that of Germany, where a tougher late-nineteenth-century law did not prevent a homosexual culture flowering, and finding freedom after 1919 and persecution after 1933; nor that of the United States, whose laws were modelled on the British ones, and often quite as draconian, but where a dynamic homosexual culture carved for itself a peculiarly prominent place in American society. As Jeremy Bentham and Hanif Kureishi – commentators from different British traditions and separated by nearly two centuries – suggest, Britain has a particularly poor record in its treatment of sexual deviants. Richard Davenport-Hines, in an important survey of British attitudes to sexuality, plumps for what he calls 'projection theory' as an explanation for this peculiarity. 'Projection' he defines as 'a form of primitive self-defence which underlies many superstitions, and is seen in extreme form in the behaviour of paranoiacs. Impulses to exclude, isolate, purify and punish malefactors are characteristic of projection'.[1] He sees the British as suffering from this complex more than other nations. Well, possibly.

Or the answer (or more probably answers) might lie in the early creation in Britain of a unitary state governing a relatively homogeneous population and the fact that Britain is one of the most heavily policed societies in the world. A cause may even be located in the cultural consequences of the disintegration of English Protestantism. Though hard-core belief collapsed as Victorian intellectuals dethroned God and demolished the authority of the Bible, believers retreated back to the moral teachings of Protestantism, which had always offered little comfort to sinners, and created a moral code far harsher than much traditional Christian teaching. The collapse of Catholicism sets up different cultural consequences which paradoxically create more permissive attitudes to sex in the secular era (as is the case in contemporary Spain, the new Weimar, and in the Irish Republic). The problem with this interpretation is to fit in Holland and Scandinavia (other areas blighted by Protestantism), where the collapse of Protestantism led to the creation of model societies. Maybe the answer lies in the experience of Empire? The list of possibilities is endless: this is a game which gives historians many hours of happy amusement as they argue it out.

In any explanation, some blame ought to be apportioned to Henry VIII, not simply for his break with Rome, his plunder and ruin of a wonderful cultural resource with the destruction of the English monasteries, and his support for the Reformation, but also for the passage of an act in 1533 that made sodomy a capital crime. This statute, although briefly repealed in the reign of his son, was reinstituted during the reign of his younger daughter and remained on the statute-book until 1861. It was a unique enactment. Henry was a particularly vicious monarch whose policies seemed to create what amounted to a reign of terror. One historian has described him as the English Stalin, a tyrant during whose reign 70,000 subjects were executed for a variety of offences. It was in this atmosphere that the act against sodomy was passed, and it created a hostile legal attitude and tradition towards homosexuality which have never been entirely obliterated.

It was bad luck for men who preferred their own sex that Napoleon's plans to invade and conquer Britain failed. Napoleon was no saint, but he was sufficiently infected by the Enlightenment to promote several liberal reforms in the territories that he ruled and conquered. He had a proper Enlightenment contempt for the past: laws and customs sanctioned by time carried little weight with him. He was responsible for the emancipation of European Jewry and freed many peasants in central and eastern Europe from the curse of serfdom. Through the Napoleonic Code (a set of laws grounded in the principles of revolutionary France) he established the notion of privacy which gave many Continental males freedoms in the privacy of their own homes that Britons did not enjoy until 1967 (and then hedged around with numerous restrictions).

The most infamous British law against homosexuality – the so-called Labouchere amendment – was passed in 1885. Henry Labouchere was a Radical MP, on the margins of national politics but with a personal constituency constructed around issues involving the improvement of national morals. He belonged to the tradition of the British Protestant reformers who had managed to abolish slavery in the early nineteenth century and had a long checklist of other evils which they wanted to eliminate. Publicly high-minded, they believed that a more strictly enforced moral code would improve their fellow men, in this way erecting a doctrine which ran counter to Christian teaching on the forgiveness of sin.

The famous amendment was tagged on to legislation primarily aimed at the protection of women. (During the late nineteenth century the age of consent for women steadily rose as a consequence of the agitation over what radical journalists described in lurid and sensational terms as 'White Slavery'.) It made all forms of homosexuality (including, for example, mutual masturbation, or even what teenage magazines call 'heavy petting') illegal. It was probably the most comprehensive act of its type ever passed, and it gave the police more power than their Continental or American colleagues for harassing the homosexual subculture.

The main effect of the legislation was a series of *fin de siècle* scandals that entertained and shocked the citizenry and brought disgrace and ruin to a number of otherwise innocent characters doing nothing more than indulging their sexual tastes – most viciously in the case of Oscar Wilde, who was destroyed by this particular instrument of British justice in 1895. Wilde's experience was used by moralists in an incredible campaign of vilification that did much to frighten (and even possibly inhibit) men attracted to their own sex. In time, however, Wilde became seen as a martyr to the cause, and during the homosexual witch-hunts of the 1950s there was an enormous revival of interest in his life, work and suffering. The Wilde case reinforced the philistinism of the broad mass of the population, who took comfort from the association between Sexual Deviance, Art and Punishment.

The amendment did not destroy homosexuality: it simply created a climate in which blackmail flourished. A homosexual subculture still existed in London, though it never matched anything which Berlin or New York might offer. The police were as arbitrary as ever, and prosecutions reflected the prejudices of individual policemen. Conditions differed from district to district, depending on the policies followed by different chief constables.

A campaign to reform the amendment did not develop until the 1950s, stimulated by the repressive policies of a Tory Home Secretary, Sir David Maxwell-Fyfe, who believed that homosexuality could be crushed. Maxwell-Fyfe enjoyed the support of the Director of Public Prosecutions and the Commissioner of the Metropolitan Police, a powerful trinity of moralists motivated by religious fervour. Their Savonarolan efforts had the effect of providing tremendously sensational copy for the popular newspapers and excited much interest in homosexuality. Lord Winterton, a reactionary backwoodsman, raised the matter for debate in the House of Lords in 1954, in a motion on 'Homosexual Crime'. The issue provided liberals (in Parliament and in the media) with the opportunity to demonstrate their liberal credentials. Bob Boothby, a maverick Tory, pressed successfully for an inquiry into the subject, and this did much to defuse Maxwell-Fyfe's campaign (which was in any case running out of steam, as the bad publicity for police methods gradually became counter-productive).

A committee of 'the great and the good' was formed under the chairmanship of a university vice-chancellor and former public-school headmaster, Sir John Wolfenden. His remit was to investigate prostitution as well as homosexuality, and, keen to spare the blushes of his female typists in the Home Office, Sir John always used the euphemism 'Huntley and Palmers' (the name of a biscuit manufacturer) instead of 'homosexuality and prostitution' when referring to the subjects being investigated by the committee, displaying that skill in language games that characterised the British mandarinate and which did much to poison British dealings with her former colonial subjects (what one mandarin described as being 'economical with the truth'). Wolfenden interviewed other members of the British Establishment and came up with a report that recommended the liberalisation of the existing law, though with plenty of 'safeguards' (for which one might read 'further anti-homosexual measures'). Wolfenden's most significant proposal was the decriminalisation of homosexual sex between men over twenty-one if conducted in complete privacy. The presence of a third party, even accidentally, rendered the act public and therefore liable to prosecution. This was liberal reform British style.

The Wolfenden Report was published in 1957, but its recommendations did not become law until 1967. Even then, further safeguards were added, and the legislation of 1967 included quite considerable Home Office input which removed a number of loopholes in the existing legislation, so making it easier to prosecute a large number of homosexual offences. As a result of the 1967 act – described by one judge as 'a buggers' charter' – more homosexual offences were punished in the quarter century following its passage than in the previous quarter century.

Despite the rhetoric, the 1967 act was only a palliative. Change came not from Westminster but from across the ocean. The fuse was lit in New York, not in London: the gay explosion of the 1970s had its roots in America.

Of course lots of liberals congratulated themselves on their virtue, on the success of their efforts to improve the position of their fellow men. The act secured Roy Jenkins, the smug Labour Home Secretary who saw it through Parliament, a permanent place in the liberal pantheon.

The parliamentary debates provoked by the passage of the act (there were several earlier unsuccessful attempts to implement Wolfenden) make amusing, almost surreal, reading today. The level of ignorance and prejudice in the Mother of Parliaments was positively medieval. The prize performance was that of British war hero Viscount Montgomery of El Alamein, who became quite apopletic in the vehemence of his opposition to this measure. Only two speakers, Dora Gaitskell and C. P. Snow (both speaking from the safety of the Lords, where they were free of any possible electoral consequences), commented on the fact that the debate was conducted as if the speakers had never themselves encountered homosexuality. Of all the speakers, and there were many in the course of these debates, only Norman St John-Stevas, a young Conservative, acquitted himself with any honour. St John-Stevas pointed out the possible impact of some of the clauses of the bill which tightened up the laws relating to what the police call 'soliciting'. His warnings were disregarded.

Throughout the debate, men who indulged in homosexual sex were depicted as 'victims'. Indeed, the 1962 film *Victim*, starring Dirk Bogarde (who had previously appeared in the movies as a clean-cut British hero), reveals the way in which many liberals wished to see homosexuality. Much was made of blackmail, and most of the speeches in favour of reform concentrated on this evil. Most speakers for the decriminalisation indulged in a ritual condemnation of the evils of homosexuality and placed themselves firmly against any form of 'exhibitionism' or 'proselytising'. Several speakers seem to have shared the social assumptions of Leo Abse, a Labour member and the Commons sponsor of the 1967 act. Abse believed that the act would lead to a diminution of homosexual behaviour. He believed that homosexuality was one of the evils of old pre-war class-obsessed Britain that would soon perish in the new egalitarian post-war Britain that the Butskellites expended so much energy in erecting after 1945.

The failure to repeal the 1885 amendment before 1967 reveals a weakness of the British political system in passing progressive legislation. The domination of Parliament by a two-party system makes it difficult to promote social reform, since both major parties are extremely conservative in their approach to social change, Labour as much as the Conservatives. The Labour Party never escaped from the shadow of its nonconformist parentage, and its agenda of social reform was dictated by the trade unions, another conservative social force that had exhausted its reforming impulse. Even the old Liberal Party had never quite overcome the moral sensibilities of its nonconformist wing in the framing of progressive legislation when it had held power.

Britain may (as Norman Stone once suggested in a mischievous mood) be the last of the *anciens régimes*, the others having perished in 1917–18. Sometimes it feels like it. Of course the intelligentsia (which has limited political clout) has certain privileges, creating oases of tolerance and enlightenment in an otherwise oppressive desert. It is little wonder that so many British artists have felt more comfortable away from Britain:

Somerset Maugham on the Riviera; Auden in New York; Isherwood, Hockney and Gunn in California.

Britain also nourished two institutions, the public schools and the scouting movement, that became veritable seminaries of vice and provided opportunities on an unimaginable scale for those who were interested. As W. T. Stead, a Victorian moral reformer, wrote after the Wilde trial, the police ought to have turned their attentions to the public schools, where they would have found many inmates guilty of Wilde's crime. Wolfenden's own son Julian had a reputation for schoolboy vice which followed him to Oxford, where, during the years when his father was pontificating on the homosexual peril, he could have been found sharing his bed with such male contemporaries as Kit Lambert (later to win fame and fortune as the manager of The Who). Julian Wolfenden, who became a journalist, later committed suicide. Another victim?

Ingrained Habits

The propensities in question here have, in the British Isles, beyond all countries, been the object of the violence of that thirst which nothing less than the heart's blood of the victim marked out for slaughter by the dissocial appetite has hitherto been able to satisfy.

Jeremy Bentham, political philosopher, 1814

Merry England

England has become a squalid, uncomfortable, ugly place . . . an intolerant, racist, homophobic, narrow-minded, authoritarian rat-hole run by vicious suburban-minded, materialistic philistines.

Hanif Kureishi, writer, 1988

Buggers

'You've been having letters from Lord Alfred Douglas.' I [John Betjeman] couldn't deny it. 'Do you know what that man is?' I said: 'No.' 'He's a bugger. Do you know what buggers are? Buggers are two men who work themselves up into such a state of mutual admiration that one puts his piss-pipe up the other one's arse. What do you think of that?' And of course I felt absolutely sick, and shattered.

from Bevis Hillier, Young Betjeman *(1988)*

Feline

Have you any views on loving one's own sex? All the young men are so inclined, and I can't help finding it mildly foolish; though I have no particular reason. For one thing, all the young men tend to the pretty and ladylike, for some reason, at the moment. They paint and powder, which wasn't the style in our day at Cambridge. I think it does imply some clingingness – a tiny lap dog, called Sackville-West, came to see me the other day (a cousin of my aristocrat [Vita Sackville-West] and will inherit Knole) and my cook said, Who was the lady in the drawing room? He has a voice like a girls, and a face like a persian cats, all white and serious, with large violet eyes and fluffy cheeks. Well, you can't respect the amours of a creature like *that*.

from a letter from Virginia Woolf to Jacques Raverat, 24 January 1925

Unfortunate Creatures

The small boys were conscious that their masters were lazy and incompetent, but nobody could explain to us that these poor freaks had been driven into their profession by necessity, crypto-homosexuality, or some other misfortune, and so we treated them without mercy.

from Kenneth Clark, Another Part of the Wood *(1974)*

Inter-War Cottages

These small unobtrusive urinals were, in many ways, the most important meeting places for homosexuals of all and every kind. Always open, usually unattended, and consisting of a small number of stalls, over the sides of which it was quite easy to spy and get a sight of one's neighbour's cock, they were ideally built for the gratification of the voyeur's sexual itch. Very frequently the sides of the stall were covered with graffiti and randy writing, which served to excite the urinating frequenter. It was pleasant indeed to add to the writing and suggest meeting someone for sexual purposes, and, in due course, see if someone had added to one's own writing and suggested a meeting.

When one considers the numbers of men, not by any means all homosexuals, who used these small urinals, it is almost certain these graffiti and suggestive writings and appointments introduced hundreds of so-called 'normal' men to the pleasures of homosexual gratification, and to an easy way of making a few extra pounds to add to their wage packets. In fact these urinals were a very important part of the social life and scene of those days. And when one remembers the vast amount of homosexuality indulged in in these small 'conveniences', it is somewhat surprising they were permitted to remain in situ and free from all the attention of the authorities for as long as they did. Many homosexuals spent hours going from one of these places to the next, spying, feeling and indulging in all forms of homosexual pleasure in each of them . . .

Frequently there would be several men in these places and they would take turns to keep a watch out against anyone coming in suddenly and disturbing the remaining others while they gratified themselves . . . This keeping 'a watch out' was very often easy, as there were perforations in the iron walls of the urinal — which allowed the watcher to see anyone coming suddenly to the scene. And in some cases the 'watching out' was even easier in the case of there being only one entrance to the place. They were generally so dimly lit that anyone coming in out of the more brightly lighted street was unable to see distinctly for a moment or two exactly what was happening, which would give the actors time to set themselves more or less to rights .

Up to about 1925, when many Tube stations started to be 'cleaned up', they were fantastic for indulging in all sorts of homosexual practices. Very many were without an attendant and in the cases where some attendant was provided he seemed utterly uninterested in what went on in the urinal and more especially in the W.C.'s . . .

Today, with hardly a single lavatory unattended, it will seem unbelievable that one could move freely from one to another without exciting any remark. Leicester Square and Piccadilly Tube stations before they were 'improved' were, of course, extremely well frequented, but very often the W.C.'s were occupied for such a length of time it seemed more profitable to go elsewhere. A rather more secluded Tube station was Down Street — very suitable should one happen to 'strike lucky' with one's neighbour in the adjoining W.C., as one could remain quite undisturbed for a long time, and without running any great risk one could go into his W.C. for complete enjoyment.

On particular evenings when trains arrived from the port with sailors on leave the stations of the main London terminuses (Paddington, Victoria and Liverpool Street) offered some possibilities.

On arrival of the train there would be scores of young sailors tumbling out of the train, all it seemed in violent need of a good piss. They ran helter-skelter into the large lavatory on the platform, and pulling down the flap of their trousers, pissed for all they were worth . . . If they happened to note some eager looker, they would exclaim: 'He's a beauty isn't he? Like him up your bum, chum?' This sally would be followed by gales of laughter from the other pissing fellows. If the pubs were still open, one at once said: 'Come along for another one, Jack, before the boozers shut.' And, once safely behind a pint at the bar, as often as not one succeeded in dragging him back to one's room.

testimony cited in H. Montgomery Hyde, The Other Love *(1970)*

On the Up

Homosexuality had been on the increase among the upper classes for a couple of generations, though almost unknown among working people. The upper-class boarding-school system of keeping boy and girl away from any contact with each other was responsible. In most cases the adolescent homosexual became normal on leaving school; but a large minority of the more emotional young people could not shake off the fascination of perversity. In post-war university circles, where Oscar Wilde was considered both a great poet and a martyr to the spirit of intolerance, homosexuality no longer seemed a sign of continued adolescence. Shakespeare, Caesar, Socrates, and Michelangelo were quoted in justification . . . True Christianity condemned it, but Relativity dismissed Christianity as a take-it-or-leave-it hypothesis. So long as one acted consistently in accordance with one's personal hypothesis, and was not ashamed of what one did, all was well. Thus homosexuals spent a great deal of their time preaching the aesthetic virtues of the habit, and made more and more converts. Their textbooks were *The Intermediate Sex*, a bright little volume by Edward Carpenter, and Havelock Ellis's massive *The Psychology of Sex*.

from Robert Graves, The Long Weekend *(1940)*

Jolly Tars

Sailors had the advantage of having a genuinely erotic uniform. It was very flattering, quite unlike the uniform of recent times. The neck of the tunic was cut in a very rough square, which gave the wearer a very masculine appeal. The faces were often bearded, which helped. The trousers must have been made to titillate. They were very tight around the waist and bottoms, but baggy around the ankles. If the sailor wore no underwear then very little was left to the imagination.

from a memoir of 'gay life' during the twenties

Sex and Character

My own experience of life has led me – as a matter of necessary practice – to treat sexual life as outside the scope of the judgements we pass on one another for social, political, business purposes. I have not found that even the most absurd aberrations are necessarily associated with any general depravity of character, or that intemperance in their practice has any other results than the intemperance in normal sexual intercourse which visibly damages many respectably married persons. I should say that a dishonoured cheque is a safer index to character for worldly purposes than inversion. But this is only a rule of thumb; for the impossibility of getting at the facts on any statistical scale puts anything like a scientific generalisation out of the question. I have all the normal repugnances to aberrations, but I have found that they are untrustworthy guides in estimating character. Normally-sexed people are sometimes as devoid of conscience as it is humanly possible to be: homosexualists are sometimes conspicuously able and highminded. Denunciations of homosexuality as depraving and detestable may have unsuspected and deeply wounding effect on one's most justly valued friends. The wisest and best inverts never tell; but they cherish a deep grudge against those who would, if they knew, turn against them, and attribute to them the general vices of which they are conspicuously innocent.

from a letter from George Bernard Shaw to the Dean of Windsor

Deceptions

Maxwell Knight – the famous 'M', a senior figure in intelligence during the 1930s – frequently spoke of his loathing of homosexuals. A young agent whom he had trained himself, Joan Miller, became his girlfriend but grew suspicious of him; she spied on M.

He put an advertisement in the local paper that went something like this: 'Gentleman requires help from motorcycle expert afternoons at weekends.' It was true that he was obsessed with the things and kept three in a barn at Camberley, including the one he had bought for me; still, I must say something about his sudden need to consult a mechanic, not to mention the way he went about acquiring one, struck me as odd. I was sure a more orthodox channel for obtaining this service existed . . .

An applicant duly appeared one Saturday and accompanied M to the barn where the two of them were closeted all afternoon. I caught a glimpse of them as they crossed the lawn. M's mechanic – a bus driver, I think – was a slim young man with a nervous way of gesticulating. Whatever he was hired to do, he did it well. M professed himself entirely satisfied with the young man's competence . . . the bus driver was back the next weekend, and the one after.

This new enthusiasm of M's left me feeling rather out of things. On the third Saturday I took a book to my bedroom and installed myself in the window-seat . . . I watched [M] make his way back towards the barn, and the bus driver was standing in the open door. M had no idea that he was being observed. For the first time he was off guard, and so fell into a posture that must have been pretty natural. I recognised it for what it was, for he had pointed it out to me himself, when we passed a couple of male prostitutes in the street.

As I sat there watching this avowed opponent of homosexuality mince across the lawn, a number of things became clear to me.

from Joan Miller, One Woman's War *(1985)*

Crashing a Garden Party

About this time I met another man whom I judged to be an eccentric, but whom I didn't much like: Lord Beauchamp, a brother-in-law of Bendor, Duke of Westminster, whom I did like. One Sunday, my host, Lord Jowitt, asked my husband if he and I would like to see one of the famous castles of the Cinque Ports. Delightedly we accepted. I don't know whether William Jowitt telephoned to ask if we might call on Lord Beauchamp, which would have been polite, all I recall is that we arrived and were shown into a garden surrounding a grass tennis-court. There I saw the actor Ernest Thesiger, a friend of mine, nude to the waist and covered with pearls: he explained that he had the right kind of skin to heal pearls. Two or three other young men were introduced to me, including a nice young man who Lord Beauchamp introduced as his tennis coach. Presently the men of the party wandered away, and as I thought they might be wanting to discuss politics I stayed behind, so did the young tennis coach.

Seeing a tennis racquet lying on a seat, I said, 'Oh, do send me some difficult services and then tell me how to reply.' Poor young man. He couldn't even pat a ball over the net. 'I'm so sorry,' I murmured, for I can't bear seeing young people embarrassed, 'I've just re-strained my wrist and can't play now.' Soon afterwards, the men of the party returned, and we left. Some time later, I read in a newspaper that Lord Beauchamp had gone abroad 'to have mud baths'. I am almost sure that he never came back to England. Perhaps, poor man, when I saw him he was physically ill, but certainly he was eccentric.

from Lady Aberconway, A Wiser Woman? A Book of Memories *(1960)*

Stock Reaction

When told by her brother, [the Duke of] Westminster, that her husband was 'a bugger', the word so mystified her that she thought her husband had become a 'bugler'. It is said that, when diagrams were drawn for her to show what happened, she had an immediate nervous breakdown.

Lady Beauchamp's reaction to the news that her husband was a homosexual, 1930

Raining Men

Talking of pederasty, Roy [Harrod] said that the late King George V when told of Lord Beauchamp's trouble, exclaimed, 'Why, I thought people like that always shot themselves.' 'Heavens,' said Billa [Harrod's wife], 'I do hope the poor darlings won't start doing that. It would be like living through a permanent air raid.'

from James Lees-Milne's diary, 23 April 1944

The Duke of Kent

That Kent was bisexual was widely known in London society in the 1930s, and references to this are even to be found in the diaries of that decade. On April 28, 1932, Sir Robert Bruce Lockhart noted: 'In the afternoon Randolph Churchill came to see me. He tells me there has been a scandal about Prince George — letters to a young man in Paris. A large sum had to be paid for their recovery.' And on July 15, 1933, Lockhart recorded that the Kaiser's grandson, Prince Louis Ferdinand of Prussia, 'liked Prince George, said he was artistic and effeminate and used a strong perfume . . .' Prince George first met Noël Coward in 1923, when Coward was twenty-three and the Prince was twenty. They became close friends. On August 26, 1942, the day after the Duke of Kent's death, Coward wrote: 'I shall miss him most horribly . . . I feel absolutely miserable . . . In memoriam I say, "Thank you for your friendship for me over all those years and I shall never forget you." ' On August 29, 1942, after the funeral, he wrote: 'I tried hard not to cry, but it was useless . . . when the coffin passed with flowers from the garden at Coppins and Prince George's cap on it I was finished. I then gave up all pretence and just stood with the tears splashing down my face . . . The thought that I shall never see him again is terribly painful.' . . . At a small drinks party in his suite at the Savoy Hotel, London, on December 10, 1969, Coward told the author, in the presence of Cole Lesley, Merle Oberon and other friends, that his relationship with the Duke of Kent had at one time been sexual: 'We had a little dalliance,' he said. 'It didn't last long. We were both very young at the time. He was absolutely enchanting and I never stopped loving him.'

from Michael Thornton, Royal Feud: The Queen Mother and the Duchess of Windsor *(1985)*

Mentor

One of the chief influences in his [C. P. Snow's] life was Herbert Edmund Howard, who joined the staff [of Alderman Newton Grammar School] in 1922 towards the end of Charles's schooldays . . . Howard, Bert to his intimates, Bill to the rest of the school, was jovial, fresh-faced and goodlooking, only five years older than Charles. Son of a postmaster in Fakenham, Norfolk, he retained some typical Norfolkese, particularly in his rages; he came straight to teaching from King's College, London. It was to be his life's work, and he entered into it with zest, starting the school debating society (with Charles), running the chess club, founding and editing the first issue of *The Newtonian* and creating the weekly *News Supplement*; besides school news this contained satire and cartoons, which attracted much attention among the boys and even some of the staff who regarded Howard with suspicion. He provided the original of George Passant, after whom the first book of the *Strangers and Brothers* series was named. He found in Charles just the inquiring, active first-class mind necessary to help establish his own ideas. Although Howard was an historian and did not come into academic contact with Charles they spent many out-of-school hours together, often at cafés late at night, when they missed the last trams and had to walk a couple of miles home in different directions. Their partnership extended over the weekends when they and one or two senior boys took junior boys for walks in the country. Theirs was a friendship for life, although Charles's career led him away from Bert's supreme insularity at Newton's where he stayed until he retired. Unlike Charles, I knew Bert as a teacher, since he was responsible for getting me direct from Newton's to Cambridge on a History Exhibition. His methods were unconventional and he inspired original thought. He ignored textbooks, encouraging classes to enact incidents of history and appointing a different person to be 'in charge', entirely without rehearsal, for the forty-minute lesson. His use came in directing us what to read and to avoid dull works. He seldom set essays and when he did he rarely looked at them . . .

His influence on boys was remarkable, but any advances in his career were inhibited by awkwardness at interviews. He achieved distinction as one of the two Midlands' representatives in the Round Britain Quiz, wrote under the name of R. Philmore six detective novels featuring C. J. Swan (a disguise for Charles) as a writer-cum-detective, and established a succession of loyal coteries of disciples. But for a man of such character he made remarkably little impact on the outside world; this may have been partly because he was bisexual, if that carries schizoid personality problems; perhaps also his intolerance played a part. He considered most people 'sunkets', a splendid East Anglian expression meaning 'despicable creatures' . . . Nevertheless, he was marvellous for Newton's and the catalyst Charles needed to widen his already strikingly broad interests.

from Philip Snow, Stranger and Brother: A Portrait of C. P. Snow *(1982)*

War Games

A sergeant in our brigade was discovered masturbating with a private in a tent, and they were both put on a charge by the sergeant major. Our colonel, who was himself a homosexual, was absent, and so the case went right up to brigade headquarters. The brigadier, who had been a boy soldier promoted through the ranks and to whom nothing in army life was a surprise, dismissed both men with a reprimand. The colonel was absolutely furious that it had gone as far as it did. 'The battalion's been out here for two years, these two youngsters have never had home leave,' he stormed afterwards in the mess. 'Out in India when I was in the ranks, reveille brought every man tumbling out of everyone else's bunks. What the hell do they want the men to do for sexual relief, go down to the brothels in the bazaar, chase Arab women and get syphilis?'

Memories of a 'desert rat' from the Second World War, in John Costello, Love, Sex and War: Changing Values 1939–1945 (1985)

Saving Beauty

One of the strangest queers who took a shine to me was a film producer who'd been a naval officer in the war. During the action in which the *Bismarck* was sunk he picked up survivors from the ship. He claimed that as the German sailors climbed up the rope ladders he'd pull the handsome ones up and pushed the ugly ones back into the water saying, 'Not you dear.'

from an article by Jeffrey Bernard in the Spectator, 20 August 1983

Outrage

A trial at Abergavenny in 1942 (reported among national newspapers only in the *News of the World*) illustrated the dangers which were faced by those who practised a criminal sexuality. Twenty-four men were charged after an investigation provoked by a youth complaining of overtures from a cinema manager. A boy of nineteen threw himself under a train before coming to trial, while at least two other defendants tried to hang or poison themselves, of whom one, a chef, was sentenced to three months' imprisonment for attempted suicide as well as ten years' penal servitude. Although the *News of the World* spoke of 'an orgy of perversion' at Abergavenny, the judge, Sir John Singleton (a bachelor with 'a detached' mind who 'could generally get from a jury the verdict he thought would meet the justice of the case', in whose court 'the slightest departure from the correct standards of decorum were apt to recoil unpleasantly on the head of the delinquent') emphasized in his summing up 'that Abergavenny is not a happy hunting ground for such people'. Singleton ordered women to leave the court before evidence was heard. Of the defendants, eighteen received gaol sentences of from ten months to twelve years, with thirteen of them receiving a total of 57 years; the younger men who received lighter sentences seem to have collaborated with the police, one of whose officers stated that with four exceptions, 'who were normal, all the accused were of a certain type' . . . There was the usual association of homosexuality with effete upper-class men, so that an 18-year-old factory worker from Barking recounted to police 'his association with men in luxury flats in the West End', for which he got fifteen months. The defendants were described in contemptuous language. A young café assistant from Chelsea 'was said to be a conscientious objector and a member of the Peace Pledge Union', both of which acts were brave in the wartime atmosphere of 1942 but could be represented to popular opinion as cowardly; he was also described as 'a timid, undersized, pathetic person'. A young actor/playwright from Hammersmith 'was described by an Army doctor as a psychopathic personality with suicidal tendencies'. The first of the defendants to be sentenced was mocked for fainting – although the sentence of ten years perhaps justified such a reaction. A middle-aged window-dresser, whom Singleton also gave a condign sentence, 'was stated by the police' to be 'detested by all decent minded men who worked on the premises with him', and was derided for keeping powderpuffs and cosmetics in his bedroom; in fact he sounds a charming queen, who was nicknamed 'The Marquis', and wrote unpublished novels under the pseudonym of Miss Amanda Flame.

from Richard Davenport-Hines, Sex, Death and Punishment (1990)

Tolerant Christian

. . . he [C. S. Lewis] said that he now realized that it was sometimes an ailment rather than a sin, and had nothing but pity for homosexuals provided they tried honestly not to give way to their unnatural desires but considered themselves in the same position as a man sworn to celibacy.

from C. S. Lewis at the Breakfast Table and Other Reminiscences, ed. J. Como (1980)

The Great Purge

In 1938 there were 134 prosecutions in England for sodomy and bestiality, 822 for attempted sodomy and indecent assaults and 320 for gross indecency. Fifteen years later, in 1952, these figures had risen to 670, to 3,087 and to 1,686 respectively. In the period between [1938] and 1955 homosexual offences known to the police increased by 850 per cent compared with 223 per cent for all indictable offences.

from Richard Davenport-Hines, Sex, Death and Punishment (1990)

Duty

Homosexuals in general are exhibitionists and proselytisers and are a danger to others, especially the young, and so long as I hold the office of Home Secretary I shall give no countenance to the view that they should not be prevented from being such a danger . . . as Home Secretary I have the duty to protect the people, especially the youth, of this country.

Sir David Maxwell-Fyfe, House of Commons, 3 December 1953

New Age

One is clearly on the threshold of a new age of conformity, an age in which the greatest crime is to do or speak differently from one's neighbour in the new garden suburb or housing estate; an age which extols petit-bourgeois values of stupidity, respectability, and moral hypocrisy.

Richard Rumbold's diary, 13 March 1954

Slipping Standards

Many of the great actors of the past, in the early days of this century, were friends of mine. I knew Sir Herbert Beerbohm Tree, Sir John Hare, Sir Cyril Maude and others. We were members of the same club. It is inconceivable that they would have been guilty of the disgusting offence of male importuning, or that the theatrical public in those days would have treated the offence with the leniency accorded to a well-known actor of the present day. In my opinion, there has been a moral declension.

Earl Winterton, House of Lords, 19 May 1954

In the Home

. . . there can hardly be any subject about which a man would more readily be excused from speaking at all . . . the whole subject is intensely repugnant, and raises intense moral indignation in many minds and perhaps some kind of primitive racial horror. Society – our society, at any rate – reacts very violently against it, because it feels that such practices are injecting poison into the bloodstream . . . the long-term solution will be found only in that moral and spiritual re-education which is the most urgent need – and, among thinking people, the consciously felt need – of our time, and in the rebuilding of family life. Behind an immense number of these cases of homosexuality there still lie unsatisfactory or broken homes. Here, as always, the most potent form of exorcism of evil will be found to be positive and creative.

the Bishop of Southwark, House of Lords, 19 May 1954

Resisting Temptation

Tolerance I believe to be one of the greatest virtues, but a tolerance which is prepared to take no notice of that which is essentially evil and wicked is not at all the sort of tolerance we want . . . we are here face to face with a terrible evil and we have to find a solution which is not based on prejudice or on merely a dislike of what is a very evil thing . . . it seems to me that the people who are cursed in this way must also resist their temptation. That is the least we can expect of them.

Earl Jowitt, House of Lords, 19 May 1954

Cruel Tricks

Nature is very unkind in many ways. There are the hunchback, the blind and the dumb; but of all the dreadful abnormalities surely abnormal sexual instincts must be the worst. It must colour the whole of a man's life, and it is a subject more for pity than for our rage.

Lord Brabazon of Tara, House of Lords, 19 May 1954

The Legacy of War

I have seen a good deal of this trouble in some of the welfare work I do in some parts of London. On the other hand, it is probably not quite so widespread as some of us feel. As I said, a good deal of it is the aftermath of the war. Gradually, perhaps, as we settle down and get back to better ways of thought and conduct, so we shall be able to grapple with it better.

Lord Ammon, House of Lords, 19 May 1954

British Justice

Wolfenden's Committee began by interviewing the Lord Chief Justice, Goddard, to seek an opinion on the relation between morality and law. Goddard was a judge who felt 'physically sick' when trying 'buggers' . . . By nature he was imperceptive and illiberal, frightened of women (as his daughter believed) but perhaps more frightened of himself. In the judgement of one contemporary, 'Goddard's influence on the cause of penal reform was almost universally malign; with a coarse callousness (his fondness for dirty jokes can hardly have been coincidental) there went not only a desperate ignorance of the springs of human behaviour (including, of course, his own) but what seemed like a positive pride in his ignorance.' . . . In trials of gross indecency, he thought that generally one of the defendants 'is an addict' to homosexuality, but 'not by any means both'. It was common to find that one of the pair had 'an irreproachable character and one just cannot understand how he came to be acting thus.' Goddard's explanation was that in gross indecency cases 'a man slightly under the influence of drink . . . hardly realizes what the other is up to.' But in buggery, 'if the parties are adults they are I believe both invariably addicts,' and he felt 'strongly that buggery ought always to be treated as a crime . . . It is such a horrible and revolting thing and a practitioner is such a depraved creature that he ought in my opinion to be put out of circulation.' Goddard saw 'a wide difference between the decadent young man who finds or thinks he finds satisfaction in good-looking youths to the extent of masturbation and the bugger who is nearly always a habitual'. He regretted that 'as a recent notorious case showed men who have good war records and can properly be classed as brave may be addicted to this vice but, if they are, they are in my opinion such public dangers that they ought to be segregated.' He wanted penalties for male importuning to be 'drastically increased' and thought for rent boys 'a whipping would probably be the best thing' (a sentiment shared by some of their clients including the occasional Tory MP).

from Richard Davenport-Hines, Sex, Death and Punishment (1990)

Modern Women

On TV I thought that women have never been more terrifying than they are now – the curled head ('Italian style'), the paint and the jewellery, the exposed bosom – no wonder men turn to other men sometimes.

an extract from Barbara Pym's notebook for 1955

Equality

It is only when there is complete equality between the sexes in all respects, beginning with economic equality between the sexes and extending throughout all aspects of life . . . that homosexuality would disappear naturally. If nature then produced an abnormality, which it might do in a number of cases, medical treatment would take good care of it.

C. Dallas in Socialist Review, December 1957

The Evil Thread

A very limited but very powerful and influential body is behind the [Wolfenden] Report, and behind the expense of the sending out of the Report. It has very wide ramifications. The evil thread runs through the theatre, through the music hall, through the Press, and through the B.B.C. It has international ramifications. While this Report tries to soften our hearts about blackmail, we must think how often we have heard of the poor fellow whose name appears in the Press and is blackmailed. But we are not told of blackmail in reverse. Have none of us heard about fellows who are passed over, in favour of someone who is willing to render service to someone up above? We have heard of contracts that are lost, or of engagements that are given for services rendered. This blackmail of the vilest type is running through our society like an evil thread.

Mrs Jean Mann, MP for Coatbridge and Airdrie, House of Commons, 26 November 1958

End of Empire

These unnatural practices, if persisted in, spell death to the souls of those who indulge in them. Great nations have fallen and empires been destroyed because corruption became widespread and socially acceptable.

Cyril Black, MP for Wimbledon, House of Commons, 26 November 1958

Twisted

He becomes bitter, his mind becomes twisted and distorted because he feels he is not as other men are . . . He is always beset by fears of discovery. The more sensitive ones wear a hunted look. They are not happy in their life.

William Shepherd, MP for Cheadle, House of Commons, 26 November 1958

At the Bottom of the Pile

Incest is a much more natural act than homosexuality.

William Shepherd, MP for Cheadle, House of Commons, 26 November 1958

Clever Guys

Anybody who knows of the actions and the personalities . . . of some homosexuals, knows that many of them are very ingratiating. They have powers, and sometimes occupy places of influence, whereby they can exercise an effect on the minds of those who otherwise would not be interested in this subject.

F. J. Bellenger, MP for Bassetlaw, House of Commons, 26 November 1958

Malignant Canker

I can well understand the pleas of those who say that those who practise this cult in private are inoffensive citizens. Perhaps they are, if it is meant that they do not break windows or behave riotously. Nevertheless, they are, in my opinion, a malignant canker in the community and if this is allowed to grow, it would eventually kill off what is known as normal life . . . I believe that humanity would eventually revert to an animal existence if this cult were so allowed to spread that, as in ancient Greece, it overwhelmed the community at large . . . I am repelled by the dirtiness of some of those whose conduct is exposed to the public gaze. I want to strip some of this false sentimentality, this false romanticism from homosexuality . . . I do not believe in this fancy talk – for that is all that it is – of love and affection for another man.

F. J. Bellenger, MP for Bassetlaw, House of Commons, 26 November 1958

Cult

It is a well-known fact that homosexuals band themselves into groups, and I fear that if the law were changed so that homosexuals did not have this fear of punishment, those groups might elevate the practice of homosexuality to a cult.

Dr A. D. D. Broughton, MP for Batley and Morley, House of Commons, 26 November 1958

Losing Out

I feel sorry for these people. They do not know what they are missing.

Dr A. D. D. Broughton, MP for Batley and Morley, House of Commons, 26 November 1958

Hidden I

. . . we should keep them out of sight of the general public . . .

Dr A. D. D. Broughton, MP for Batley and Morley, House of Commons, 26 November 1958

Hidden II

All decent people long to see a cessation of the discussion. Behind a drawn blind a corpse may be rotting; the blind will not stop the smell, but at least it will hide from the passer-by the horrors of putrefaction.

Lady Lloyd in a letter to the Daily Telegraph, 5 July 1960

Splendid Isolation

What I particularly admired about the debate was the way that every speaker managed to give the impression that he personally had never met a homosexual in his life.

Caption under a July 1960 Osbert Lancaster cartoon of two women talking at a party

Victim

It [*Victim*] was the first film to treat homosexuality seriously. It was the first film in which a man said: 'I love you' to another man. I wrote that scene in. I said 'There's no point in half-measures. We either make a film about queers or we don't.' I believe that pictures make a lot of difference to a lot of people's lives.

Dirk Bogarde, in Jeremy Pascall and Clyde Jeavons, A Pictorial History of Sex in the Movies (1975)

Unwell

The film [*Victim*] embarrassed audiences outside the metropolitan areas. There was a scene where Bogarde comes out of his house to discover a notice saying that he is 'queer' daubed on his garage wall. North of the line from Birmingham to the Wash, they couldn't understand what 'queer' meant. They thought he was feeling unwell.

Alexander Walker in Gay News, August 1976

An Interesting Discussion

Immediately Mr Davis left the room everyone stops work and starts talking. Discussion came round to 'little boys' – very interesting. Smith talked of Cooper, Peters of Markson (jokingly discussing his figure). Then we spoke of Aston (a prefect) and Travers (a junior). Aston asked me to send Travers along to him in

Prep, so I sent someone else. When he came back he told me Aston wanted to see Travers, so T. went. There was uproar from the form that Aston takes when he walked in: they know about the affair. Half the school heard it. Everyone in VI 2 was most amused. The 'Puritans' in the Common Room were discussed by Aston and me. Discussion lasted all period. Also discussed Mr Simon's homosexual tendencies when he takes showers, and how he went down to fetch his glasses so that he could see more clearly. Mr Wallace's keen interest in Fenton was also mentioned and Mr Gower's favours to Martin.

Discussion turned to politics and the state of the country. I said that we were a second-rate power . . .

Boy, seventeen, independent school, in Royston Lambert, The Hothouse Society: An Exploration of Boarding School Life *(1968)*

A Day in the Life of an English Public School Boy

Woken up 6.45 and think I haven't done my bloody English essay. Watch all the plebs making their beds, no bloody talent in this house except for old prosy Symes, who gives me a smile. Still he can get stuffed I'll stick to Dick (my 'friend' in Forde's House). Time to go into showers and feel that my pyjamas are still wet then I remember that I had a wet dream about Nicholson of Westons's – a school tart. I dreamt I had a snog with him – funny that as I've never spoken to him before. Housemaster makes sarcastic comment on way into showers – bastard. Get dressed same old routine. Supervise jobs making sure they are good today as the Matron won't spare me. Am on duty today, clean my shoes which are caked with mud.

Go up to Dining Hall and try to arrange it so I meet up with my 'friends'. Saw Dick in D.H. and he gives me a smile, and walked halfway back house with him which cheered me up. Go back house – no letter – got books for school. Have to go to Chapel. Walk down corridor with friends keeping eyes open for talent. Johnson told Paul (a pal of mine) to keep away from him – reason J asked P how much he wanted for his fur hat – P said 'half an hour'. Double French first two periods – bugger – can't stand it although I am doing it for 'A' level . . . French is over – couldn't stick that any more. Got maths and see Nicholson walking in front of me (corr he ain't half got nice legs – we the group gave him 8+ out of 10 for them – wish that dream came true) . . . 11.00 break usually see Dick but he is having an exam so stay in VI form and had usual sex conversation with the boys. We have Mr Jones for English next – always a laugh – never do any work. Paul comes in late as usual – saved him a seat and tell him about my dream – he thought it was funny and also that he had been chatting N. up the night before. Didn't do any work that period – late for the next period as saw Dick and had little chat with him. The master taking us didn't do anything though – meant to hand in essay but hardly any of us had done it so he set us another one – bastard. Five minutes after I had come in had to go for my haircut. Wondered if I could get a good one off him – wasn't too bad.

End of morning school soon came after haircut. Back to house – good meal today – punished 'prosy' Symes – he shouldn't take the mick out of Dick – he's jealous. Great day outside, sun shining. Got trial for 2nd rugby team. No talent in the rugby teams except for Pratt – but he is too fast for me – never catch up with him – pity. Bloody Richards swings his fist straight into my nose in a loose scrum gives me a nosebleed . . . thank Christ that match over – never thought it would end. Saw Symes going back house – don't know how I control myself still only another 5 weeks to go – 5 weeks! I'll never last. Took my shirt off and walked into the bootroom where I saw Eldon Jr. playing around – get everybody upstairs except him – have a scrap with him – the sex maniac. Back into showers – wish I was in Forde's with Dick – it would be a right old sex orgy. After got dressed noticed Symes has a clean pair of very tight trousers – give him a wolf-whistle – just gives me a dirty look. Comb my hair and have a chat with the boys who want to look at these notes – tell them to get stuffed.

I don't mind Tuesday afternoon lessons – only music and a free period. Free period with Paul. We read each other's girlfriends' letters – can't wait to get home. D.H. again – not a bad tea – see Dick afterwards. After that walk down corridor with Paul and others and see the three junior tarts standing outside their class as we do every bloody night of the term except Sundays. All of them are very nice – make a number of comments about them whereupon they turn round and smile at us – funny. Take prep – never do any work as they are always making some sort of noise or else annoying you. Saw Dick after prep had great chat with him.

Went up to his dorm to see him at 9.15. Great talking to him. The lights went out – still talking. Another prefect came in. Said jokingly he had 'caught me'. Made feeble excuse 'listening to records'. He went to see a 'friend' of his. Then yet another prefect came in. He had me worried for he still had his uniform on and the master on duty had a dark uniform. He had come to see a 'friend'. The trouble with Dick is that he is so sensual in bed. He writhes and wriggles fantastically.

Went back to House and had a cup of coffee.

Conversation as usual ended on 'little boys'.

Looking back on the day I seem to have done no work and talked and thought about 'little boys' all day. You'll find this is typical of this place.

Boy, seventeen, in Royston Lambert, The Hothouse Society: An Exploration of Boarding School Life *(1968)*

Helping

Needless to say, Mark, the House tutor, noticed my behaviour and put two and two together, but wasn't worried in the least, even encouraging the relationship in quite extraordinary ways. He said the friendship might do us good providing we didn't go too far. He even 'lent' us his room by going out and leaving us two together alone. He knew it was the only place in school we could be private.

Boy, sixteen, in Royston Lambert, The Hothouse Society: An Exploration of Boarding School Life *(1968)*

Long Night

Dormitory orgies have included, in those in which I have participated in
1. Doing naked war dances by torch lights.
2. Projecting erect penises on to the ceiling and walls by torch.
3. Wearing scanty swimming trunks in dormitories and dancing in them.
4. Getting as many in one bed as possible.
5. Each getting into each other's beds, and feeling erections, and lustful paintings, etc. Nothing serious.

Boy, eighteen, in Royston Lambert, The Hothouse Society: An Exploration of Boarding School Life (1968)

Monty's Last Stand

To condone unnatural offences in male persons over 21, or, indeed, in male persons of any age, seems to me utterly wrong. One may just as well condone the Devil and all his works. I am entirely opposed to this Bill . . . My main reason is that a weakening of the law will strike a blow at all those devoted people who are working to improve the moral fibre of this country. And heaven knows! it wants improving. . . . Do not let us forget that it is the present young generation who will have to handle the problem that lies ahead in this distracted world of politics, war and mixed-up values. They will need all the help and guidance that we older ones can give them. The first category I take is the boys and young men in our schools and universities, whom I suppose number some millions, although I do not know the exact figure. What influence on their minds and characters will follow if they know that their masters and tutors are indulging in unnatural practices, and if they know that the law of the land allows it? What effect will this have on the moral fibre of these boys, some of them quite young and under 21? The practices are illegal; and yet, suddenly on the morning of their 21st birthday, they can do what they like, and they are legal.

[The sponsor of the bill, Lord Arran, interrupts with a question for Montgomery: 'My Lords with great respect to the noble and gallant Viscount, does this not apply equally to the age of consent for girls? Suddenly, over the age of sixteen, it is all right.']

I am not very expert on girls. No doubt the noble Earl knows more about them than I do.

The second category I take is the youth organisations throughout this country. I will mention just a few, about which I know quite a lot: the Boy Scouts, the Boys Brigade, the Church Lads' Brigade, the Cadet Forces, the National Association of Boys Clubs – and there are other such organisations. In Canning Town in the East End of London you have David Sheppard and his Mayflower Centre. Many London gangs come from that area. I have been there. I have sent boys from the centre to the Outward Bound schools, magnificent places for the building of character. A boy is taken from his home area and spends a month having his character developed in an entirely different atmosphere by the sea, in the mountains and so on. I sent one boy from that school who was leader of one of the worst London gangs. I saw him before he went: I saw him when he came back, and he was a changed boy . . . Far from helping these unnatural practices along, surely our task is to build a bulwark which will defy evil influences which are seeking to undermine the very foundations of our national character – defy them; do not help them. I have heard some say – and indeed, the noble Earl [of Arran] said so himself – that such practices are allowed in France and in other NATO countries. We are not French, and we are not other nationals. We are British, thank God!

Lord Montgomery of El Alamein, House of Lords, 24 May 1965

Cottages

When I left I took the Piccadilly line to Holloway Road and popped into a little pissoir – just four pissers. It was dark because somebody had taken the bulb away. There were three figures pissing. I had a piss and, as my eyes became used to the gloom, I saw that only one of the figures was worth having – a labouring type, big, with cropped hair and, as far as I could see, wearing jeans and a dark short coat. Another man entered and the man next to the labourer moved away, not out of the place altogether, but back against the wall. The new man had a pee and left the place and, before the man against the wall could return to his place, I nipped in there sharpish and stood next to the labourer. I put my hand down and felt his cock, he immediately started to play with mine. The youngish man with fair hair, standing back against the wall, went into the vacant place. I unbuttoned the top of my jeans and unloosened my belt in order to allow the labourer free rein with my balls. The man next to me began to feel my bum. At this point a fifth man entered. Nobody moved. It was dark. Just a little light spilled into the place from the street, not enough to see immediately. The man next to me moved back to allow the fifth man to piss. But the fifth man very quickly flashed his cock and the man next to me returned to my side, lifting up my coat and shoving his hand down the back of my trousers. The fifth man kept puffing on a cigarette end and, by the glowing end, watching. A sixth man came into the pissoir. As it was so dark nobody bothered to move. After an interval (during which the fifth man watched me feel the labourer, the labourer stroked my cock, and the man beside me pulled my jeans down even further), I noticed that the sixth man was kneeling down beside the youngish man with fair hair and sucking his cock. A seventh man came in, but by now nobody cared. The number of people in the place was so large that detection was quite impossible. And anyway, as soon became apparent when the seventh man stuck his head down on a level with my fly, he wanted a cock in his mouth too. For some moments nothing happened. Then the eighth man, bearded and stocky, came in. He pushed the sixth man roughly away from the fair-haired man and quickly sucked the fair-haired man off. The man beside me had pulled my jeans down over my buttocks and was trying to push his prick between my legs. The fair-headed man, having been sucked off, hastily left the place. The bearded man came over and nudged away the seventh man from me and, opening wide my fly, began sucking me like a maniac. The labourer, getting very excited by my feeling his cock with both hands, suddenly glued his mouth to mine. The little pissoir under the bridge had become the scene of a frenzied homosexual saturnalia. No more than two feet away the citizens of Holloway moved about their ordinary business, I came, squirting come into the bearded man's mouth and pulled up my jeans. As I was about to leave, I heard the bearded man hissing quietly, 'I suck people off! Who wants his cock sucked?' When I left, the labourer was just shoving his cock into the man's mouth to keep him quiet. I caught the bus home.

from Joe Orton's diary, 1966

A Hard Night

Friday, 11 February 1966
[After a late-night meeting with the National Union of Railwaymen, who had retired to another part of Whitehall to consider their position,] we [cabinet ministers and officials] had retired to the room of George Brown [Secretary of State for Economic Affairs], leaving the NUR to chew it over. For four hours the minutes ticked by while we waited. George and the rest started to drink, while I worked on some office papers. George's manner began to change rapidly; he got noisy and aggressive, abusing his officials in what he no doubt considered a jocular way and shouting at everyone. At 3pm I said mildly I hoped I shouldn't be prevented from voting at 4pm on the Second Reading of the Sexual Offences Bill. This set George off on a remarkable diatribe against homosexuality. As an Anglo-Catholic and Socialist, he thought society ought to have higher standards. As Eric Roll [Treasury mandarin on secondment to the Department of Economic Affairs] and the officials argued with him good-naturedly, he got very passionate: 'This is how Rome came down. And I care deeply about it – in opposition to most of my Church. Don't think teenagers are able to evaluate your liberal ideas. You will have a totally disorganized, indecent and unpleasant society. You must have rules! We've gone too far on sex already. I don't regard any sex as pleasant. It's pretty undignified and I've always thought so.' . . . Just as we were feeling the long wait would never end, Sid Greene came in to say we had lost by twelve to eleven. George was deeply disappointed. I left him phoning Harold [Wilson] and went to vote. The Second Reading was carried by a comfortable majority of 179 to 99. I then heard Harold had cancelled his trip to Liverpool and we were to go to No. 10 for a meeting with the NUR Executive at 6 pm.

from Barbara Castle, The Castle Diaries (1984)

Taking a Stand

Tuesday, 20 December 1966
I asked Dick [Crossman, Leader of the House] how the Sexual Offences Bill got through without a vote. He said that Dance, leader of the opposition to it, had been so sozzled he had failed to rise at the right moment.

from Barbara Castle, The Castle Diaries (1984)

Recruiting

. . . people who indulge in this filthy business do not confine it to themselves but are great proselytizers, and are always trying to attract other people, especially other younger men, into this filthy business.

Ray Mawby, MP for Totnes, House of Commons, 22 June 1967

Sterling Service

Monday, 3 July 1967
All-night sitting on the Sexual Offences Bill. It was a good job I stayed, tired as I was. At one stage we only carried the closure by three votes. Trailing through the lobby at 4 am, I ran into Lena Jeger who put her arms round me and said in a piercing voice, 'Aren't we good, doing our bit for the boys!' She really is a joy.

from Barbara Castle, The Castle Diaries *(1984)*

Unnecessary Gamble

3 July 1967
Frankly it's an extremely unpleasant Bill and I myself don't like it. It may well be twenty years ahead of public opinion; certainly working-class people in the north jeer at their Members at the weekend and ask them why they're looking after the buggers at Westminster instead of looking after the unemployed at home. It has gone down very badly that the Labour Party should be associated with such a Bill.

from Richard Crossman, The Diaries of a Cabinet Minister, *Volume 2 (1966–8) (1976)*

Decline (and Fall?)

For twenty years I was a tutor and head of a Cambridge college and I am now head of a college at London University. One of the happiest parts of my duties has been to get to know undergraduates and how they live their lives. One gets to know something also of their lives at school, and particularly at boarding school. Of all the changes that I have seen during these years, nothing has been more striking than the decline in homosexuality or, to be more accurate, the decline in young men who are pretending or flirting with homosexuality. This is an immense change and the reason for it is obvious: to-day boys in their teens go out with girls: the old days of the segregation of the sexes, of shyness and awkwardness and of formal relations between them are over.

Lord Annan, House of Lords, 13 July 1967

Consequences

Thursday, 13 July 1967
Into Cabinet for my great battle on the carriers' licensing . . . Dick [Crossman] supported me 'on the margin and on political grounds'. But Jim [Callaghan] was grudging. Of course he was in sympathy with my aims, etc., but . . . Dick Marsh supported him and my heart began to sink. I appealed to Roy [Jenkins]: 'Back me up.' And purely on quid pro quo grounds for my support of the Sexual Offences Bill, he did! . . . [She passed her business.]

from Barbara Castle, The Castle Diaries *(1984)*

A Public Warning

I ask one thing and I ask it earnestly. I ask those who have, as it were, been in bondage and for whom the prison doors are now open to show their thanks by comporting themselves quietly and with dignity. This is no occasion for jubilation; certainly not for celebration. Any form of ostentatious behaviour, now or in the future, any form of public flaunting, would be utterly distasteful and would, I believe, make the sponsors of the Bill regret that they have done what they have done. Homosexuals must continue to remember that while there may be nothing bad in being a homosexual, there is certainly nothing good. Lest the opponents of the Bill think that a new freedom, a new privileged class, has been created, let me remind them that no amount of legislation will prevent homosexuals from being the subject of dislike and derision, or at best of pity. We shall always, I fear, resent the odd man out. That is their burden for all time, and they must shoulder it like men – for men they are.

Earl of Arran, House of Lords, 21 July 1967

Gangland Pleasures

He began getting what he seemed to want – the pretence of friendship, the appearance of respect, even of social success; these were the people who could introduce him to the smart life if he wanted it. They took him to their homes, their London clubs, dined him in the House of Lords, introduced him to celebrities. It was surprising how cheap the rich world was, and it gave Ronnie [Kray] a new role – the playboy gangster in a sophisticated world.

As usual he began dressing for the part – sharper suits, heavier jewellery, better-cut overcoats. Then he moved into the West End, taking the lease on a top-floor Chelsea flat in payment for a gambling debt. He took the whole place over – furniture, pictures, the former tenant's young boyfriend. Then for a while he became something of a character on the Chelsea scene, the King's Road's own gangster-in-residence . . .

Ronnie disliked women more than ever; now he was out of the East End he made no bones about his homosexuality. It was a relief to be able to admit it.

Now he discovered its advantages. It was quite smart, a sort of eccentricity to be made the most of, and he had the entrée to the useful freemasonry of the similarly inclined.

There was no hint of effeminacy about him. 'I'm not a poof, I'm a homosexual,' he would say, and was genuinely put out by the antics of effeminate males. 'Pansies,' he used to say, with the same cockney contempt with which he pronounced the word 'women'.

He liked boys, preferably with long lashes and a certain melting look around the eyes. He particularly enjoyed them if they had had no experience of men before. He liked teaching them and often gave them a fiver to take their girl-friends out on condition they slept with him the following night. He always asked them which they preferred. He was something of a sadist, but was generous with his lovers. The gifts he gave them were his main extravagance. He never seems to have forced anyone into bed against his will and, as he proudly insisted, was free from colour prejudice . . . An important part of the compulsive pederasty which had begun to dominate his life was his growing fear of the dark. He dreaded sleeping alone.

During the period at the Barn he fell in love. This was not something he actually approved of: love, especially when combined with sex, was usually a means women employed to keep men at home and relieve them of their money. So it might be more accurate to say that Ronnie began the luxury of continued tenderness for the first time in his life.

Vanity came into it. He enjoyed taking the boy out and being seen with him at the best restaurants: the boy was beautiful and behaved like a petulant young mistress. Ronnie enjoyed indulging these shows of temperament. He liked taking him to his tailors, selecting all his shirts and ties and doing what he could to curb the excesses of his youthful bad taste. He was extremely jealous: one man the boy had flirted with had his face cut open. The boy was 'his' boy.

He called him 'son', referring to himself as 'your old Dad'. Any extravagance was allowed him . . .

But it was no good. Everybody round him seemed to find happiness; not Ronnie . . . Boys were like drink. They helped him to forget; next day the hopelessness returned.

from John Pearson, Profession of Violence *(1972)*

Sad Pleasures

As a Member of Parliament myself, I voted for the Sexual Offences Bill not because of some of the self-interested lobbyists, many of them in high positions, who made of their private concerns a public crusade, but because I found it impossible to support a status quo which presented homosexual men as a natural prey for the blackmailer . . . [it is difficult] though to think of homosexuality as anything but a troubled condition, shot through with anxious pleasures and the sad orgasms of the lower sensory system.

Maurice Edelman, MP for Coventry North, in the New York Times, *5 July 1970*

Tasty Stills

Films and Filming of course occupies a curious but not insignificant niche in gay history. During the late 60s and early 70s it could be relied upon to present, month after month, a generous selection of tasty stills of male stars in states of undress. This was partly due to the kinds of film that were being produced at that time . . . But there was more to it than that: the number of stills, their selection sometimes made *Films and Filming* the next best thing to a thoroughly-composed male nude mag.

Roger Baker in Him/GR, October 1983

CHAPTER TEN

The Gay Movement

The Gay Movement of the late 1960s and early 1970s created a public face for homosexuality with the emergence of young men prepared to be identified in the street and on the screen as homosexual. This gave homosexual men a public presence and a voice, where previously they had largely been hidden and silent.

Though the early partisans imagined that they were the heralds of a mass movement which would soon imitate them and throw off their masks, the activist core has remained relatively small in relation to the number of men who enjoy the facilities of the ghetto. The activists operate as a sort of priesthood. Though they are often seen as spokesmen for homosexuals, the degree of representativeness is limited. Like all priests, they have a different perspective from the sinner out in the clubs and the bars. They resemble the sectarian element often associated with Protestant nonconformity, forever bickering among themselves over apparently abstruse points of principle and prone to the most extraordinary amount of factionalism. Communicating through the medium of tatty newsletters, they were (or are?) sustained in their faith by the expectation of a glorious tomorrow and the superiority that comes with the feeling that one belongs to the elect. There are, of course, many parallels – and, indeed, much kinship – with the extreme fringes of the Left. But while the overlap has often been considerable, many gay activists have resented their marginalisation by their brothers and sisters of the broad Left.

The change that brought this priesthood into existence was clearly associated with the profusion of radical groups emerging at that time, challenging conventional values and the traditional order. Women, blacks, students and gays all took to the street affirming their commitment to revolutionary social change. They imitated the tactics of the Civil Rights Movement and the campaign against the Vietnam War, and the media provided them with enormous publicity for all their antics. Beginning in America, such movements spread across the democracies. For the protesters this was an exciting period; they seemed to be harbingers of a new age.

Their hopes were quickly dashed, their utopian impulses soon defeated. The movements themselves quickly fragmented, and it proved impossible to create a coalition of the discontented. The forces of the traditional order were more powerful than they appeared. For some this setback was a disillusioning experience, but the radical spirit survived among the thousands who committed themselves to their cause. They had found a voice – a public presence – and the Movement continued.

There came into existence a class of professional agitators, inspired by the events of the 1960s, who have become a permanent feature of the political landscape. They propagandised, they educated, they wrote, they protested, and they lobbied. Newspapers and magazines were established, providing them with a platform. Organisations were set up to promote the cause at a local level, and proved to be particularly powerful in colleges and universities. Institutions were created to direct the efforts of the agitators, and with the foundation of counselling and information services it became possible for many isolated individuals to make contact with other men who shared their tastes. Such services became the glory of the Movement. All relied on groups of men willing to give some of their time to the cause.

Gay Liberation (the most radical manifestation of the Movement) lasted for three or four years before its groups disintegrated in the early 1970s. The example of the Americans was imitated elsewhere in the West, with a Gay Liberation Front coming into existence in London during 1970 at the London School of Economics, already at that time a centre for a viciously radical student movement that did much to damage the reputation of that famous institution.

The Liberationists were extreme left-wingers who sought a complete social revolution and advanced a set of aims that would, if implemented, have transformed society. They won the allegiance of only a fraction of men who indulged in homosexual acts and never even came close to achieving any of their aims, but they had a significant impact on society, radicalising and educating a group of men who would thereafter devote themselves to homosexual causes, the activists, the gay priesthood. These were the men who created the newspapers, led the campaigns to achieve rights for homosexuals, and established a visible homosexual presence in public life.

This was a turning-point in the history of homosexuality. Though homosexual reform groups had existed before, they had usually operated clandestinely, shunning the attention of the media and working towards extremely limited goals within the existing social and political order. There had been much emphasis on appearing respectable and showing the makers of opinions that homosexuals were worthy citizens and could be just as dull as the rest of the citizenry. The radicals saw themselves as outsiders and were indifferent to and uninterested in respectability.

In the United States the Gay Movement has grown into a powerful political element, homosexuals being accepted as a minority group which in a number of cities has substantial political muscle. Annual gay pride marches in North America attract considerable support and are now part of the urban calendar, with the participation and blessing of political leaders courting the gay vote. In Britain, where the political structure is unaccommodating to minorities, the Gay Movement has remained peripheral, with little to show for two decades of agitation. The campaign to lower the age of consent for homosexual acts has so far been a flop; this age still stands at twenty-one, where it was set in 1967.

The activists have always had a rather odd relationship with the wider body of men who practise homosexual sex. They often allude to the 'gay community', a term that they and the media take to comprehend all homosexuals. As a result, activists often describe themselves – and their description is accepted by broadcasters and journalists – as spokesmen for 'the homosexual community'. This is absurd. They represent only themselves and the small groups to which they belong, and, though they might on occasions enjoy the support of slightly wider groups, they never comprise more than a tiny number of men who might participate in homosexual activity. They do not represent homosexuals in the broadest sense, though they often act as if they do. The proposition that homosexual inclinations, thoughts or actions make an individual either political or radical is one of the more idiotic items in the gay creed.

The activists often have a curiously ambivalent relationship with the commercial gay scene. In the 1970s many activists found themselves attacking the materialism of the clubs and the bars; however, such commercial outlets attracted many more men than protest meetings or demonstrations. The activists lived in hope that their brothers would come to realise the error of their ways, but their rhetoric has had little impact.

It was hoped that, as time wore on, more and more prominent people would come out as gay. In the 1970s and early 1980s few men did, and though the number of famous folk who are openly gay has been much expanded, it is still only a fraction of the number of gays who occupy all sorts of important positions in society. In Britain, in fact, it has largely been figures in show business who have announced their sexual proclivities to the world.

To the activists the act of 'coming out' was a critical rite of passage in which an individual became at last an honest soul. Coming out would, it was hoped, bring all sorts of benefits and especially achieve much greater tolerance of homosexual behaviour in society. That so few prominent homosexuals have come out has been one of the greatest disappointments for the activists, and in 1989 a small but militant group in New York started to 'out' celebrities, movie stars, powerful columnists and journalists by announcing their homosexuality in posters distributed across the city. This was a phenomenon that sparked off articles in the press for a few months but then quickly fizzled out. Those concerned enjoyed their fifteen minutes of fame but had little discernible effect on the lives of the men on whose behalf they apparently acted. Indeed, it is difficult to see quite how the revelation of the homosexuality of a film star or a pop singer, usually the prerogative of the tabloid press, could have much impact on anyone except the star concerned. Most stars sensibly ignored the posters or denied the allegations made. A British attempt to imitate the New Yorkers led in the summer of 1991 to a complete fiasco. After a first press conference, the activists concerned got cold feet and quickly retracted their claims, except for a peculiar attack on teen idol Jason Donovan, who went to the High Court in 1992 and showed they had been mistaken: he was not a homosexual. A magazine had foolishly printed a picture of their poster, giving him the opportunity to sue and clear his name.

The police raid on the Stonewall bar in Christopher Street in New York's Greenwich Village on 27 June 1969 is an act which occupies an important place in the calendar of the activist, like Bastille Day for the French. The bar catered for a homosexual clientele and so was prey to periodic raids by the New York Police Department. Raids followed a regular pattern: the owner and his staff were arrested along with a number of patrons and were taken downtown in a paddy wagon; the other patrons had their names taken and were cautioned. Next morning, after a night in the cells, the men who had been arrested were charged before a court for a variety of minor misdemeanours to which they usually pleaded guilty. They were then fined and released. The bar-owner would repair and renovate his premises after the raid, reopening a few weeks later, and try to attract back his clientele, who had in the meantime moved on to other bars.

On the evening of 27 June the patrons resisted arrest and fought back, producing several evenings of riot in Greenwich Village. The importance of the event for the activist is that it was the first act of resistance, the first public manifestation of gay pride. Many heroic accounts of these riots have been written by activists – indeed, the doyen of American gay letters, Edmund White, makes Stonewall the climax of one of his gay novels, in which it becomes a rite of passage not simply for the Movement but for the hero and, one presumes, for Mr White himself. What all the narrators like to emphasise in their accounts of this epic is the part – the noble part – played in this act of defiance by the effeminate patrons, many of them in female attire and some of them fully paid-up members of the transvestite guild. The weakest and most despised part of the Movement had thrown the first stone. Appropriately enough the day is commemorated by parades and festivals in the great cities of the West. One day, one imagines, it will be honoured with a postage stamp.

In 1989 Ian McKellen and some chums from British theatreland established a group to lobby for improvement in the position of homosexuals in British society. They named their group Stonewall, even though Sir Ian and his friends had no intention of dirtying their hands. Words, not sticks and stones, would be their weapons.

The Good Old Cause

Since June 1969, when a police raid of a Greenwich Village gay bar sparked several nights of rioting by male homosexuals, gay men and women in the United States have enlisted in ever growing numbers in a movement to emancipate themselves from the laws, the public policies, and the attitudes that have consigned them to an inferior position in society. In ways pioneered by other groups that have suffered a caste-like status, homosexuals and lesbians have formed organizations, conducted educational campaigns, lobbied inside legislative halls, picketed outside them, rioted in the streets, sustained self-help efforts, and constructed alternative separatist institutions on their road to liberation. They have worked to repeal statutes that criminalize their sexual behavior and to eliminate discriminatory practices. They have labored to unravel the ideological web that supports degrading stereotypes. Like other minorities, gay women and men have struggled to discard the self-hatred they have internalized. Many of them have rejected the negative definitions that American society has affixed to their sexuality and, instead, have begun to embrace their identity with pride.

from J. D'Emilio, Sexual Politics, Sexual Communities: The Making of a Homosexual Minority in the United States 1940–1970 *(1983)*

Against the Current

. . . in so far as the origins of prejudice can be traced, gay love has been accepted or despised to the degree to which it supports (or at least does not threaten) the values of those in charge. It is for this reason that gay people must be politically aware.

from Stephen Coote's introduction to The Penguin Book of Homosexual Verse *(1983)*

Stonewall

The forces of faggotry, spurred by a Friday night raid on one of the city's largest, most popular, and longest lived gay bars, the Stonewall Inn, rallied Saturday night in an unprecedented protest against the raid and continued Sunday night to assert presence, possibility, and pride until the early hours of Monday morning. 'I'm a faggot, and I'm proud of it', 'Gay Power!', 'I like boys!' – these and many other slogans were heard all three nights as the show of force by the city's finery met the force of the city's finest. The result was a kind of liberation, as the gay brigade emerged from the bars, back rooms, and bedrooms of the Village and became street people.

from Village Voice, *1969*

Inventive

People invent categories in order to feel safe. White people invented black people to give white people identity . . . Straight cats invent faggots so they can sleep with them without becoming faggots themselves.

James Baldwin, 1971

Kidnap and Rape

. . . the kidnapping and debauching of the innocent word 'gay' . . .

Roger Scruton in The Times Literary Supplement, *1980*

Label

Most 'gays' are unhappy with the label, although no one is miserable about it. Their experiences . . . testify to the irony of the term. For all its limitations, 'gay' is the only unpompous, unpsychological term acceptable to most men and women, one already widely used and available to heterosexuals without automatically implying something pejorative. Perhaps one limitation more felt than expressed is implied by grammar: used as a noun 'gay' sounds awkward; as an adjective it is also somewhat stiff: it seems overpolite to emphasize 'gay men and women'. For a group in search of their identity, 'gay' offers little help in self-definition.

from Seymour Kleinberg, The Other Persuasion *(1977)*

Our Word

'Homosexual' is medical in origin, pathologising in tendency, imposed from the outside and, linguistically speaking, a pseudo-Graeco-Roman mess. 'Gay' is self-chosen, affirms its own mental health and, linguistically speaking, is plucked from the heart of the language, for which its enemies can never forgive it (as in 'They've stolen our beautiful word.').

Alison Hennegan, former literary editor of Gay News, *in the* New Statesman, *December 1983*

Two Objections to the Appropriation of the Word 'Gay' from a Progressive Historian

The first objection is political. A minority is doubtless entitled to rebaptize itself with a term carrying more favourable connotations so as to validate its own behavior and free itself from scandal. But it is scarcely entitled to expect those who do not belong to that particular minority to observe this new usage, particularly when the chosen label seems bizarrely inappropriate and appears to involve an implicit slur on everyone else . . . The second objection to 'gay' is linguistic. For centuries the word has meant (appropriately) 'blithe', 'light-hearted' or 'exuberantly cheerful'. To endow it with a wholly different meaning is to deprive ourselves of a hitherto indispensable piece of vocabulary and incidentally make nonsense of much inherited literature. Are we now to think that the child that is born on the Sabbath day is blithe and good, bonny and – endowed with an erotic preference for its own gender?

from a review by Keith Thomas in the New York Review of Books, *December 1980*

Uncle Tom and the Fair-Minded Citizen

Why oh why must the minority of gay campaigners use foul language, clown-tactics, and general public rudeness . . . Instead of constantly criticising and giving abuse to Court and Government decisions, no matter how unjust, why not try appeals for reasoned public support.

If the law is unjust or a bad one then the public will have it changed in time. Don't treat the public as a moronic TV audience but get about and inform them of the facts, as we see them, ask, politely, for their help. It is amazing how many people, when informed of a wrong, will give help and advice. All it takes is a PLEASE, something that seems to be lacking.

from a letter in Gay News, *1972*

Trapped in Old Values

Homosexuals suffer greatly for their heterosexual upbringing. Expressed simply this means that gay people inherit sets of standards and values that could equip them very well if they grew up straight and conform to the principles of marriage and so on, but which are not just useless but downright damaging to the individual who wishes to realise his potential as a homosexual. In this specific context he inherits a sexual outlook that is hemmed in by severe repression . . . It is rather like having VD and finding oneself with people who are talking about the ailment in tones of horror and disgust.

from Gay News, *September 1973*

A Poor Visionary

My thoughts at the moment are those of re-education. People must learn not to despise Gays: Gays and 'straights' need equal opportunities for loving and making love . . . Everybody has a degree of gayness which they are taught to repress . . . I'd like to see the break-up of the nuclear family . . . My idea of perfection is four (at least but preferably an even number i.e. 2, 3 or 4 couples) living together in an interchangeable bisexual relationship . . . Before anything can be done to society in general, we shall all have to get our personal lives together. If it means breaking a few laws that's our problem. Eventually we'll have no laws to break . . . I suggest to all bisexuals that they leave their suburban homes and come out. We can do something when we're united . . . If every Gay/ Woman/Black/Freak went on strike our joint proposal for a new society would have to be listened to . . . I'd like to hear from anybody with views on the oppression of bisexuals or getting all groups in favour of restructuring society together, but I can't promise to write back unless you enclose a stamped addressed envelope (I can barely afford paper and biros) and can't be prompt in writing if many people write. Let's all get together and try to do something for once, it'd make a change from sitting on our arses and just talking.

Chris Robbins in Gay News, *September 1973*

The College Scene

In defiance of taboos that have prevailed for generations, thousands of college students are proclaiming their homosexuality and openly organizing 'gay groups'. No one knows exactly how many are involved, but in growing numbers they are forming cohesive campus organizations for educational, social and political purposes, often with official sanction and with remarkable acceptance from fellow students. However a number of psychiatrists and psychologists are somewhat uneasy about the ready availability of homosexual social activities in the presence of impressionable adolescents whose sexual identities are not fully crystallized.

By organizing, the gay students hope to build a sense of community among gay men and women and to disabuse their heterosexual classmates and the outside community of what they feel are damaging myths about homosexuality. From conversations with officials and homosexual students on half a dozen campuses from Boston to Los Angeles, as well as reports from campus correspondents at thirteen other schools, it would appear that the gay students have made substantial strides in changing attitudes. The groups appear to be most successful at schools isolated from large urban areas and where there are few social outlets. Thus strong gay organizations exist at Cornell, Massachusetts, Rutgers, Maryland and Colorado.

from the New York Times, *15 December 1971*

Exhibitionism

We learn that at the University, that seat of learning . . . a Gay Society was formed last term. It has, according to its vice-president, a membership of 10 and is still growing.

At St Luke's College, Exeter, another proud institution that has turned out many good teachers in the past, 'there is a movement towards gay rights' and at Exeter College there is 'a fair chance' of a gay society being formed in the future.

What is so nauseating about these disclosures is not that such a situation exists in Exeter . . . but that the students are so brazen about it. They want the whole world to know, apparently, about the activities and proclivities of some of their number.

They are very much like the child who does something because he knows it is naughty, and has to draw attention to himself . . . We are not moralising here; everyone to his own choice but . . .

from the Exeter Express and Echo, *May 1973*

Solidarity

I discovered my own gayness, I realized it would make me an outsider in society. I began to identify with other groups of outsiders, people who had no control over the wealth and power in society, let alone control over their own lives. I identified with women in their struggles against oppression, with the working class in their struggles against exploitation and with the Third World in their struggles against imperialism and poverty.

Bob Cant

Superior Persons

. . . to be honest, gay persons are not just plain folk, we are quite extraordinary . . . We are not – heaven forbid – 'the same as' heterosexuals, but are uniquely different with our own positive and lasting contributions to humanity. Some of us are pederasts. Some of us are sado-masochists. Some of us are hustlers. Some of us are frenzied fairies in drag. In other words: we have amongst our ranks – in our culture – a wealth and variety of collectively liberating experience undreamt of by merely mortal heterosexuals. We are Hamlet and his father in heaven and hell, while they are Horatio with his plodding commonsense.

Rictor Norton in Gay News, *May 1974*

Gender Bending

Masculinity is an ideology: a set of values and a way of looking at the world. Its principal propagator is the mass media, from which issue forth like storm gods the bellowing prototypes of society's strictly dichotomous images of sex roles. The gay movement, along with such explicitly countercultural groups as the Beats and the Hippies, have done much to break down the rigid boundary line separating masculinity from femininity, but the cultural definition of the heterosexual majority still exerts very considerable pressure towards conformity.

Jack Babuscio in Gay News, *August 1975*

The Holocaust

Public outcry against the Nazi atrocities retains a mute silence concerning the gay victim, and for a very simple reason: modern attitudes towards gays are little different from those of fascist Germany. The question 'Why did it happen?' becomes the question 'Can it ever happen again?'

from Gay News, *November 1975*

Hope

Time and the younger generation are on our side.

Ian Harvey in Gay News, *January 1976*

A Complete Experience

To me, of course, my gayness is very important, twenty-four hours a day, seven days a week.

Jeffrey Weeks in Gay News, *January 1976*

The Big Orgy

. . . the fear that gayness, if sanctioned or condoned, will reveal its true potency and general popularity; freed from the confines of a barbaric law, man would turn irrevocably from woman to the superior attraction of homosexuality with the whole country brought to its birthless end as an orgy of gay sex.

Nicholas de Jongh in Gay News, *January 1976*

Normal

[Quentin Crisp] has set the 'gay' world back twenty years I should think. Here we are all doing our nuts saying to the hets 'Let us live our lives as we want to as normal as we can' . . . [Because] as far as I am concerned, being 'gay' means that I am perfectly normal with one slight difference. I prefer to love another man. I am not and see no point in trying to ape a female. There are a great deal like me. Our local has a good number of 'affairs' and, although in the 'Camp' life it would be boring, our lovers chat about food, clothes and the men about cars, television etc. just as normal couples do, even to noticing a nice young thing just as Dad would fancy a young bit of skirt. I put this in to show how normal we really are. There is no need to slap us and the hets in the face with 'high camp' . . . Quentin, keep it to yourself. No need to write books about it, have it on the box. Who wants to know? Certainly the hets will have many false ideas about us and make it that bit harder for the ordinary homo to be accepted by them. Please don't print my name, I have no desire, unlike Quentin, for publicity and self-importance.

from a letter in Gay News, *January 1976*

Straight Talking

Live your life openly as being gay. Let other people see you are an ordinary guy and that you and your boyfriend can be and are as happy with one another as your straight friends and colleagues are with their husbands or wives. If you encounter any anti attitudes then ask the person concerned why he or she feels the way they do. You'll be very lucky to receive a coherent reply! – and when you tell them you are a gay, they will, in all probability, say they either don't believe you or drop out of the conversation with a weak apologetic smile . . . I wish other gay people could realise that to overcome any prejudice they may encounter will only be put right by careful discussion and total honesty. You can always be respected for it. Never despised. Always think carefully before answering a question, though, and I have found to my cost that it is never a good idea to be flippant. You won't be taken seriously, and then your whole case will completely collapse. You'll immediately be slotted into one of the convenient holes of being a stereotyped gay.

Jeffrey Weeks in Gay News, *January 1976*

Great

I live my gayness with pride and joy. Yet the more convinced I become of the extreme goodness of homosexuality and of the great social importance of the gay liberation movement the more misgivings I have about welcoming sado-masochists, transvestites, transexuals and pederasts as fully equal sisters and brothers in our fight for freedom . . . I believe homosexual love is potentially great and ennobling. I believe that when a woman and a woman, or a woman and a man or a man and a man meet together physically and emotionally, high and good things happen . . . My sexuality is socially important. It takes no account of gender roles. It is not justified because of its reproductive possibilities. It can give a powerful support to the women's movement. It can show the way to newer and more joyful sexual behaviour for all human beings. I believe that transvestism, transexualism, pederasty and sado-masochism do not have this potentiality. Furthermore I believe that all of them . . . would disappear in a truly sexually free society.

from Gay News, *February 1976*

Bad Images

I can't think of a single film or play on the subject of homosexual relationships which has ever had anything constructive to say about us. We are always portrayed as vain, neurotic, stupid or just plain nasty – and definitely unhappy!

It happens in the theatre, in films and on television. The tragic thing is that even some of our own kind only portray us in this way, be they directors, producers, writers or actors . . . [they produce] the unacceptable face of homosexuality . . . [One day] the other, equally true side of the coin will be revealed.

David McClure in a letter to Gay News, *February 1976, after seeing* Fox and his Friends, *a film directed by Reiner Werner Fassbinder*

Good Images

A film about gays that is honest, positive, funny and sexy. A film that does not take place in an atmosphere of exploitation and seediness ([Fassbinder's] *Fox and his Friends*) or a world so removed from most people's lives (Hockney's in *A Bigger Splash*) that it is meaningless. A film about people and not stereotypes. A film that would appeal to both gays and straights . . . the first real gay feature film called *Nighthawks* . . . [using] actors who need not have any previous acting experience . . . about a 32-year-old geography teacher at a comprehensive who comes out. A teacher was chosen as the main character because teaching is a profession where it is traditionally very difficult to come out. And geography was chosen as his subject because, unlike arts subjects, it is very difficult to talk about one's gayness to a class of children if you are trying to explain soil erosion . . . [Ron Peck, the director and writer, hopes] . . . that people who see *Nighthawks* will come away 'with a sense of how large, how rich and how full of variety gay life is. And that is another area of sexuality that can be very exciting and positive . . . Films like *Midnight Cowboy* are very dishonest' . . . Ron hopes to use real pubs and clubs and schools when he starts shooting in May. And real gay people to fill them.

The film will be improvised with a very carefully worked out structure . . . Ron will need several hundred people either as actors or extras, so if you want to get into the picture write now!

from Gay News, *February 1976*

Two Parades

June 28 – the seventh anniversary of New York's Stonewall riots – was celebrated on both sides of the Atlantic. In London a disappointing 200 people turned up for a march through the West End . . . Banners on the march marked the presence of Wages Due Lesbians, University London Gaysoc and Brighton CHE . . . organisers blamed CHE and *Gay News* for the poor turnout, saying they should have given the event more publicity . . . in San Francisco, where police estimated the gay rally turnout to be a staggering 90,000 . . . the parade was the biggest and best attended yet . . . the San Francisco parade was a celebration rather than a protest; a circus or Mardi Gras rather than a political rally.

from Gay News, *June 1976*

Filthy Lucre

It is difficult to sum up Cambridge . . . it is one of the strongest gay scenes in the country and perhaps this is due to its rather puny commercial facilities.

Stephen Airey in Gay News, *November 1976*

Perfect

Resolutions imply that people need some improvement; gay people don't need any improvement; they're so complete, so intact, so well-developed.

David Starkey in Gay News, *January 1977*

Passing

In the past, the common denominator has been the unique pressure of 'passing', of spending a little if not a good deal of one's life masked as a heterosexual: for some, the only moments without hypocrisy were in bed; for others, the mask became the private face as well.

from Seymour Kleinberg, The Other Persuasion *(1977)*

Bright Spark

Alan Burnside . . . is now paying the price for speaking out publicly against discrimination. Twenty-year-old Alan, an electrician at Blackhall Colliery near Durham, is now regarded by former 'friends' and colleagues as the carrier of a vile, contagious disease. Men whom he has worked alongside for years will not even speak to him now – except to insult him. The reason is that Alan wrote a letter to *Coal News*, the National Coal Board newspaper, in which he called for an end to discrimination against gays in employment and in society at large. 'Homosexuals whether male or female are just ordinary people doing ordinary jobs,' he wrote. 'They should be allowed to live their lives freely without persecution' . . . 'I've been trying to get that letter published for two years,' Alan told *Gay News* . . . [Since publication of the letter] Alan has been totally on his own at work, facing a barrage of insults and swearing, and seeing his name daubed in crude printed graffiti. 'I was quite popular – on speaking terms with nearly everyone at the colliery,' he said. 'Now I'm completely snubbed . . . They don't want to be seen talking to anyone gay' . . . There is one thing that Alan has found particularly hard to take. He said that there are three other gay men that he knows at the colliery – and they are not talking to him either.

from Gay News, *September 1977*

The Power of Personality

Out there in the desperate world of compulsive cruisers there's a wealth of experts ready to advise on whether Wranglers, Levi's, FUs or Falmers jeans are the right cut for your particular body . . . I've always suspected such dressing as having about it elements of narcissism, for even if you have close and trusted friends guiding you, the decisions you make about what assets you have and how best to display them to sexual advantage must be subjective, and must show sophisticated sexual awareness of your own body . . . The gay scene is a market, I suppose, and both sellers and buyers have become used to the coinage of appeal and neither can change it without losing out.

The way the compulsive cruisers present themselves is geared to the way the buyers choose: looking no further than skin-deep, ignoring what might or might not be underneath. It all takes place on a simple, animal level, and those taking part may as well be walking around with nothing on because it's sexuality in the crudest form that's involved, and not eroticism.

Gay bars and discos packed with such people can be a degrading spectacle . . . I'm urging the *new* revolution – the revolt out of all style at all – where the clothes we wear, the way we look, will be immaterial. Our sexual attractiveness will come from within. The majority of gays are placing their cosmetic selves on the line. Until they can come to terms with their real identities they won't be able to come to terms with the reality of gay liberation. Liberation can come only when gays no longer use the masks of false identity to hide their insufficiencies.

You might argue that within clothes liberation there should be scope for eccentricity. I agree there should be that scope. But if we had a successful revolt out of style there'd be so many happy eccentricities in clothing and looks that, by definition, there'd be no eccentricities.

Robin Houston in Gay News, *November 1977*

The Promised Land

The gay community doesn't exist yet but once or twice over the last two years I think I've glimpsed it. And it's worth fighting for.

Drew Griffiths in Gay News, *August 1978*

Porn

. . . gay pornography . . . is by and large a positive fulfilment that counteracts the nightmarish fears of our adolescent years and, as such, is politically progressive.

Michael Denneny, 1979

Horrors

What in homosexuality particularly horrifies homo normalis, the policeman of the hetero-capitalist system, is being fucked in the arse: and this can only mean that one of the most delicious pleasures, anal intercourse, is itself a significant revolutionary force. The thing that we queens are so greatly put down for contains a large part of our subversive gay potential. I keep my treasure in my arse, but then my arse is open to everyone.

from Mario Mieli, Homosexuality and Liberation *(1980)*

Experience

There is more to be learned from wearing a dress for a day than there is from wearing a suit for life.

from Mario Mieli, Homosexuality and Liberation *(1980)*

Marriage

The men, both 42, have led the way in taking advantage of a new law in Denmark that allows homosexuals to become 'registered partners', giving them the same rights and responsibilities as traditional married couples. For Ivan Larsen, a Protestant priest, and Ove Carlsen, a child psychologist, it was a logical step. They have lived together for two years, and making their relationship official was attractive: they can now inherit each other's possessions and get tax advantages.

Their main reason was old-fashioned. 'Like any other couple taking this step, we love each other,' said Carlsen.

Their wedding was held two weeks ago at Copenhagen Town Hall along with ten other male couples. Both dressed in black trousers, white dinner jackets and bow ties – Larsen's blue, Carlsen's pink. Each was asked: 'Do you take this man to be your lawful partner?' Holding back the tears, each replied simply: 'Yes' and then signed the register. As they left arm in arm, cheering guests showered them with confetti . . . The 90 guests included Carlsen's two children, aged seven and ten, from his previous, heterosexual, marriage. 'They have accepted what the situation is,' he said. 'They understand.'

from the Sunday Times, *15 October 1989*

Outing

The American language is usually more than ready for a new word, but the verb 'to out' is having some difficulty gaining acceptance. To be 'out' is to be an admitted homosexual, and to 'come out' is to declare the fact. To be 'outed', however, is to be exposed as a homosexual against one's will. In the old days, this was known as fag-baiting or queer-bashing, and was done by 'crusading' moralists. To be subjected to an outing today, however, is to be outed by homosexuals intent on making a point.

Christopher Hitchens, in the Sunday Correspondent, 22 April 1990

Nasty

Outing is a nasty word for telling the truth.

Armistead Maupin, June 1991

Reclamation

I wrote the Malcolm Forbes exposé for three reasons – so that history wouldn't be distorted, so that it's clear that gays are everywhere, not just at the bottom of the pile, and because a powerful man like Forbes felt unable to speak out over the Aids crisis because he wanted to remain in the closet. There is an element of revenge in it, but it's also about claiming figures in the political establishment. I don't want to help gay people remain emblems of heterosexuality.

Michelangelo Signorile, New York gay journalist, justifying outing, in Gay Times, June 1990

Ethical Lives

Outing is about getting people to a point where their lives are ethically led. It is about providing the gay community with role models. There are just too many gays trying to pass as straight; as activists we have to do what we have to do: it's as simple as that . . . There is a basic line of dissent in the movement now between true activists and what I call assimilationists – the ones who want to serve as faggot waitresses at the great heterosexual banquet. When you don't come out, your cowardice impacts on other people – fellow gays – just as it would impact on the black community if you were of colour and tried to pass as white. Outing people is about giving the gay community the strength of numbers, the role models that it badly needs.

Rick Wilson, media liaison officer for the New York chapter of Queer Nation, June 1991

The Gay Gaze

Gay men are able to subtly communicate their shared worldview by a special gaze that seems to be unique to them. Although it is not always possible to tell who is gay – some men are very effective at hiding it and one therefore occasionally mistakes a gay man for a straight man – most gay men develop a canny ability to instantly discern from the returned look of another man whether or not he is gay. This gay gaze is not only lingering, but also a visual probing, a sometimes satisfying search for recognition. Almost everyone I interviewed said that they could tell who was gay by the presence or absence of this look . . . Young homosexual boys can become aware of this gay gaze without quite comprehending its significance. A swimmer told me: 'I remember that, when I was a boy, I would meet some of the men friends of my parents and they would look at me in a knowing way, and I wondered what it was that they knew. And now, of course, I know.' In Stanley Kubrick's film *The Shining*, there is a similar recognition between an older man, a chef, and a little boy. Their recognition is not a gender paradox, but it is of a special gift of insight . . . The gay look and deportment are the products of the knowledge of paradox and estrangement, and of adjusting oneself to a world which doesn't fit. Having had this experience, gay men can recognize it in each other. 'It takes one to know one.' . . . The gay gaze is an ironic clue to paradoxical masculinity . . . with just one look, that masculine façade is peeled away, revealing the truth of the paradox. By this ironic gaze, gay athletes usually know of their sometimes silent, paradoxical fraternity.

from Brian Pronger, The Arena of Masculinity *(1990)*

Good Games

The Third Gay Games and Cultural Festival, held in Vancouver in August 1990. It was an almost magic time, during which intensely happy, healthy lesbians and gay men came together and delighted in their lives and being together. The mood was often euphoric. In mainstream competitive sports the athletes seldom look this cheerful just before beginning a gruelling event such as the triathlon, but the joyful spirit of the game overwhelmed much of the anxiety of the competition.

from Brian Pronger, The Arena of Masculinity *(1990)*

Cold Confessions

The night the snow storms hit the country last month, 200 people braved a bitterly cold wind to join the London group OutRage in a protest against Clause 25 of the Criminal Justice Bill outside the capital's Bow Street police station. One lesbian and eleven gay men, including the film-maker Derek Jarman, had come to the station to confess to the sex crimes covered by the clause. Bow Street police called a halt after twelve confessions and formal statements. But no charges were pressed and the papers were forwarded to the Crown Prosecution Service.

from Gay Times, *March 1991*

Queer Politics

'We're here! We're queer! Get used to it!' Some of us are quite happy to call ourselves queer. A once-despised word no longer makes us recoil in fear. Indeed it is fast becoming a proud symbol of the angry and assertive New Queer Politics of the 1990s . . . A quarter of a century [after the passage of the 1967 act] . . . thousands of lesbians and gay men are still sacked from their jobs, convicted for consensual sex, beaten-up by queer-bashers, denied custody of their children, and driven to attempt suicide.

The New Queer Politics is about seizing the vocabulary of oppression and transforming it into a language of liberation; appropriating a traditional term of homophobic abuse and redefining it as an expression of pride and defiance. By proclaiming ourselves queer, we subvert the derogatory meaning of the word and undermine its effectiveness as an insult. Responding to taunts with an unexpected 'Yes, I am queer, so what?' deflates the power of the abuse, disarms the abuser, and empowers the intended victim.

Adoption of the Q-word is also a conscious attempt to ditch the politeness of 'gay' in favour of the unpleasantness of 'queer', which reflects more accurately the way we are still perceived and treated by society. Whereas the term 'gay' masks the reality of homophobia, 'queer' forces people to face up to it. 'Queer' is the brutal truth . . . the celebration of sexual diversity . . .

Some think queers should present a respectable image and emphasise that we are just the same, and just as good, as heterosexual men and women. But why should we have to lead blameless lives, or be able to pass as hetero, in order to win equal treatment?

Blurring the distinction between heterosexuals and homosexuals is profoundly dishonest. Queers are not the same as heterosexuals . . . The New Queer Politics rejects the stereotype of queers as victims. Being lesbian or gay is not just an endless story of discrimination and suffering. It has advantages. Compared with most heterosexuals we tend to have a wider range of sexual partners and to be more sexually adventurous. We've adapted better to safer sex. We find intimacy and openness with new partners easier. We generally have a broader network of friendships, which cut across class and race. We're less compulsive about parenthood. We don't need marriage to sustain our relationships. We are likely to stay on friendlier terms with former partners. All these worthwhile aspects make me thankful to be queer . . .

The New Queer Politics looks beyond equality, and challenges the assumption that lesbian and gay desire is an intrinsically minority sexual orientation. It argues that everyone is potentially homosexual (and heterosexual). While some biological factors may predispose individuals to a sexual preference, all the psychological and anthropological evidence suggests that sexuality is primarily culturally conditioned and is not rigidly compartmentalised. None of us is wholly attracted to one sex or another. 'Queer' emancipation is therefore in the interests of heterosexuals too.

Peter Tatchell in the Independent on Sunday, *July 1992*

Sane Crusader

I am aware of the theory that poisonous words can be detoxified if they are defiantly adopted by those who they are intended to insult. Lesbians have been calling themselves dykes for some time now, and many seem happy with the word. But hearing an up-front lesbian calling herself a dyke is a different thing altogether from hearing a hostile heterosexual male calling her the same thing.

I tried many years ago to persuade newspapers to stop using words like 'poof' and 'poofter'; my main purpose in doing this was to draw attention not so much to the words themselves, but to the aggressive contexts in which they were being used. No-one in the straight world seemed to have noticed that homosexuals were being vilified and abused on a daily basis by scummy but powerful newspapers. By making a fuss about the insulting words, I was also drawing attention to the almost unbelievable persecution of which the words were only a part.

People, of course, are entitled to call themselves whatever they like, but if our community does decide to consign the word 'gay' to the scrapheap, I feel we will be throwing away one of our finest achievements. Whatever the members of OutRage or Queer Nation might say, 'gay' has attained a wonderful universality – the terms black gay man or disabled gay man or working-class gay man all have the ring of authenticity. 'Gay' is a word that belongs to us all.

Just because some tyro activist says 'gay is middle-class' doesn't make it so. I think whoever is responsible for such a preposterous idea is fighting a different cause to the rest of us. The more-politically-pure-than-thou brigade should not be allowed to demean our accomplishments.

Terry Saunderson, Mediawatch columnist, Gay Times, May 1991

CHAPTER ELEVEN

The Golden Age?

Out of the homosexual subculture a 'gay community' emerged in the late 1960s and the 1970s. In America there were gay districts in San Francisco and New York, resorts at Fire Island and Key West, and what pundits called the 'pink economy'. Most of the men who supported this economy – what in Britain was called 'the commercial scene' – were interested less in politics than in pleasure. Bathhouses flourished in North America and on the Continent, back rooms were constructed and bars multiplied. All were overshadowed, though, by the creation of the disco, which became the central arena of sexual commerce, in which the sexual actors hunted for their partners to the sound of a distinctive beat that would eventually become HiEnergy. The patrons of the clubs danced; the dancing began during the glorious and revolutionary summer of 1969 and never seemed to stop until some of the dangers of this hedonism began to impinge in the early 1980s.

The club became the centrepiece of a distinctive urban lifestyle for many men under forty-five. For, in spite of all the rhetoric of the gay priests, this was a society in which the only acceptable currency was beauty. A few brave souls who had passed the point of no return tottered in, some in the process becoming club mascots, lamenting to the listeners at the bar the fact that, like sexual intercourse for Philip Larkin, liberation had come 'rather late' for them. Club-owners, who made a mint, could afford to be generous and let in the occasional 'wrinklie' – after all, they would sometimes admit lesbians. Pillars of the pink economy, they needed few lessons in either politics or charity.

That world has now passed, is lost for ever: never glad confident morning again. It is not easy to recapture a world that we have lost. A shadow, a dark shadow, has passed across those years, and it is hard to evoke the crazy decade of the 1970s without the thought of the dancers who met horrible deaths in the years that were to follow.

It is never easy to banish hindsight. Historians try, but it is a largely futile act. In the 1970s the men who sought their own kind were on the verge, it seemed, of the promised land. There were, however, many intimations of disaster, and the gay Jeremiahs filled the pages of their new newspapers and magazines with dark forebodings. In 1977 Seymour Kleinberg, a New York intellectual and gay activist, told those who would listen that they should remember the fate of Warsaw, a Jewish city in 1940 but for not long afterwards.[1] New York might seem to be a gay town, but the Movement had many enemies. Apocalyptic parallels were drawn – many of them, like Kleinberg's, with the Holocaust. They made some anxious about what might follow if the dancing ever stopped. It was this atmosphere that produced Martin Sherman's rather wooden piece of agitprop *Bent*, a much performed drama set in a concentration camp, and often put on as a way for the Movement and its liberal allies publicly to affirm their faith in the gay cause – as well as providing directors with the opportunity of peopling the stage with several scantily clad hunks. There were warnings aplenty. The enemies identified were political and evangelical, never biological.

The dancers assumed (with almost everyone else) that biology had been conquered, that Howard Florey, Alexander Fleming and the scientists had tamed that particular beast. Penicillin was the panacea that would combat all the infections and minor ailments that seemed to punctuate the careers of even the most prudent dancers. It gave the dancer a well-earned (and much needed) rest while the magical tablets lifted the spell, and he could then return to take his place in the dance again. The doctors who warned (and there were some) were ignored. Promiscuity as practised by these urban warriors, they pointed out, could seriously damage health; the human body, tough and resourceful though it is, is most vulnerable in the intimate acts of sex. Those few who heard the doctors scoffed at them as wet blankets animated by some outdated religious creed, who just wanted to spoil the fun for those at the carnival. Who can blame them for their scepticism? The doctors had so often cried wolf before, and nothing cataclysmic had ever happened. What happened, of course, was that the dancers confused morality and biology. It was, for many of them, a fatal confusion.

The homosexual subculture had never been so visible. San Francisco – 'our town' they called it – where self-identified homosexuals were once estimated as a quarter of the total population, became the gay capital of the world, with New York, Sydney and Amsterdam as serious rivals. Armistead Maupin beautifully chronicled this urban paradise, the area around the golden bay, in his tales from the city,[2] an important addition to the homosexual canon.

Few writers captured the mood of the moment as successfully as Edmund White. In fiction and in essays, he celebrated the brave new world ushered in so auspiciously by the rioters in Greenwich Village. In 1980 White produced a travel journal which soon became a historical document. He celebrated the bizarre world that men (from every possible settlement across America, practising every trade and profession imaginable, and descended from almost every possible race and nation) could make without women. The only women were tokens – the sisters in the movement (who were generously allowed by their triumphant brothers occasionally to share their social space) and the 'fag hags'. White does not conceal his wonder and delight at the world that his brothers had made. *States of Desire* he entitled the book; 'Travels in Gay America' was the subtitle. William Burroughs thought that 'we may have found our gay de Tocqueville', while Michael Perkins in *Screw* believed that White had made 'some sense about people and their adjustments to life in a nation that remains staunchly anti-sexual; the 'news is that homosexuality in America is flourishing, despite political setbacks'. That was how things stood in the spring of 1980. The first dancers were already infected with the virus that would soon kill them.

The ubiquitous White even produced a manual, a do-it-yourself guide in the best American tradition, *The Joy of Gay Sex*. The original edition is now a collector's item.

One of the most curious features of the 1970s was what Peter York in an article in *Harpers and Queen* described as 'the masculinisation of the American male'.[3] One of the most visible manifestations of this development was that some men started to dress up in particular costumes far removed from those of their everyday life, but with none of the negative connotations associated with drag. Bankers, lawyers and doctors dressed themselves up as cowboys, construction workers or leather men. The most popular look was undoubtedly what was called the 'clone look', in which the man wore his hair close-cropped but compensated for this by plenty of facial hair. Moustaches and beards became tremendously popular. Such a look could be worn with a variety of macho outfits, though jeans and boots were usually essential. It all added to the gaiety of nations, but it was odd to see a man wearing the uniform of the clone attacking the process of social stereotyping. The clone look had the great advantage that it allowed the older dancers to make the transition to their thirties, and even early forties, with dignity. They could remain in season for a much longer period of time – or, as Edmund White prefers, 'hot' for much longer.

An Invitation

Sodomy, fellatio, cunnilingus, pederasty,
Father, why do these words sound so nasty?
Masturbation can be fun,
Join the orgy everyone.

from Gerome Ragni and James Rado's lyrics for the musical Hair *(1968)*

Busy

I knew one guy who worked for a Wall Street law firm – he'd come home have his 'disco nap' until 11 o'clock then he'd go out until about five in the morning, have another nap, then get his suit on and go to work. And that was all he did.

Susan Sontag, 1991

An American Lifestyle before the Plague: Michael Tolliver's Dirty Thirty Valentine's Resolutions for 1977

1. I will not call anyone nellie or butch, unless that is his name.
2. I will not assume that women who like me are fag hags.
3. I will stop expecting to meet Jan-Michael Vincent at the tubs.
4. I will inhale poppers only through the mouth.
5. I will not spend more than half an hour in the shower at the Y.
6. I will stop trying to figure out what color my handkerchief would be if I wore one.
7. I will buy a drink for a Fifties Queen sometime.
8. I will not persist in hoping that attractive men will turn out to be brainless and boring.
9. I will sign my real name at The Glory Holes.
10. I will ease back into religion by attending concerts at Grace Cathedral.
11. I will not cruise at Grace Cathedral.
12. I will not vote for *anyone* for Empress.
13. I will make friends with a straight man.
14. I will not make fun of the way he walks.
15. I will not tell him about Alexander the Great, Walt Whitman or Leonardo da Vinci.
16. I will not vote for politicians who use the term 'Gay Community'.
17. I will not cry when Mary Tyler Moore goes off the air.
18. I will not measure it, no matter who asks.
19. I will not hide the A-200.
20. I will not buy a Lacoste shirt, a Marimekko pillow, a second-hand letterman's jacket, an All-American Boy T-shirt, a razor blade necklace or a denim accessory of any kind.
21. I will learn to eat alone and like it.
22. I will not fantasize about firemen.
23. I will not tell anyone at home that I just haven't found the right girl yet.

24. I will wear a suit on Castro Street and feel comfortable about it.
25. I will not do impressions of Bette Davis, Tallulah Bankhead, Mae West or Paul Lynde.
26. I will not eat more than one It's-It in a single evening.
27. I will find myself acceptable.
28. I will meet somebody nice, away from a bar or the tubs or a roller-skating rink, and I will fall hopelessly but conventionally in love.
29. But I won't say I love you before he does.
30. The hell I won't.

from Armistead Maupin, More Tales of the City *(1980)*

Stylised

If you take a New York or San Francisco or Houston man who looks gay and lives a gay life and you strip away the accoutrements, you have just an ordinary man. It's all been put in, it's all styled on top; all surface — the man's haircut, clothing, where he goes dancing, the choice of drugs he takes, and what he will try out in bed.

from an interview with Felice Picano in The View from Christopher Street, *ed. M. Denneny, C. Ortleb and T. Steele (1984)*

More Thoughtful

The nature of gay life is that it is philosophical. Like Nietzsche, though in a different sense, we could speak of 'gay science', that obligatory existentialism forced on people who must invent themselves . . . Once one discovers one is gay one must choose everything, from how to walk, dress and talk to where to live, with whom and on what terms.

from Edmund White, States of Desire: Travels in Gay America *(1980)*

Vanity

The desire to make a good appearance, of course, is typical of singles everywhere, whether straight or gay. Vanity, alas, is less characteristic of couples of either variety. Domestic bliss usually creates an eyesore.

from Edmund White, States of Desire: Travels in Gay America *(1980)*

Life in the Ghetto

The really horrible thing about the phenomenon of present-day homosexuality . . . is that today's unlucky deviate can only save himself by the most tremendous exertion of all his forces from falling into an underworld in which he never meets either men or women, where it is impossible to have either a lover or a friend, where the possibility of genuine human involvement has altogether ceased. When this possibility has ceased, so has the possibility of growth.

James Baldwin

Rates of Exchange

The gay world in America, at least, is the only classless society, although its
egalitarianism is hardly utopian. What replaces money and education as the
basis of privilege is youth and beauty, two more fragile commodities. It would be
nice but stupid to say that these values are almost universally accepted by gay
men and women because their society is materialistic or shallow. It is true that
the obsession with youth and beauty is excessively American but the fact that
gays unquestionably accept and identify with these values is undeniably part of
their history.

from Seymour Kleinberg, The Other Persuasion *(1977)*

Advice from San Francisco

Cruising, he had long ago decided, was a lot like hitchhiking. It was best to dress
like the person you wanted to pick up.

from Armistead Maupin, Tales of the City *(1978)*

A Way of Life

'Do you ever get bored of all this?'

'The nursery you mean?'

'No, being gay.'

Ned smiled. 'What do you think?'

'I don't mean being homosexual,' said Michael. 'I wouldn't change that for
anything. I love men.'

'I've noticed.'

'I guess I'm talking about the culture.'

Michael continued. 'The Galleria parties. The T-shirts with come-fuck-me
slogans. The fourteen different shades of jockstraps and those goddam mirrored
sunglasses that toss your face back at you when you walk into a bar. Phony
soldiers and phony policemen and phony jocks. Hot this, hot that. I'm sick of it,
Ned. There has gotta be another way of being queer . . .'

'. . . nobody's *making* you go to the gym, Mouse. Nobody's making you act
butch. If you wanna be an effete poet and pine away in a garret or something
you're free to do it . . .'

'It's just so fucking packaged,' said Michael. 'A kid comes here from Sioux
Falls or wherever, and he buys his uniform at All-American Boy, and he teaches
himself how to stand just so in a dark corner in the Badlands, and his life is all
posturing and attitude and fast-food sex. It's too easy. The mystery is gone.'

from Armistead Maupin, Further Tales of the City *(1982)*

Hot

Perhaps no other word so aptly signals the new gay attitude as *hot*. Whereas *beautiful* in gay parlance characterizes the face first and the body only secondarily, *hot* describes the whole man, but especially his physique. One may have a lantern jaw or an asymmetrical nose or pockmarked skin and still be 'hot', whereas the signs of the 'beautiful' face are regular features, smooth skin, suave colouring – and youth. The 'hot' man may even fail to have an attractive body; his appeal may lie instead in his wardrobe, his manner, his style. In this way 'hotness' is roughly equivalent to 'presence' with an accent on the sexy rather than the magisterial sense of that word. In addition, 'hot' can, like the Italian *simpatico*, modify everything from people to discos, from cars to clothing. Gay chartered cruises promise a 'hot' vacation and designers strive after a 'hot' look.

from Edmund White, 'The Political Vocabulary of Homosexuality' in The State of the Language, ed. Leonard Michaels and Christopher Ricks (1980)

Inferno

They seem to live in a modern-day inferno, where they despise their own ageing flesh, where they inflict ceaseless physical and psychological harm on themselves and one another, all in the name of happiness.

Paul Cowan, writer, reviewing States of Desire in the New York Times, 3 February 1980

A Critical Thought

Do they really think that because we're gay, young, and urban we don't have the same need for fidelity and intimacy that any other human beings do? When sex is as easy to get as a burger at McDonalds, it ain't too mysterious or marvellous, believe me.

Andrew Holleran in The View from Christopher Street, ed. M. Denneny, C. Ortleb and T. Steele (1984)

Without Foundations

Most heterosexual relationships are built by, first of all, the meeting relating to the reality of one another. Next comes seeing the person again, getting to know the person. You go through all these levels, until finally it has grown into a relationship that, in order to find a greater closeness, moves into the beautiful sexual areas. You stay together the night, you make it, and next day you explore all the levels of the relationship you've already built up. The base is there. In the gay world, we begin by mumbling a few words to each other, if that. Suddenly we're making sex. Then we just as suddenly split to the next person. You see, we've begun with the intimacy without ever having gone through any tenderness or gentleness. I think this is the reason why so few lasting homosexual relationships exist.

from an interview with John Rechy in Gay News, *1976*

Buying the Christmas Tree

'Do you believe in marriage, Mary Ann?'

She nodded. 'Most of the time.'

'Me too. I think about it everytime I see a new face. I got married four times today on the 41 Union bus.'

There was an embarrassment in Mary Ann's laugh.

'I know,' said Michael unaccusingly. 'A bunch of fairies in caftans, tripping through Golden Gate Park with drag bridesmaids and quotations from "Song of the Loon" . . . That's not what I mean.'

'I know.'

'It would be like . . . friends, someone to buy a Christmas tree with.'

from Armistead Maupin, Tales of the City *(1978)*

The Perfect Match

[Reverend] Troy Perry [founder of a church, the Metropolitan Community Church, that catered almost entirely for gay Christians] . . . has been married twice. First time around it was at the age of 19 to the attractive blonde daughter of a Pentecostal minister.

He says: 'I came from the south of the USA, and there the attitude was get yourself a good girl, and that will sort you out if you thought you were gay. It doesn't work.'

The marriage split up when he told her he was gay and she got a court order to stop him seeing their children, both of them boys.

His second marriage was in January this year [1972] to a Roller Derby star, Steve Jorck. Troy describes him: 'He's just 5 ft 8ins tall, 23, Mexican American and beautiful. We are very happy.'

from Gay News, *1973*

A Sad Condition

I have been told by lots of acquaintances that quite a lot of youngsters prefer older men for company, but whilst I am not senile! (just over 40) I have tried unsuccessfully by means of ads, visits to pubs (which I am not very fond of), joining CHE, rather boring at times, without success. I wouldn't say I was ugly but as far as I can see most youngsters prefer people their own age or thereabouts and I am not blaming them, however unfortunately I am one of those gays who are much happier in young people's company, provided they are genuine and not making it obvious that they are tolerating one for their generosity or what they can get out of them.

Charles G. Brown in Gay News, *1973*

Mean Streets

What is autobiographical in the film [Terence Davies's *Madonna and Child*], and what I think is true, and this I will defend because I believe it passionately, is the implication behind it: what do you do if you're not good looking, you haven't got a good body? What do you do then? There are a lot of very, very miserable gay men around for that very reason. Because life on the gay scene seems to be totally based on what you look like. I mean, when I first moved near *The Bacon Factory* two years ago, I went to the *London Apprentice* twice – twice is enough! I mean, that relentless brutal cruelty – the way they cruise and look at one another and then just walk away – it's inhuman. You think, how can they do that to one another?! Because surely we should stick together – in a sense say, look we shouldn't do that. But everybody tacitly agrees to it by collusion. And everyone rails against it, but doesn't do anything about it . . . I'm not good looking, I haven't got a good body. You are miserable. And most of the time you are lonely. And I think that that is what is true about [his] film trilogy too.

from an interview with Terence Davies in Him, *no. 74*

Murderous Thoughts

I was left with an endless search through the soul-destroying pub scene and its resulting one-night stands . . . passing faces and bodies, the unfulfilled tokens of an empty life. A house is not a home and sex is not a relationship. We would only lend each other our bodies in a vain search for inner peace.

confession of Dennis Nilsen, mass-murderer, from Brian Masters, Killing for Company *(1985)*

MCC

. . . in its very early days the Metropolitan Community Church London had to contend with an influx of gays who looked upon it simply as an extension of the gay scene as a whole, a place to which so many came simply to pick up young trade and take them to bed. I am not moralising. I am simply stating as a fact that such was not the purpose of MCC's existence. One of the greatest mistakes made about MCC London (and made by all sections of society who have heard about us), is in thinking we are a gay church. This is simply not true, and has never been so. We are first and foremost a Christian church, one whose majority of members and attenders happen to be gay.

from Gay News, *February 1977*

Saving the President

A disabled former Marine who said his life was ruined after he thwarted the possible assassination of President Gerald R. Ford in 1975 has been found dead in his apartment . . . Oliver W. Sipple, 47, died of natural causes . . . Sipple, who was wounded in Vietnam, was in the crowd outside San Francisco's St. Francis Hotel on September 27, 1975, as Ford emerged . . . Sipple saw Sara Jane Moore's outstretched hand holding a chrome revolver aimed at the President.

A shot was fired that missed Ford, apparently because of Sipple's deflection . . . Sipple, who was retired from the Marines on full disability pension, received a letter from Ford expressing 'heartfelt appreciation' for his actions.

Less than a week later, as the media thronged about him, it was reported that Sipple was a homosexual.

His attorney John E. Wahl filed a $15 million invasion of privacy suit against seven major newspapers . . . The suit alleged that Sipple's relatives stopped speaking to him and that he was exposed to contempt, ridicule and humiliation.

San Francisco Superior Court Judge, Ira Brown, dismissed the suit and his ruling was upheld on appeal.

'They decided against him wrongly I think,' Wahl said . . . 'They said that because he had thrust himself in the limelight by saving the President's life he became a public figure.'

from the Los Angeles Times, *6 February 1989*

Public and Private

Only fifty or sixty selected journalists, all issued with personalized passes, were permitted to attend the press conference at the National Liberal Club at which Jeremy Thorpe intended to make a final and definitive statement to end speculation about his relationship with Norman Scott . . .

After the nine-minute statement was over, a BBC reporter Keith Graves was one of the first with a question.

'The whole of this hinges on your private life. It is necessary to ask you if you had a homosexual relationship.'

The question infuriated Marion Thorpe. 'Stand up and say it again,' she almost shouted at Graves. Twice she challenged Graves to repeat his question. Graves did.

It was the turn of Jeremy Thorpe's lawyer John Montgomerie to intervene: 'I cannot allow Mr Thorpe to answer that question. I do not propose to say why. If you do not know why it is improper and indecent to put such a question to a public man you ought not to be here.'

Keith Graves registered a protest. The press conference had been called to clear up allegations that had been made about Mr Thorpe's behaviour. The main allegation was of Mr Thorpe's homosexuality . . .

Robin Day asked why, having denied both a homosexual relationship with Norman Scott and any involvement in a plot to murder him, Mr Thorpe had not sued for libel. Mr Thorpe replied ' . . . the best thing to do is to wait until the cataract of innuendoes and accusations is concluded and then the position will be considered.' He was not a 'suer' he said.

from Gay News, *November 1977*

Muscle Men

Of course many bodybuilders are gay. I love the muscular aspect of myself. Yet, in effect, though different, it's similar in reversed purpose to drag. It's the opposite side but from almost the same source. The queen protects herself by dressing in women's clothes and the bodybuilder protects himself in muscles — so-called 'men's clothes'.

from an interview with John Rechy in Gay Sunshine, *1978*

Coming

Pumping iron is like coming, but coming continuously.

US bodybuilder Arnold Schwarzenegger in the film Pumping Iron *(1977)*

Decadent Exercise

Homosexuality and mental derangement are being caused by the growing cult of bodybuilding the official government sports committee newspaper *Sovetzky Sport* has claimed. In a vehement attack on the growing number of eager Soviet bodybuilders, the newspaper condemned bodybuilding as capitalist-influenced and socially harmful. The government sports committee has consistently refused to acknowledge bodybuilding as a sport, but the public attack on bodybuilders is thought to result from official alarm at the growth of private clubs in premises obtained by illegal deals with local housing officials, which sports officials claim exploit 'weak-minded adolescents' for profit . . . *Sovetzky Sport* reported that homosexuality is being practised by devotees who are introduced to bodybuilding through the 'no questions asked' cellar clubs which supply young enthusiasts with pictures of 'Mr America', 'Mr Universe' and American pornographic pictures. Bodybuilding also leads young Russians to neglect their studies, to bully their fellow workers, and even to commit murder.

from Gay News, *October 1977*

Midnight Express

The emotional coldness of prison life was worse than the physical cold. Loneliness is an aching pain. It hurts all over. You can't isolate it in one part of your body.

The weekly bath came to mean more to me than just washing and hot water. It meant a chance to touch another human being. To be touched. I soaped the muscles of Arne's shoulders with my hands. He washed my back. It seemed strange that I was enjoying the touch of a man's hands on my body. I never had before. This wasn't supposed to be right.

Then why did it feel right?

We began to give each other massages in the evening. I'd take off my T-shirt and stretch out across Arne's bed. He had hung a sheet down from my bunk above for privacy. Arne's long fingers felt good kneading the tired muscles of my back and shoulders. I liked the human warmth of his hands on my back. He was Swedish, and he knew how to give a massage. He handled my body like he handled his guitar. Gentle strength. Easy rhythm.

Some days the pressure of prison was so great I thought I'd burst inside. I lay on Arne's bed after just such a day. He knew how I felt. My head was turned to the side. My eyes were closed.

His hands stopped moving.

'Willie?' he questioned.

I opened my eyes. A long erection stood up out of his shorts.

I rolled over on my back. He held me in his hands and lowered himself on to the bed.

'It's all right, Willie. It's only love,' he said.

from Billy Hayes and William Hoffer, Midnight Express *(1977)*

Shoot

Defence Under-Secretary Robert Brown has told the Commons that pictures of serving guardsmen appearing in *Him* magazine would be the subject of an army investigation.

Guardsmen pictured in uniform and underwear would be questioned by the Army's Special Investigation Branch. The Branch would also be investigating further allegations that one of the men photoed was responsible for running a gay procurement service, supplying young troopers and NCO's to gay clients. The story was first broken by the *Daily Mirror* which devoted almost the whole of its front cover to the publication of the photos in *Him*. Two days later it returned to the fight with charges that a call-boy service operated in the Life Guards regiment of the Household Cavalry. The man who ran the service, says the paper, was Corporal Tom Pitman. Pitman himself has dismissed the suggestion as ridiculous.

If the *Mirror* charges have caused anxiety amongst members of the establishment who are alleged to have made use of the young soldiers, the story has been greeted with amusement in other places.

from Gay News, *November 1975*

Soldiers

The accused were slight and young and pale-faced and charged with gross indecency with each other . . . They are both 22 and single and look as though they haven't started shaving yet . . . one serving with weapons intelligence, the other on 'close protective duties', his last duty in Northern Ireland that of bodyguard to the UDR's commanding officer. Both are corporals and have been in the army since they were 16 and 17. The red-haired one is from London and the blond from Glasgow . . . their own counsel describes it as 'a strange case'. They are charged with gross indecency on three occasions in Belfast, Glasgow and London . . . On the first day of the case the prosecution explained that their defence to the indecency charges was that they had fabricated a homosexual relationship to get out of the army in a hurry; because they had become disillusioned with service life in Northern Ireland . . . But the prosecuting officer . . . scorns their story in his summing up. He points out that letters suggesting a homosexual affair were only discovered in the red-haired corporal's lodgings during an investigation into improperly-held ammunition . . . He then made statements to the Special Investigation Branch admitting an affair, and detailed three occasions when indecency had taken place . . . A similar statement had come from the other corporal.

The letters had been enough to suggest a relationship . . . he read excerpts. They were sentimental young-love letters . . . Both young accused faces stayed pale and expressionless . . . [They were both found guilty.] . . . Both were dismissed from the service, directed to be placed in detention for 56 days and reduced to the ranks.

Fionuala O'Connor in the Irish Times, *July 1980*

Abbreviations from the Classified Section of the *Advocate*

B&D   = Bondage and Discipline
S/M   = Sadomasochist
Ms   = Masochist
clean   = circumcised
Gr act = Greek active; i.e. anal insertor
Gr pas = Greek passive; i.e. anal receptor
Fr act = French active; i.e. oral insertor
Fr pas = French passive; i.e. oral receptor

lt S/M   = light (mild) sadomasochism
W/S   = water sports; i.e. urinating
J/O   = jack-off; masturbation
FF   = Fist Fucking
Lv's   = Levi's including denim and cords
fone frk = phone freak; i.e. dirty talk
gdlk   = good-looking; i.e. godlike
LIAHO   = Let it All Hang Out

compiled by Rictor Norton in Gay News, *April 1975*

Getting in Touch

At twenty, I finally realized I was homosexual and I wanted to have sex with somebody. I knew I had to do something about it. The opportunity came up one day when I went to see *Something for Everyone*, a film which involved Michael York in all sorts of sexual activities. The audience was liberally sprinkled with gay guys (I was with a straight friend). Soon a guy next to me touched me – no big deal, it was crowded. I wasn't even aware of him, at first. Then he started running his hand over my foot, and into my shoe. Well, I had never had my foot fondled by another guy before, besides which I was with a straight friend who thought I was straight as well, so what could I do? I was so petrified, I was afraid to even look at the guy. Finally, my friend looked over and noticed what was going on. I must have given him a totally helpless look, because he chased the guy away for me.

All the way home I felt miserable. Here was my opportunity, and I blew it. As a joke, I said 'Now I understand those ads in the *Village Voice* that read "Will the guy who fondled my foot at the Elgin last night please call . . . " ' But it wasn't a joke to me. That's exactly what I wanted to do. The idea obsessed me. So I did it.

The next week was a nightmare. The phone rang at any hour of the day or night. (God was I stupid and naive. I really thought that only the guy would call, and that he would call at the time specified in the ad). Fortunately my family bought the story the ad was a misprint, which a very nice girl at the *Voice* agreed to tell them. (This sounds so dumb, but it really seemed like a good idea at the time.)

During the day, home alone, I was answering the calls hoping to find my fondler. But after three calls I realized this wasn't going to happen. Half of the guys who called thought they'd be getting a girl. But I finally got one guy who sounded sane and nice. I knew after a few sentences that he wasn't the guy at the theatre, but he seemed normal enough, and this was the best chance I figured I'd get from this fiasco, so I agreed to come over to his place. He was very kind to me and patient with me, and he taught me everything I know.

from James Spada, The Spada Report *(1979)*

Explanations

I've been a hustler in the past, and can give several reasons for being one.

A. As a penniless artist it was a way of eating.
B. I was exploring my feelings or hang-ups about prostitution.
C. I was meeting the needs of certain people.
D. It was more honest than most gay-one-night-sex-games, played in the name of love.

from Gay News, 1973

Numbers

. . . hustling is linked to narcissism and being paid is proof that one is very strongly desired and desirable. So is the 'numbers' trip: a lot of people digging me. (I'm not talking about an orgy situation. That's fine if I am the *absolute* centre of the orgy, which I usually am. But if people start getting interested in each other, then I split. I can't *stand* it, but that doesn't often happen.) The numbers trip: I was estimating a while ago that I'd been with at least seven thousand people . . . [I'm] aiming for ten thousand . . . sometimes I feel only despair about the whole promiscuous scene. It has nothing to do with morality. All I know is that sometimes when I come back home very late – maybe the sun is coming out and I don't know what I've been looking for all night and into the morning – and the only thought that I have in my mind is to gobble down a lot of sleeping tablets and die . . . although I may never kill myself the concept of suicide is a very real one with me . . . Granted I may never kill myself but simply the idea of doing it has moulded my life. (I guess a contradiction of that is working out with weights. The only thing that has any continuity for me is making my body more and more muscular.)

from an interview with John Rechy in Gay News, December 1975

Pin-ups

On the whole, the assumptions behind homosexual pin-ups are not very different from heterosexual ones. One favourite type is the slim and delicate adolescent, sometimes hardly into puberty, who is posed in different ways, like any playmate, to emphasize his buttocks or his legs or his provocative face. But there is always the reassuring bonus, the large and prominently displayed penis (Mark Gabor claims in his *History of the Pin-up* that male models sometimes masturbate just before photo sessions, then hold the penis down with an invisible string so that it appears enviably large in a relaxed state). There is a long tradition, sanctified by art, of passive but provocative poses for the female nude. The boys, on the other hand, inevitably appear rather self-conscious; they often hover between an easy nonchalance, a determined seductiveness, and an aggressive look-what-I've-got stance . . . The other favourite type is of course the superstud, and whole magazines are straightforward celebrations of virility . . . The he-man is shown bursting out of his jeans, or stomping around in nothing but boots and leather jacket.

from Margaret Walters, The Nude Male (1978)

Kip

Kip Noll has freshfaced blond good looks . . . His photos are bestsellers in gay bookshops all over the world . . . he has been doing porno since he was 19 – he is now 24 – but he still works as a machinist in San Diego and hopes to complete his apprenticeship. 'It would be something to fall back on; as I'm a pretty good handyman.' On the other hand he'd rather be a fashion model or do television commercials. He has six brothers and sisters and his family all know what he's doing and support it. 'I didn't get on with my parents so well till I started making movies,' he says. 'Then I became happier and more relaxed, and found I got on with them better. One day my mother asked me what I was doing, I told her, and she asked me if I felt I was doing it well. I said yes, and she said in this case she would always support me.' Kip adds that his mother hasn't seen any of his movies. He thinks they might upset her but he intends to show her some of his magazine pictures. 'My girlfriend – I'm bisexual – doesn't know what I'm doing yet, but I'm going to tell her. She won't mind, she always supports whatever I do.'

Oleg Kamensky in Gay News, November 1980

A Favourable Report

Both films displayed extremely pretty young men, copious amounts of masturbation, detailed accounts of fellatio and the occasional anal penetration. My favourite episode (which was from *Sex Garage*) involved a comely young stud in a shower-bath masturbating, whilst the sound track issued *Jesu, Joy of Man's Desire* in the piano transcription of the late Dame Myra Hess.

Elsewhere the bodies were all attractive and the activity which the bodies performed caused me to feel wistful and just slightly covetous.

from a review of two films directed by Fred Halstead, Gay News, June 1973

Satisfying his Public

All Peter [de Rome's] films feature orgasm. He is quite adamant about this: 'It's just a little idiosyncrasy I have, I think audiences feel cheated if they don't see an orgasm. Personally I like to see a lot of it.' Doesn't this present problems for the porno actor who can't produce a large volume of semen? No problems, says Peter: 'We just use flour and water or I shoot it from about three different angles so that it looks more than it is.'

from Gay News, November 1976

Homecoming Queen

The plots of many gay pornographic stories, novels and films are erected around the notion that frustration can push even the most hardened heterosexual towards homosexuality if his girlfriend says no too often: the apparently straight guy whose girlfriend refuses his invitations to sex. In one Californian video of 1979 entitled The Idol, in which the action takes place on an American college football team, young Gerry (the idol of the title) reveals his frustration to a team-mate. Gerry's girlfriend is too nice a girl; she won't sleep with the hunk.

FRIEND: Why don't you let one of the boys get you off?
GERRY: You're out of your head – you know I'm not into that scene.
FRIEND: Nobody's asking you to switch: all you do is get your rocks off. You should see what goes on in the locker room. Half of the guys aren't there to make the team; they're there to *make* the team – get it?

Gerry ends up hooked; smitten, he falls for one of his team-mates. On the last line of the video he faces the camera and smiles. 'Joe College', he says, 'becomes Homecoming Queen.'

dialogue from The Idol (1979)

Catholicism

It is so wrapped up in symbolism, and indeed drag, the priests in their robes, the colourful saints, the beautiful cathedrals. I think stylistically it made my writing very elaborate, filled it with metaphors and symbolism. Beyond that my books are formed around the theme of confession.

from an interview with John Rechy in Gay News, December 1974

Fun

It's fun to stay at the YMCA
They have everything there for young men to enjoy
You can hang out with all the boys

lyrics from 'YMCA' by Village People (1979)

False Impressions

We never have been openly gay. I don't know where the press got that one from. The Village People fought the press on that one from Day One. We've never come out and made a statement that we're gay. Never, ever. Some of the songs have pretty obvious words, but YMCA is used at every kid's party; lots of those kids under High School age have no idea what those words mean. I don't know why people think we're blatantly gay because it's never been presented in that way . . . Our Las Vegas show, which sells out consistently, it's all women screaming and carrying on. And they really don't know. They don't catch on.

Mark (the construction worker) of Village People, in Gay Times, March 1985

Judicial Opinion

Cases such as these are all the more grave in these days because, some years ago, Parliament committed itself to pass a Buggers' Charter which enabled perverts and homosexuals to pursue their perversions in private if their partners are over 21.

Justice Melford Stevenson during a trial in 1978

Wishful Thinking

An 18-year-old labourer has been sent to Borstal for sexual offences involving young boys. The court heard that the defendant had lured a young boy to a lonely barn, trussed him up like a chicken, and sexually assaulted him before leaving him there overnight. Passing sentence at Lewes Crown Court, Mr Justice Eveleigh commented: 'I would have liked to have given you a taste of your own medicine.'

from Gay News, January 1976

The Enemy Within

A Glasgow reader of *The Guardian* was upset to read a news story in the paper under the headline 'Airmen in vice enquiry'. The 'vice' in question turned out to be homosexuality.

But Gurney Buxton, the offended reader, was even more upset when he wrote to complain of homosexuality being described as a vice. 'With respect,' wrote Executive Editor John Ryan, 'a great many people including myself would think that it was a vice. That is not to say that *The Guardian* should not show sympathy and understanding to those afflicted.'

from Gay News, July 1976

Sex on the Rates

To ask ratepayers to subsidise homosexuals is like asking them to subsidise prostitutes or negroes or Jews . . . [should we] saddle ourselves with giving aid and comfort to people who, rightly or wrongly, they may strongly disapprove of?

Lord Arran, March 1975

Brutal

Lay one finger on my little son's innocent mind – not to mention his hopefully heterosexual body – and I'll tear the lovely lot of you limb from lily-white limb.

Jean Rook in the Daily Express, May 1974

Help

Ms Elsie Donaldson of Woking wants local homosexuals to call at her home and confess their 'sinful' practices. Ms Donaldson, in her fifties and one of the Festival of Light brood, is to clear-up single-handed the notorious 'serious homosexual problem' in Woking. The way the scheme operates is as follows: 'When a homosexual feels the urge to commit indecency I want him to phone me. I will give him a sympathetic hearing and will try to dissuade him from indulging in sinful activity.'

The plan sprang to mind after Ms Donaldson conducted a survey of public morals in Woking. 'There are a lot of homosexuals in Woking. I know this from conversations I've had with people in the streets of the town and on the buses. It is a serious problem and is getting worse every day . . .'

Ms Donaldson is calling her crusade 'Homosexuals Anonymous' . . . 'My telephone service will be confidential. I will help them all I can. I want them to talk about their problems in the hope that they will get their feelings out of their system.'

Asked about Woking's 'serious homosexual problem', Supt John Green, deputy chief of Woking police, told the *Cobham and Windlesham News and Mail* that last year there had been no cases of buggery or gross 'indecency' in the area, but there had been one case of attempted buggery.

from Gay News, February 1976

The Opinions of a Public Servant

You know what I'd do to the homosexuals who pollute our lovely countryside with their presence? . . . I'd put the Edinburgh Corporation police dogs on half rations for a week – make them right vicious – and then you know what I'd do . . . I'd set them loose and let them sink their fangs into those nancy boys up there; make right mincemeat out of them they would . . . I said as much in the Council Chamber . . . It's not a disease you know its – filth . . . They're like all those alcoholics and drug addicts who never do an honest day's work in their life – they contribute nothing to the life of the Nation . . . They should all be bloody well burnt. Hitler may have had his faults . . . if they must have sexual outlet they can always get it for five shillings from a woman in the streets . . . It spreads you see. We have to stop it spreading to the schools – we have to protect our children . . . We have millions and millions of good youth. We must protect them from filth . . . I'd put them to real hard work on the roads. Or in the Army. To make men of them. National Service will come back when we're in the Common Market. I'd put them to marching all day. In my six years in the Army, I never once came across a homosexual. You're too tired for sex in the barrack room. You just want to get into bed . . . I'm a family man and I've been 25 years in the public service . . . The great thing about service in local government is that you learn to give not take . . . I'd like to be an MP. The trouble is, every party is agin me. I speak too straight for them. But many people do share my views . . . it's the opinion of millions.

from an interview with Edinburgh City Councillor Kidd in Gay News, *1973*

Niggerdom

[If my sons were gay] I should know them condemned to a permanent niggerdom among men, their lives, whatever adjustment they might make to their condition, to be lived as part of the pain of the earth.

Joseph Epstein in Harper's, *1970*

A Pattern

That Auden and Burgess were both homosexuals clearly had something, perhaps everything, to do with their need 'completely and finally to rebel against England' . . . homosexuality represented to these young men of the English upper class . . . the refusal of fatherhood and all that fatherhood entailed: responsibility for a family and therefore an inescapable implication in the destiny of society as a whole . . . The list of these young men is almost endless, ranging from the dandies and aesthetes of the Twenties like Brian Howard and Harold Acton, to expatriate writers of the Thirties like Auden and Isherwood, to Soviet agents like Burgess and Maclean. It was through their writings, their political activities, and the way of life that they followed that an indispensable element was added to the antidemocratic pacificism of the interwar ethos: a generalized contempt for middle-class or indeed any kind of heterosexual adult life . . . Anyone familiar with homosexual apologetics in America will recognize these attitudes. Suitably updated and altered to contemporary American realities, they are purveyed by such openly homosexual writers as Allen Ginsberg, James Baldwin, and Gore Vidal – not to mention a host of less distinguished publicists – in whose work we find the same combination of pacificism (with Vietnam naturally standing in for World War I), hostility to one's country and its putatively dreary middle-class way of life, and derision of the idea that it stands for anything worth defending or that it is threatened by anything but its stupidity and wickedness . . . the Soviet Union [is today] the most powerful of all the Communist states, it is by that very fact the most dangerous enemy of liberty, democracy and human rights on the face of the earth . . . the democratic world is under siege, the conviction that it is worth defending, and the understanding that American power is indispensable to its defence . . . the parallels with England in 1937 are here, and this revival of the culture of appeasement ought to be troubling our sleep.

from Norman Podhoretz, 'The Culture of Appeasement', in Harper's, *October 1977*

Opinions

The following were among the responses to a 1975 NOP survey of people's opinions on the causes of homosexuality.

A result of inbreeding amongst the upper classes.
female respondent

The middle class mostly. Their ideas are always avant-garde and forward-thinking. They are mostly well-educated and have learned to see two sides to a question. The working class are more puritanical.
male respondent

Could be a class thing. I don't think working-class people would tolerate behaviour like that. They would knock it out of their sons if they showed any tendency that way.
male respondent

I don't think the young ones are so much affected as the older ones. Perhaps they've had an unsatisfactory life in some way or been rejected in some way.
female respondent

I think it's an older man's game. I should think a younger man is satisfied with his wife, and when her charm fades he turns elsewhere.
male respondent

Careless Talk

I have a teenage boy of 15 and they know more about these things than we do. The way I look at it, you talk about anything and you encourage it . . .
comment from a Conservative council candidate in Preston, reported in Gay News, May 1973

Save the Children

. . . recruitment of children is absolutely necessary for the survival and growth of homosexuality – for since homosexuals cannot reproduce, they must recruit, must freshen their ranks.
Anita Bryant in the Miami Herald, 20 March 1977

Drawing the Line

It's been a great day for the country. A line has at last been drawn.
Mary Whitehouse in the Guardian, *after the 1977 blasphemy trial in which she successfully brought a suit against Gay News for publishing a poem by James Kirkup that she persuaded the court was blasphemous*

Handicapped

I am not being insulting when I refer to you as handicapped.
    Lord Longford, December 1979

God Bless America

I think that at the moment gays must remain alienated, a group which maintains its distance from society; it must repudiate society and to some extent hate it. But while gays have to reject society, at the same time the only thing that they can actually hope for is to achieve a sort of social space where they can come together in groups like in the United States.
    from Jean-Paul Sartre's last interview, Gai Pied, 1980

Beware

If New York sometimes seems to be entirely gay, that is a comforting illusion: Warsaw looked very Jewish in 1940. Most gays in America do not live in New York or San Francisco, and though most live in cities, Los Angeles and Washington and Chicago still insist that their lives be covert. In New York, where life is overt or covert by choice, the establishment's revenge is expressed by repeated failure to pass a simple, constitutionally guaranteed civil-liberties bill specifically protecting gays from prejudice in housing and employment.
    from Seymour Kleinberg, The Other Persuasion (1977)

Public Warning

This sort of thing happened in Sodom and Gomorrah and it was wiped out. The same thing happened in Babylon, the Roman Empire and Ancient Greece. I fear for this country . . . We will slip so far into degradation that there will be a judgement of some kind.
    a vicar from Accrington reacting to the opening of a gay night at a nightclub in Blackburn in November 1980

CHAPTER TWELVE

Show Business

Few industries have the power to influence social attitudes and shape human identity as much as 'the entertainment industry', which has grown to occupy such a dominant position in modern culture. Films, for example, can reach millions of viewers across the planet. The profits of the entertainment industry can be immense, the level of the fame for the performers on a scale that had never before the twentieth century been imagined.

As a consequence, the moralists have always made this industry a special target. Studies have been commissioned and publicised that show the relationship between the industry and various aspects of social behaviour. Invariably such studies have demonstrated the often pernicious impact of the entertainment media. Such reports often rest on an idealised vision of the past, a society which has now passed, when folk were more industrious, more deferential, much more responsible, less violent and certainly not as foul-mouthed as they are today. Unfortunately such a society (which would in any case be rather dull) is difficult to find. A social historian might, after reading about the past, be driven to the conclusion that the rot really started when Adam and Eve left the Garden of Eden. Past societies often look more respectable because we did not have to live in them. Some moralists speak approvingly of the Victorians, but much of the historical effort of the last fifty years has smashed the rather cosy and sentimental views that once surrounded that society. It is difficult in any case to measure human behaviour and plot it on a graph like the profits of a business. This does not stop the moralists thundering away about all their pet hates – whether heavy-metal lyrics played backwards or the sexual antics of Madonna – in the process making the entertainers concerned seem more subversive than they really are, and also more attractive to their fans. Modern culture provides all sorts of groups with the opportunity to witness to their beliefs through condemnation; it is their way of waving their banner and drawing attention to their point of view. What impact it has is hard to say.

In the twentieth century, Westerners have been converted into consumers on a terrific scale. The wealth of the West has allowed a standard of living that gives citizens time and money with which to amuse themselves. Some people possibly use that time and money unwisely, certainly from the point of view of the moralist or the bourgeois intellectuals. It is this income that the entertainers and their managers and promoters chase, for, whatever rhetoric they might like to mouth about art, entertainment is chiefly a business and the stakes are high. Of course there are artists who reject the glitter of Hollywood and follow the virtuous path, pursuing art rather than gold. But the temptations are great, and who can blame a performer if he succumbs? Everyone has a right, surely, to make a livelihood.

Entertainments are not real life: they do not mirror the world in every detail or with much accuracy. They are constructed according to styles and conventions which are part of the shared understanding that can exist between all those involved. They often pander to our worst emotions; they allow us to believe that happiness can be achieved or that men and women have a power to shape their destiny which in reality they rarely possess. They are often escapist, and they are often extremely successful in achieving their ends of entertaining us and making money at the same time. The talent and ingenuity of the performers is one of the wonders of the modern world.

Homosexuality is rarely depicted. Until recently the writers of movies seemed to inhabit a world akin to that of British parliamentarians, a society in which cases of homosexuality were extremely rare. A film about a dance troupe, for example, might depict all the characters as completely (not even partially) heterosexual. When a writer wanted to present a character who might have homosexual interests, he usually fell back on the sissy. Writers traded in stereotypes, and it was one of the conventions of the genre that all homosexually inclined men had a more pronounced feminine side to their character. This is one of the most ancient of all myths about homosexuality – the idea that the homosexual is a womanly man.

When Gay Liberation emerged, the movies and television became a particular target of its venom. They knew, the activists said angrily, that many of the stars were not as they were depicted in the hype; they knew actors/directors/producers/writers/ agents or whoever who slept with members of their own sex. This, they cried, was hypocrisy on a tremendous scale. They wanted more positive homosexual images in the movies. When film-makers depicted homosexuality negatively, as they did in the film *Cruising*, the activists demonstrated and became very angry.

Gradually film-makers added 'homosexual' characters. Occasionally – very occasionally – they even devoted whole films to the subject of homosexuality. They did this not because they were suddenly converted to the cause of depicting real life on the screen or because they wanted to promote more positive images of homosexuality but because a market for such images existed. Most such films were largely art-house movies in any case. As Frank Capra found in the 1930s, the audience can sometimes like the feeling that they are being liberal, tolerant or enlightened. Oliver Stone and, to some extent, Kevin Costner have made much money from such phoney liberalism.

What has happened is that film and TV writers have extended their repertoire of homosexual characters. The perennial sissy or outrageous queen is still there, and often more baroque than before: Oliver Stone's *JFK* featured several, New Orleans supplying the perfect setting for cross-dressing (Mardi Gras has a lot to answer for). Now, however, the writers have also added the Good Gay, who is the opposite of the old screaming sissy. The Good Gay is always played by a handsome actor who will in the course of promoting the film emphasise his heterosexual credentials and point out what a challenge the role was, etc, etc, – all with considerable dexterity and skill. He might even announce that he has homosexual friends. His character will be 'normal', the very model of the Hollywood hero: it's just that he prefers guys to dolls, just one of those little quirks. This produces wonderful American films such as *Parting Glances* or *Longtime Companion*, from which a viewer might be deceived into believing that one might spot a homosexual chiefly by his good looks. Even then the activists aren't happy. The world of the Good Gay is almost always professional and middle-class. What about the blue-collar guy? Or the guy with no money? Why can't the movies be more like real life?

This pattern has been true of the cinema and the television but less true of the theatre, where it has been possible to inject more subtlety and diversity into the stories presented. The nature of the enterprise and the relatively lower overheads have made the theatre more accessible to a wider range of writers. As a consequence, there is a strong political content in a number of modern plays. Homosexuality has been much discussed and depicted in recent decades, and the plots and characters satisfy the agitators more than anything they see on the screen.

Britain has been peculiarly prominent in the portrayal of homosexual sex in all types of drama. My Beautiful Launderette, Maurice and Prick Up Your Ears have been important additions to the cinematic canon.

Most performers and promoters strive to maximise the audience that they reach and as a consequence project a sufficiently ambiguous set of messages to reach the widest possible number of punters. A producer making a film starring Matt Dillon will be aware that Dillon is an important homosexual icon, and the film will be marketed with this in mind. A homosexual following has helped many stars make it, and, though it establishes no obligation between actor and admirers, this is a factor that a promoter would be foolish to ignore.

The problem comes when we project a moral or political agenda on to the entertainment industry; when we demand, for example, that a movie star who sleeps with other men must stand up and be counted. This assumes that he can or should always be honest. Considerations other than a loyalty to a spurious gay community are more important in the answers that he gives to the journalist or the chat-show host. In a world that is constructed around illusion, why should an entertainer risk his future livelihood simply for an act of solidarity which will possibly destroy his career?

Ironically, it may be easier for an actor to announce his sexuality in Britain than it is in the United States, and easier still for actors who earn their living primarily from the theatre. Sir Ian McKellen is often cited as an example of a self-identified homosexual who goes from strength to strength as a result of coming out. McKellen's action has frequently been presented in heroic terms. (It was in fact the second time McKellen had come out; the first is buried away in a gay magazine, Sebastian, of 1969 which has not made it to the cuttings library.) McKellen is also safeguarded by his position at the National Theatre, a place with a strong gay presence, and in which his succession of outstanding performances has given him sufficient standing to dictate his own terms. McKellen was also quite old by the time of his second coming, and the possibility of a Hollywood career had already passed. Whether a famous actor announcing that he is a homosexual makes a difference remains an open question.

Music is different. During the 1970s, in a deliberate effort to enhance their reputation as subversive or dangerous characters, a number of pop performers claimed that sometimes they slept with men. Homosexuality only added to the allure of stars like David Bowie or Marc Bolan, who accrued tangible benefits from the occasional expedition to the wild side.

Entertainment has also played a tremendous role in promoting homosexuality through the eroticisation of the male, regardless of whether or not the screen partner is male or female. It can provide an opportunity for men of all ages to establish, modify or expand their sexual identity and interest. Homosexual culture would be particularly impoverished if Hollywood and its satellites had deprived us of Paul Newman, Terence Stamp, Alain Delon, Jan-Michael Vincent, Richard Gere, Christopher Atkins, Kevin Bacon, Rob Lowe, Tom Cruise, Antonio Banderas, Patrick Swayze, Keanu Reeves, Johnny Depp and River Phoenix – not forgetting, of course, either Matt or James.

Total honesty might also deprive us of the sport of imagining that all sorts of screen idols really are actively pursuing other men, of imagining Beverly Hills as a sort of homosexual saturnalia. This sport brings amusement to the conversation of the initiated wherever they gather throughout the West. Frequently based on some nugget of information passed on so often by word of mouth that it becomes distorted at every retelling, all kinds of elaborate tales are embroidered. Interviews are scrutinised for some hint or sign. Denial is not significant: what matters is the way in which the denial is phrased. It is a theological art. The game was much assisted by Kenneth Anger's scurrilous exposures of Hollywood which fed the fantasy that really most of the stars are secretly homosexual.[1]

The entertainment industry provides opportunities for homosexual sex and fantasy on an incredible scale. Many of the great movers and shakers of the industry have been driven by homosexual passions. Examples include Henry Willson, Hollywood agent, who christened and discovered a stable of stars – Rock Hudson, Tab Hunter, Rip Torn and Troy Donahue – Larry Parnes, pop impresario, who named and managed a succession of pop singers – Tommy Steele, Marty Wilde, Vince Eager, Duffy Power, Billy Fury and Georgie Fame. One might add for good measure Brian Epstein and The Beatles, Kit Lambert and The Who, Tam Paton and The Bay City Rollers and Simon Napier-Bell and Wham!

Many forms of entertainment exploit what has been called 'camp', a particular form of cultural expression which began in the homosexual subculture. There have been many attempts to define this nebulous concept, though with no particular success. Susan Sontag, high-powered American intellectual, once wrote a much cited essay on the subject;[2] like many of Ms Sontag's essays, it is hard to understand and in the end does not illuminate. In Britain, most people's experience of camp comes through comedy – especially that national institution the 'Carry On' films.

One of the odd things about camp is that it is often associated with extraordinary devotion by gay men for female stars. Many of them, like Bette Davis or Joan Crawford, hail from the golden age of Hollywood. Dietrich, Piaf, Bankhead, Springfield, West, Midler and company have all attracted similar cults. Certain films also acquire a classic camp status, such as Mildred Pierce, Sunset Boulevard, All About Eve and Whatever Happened to Baby Jane. One of the greatest followings has been that attached to Judy Garland. Was it coincidence, one wonders, that it was on the night Judy died that the boys in Stonewall fought back?

Entertainment can satisfy the spectator in many different ways. It generates more signs and symbols for him to decode and provides him with more material to explore as he tries to see behind the mask. In this way show business has enhanced the cultural complexity produced by the evasive manner in which actors, directors, producers and writers insinuate homosexuality and cultivate homoerotic images.

Indulgence

Show business is one business in which we don't care what people are: there is no prejudice towards homosexual, lesbian or colour. We are as one.

Cilla Black, quoted in Ray Coleman, Brian Epstein *(1989)*

Tarzan

[Lindsay Kemp, mime artist and dancer,] says he knew he was gay from the age of five. 'I used to go to the kiddies' matinees at the movies in Talahassee, Florida, and Tarzan used to turn me on. That's when I knew I was different from the rest of the boys.'

from Gay News, 1973

Theatrical Attractions

I also wanted to be an actor because I thought I could meet queers.

Sir Ian McKellen, March 1991

Energy

'Just because it wiggles, you don't have to fuck it.' 'Oh I do,' Rock would say.

Mark Miller, from Rock Hudson: His Story *(1986)*

Common Sense

Man is made for woman and anybody who pretends that two men can live together happily like man and wife is talking a load of rubbish. Let's not kid ourselves, there would be no life in that kind of relationship.

Kenneth Williams in the News of the World Colour Magazine, *February 1984*

Out in the Open

[Cary Grant] and [Randolph] Scott seemed quite content to be photographed for fan magazines in and around the swimming-pool, playing beach-ball, cooking in matching aprons in the kitchen, washing the dishes together, and fooling around on the patio in a manner that left little to the imagination. They were still confident that the public would never suspect anything and the more they flaunted their relationship the more everyone would think that if they had anything to hide they would not allow themselves to be pictured or written about in their habitat.

Charles Higham and Roy Moseley, Cary Grant *(1989)*

The Odd Couple

. . . in 1950 Danny Kaye effectively insinuated himself into Olivier's intimate life. He spent many weekends with them both in Los Angeles and London; he arranged his own work to coincide with Olivier's commitments; he turned up in foreign cities where they were travelling; he hosted an inordinate number of parties and dinners in their honour; four times, he corralled the Oliviers into performing vaudeville numbers with him at charity benefits; and he acquired invitations to an astonishing number of events on their schedule. All this and the fact of the affair would perhaps remain unremarkable had not Olivier written a letter to Vivien in 1961, weakly describing as transitory and unimportant the sexual intimacy between himself and Kaye. The letter, written to Vivien when she was living with an actor named John Merivale, survived her death and remained with Merivale until his. Additionally, the first draft of Olivier's autobiography (written in 1981) frankly admitted the numerous homosexual escapades of his adult life – events his third wife prevailed on him to remove from the book. As for the relationship with Kaye, it was certainly everything Vivien suspected and far more than Olivier admitted. She was singularly unamused when she saw photographs taken at one riotous all-male gathering at the Caribbean home of Noël Coward. Kaye and Olivier had performed impromptu song-and-dance duets, dressed alternately as bride and groom. This was pure British music hall, but to Vivien it betokened something true about the relationship, and something with which she could not compete.

Donald Spoto, Laurence Olivier: A Biography *(1991)*

Need

When I was fourteen, sex suddenly became all-important to me. It didn't really matter who or what it was with, as long as it was a sexual experience. So it was some pretty boy in class in some school or other that I took home and neatly fucked on my bed upstairs.

David Bowie, Playboy *interview, 1976*

Domestic Pleasures

On June 11th [1967], John Jones [Bowie's father] took David and his belongings to Manchester Street [to the flat of his new manager, Ken Pitt] . . . Pitt soon found the meticulous order in which he preferred to live had been violated by the clothes, books and sheaves of paper littering the floor of David's room. After failing to mend David's ways, he simply ensured that David's door was kept shut and tried to forget the chaos behind it.

Pitt now embarked on his self-appointed task of improving David's mind. He dismissed the beat writers Terry [Bowie's brother] had recommended as 'juvenalia', and showed him the more cultivated authors on his bookshelves: among them André Gide, Antoine de Saint Exupéry, and Oscar Wilde. David was captivated by both *The Picture of Dorian Gray* and *The Little Prince*, which he read again and again. Pitt looked upon him disapprovingly as a product of the first television generation, and often took him to the theatre, from the classics to pantomime . . . Pitt describes the year David spent living with him in Manchester Street as 'one of the most stimulating periods of my life'. Their relationship was close and relaxed: David would walk around naked, 'his big dick swaying from side to side' says Pitt, which prompted him to paper over the kitchen window to block the view obtained by the women in a neighbouring flat. Once when Ken emerged from the bathroom without any clothes, David produced a ruler to measure his penis and exclaimed in mock-awe, 'Ye gods'. How much closer the relationship became, however, Pitt declines to say: 'That is something that belongs to him and me.' He agrees that it was 'strong and affectionate', adding: 'I think most people who knew us accept that.' For all the intimacy, David, then twenty, retained a large degree of control over the relationship.

from Peter and Leni Gillman, Alias David Bowie (1986)

Creative Urges

I honestly feel that if Brian [Epstein] had not been homosexual, if he hadn't had this drive within him, there would not have been the same dedication. His motivation was *paramount*. A homosexual cannot indulge, or doesn't wish to indulge, in certain procreation. So a male homosexual goes and finds an image and they are then his creation. The Beatles existed as an entity before Brian Epstein, but he created them. He was driven on by this: 'They are *mine*.'

Bob Wooler, in Ray Coleman, Brian Epstein (1989)

Tease

The merciless streak inside Lennon, which exposed anyone's clear vulnerability, caused a ripple when Brian [Epstein] was preparing the book . . . Asked by Brian for a title for his autobiography, John said, 'Why don't you call it *Queer Jew*?' When Epstein told him he had decided on *A Cellarful of Noise*, Lennon taunted that it should have been called *A Cellarful of Boys*.

from Ray Coleman, Brian Epstein (1989)

Adjusting

The patient was homosexual but had been unable to come to terms with this problem.

Dr Norman Cowan, the GP of pop manager Brian Epstein, giving evidence to the inquest after Epstein had taken his own life on 8 September 1967

Good Buddies

The only person sleeping aboard *Ocean Sabre* (Cassidy's yacht moored in mid-Thames) other than the crew and John Monte, David's road manager, was a rangy, wavy-haired classically good-looking boy who had been described everywhere as Sam Hyman, David's best friend. 'It started off', David wrote in his British fan magazine, 'just like any other friendship between schoolkids. We played baseball together, spent days down on the beach just goofing around . . . we rode our bikes for miles . . . I reckon I know Sam almost as well as I know myself . . . and I guess he feels the same way about me. Actually, the way I figure it, a good buddy can sometimes know a guy better than he knows himself.'

from Gay News, *January 1973*

Impresario

Once you've rearranged the entire seating of Lancing College Chapel to sit next to the boy you fancy, anything is possible.

Kit Lambert, in Andrew Motion, The Lamberts *(1986)*

No End of a Lesson

The last big boyfriend was, of course, Culture Club drummer Jon Moss. 'Maybe I should say people were right when they called me [Boy George] closeted back in those days, but part of the reason for that was because I was having a sexual relationship with a so-called straight man called Jon Moss. I was very much in love with him and didn't want to lose that, and it was much more sacred to me than announcing my homosexuality. I suppose I thought if I announced 'Hey everybody, I'm having an affair with the drummer – isn't he lovely?' everybody would go off me . . . we're quite friendly again now. It's funny, a while ago at a press conference in Italy they asked me what my relationship was with Jon and I said, 'He was a great fuck.' And I spoke to him a couple of weeks later and coincidentally he'd been asked the same question and he'd said, 'George was a great fuck!'

It's okay between us now, even though when I was a heroin addict he didn't do anything to help me. He just walked away. But then, looking back, he couldn't have helped me because I was completely helpless . . . I learned a lot from Jon Moss. Like never to fall in love with someone who says they're heterosexual. *Ever.*

from Gay Times, *January 1988*

Peter

[Little Richard] confessed that he has always enjoyed being gay ('I've been gay all my life and I really enjoyed it, though I don't do it no more since God filled me with his power. But I loved sex, I loved big penises. If there was anything I loved better than a big penis it was a bigger penis.') and defended gay people as 'the sweetest, kindest, most artistic, warmest and most thoughtful people in the world. And since the beginning of time all they've ever been is kicked' . . . life on the road was, according to Richard, one big orgy and his own favourite pleasure was hand-shandies: 'I was pumping so much peter in those days, sometimes eight or nine times a day. I was creaming, steaming and beaming,' he told me with another beam, presumably at the memory of it.

from an interview with Little Richard in Gay Times, *May 1985*

Gay Pride

Status Quo rock star Francis Rossi yesterday told of his 'proudest moment' when his son Simon pulled him to one side and admitted: 'Dad I'm gay.' Singer Rossi, 38, said his relationship with 20-year-old Simon was transformed by the confession. He added: 'Until then I didn't really like him very much. I thought he was a big fat lazy git, a real spoiled brat. But it took immense courage for him to tell me and I admired him for it. Coming out of the closet suddenly made him more mature. We can talk to each other, man to man. I know it sounds funny to say that, but it's absolutely true.' . . . Drama student Simon, the eldest of divorced Rossi's three sons, lives in Kensington with a lover called Stephen . . . 'I even call him a big faggot. It's not an insult . . . There are loads of faggots in show business and I've always found them to be great people. They are capable of being honest.'

from the Sun, *8 March 1988*

Furious 20-year-old Simon Rossi stormed: 'This could ruin my career. I just couldn't believe it when I saw in the papers that my father had called me a big faggot. All I can think is that he's desperate for publicity for his new single . . .' Simon, who has a live-in boyfriend called Stephen, added: 'My better half was livid.'

from the News of the World, *13 March 1988*

Parasites

'I made an issue out of the Pet Shop Boys,' says Jimmy Somerville, 'because they are consciously using their gay background and gay culture for career purposes, and they're not putting anything back into gay culture except disco music. They could be voicing opinions and ideals which would influence young gay men and lesbians.'

from Gay Times, *June 1990*

Mommy's Boy

In 1956 the *Daily Mirror* published an article which, he claimed, implied Liberace was a homosexual. He sued, and the case came to court in 1959. Liberace was awarded £8,000 in damages and costs; his 'reputation had been vindicated'.

Q. Are you a homosexual?
LIBERACE: No, sir.
Q. Have you ever indulged in homosexual practices?
LIBERACE: No, sir, never in my life. I am against the practice because it offends convention and it offends society.
Q. Was there anything sexy about your performance at all?
LIBERACE: I am not aware of it if it exists. I am almost positive that I could hardly refer to myself as a sexy performer. I have tried in all my performances to inject a note of sincerity and wholesomeness. I am fully aware of the fact that my appeal on television and personal appearances is aimed directly at the family audience.
Q. Do you ever tell what we know as dirty stories?
LIBERACE: I have never been known to tell any so-called dirty stories.
from cross-examination of Liberace, the High Court, 1959

Sell-By Date

For a dozen years, Liberace had taken on live-in lovers, usually blond, blue-eyed young men with strong physiques, easily found through his acquaintances in the gay milieu of West Hollywood and Las Vegas. They provided comfort and companionship during the long weeks on tour and enhanced Lee's periods of rest at the homes in Palm Springs and Malibu. Inevitably each liaison ended, usually because of Lee's boredom with his empty-headed lover. The parting was assuaged with gifts of jewelry and cash.

Sometimes a lover departed of his own accord, bored by life with the aging star . . . Now in his sixties, he realized his diminishing capacity to attract young men. Both for them as well as his stage appearance, he embarked on severe diets, wore more youthful hairpieces to cover his baldness, underwent surgery to remove the lines in his face, and used more and more make-up. . . .

[Scott Thorson met Liberace and became his lover in 1978. A veterinary nurse, he had graduated from Walt Whitman High School in Los Angeles a year earlier.] It was the longest-lasting of Lee's relationships, but it was destined to end, like all the others. Not that he wanted it to end; he believed that he had found his lasting love. But after four years of closeness, Lee believed that Scott had developed a Jekyll–Hyde personality, and he blamed the change on liquor and drugs. When Scott's behavior became too erratic to tolerate, Lee decided to erase Scott Thorson from his life. The process wasn't easy. Scott didn't want to leave the Beverly Boulevard penthouse he shared with Liberace. Then one violent predawn morning in April 1982 . . . several burly men awoke him in his bed, maced and beat him, expelled him from the penthouse, and had the locks changed so he could not reenter.

from Bob Thomas, Liberace: The True Story *(1987)*

Reputation

In a tearful scene [on his deathbed] Liberace told [his former lover], 'I don't want to be remembered as an old queen who died of AIDS.'

from the News of the World, *11 October 1987*

Dream Boy

Ask him about the drugs stories and the speculation about his sexuality and he [Jason Donovan] immediately puts his guard up, leans back, arms folded. There is a pause while he ponders what to say and I wonder whether I'm about to be ejected. When he does speak, he forms his words slowly and deliberately. He's been here before. 'The success of this show [*Joseph and his Amazing Technicolor Dreamcoat*] and the single just goes to show how thin those rumours were. If people were to have believed what they read, I'm pretty sure they wouldn't have taken to what I've done as well as they have.'

He pauses again. Perhaps he realises that this line of argument is getting neither of us anywhere. He tries another tack. 'Look, it's unfair for people to say things like being gay, or the drugs thing, y'know? I don't take drugs, and I'm not gay. Some of my best friends are gay, I'm not denying that, but it's not the way I choose to live my life. To convince people of that just isn't worth the bother. Let them think what they want to think.'

It is a far cry from the statements he's given previously. What no mention of his affair with Kylie, no surfing tales? 'I just said "this is the situation",' he insists. 'Believe it, or don't believe it. That's me about my career. That's my image. If you like it, buy it. If you don't, don't.' Some people aren't buying it. A couple of weeks ago a spate of posters appeared across town. They represent the arrival of an 'outing' campaign similar to those currently being waged in the United States. Donovan is depicted with the slogan 'Queer As Fuck' emblazoned across his chest. Was he aware that he had become the target of gay activism.

He mumbles a vague 'no', accompanied by much rearranging of hair. 'In, er, London? Really? In what way? What's it all about?' I dutifully explain the principles of outing, though I have a recollection of seeing Jason discussing said campaign with Michelle Collins on *The Word*. Perhaps it slipped his mind. 'So it's basically gay rights,' he interrupts. 'It's funny. The thing is, without getting into this, because I really don't want to, the thing is there is nothing wrong with homosexuality, absolutely nothing wrong with it at all. I don't deny people the privilege or the right to do whatever. It's a free world. It just frustrates me that people in that position would want to think of you as one of them. That's what frustrates me, when you know damn well, and they know damn well, that you're not gay. That's where it gets my back up a bit. C'est la vie.' We spend the remaining ten minutes negotiating our way towards a polite departure point, briefly discussing his immediate plans (a holiday) and future direction . . . He barely has time to compose himself before the man from the *Daily Express* appears at the door. I'm half-way back to the office before I remember the photographs of Chesney Hawkes plastered around his bathroom mirror. Nice to see our Jase taking the competition so seriously.

Paul Burston in City Limits, *July 1991*

Best of British

We showed *Withnail and I* to this New York Pensioners Film Club – not one of 'em under 70 . . . [At the end, Bruce Robinson, the director and writer of the film, answered the audience's questions.] One old woman stood up and said, 'Mr Robinson, could you tell why it is that nowadays all the films we see coming out of England are about homosexuality?' And of course when you look at them – *My Beautiful Launderette, Maurice, Another Country,* even *Withnail and I* – they are all in some form or other. And all I could say to her was 'Fuck me, you've really got me there' . . . but maybe one reason why the latest wave of British movies use homosexuality so much is because we're living in more and more repressive times, and of its nature the people who make films are people who are anti the repression.

from Gay Times, *February 1988*

Irrelevance

My Beautiful Launderette: Funny, perceptive study of a Pakistani marred by a homosexual element that seems irrelevant to the story.

from the Daily Express *TV guide, 9 April 1988*

Virtue

In *Launderette* I wanted their sexuality to be a virtue; I didn't want it to be a big deal. It just seemed right, perfectly natural that they were gay. Those blokes were gay just as other people were straight.

Hanif Kureishi in Gay Times, *April 1990*

Making Love

Arthur Hiller's *Making Love* is one of those movies about gays which tries too hard to be fair and decent and honest. So hard, in fact, that long before the end one is willing to accuse it of all sorts of fudging. It's fudging, for instance, even to suggest that a marital break-up, caused by the husband's coming slowly and cautiously out of the closet, will be alright in the end because there are bound to be two Mr Rights lined up for both partners just around the corner.

Hiller . . . who perpetrated *Love Story* on a surprised world a decade or so ago . . . is a nice man who has made good movies. But he can also make terrible ones. *Making Love* is a big fairy story . . . you do not feel they are real people at all but some cocaine-fazed Californian approximations of human beings . . . what do you make of a writer who says, like Bart, that he's an artist and 'has to open himself up to new things'? A great titter rolled around the audience when I saw the film at this point, and who would blame them? The writing is sheer blancmange . . . It is a total misconception to paint the gay world in these soft colours and then say, ad nauseam, that we are just the same. The rough edges of real humanity, homosexual or heterosexual, are only very briefly to be found in *Making Love*, which, though palpably sincere, undermines its problem picture status with every feeble half-truth known to Hollywood.

Derek Malcolm in the Guardian, 10 June 1982

High Energy

William Haines, the silent star, had been ruined when Louis B. Mayer discovered Haines had been involved with a sailor. If Jack Warner, who had a soft spot for Errol [Flynn], chiefly because of Errol's famous success with women, had found out, he would probably have destroyed Errol's career. Errol discovered when he first went to Mexico that at last there was a safe way of indulging his needs: all he had to do was cross the border. He met an Australian millionaire whom he had known before and who lived in a mansion in Cuernavaca and knew how to obtain boys for small amounts of money. Errol would always go to Cuernavaca for these boys. No one got onto it. Not even the most ardent gossips.

I knew a boy, a hustler, who was at one of the Australian millionaire's parties. I asked him about it afterward. He told me that Errol invited him to his room and performed fellatio on him and vice versa. The boy said Errol was so handsome, superbly built and passionate that for the first time in his career as a male prostitute he was genuinely turned on by a client. He was amazed by Errol's staying power, virility, and sheer energy in bed.

'A prominent director' quoted in Charles Higham, Errol Flynn: The Untold Story (1980)

In Hiding

At the outset of the production, du Maurier asked him: 'Laughton are you a bugger?' To which Laughton stammeringly replied: 'N–no, Sir Gerald. Are you?'

Du Maurier's question was presumably a reference to the hysterical and malicious qualities Charles had brought to Walpole's Crispin. But it must have given him a nasty turn. Because of course he was. He had not spoken of it to anyone, least of all to Elsa. If he had hoped that marriage would divert his desires, he was disappointed. His need for sex with men had not cleared up like acne, he was still impelled to find young men and sometimes even to bring them clandestinely home. Elsa Lanchester believes that these encounters were furtive and inspired by self-lacerating guilt: that Charles needed to sin, like a minor key version of that figure of whom he sometimes seems to be a thwarted alter ego: Oscar Wilde.

from Simon Callow, Charles Laughton: A Difficult Actor *(1987)*

Montgomery Clift and Innocence

[Clift's] real passion was reserved for an aspiring actor he'd met at Klein's gym. [The actor, who was called Josh, remembered that he had been Clift's lover for two years.] 'Our affair was for me the most beautiful experience in my life,' he said. 'I'll never forget it. We were still sexually pure and innocent. We laughed a great deal, and played together. We hadn't started cruising yet, and neither one of us had ever gone to a public toilet or bathhouse to make contact. We didn't hang out at Forty-second Street movie houses. We'd never seen a drag show, and I for one didn't know what a male hustler was.' . . .

When they were together they rarely brought up the subject of homosexuality. They had both been raised to believe that homosexuality was a form of mental illness, a psychiatric disorder.

'When we were alone it was like Monty and I were shut away from reality for a couple of hours. It was a disorienting experience. Alone we could be emotional and passionate but outside we had to hide our feelings.

'Naturally we felt guilty about what we were doing, but we couldn't help ourselves. We were violently attracted to each other and knew we had fallen in love . . .

'One of the things that was starting to torture Monty back in 1940 was the fact that he had to hide his sexual feelings. He despised deception, pretense, and he felt the intolerable strain of living a lie. He was scrupulously honest with himself, and he had a tremendous sense of morality about what is right and wrong. I think that's one of the reasons he was in such conflict about his homosexuality. There was no tolerance for it back then. Gays were totally oppressed.' . . .

Josh said that their affair ended when he joined the Navy in 1942 . . .

from Patricia Bosworth, Montgomery Clift: A Biography *(1978)*

Ambidextrous

When James Dean was asked by someone if he was gay, he coyly replied: 'Well, I'm not going through life with one hand tied behind my back.'

from Graham McCann, Rebel Males: Clift, Brando and Dean *(1991)*

Fags

Dean had taken to hanging out at the Club, an East Hollywood leather bar. The predatory night prowler, who dug anonymous sex, had recently discovered the magic world of S and M. He had gotten into beating, boots, belts and bondage scenes. Regulars at the Club tagged him with a singular moniker: the Human Ashtray. When stoned, he would bare his chest and beg for his masters to stub out their butts on it. After his fatal car crash, the coroner made note of the 'constellation of keratoid scars' on Jimmy's torso.

Dean had avoided service in Korea by levelling with his draft board – he informed the Fairmount Selective Service Unit that he was gay. When Hedda Hopper asked him how he had managed to stay out of the Army, he replied: 'I kissed the medic.'

Shortly after arriving in Hollywood, Dean had adopted the route taken by many other broke, aspiring actors – he moved in with an older man. His host was TV director Roger Brackett, who lived on posh Sunset Plaza Drive. The fan magazine spoke of their father–son relationship. If so it was touched by incest . . .

Dean was withdrawn, compulsively promiscuous, but friendless, suspicious, moody, uncooperative, boorish and rude. He could, on occasion, be charming; on most occasions he was annoyingly nuts. He betrayed a psychopathic personality with fits of despondency that alternated with fits of wild jubilation. A classic manic-depressive . . . On the eve of his death, he had attended a gay party at Malibu, which had ended in a screaming match with an ex lover, a man who accused him of dating women just for the sake of publicity.

from Kenneth Anger, Hollywood Babylon II *(1984)*

With the Masses

I,ike the vast majority of men I've had several homosexual experiences and I'm not remotely ashamed of it.

from an interview with Marlon Brando in Cine-Revue, *1975*

Cameron Mackintosh

He is a concentrated, stocky man. His staff joke about the claim in his passport that he is 5ft 8in. The will, which is iron, is wrapped in theatrical charm – it is an unforced performance, whose core is to give away nothing unnecessary: discretion as a negotiation technique. What makes him famous is that he put *Cats* on stage, and *Phantom of the Opera* and *Les Misérables* and *Miss Saigon* . . . He is one of the 200 richest men in Britain . . . Theatrical gays sent a letter to *The Guardian* defending Ian McKellen's decision to accept a knighthood from a government not famously kind to gay people. Mackintosh signed. He did not see it as any kind of coming out, not even as much of a decision: 'I just think Ian thoroughly deserved his knighthood.'

He pushed away the notion that this could be political. He makes a joke that is over-rehearsed: 'I do not burn bras,' he says, 'nor do I wear them.' He does not find it funny. 'I do not talk about my private life – it's just that, my private life.' But the effect is to make his nine-year lover, a London photographer, seem much more of a dark secret than the wife or mistress of your average mogul.

That is the theatre tradition: do what you like, but do not tell the punters.

from a profile of Cameron Mackintosh by Michael Pye in the Independent on Sunday, *1990*

Dream On

In Gus Van Sant's *My Own Private Idaho*, River Phoenix played a male hustler who falls in love with his friend, played by Keanu Reeves.

Q. Define 'Best Friend'.

RIVER: Someone you can tell all your secrets to. For me it's a guy you enjoy being with, a guy you love and a guy you care about. Keanu is my buddy, dude.

KEANU: I've always loved you River. River is my best friend and I don't have many of them.

RIVER. That's really sweet, Keany.

Q. Is there anything you wouldn't do in a film?

RIVER: Didn't we answer that already?

KEANU: Where have we heard that before? I'm not against gays or anything, but I won't have sex with guys. I would never do that on film. We did a little of it in *Idaho* and it was really hard. Never again.

RIVER: I thought you liked that. Was it something I did?

KEANU: Shut up, dude!

Winfield Scott in City Limits, *January 1992*

Camp I

Camp is a kind of wit common to but by no means exclusive to male homosexuals. A definition of the concept is elusive, but it may be tentatively circumscribed by saying that camp consists of taking serious things frivolously and frivolous things seriously. Camp is not grounded in speech or writing as much as it is in gesture, performance, and public display . . . The targets of camp are good taste, marriage and the family, suburbia, sports and the business world. Camp is thus a less hostile continuation of the trend of nineteenth-century Bohemia to *épater le bourgeois*, to bait middle-class respectability . . . To a large extent camp is in the eye of the beholder . . . Perhaps it is not too much to say that camp aspires to fulfill Friedrich Nietzsche's precept of the reversion of all values. It certainly serves to bring into question established hierarchies of taste . . . The world of camp then serves to deconstruct the cult of seriousness and 'values' that sought to fill the gap produced by the fading of religion and traditional class society in the West.

Significantly, no equivalent of camp seems to exist in the Third World.

Wayne R. Dynes, The Encyclopedia of Homosexuality *(1990)*

Camp II

Camp is a lie that tells the truth
Philip Core, Camp (1984), after Jean Cocteau's 'I am the lie that tells the truth'

Camp III

First off, a partial definition: camp is NOT a person, situation or activity; it is, rather, a relationship between these things and homosexuality . . . those elements in a person, situation or activity which express a gay sensibility or viewpoint. Camp, in fact, is the product of oppression, a *creative* means of dealing with an identity that is loaded down with stigma. As soul (or blues) is to the black community, so camp is to the gays . . . there are four basic properties inherent in camp: first, irony – especially in regard to incongruous contrasts (masculine/feminine, sacred/profane, youth/old age); second, aestheticism – in the sense of an emphasised style; third, theatricality or the perception of life as theatre and role-playing; and finally, humour – for camp, as the world well knows, is funny, it is witty. And it is also indulgent, obliging, and often extravagant . . . [it is] a creative strategy for dealing with social pressures.
Jack Babuscio in Gay News, *March 1976*

Camp IV

You can't camp about something you don't take seriously, you're not making fun of it, you're making fun *out* of it. You're expressing what's basically serious in terms of fun and artifice and elegance.
from Christopher Isherwood, The World in the Evening *(1954)*

Flying and the Flood

Since coming out, I feel buoyant, self-content and deeply happy and what I hadn't realised was that deep inside me was the weight that I've now thrown out . . . I think my next contribution to the campaign against Clause 29 and what it represents is to help many other famous people in Britain to come out – not just in theatre and television. The way I want to try and help is to convince those of us who have been teetering on the edge and are ready to jump that flying is a delightful experience.
from an interview with Ian McKellen in Gay Times, *April 1988*

Collaboration

The queers of the sixties, like those since, have connived with their repression under a veneer of respectability. Good-mannered city queens in suits and pinstripes, so busy establishing themselves, were useless at changing anything.

To be queer was never respectable – even though you wore a suit. The more conventional, the more desperate a hidden life. Pushed to the fringes, our world existed in the twilight of Heterosoc; that was the reality, and if anyone raised their voice in protest they were accused of endangering the peace of anonymity. A demonstration was likely to frighten the closeted, their inactivity reproached.

Stonewall was a RIOT which occurred in the summer of 1969 in Christopher Street, New York, outside a bar of the same name. For the first time the queers fought back with bricks and bottles and empty beer glasses and burned cars. The best fighters were the trannies – a dress was a badge of courage. This riot sparked a revolution in consciousness. A community of interest was established and a debate was entered. The harder it was fought the more our case was furthered.

Everything that made our visible reproached the closeted. One day it might be as silly as moaning about Quentin Crisp's blue rinse as a BAD ROLE MODEL, or, on another, complaining of a rowdy Gay Liberation Front meeting. For them, we were not them. They took everything and did nothing, sat in their interior decoration, attended the opera and did fuck all to help change; their minds as starched as their shirts.

Twenty years later, Stonewall – the self-elected and self-congratulating parliamentary lobby group – have made more than enough compromise with convention. Did those who rioted at the Stonewall bar fight so that we could so easily be co-opted by a gay establishment? Do they represent our best interests in Heterosoc?

Do they represent us?

Why did one man go to Downing Street to put our case? Why were there no women? Weren't the rest of us acceptable? It was as if no queer had ever been in number 10 before, the fuss everyone made . . . Was lone McKellen's visit an election ploy? Gay votes would make the difference between a Tory or a Labour government; we were at least one in ten of the population. Was McKellen representing only himself as he maintained? If so, it wasn't seen that way. At the last general election [1987] a poll in the gay press showed that support was evenly divided between the political parties, but who could vote Tory after Section 28?

Perhaps you could if you could accept honours from them. Honours support a dishonourable social structure. Barbara Cartland, Ian McKellen and James Anderton; there's no merit there. To have accepted them showed a terrible vanity. And there's our only 'out' gay MP (Labour) crawling in this sycophantic trough, criticising me in the press. All the hard work put in by activists for a different world – not the same old world – was betrayed at this moment.

McKellen is a charming and intelligent man and that's the problem. Oh, the shark has pearly teeth, dear, with eighteen minnows following. One of them, [John] Schlesinger, is making promos for the Conservative Party; the party that ruined the eighties and made our lives hell.

Part of the con was to steal the name Stonewall and turn our riot into their teaparty. We are now to be integrated into the worst form of British hetero politics – the closed room, the gentleman's club – where decisions are made undemocratically for an ignorant population which enjoys its emasculation.

So they – Stonewall – won't acknowledge this criticism. They'll pretend there isn't a debate. The only way they can succeed in their politics is through the myth of homogeneity and the 'gay community'. But our lives are plural. They always have been – sexuality is a diversity. Every orgasm brings its own liberty.

from Derek Jarman, At Your Own Risk: A Saint's Testament *(1992)*

Supporting the Cause

As Gay and Lesbian artists, we would like to respectfully distance ourselves from Derek Jarman's article [criticising Ian McKellen for accepting a knighthood from the same Conservative Government as passed Clause 28]. We regard [McKellen's] knighthood as a significant landmark in the history of the British Gay Movement. Never again will public figures be able to claim that they have to keep secret their homosexuality in fear of it damaging their careers. Ian McKellen provides an inspiration to us all, not only as an artist of extraordinary gifts, but as a public figure of remarkable honesty and dignity.

Signed: Simon Callow, Michael Cashman, Nancy Diuguid, Simon Fanshawe, Stephen Fry, Philip Hedley, Bryony Lavery, Michael Leonard, David Lan, Tim Luscombe, Alec McCowen, Cameron Mackintosh, Pam St Clement, John Schlesinger, Anthony Sher, Martin Sherman, Ned Sherrin, Nick Wright

from the Guardian, *9 January 1991*

CHAPTER THIRTEEN

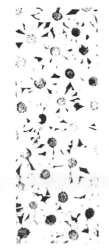

Living in the Shadow of the Plague

We know little about Aids. The *New York Times* alerted the world to the menace in an article that appeared on 3 July 1981. By that time doctors were diagnosing similar symptoms in patients on both the east and the west coast of the United States. Many of the men were actively homosexual, and this led to the creation of the most powerful and most persistent myth about the disease; that it was a gay plague. Though this was soon disproved as the 1980s advanced, it has become a difficult myth to dispel. The disease did hit gay ghettos across the West, but other high-risk groups such as drug-users, and the thousands of sufferers in the Third World, were not infected through homosexual sex. One of the more ludicrous features of the reporting of Aids has been the indifference shown by the media to the progress of the disease in Africa, Asia and Latin America.

In 1984 a French research team identified the HIV virus, which they believed was responsible for the development of Aids. A group of American scientists also came to this conclusion. This theory has been generally accepted, though there have been a number of dissenting voices inside and outside the world of medicine.

If one ever wanted to show that the world was not a particularly rational or humane place, then the Aids epidemic would provide plenty of evidence. From the start, many interest groups have tried to use the development of the disease to advance their own particular messages. Moralists, rarely silent, see in the progress of Aids an indictment of the permissive society and the unnaturalness of homosexuality – divine punishment, some Christians have suggested, on deviants. It's strange that God should seem to ignore the lesbians, practising the safest sexual option at the moment. Right-wing newspapers have had a wonderful time. In the mid-1980s they built up an incredible public hysteria that led some health-workers to refuse to treat patients suffering from Aids and frightened their readers about the spread of the disease. In the 1990s they misled their readers by telling them the danger had passed. Aids allowed many old scores to be settled, and the Conservative press was exposed once more for its susceptibility to propaganda.

The gay ghettos of the West at last found a cause that really did create something like a homosexual community. The counselling and caring provided by organisations in all the developed nations have been a rare testimony to the nobility of the human spirit when facing a major tragedy. Unfortunately, political divisions have re-emerged and Aids has been used by some campaigners as a vehicle for expressing their hostility to the political and social establishment. Drug companies have been a regular target. Protesters believe that science has been dragging its feet and that the pharmaceutical companies have been too interested in profit rather than in saving lives. Too much faith has been placed in the development of a 'magic bullet' that will make this epidemic go away. AZT, which seemed for a while to fit the bill, is now largely discredited and may indeed have made the suffering worse for those victims treated with it. At one time protesters pressed companies to release the drug before it was properly tested; now they demonstrate against the same companies for distributing the drug.

Many concerned have looked for someone to blame, but Aids was really nobody's fault. The idea advanced by moralising journalists that Aids patients were murderers is as absurd as the notion advanced by some gay activists that governments deliberately let people die because they found their lifestyle distasteful. If anything, the disease reveals the fragility of people's control of their environment and the circumstances of their life. For centuries bubonic plague devastated human society before suddenly retreating, and man was powerless to affect its progress. Perhaps we know a little more than our ancestors, but not that much.

Aids hit the West, at least, at a time when it was believed that the age of infectious diseases had passed. The last major epidemic had been the influenza which appeared at the end of the First World War. Western doctors, researchers and health services had come to focus their energies on non-infectious diseases. Aids completely invalidated their assumptions. The failure to react sufficiently quickly was probably due to the fact that for nearly seventy years resources and attention had shifted away from infectious diseases to chronic ones.

Aids brought many men and women to become more open about their homosexual inclinations. Some, like Rock Hudson and Liberace, had little choice. The disease possibly brought more candour to public discussions about sexuality. Even so, the Catholic Church showed itself to be peculiarly medieval in the way that it consistently campaigned against greater sex education even though this might save more lives.

There was considerable progress in the decriminalisation of homosexual sex across the globe. The election of Bill Clinton to the American presidency in the autumn of 1992 raised great expectations in the United States of the advance of legislation that would bring benefits to American gays, who emerged during the election campaign as a powerful and sophisticated political lobby, delivering votes and funds to Clinton at a time when he desperately needed them. Clinton's attempt to allow servicemen to openly practise homosexual sex and announce their inclinations and interests has become a major test of strength that has at least directed more attention to sexual issues and has done much to reveal the pervasiveness and persistence of homosexuality in human society.

The Beginning

Doctors in New York and California have diagnosed among homosexual men 41 cases of a rare and often rapidly fatal form of cancer. Eight of the victims died in less than 24 months after the diagnosis was made.

The cause of the outbreak is unknown, and there is as yet no evidence of contagion. But the doctors who have made the diagnoses, mostly in New York City and the San Francisco Bay area, are alerting other physicians who treat large numbers of homosexual men, to the problem in an effort to identify more cases and to reduce the delay in offering chemotherapy treatment.

The sudden appearance of the cancer, called Kaposi Sarcoma, has prompted a medical investigation that experts say could have as much scientific as public health importance because of what it may teach about determining the cause of more common forms of cancer.

Doctors have been taught in the past that the cancer usually appeared first in spots on the legs and that the disease took a slow course of up to ten years. But these recent cases have shown that it appears in one or more violet-coloured spots anywhere on the body. The spots do not generally itch or cause other symptoms, often can be mistaken for bruises, sometimes appear as lumps and can turn brown after a period of time. The cancer often causes swollen lymph glands and then kills by spreading through the whole body.

In a letter alerting other physicians to the problem Dr. Alvin E. Friedman-Klein of New York University Medical Center, one of the investigators, described the appearance of the outbreak as 'rather devastating' . . .

In the United States it has primarily affected men older than 50 years. But in the recent cases, doctors at nine medical centers in New York and seven hospitals in California have been diagnosing the condition among younger men, all of whom said in the course of diagnostic interviews that they were homosexual. Although the ages of the patients have ranged from 26 to 51 years, many have been under 40, with the mean at 39 . . . According to Dr. Friedman-Klein, the reporting doctors said that most cases involved homosexual men who had multiple and frequent sexual encounters with different partners, as many as 10 sexual encounters each night up to four times a week . . .

Cancer is not believed to be contagious, but conditions that might precipitate it, such as particular viruses or environmental factors, might account for an outbreak among single gays . . .

Dr. Curran [of the Federal Center for Disease Control] said that there was no apparent danger to nonhomosexuals from contagion. 'The best evidence against contagion,' he said, 'is that no cases have been reported to date outside the homosexual community or in women.'

Dr. Friedman-Klein said he had tested nine of the victims and found severe defects in their immunological systems . . . But Dr. Friedman-Klein emphasized that the researchers did not know whether the immunological defects were the underlying problem or had developed secondarily to the infection or drug use.

from an article by Lawrence Altman, 'Rare Cancer Seen in 41 Homosexual Men', in the New York Times, 3 July 1981

Murder

Last year, according to detectives in the Hollywood division of the Los Angeles Police Department, sexual preference was a factor in 10 of 42 murders in their 19-square-mile jurisdiction. Detectives say the victims are frequently runaways who leave less tolerant environments in the Middle West to come here to live in a community of homosexuals whose size is unknown but which has been estimated at 20,000 to more than 150,000. Many of the runaways, according to social workers here, end up earning their living as homosexual prostitutes, making contacts with customers in homosexual bars or as hitchhikers

from the New York Times, *21 September 1981*

Adrian Mole

December 23, 1982
Went to the 'Off the Streets' Youth Club party with Pandora. Nigel caused a scandal by dancing with Clive Barnes who was wearing lipstick and mascara! Everyone was saying that Nigel is gay, so I made sure that everyone knew that he is no longer my best friend.

from Sue Townsend, The Growing Pains of Adrian Mole *(1984)*

Battle of Bermondsey

I'm intrigued by the book's reference to 'other figures in the Bermondsey by-election who were homosexual'. Is he referring to other candidates? 'I can't answer that, because of the libel laws,' he says.

Kris Kirk in Him/GR *no. 63, interviewing Peter Tatchell, who lost the Bermondsey by-election after he was the victim of a vicious campaign of vilification and character assassination by the tabloids and the Liberals who took the seat*

The Fallen

Aids is not simply removing our friends and lovers, the virus is also ripping untimely from life many of the men who contribute to our cultural lives. Just as the First World War removed the flower of British youth, so Aids is destroying many who had much to contribute, much to say – which makes their loss doubly sad.

Peter Burton in Gay Times, *September 1988*

The Damned

AIDS has been sent by God to punish homosexuals.

Donna Summer, 1984

Lies

Bob Dolphi asked Rock if it was difficult being well-known and reading articles about himself in the *National Enquirer* and magazines of that ilk. Hudson said it was water off a duck's back: 'You should hear what the *Enquirer*'s saying about me now. They're saying I've got AIDS. Well I hate to disappoint the fucking bastards but I don't have.'

from T. Parker, The Trial of Rock Hudson (1990)

An American Liberal

Because, you see, I am a homophobe. Not like the thugs, of course. Not me, I'm a liberal. Tolerant. Some of my best friends . . . I'm the other kind of homophobe, the polite kind: It's fine with me, only why do 'those people' have to be so blatant? Why do they have to parade their sexuality? . . . When I looked at the Christopher Street culture, that was something else. It threatened me as a woman.

It threatened me because I saw in it a satirical mirror of femininity, the very kind of femininity that feminism struggled against: a precious little-girlism, giggly and fey and cruel. There was a hate of women behind it, and I felt it . . .

I was disgusted by the promiscuity and boy pornography and sadomasochism that seemed so much a part of that scene. But why more disgusted than by heterosexual promiscuity and child abuse and violence? Homosexual men had to be good to earn my tolerance: I couldn't see that being homosexual is as little a guarantee of sanity or decency as being Jewish, Catholic, black or white is . . . I do know, however, that I am not the only one faced with this dilemma. Among the most liberal of us, there is a public discomfort with public forms of homosexuality.

Lesley Hazleton in the New York Times, 15 May 1986

Solemn Art

If art is to confront AIDS more honestly than the media have done, it must begin in tact, avoid humour and end in anger.

Edmund White, January 1987

Bad Taste

Condom commercials are seen as a breach of morality and good taste; viewers will be offended.

John Carry in the New York Times, 8 February 1987

Medicine and Morality

When it comes to preventing AIDS, don't medicine and morality teach the same lessons?

Ronald Reagan, 2 April 1987

Divine Retribution

There is a link between sin and sickness. God has spoken on the thing . . . God's judgement is written into the way things are. If we misuse our bodies we take the consequences.

Revd Tony Higton, a leading member of the evangelical wing of the Church of England, quoted in the Guardian, *4 September 1987*

Racist

The theory that AIDS originated in Africa is a stalking horse for anti-black racism, charged Lieut. Col. Abdul Mumini, governor of the Nigerian state of Borno. This theory, the governor said, 'is reminiscent of a colonial mentality which capitalizes on our weakness and underdevelopment, to unjustifiably attribute everything that is bad and negative to the so-called dark continent.'

from the New York Times, *19 November 1987*

Angry Dame

I am quite prepared to affirm that it is quite right that there should be an intolerance of evil . . . I believe that intolerance of evil should grow.

Dame Elaine Kellett-Bowman MP, House of Commons, 15 December 1987, reacting to the arson attack on the offices of Capital Gay

Free Will

Homosexuals are not a lot of passive victims condemned by their nature to suffer a dreadful fate which they can do nothing to avoid. They are individual men and women – rather than collective members of an oppressed community – and can save themselves by an effort of free will. If only the Jews had been able to escape their tragic fate with comparable ease.

Peregrine Worsthorne in the Sunday Telegraph, *31 January 1988*

Boys in Blue

A secret probe into claims of a sex orgy at a top police college has been launched by Scotland Yard. Detectives swooped on the Metropolitan force's Peel Centre in Hendon, London, after seeing photographs of young bobbies caught with their trousers down. At the centre of the inquiry are a dozen recruits aged between 16 and 18. Among the allegations being investigated is one of homosexual practices among some of the trainees.

The Yard were called in after a girl student at the centre complained about goings-on in the recruits' bar. Senior officers at first shrugged off her claims. But a full-scale investigation was ordered after she revealed she had taken photographs of the orgy, which started after heavy drinking. Officers of the Yard's anti-corruption squad seized her roll of film. They have spent all week at the centre interviewing recruits and searching their quarters.

One policeman said: 'This was not a case of coppers dropping their trousers and mooning. We are talking about sexual acts taking place between men in the bar. This is very serious. People like that are not fit to become police officers.'

from the News of the World, *7 February 1988*

Civil Rights

I have been an activist for 20 years and I see this as an important issue of sexual freedom. Liberace never went to the baths. The large majority of people at bathhouses are having safe sex. But I also support people's right to have unsafe sex.

John O'Brien, bathhouse patron, on moves to close bathhouses in San Francisco, in the Los Angeles Times, *23 February 1988*

Seduction

It's not a condition, it is something which is acquired by seduction in youth.

Paul Johnson, journalist and conservative polemicist, quoted by the New Statesman, *11 March 1988*

The Guilty and the Innocent

I am fed up being continually bombarded with the AIDS problem. The majority of victims have only themselves to blame because of their sexual activities and needle sharing. I abhor the amount of money being spent on them and feel no sympathy for them whatsoever.

I feel sorry for the innocent victims who contract the disease through blood transfusions and the babies born with AIDS because their parents have it. We should spend the money on them, but give the rest of it to the NHS.

from a letter published in the Daily Express, *16 March 1988, from Mrs Celia Johnson*

Christian Thoughts

[The Church] supposes that God created numbers of people whose sexual inclinations were for ever to remain unfulfilled; whose lives were to demonstrate perpetual sacrificial qualities not of their own choice. Compulsory celibacy is seen as a guarantor of purity. In every other dimension of contemporary theological speculation, it should be noticed, modern churchmen are fussily anxious to establish that you cannot, without grave error, separate the idea from the practice . . . Actual experience of life in liberal society also suggests that the moral and spiritual accompaniments of human love are as capable of germinating and flowering in relationships once called deviant as they are in sexual associations which, for all their apparent orthodoxy and normality, in reality disclose an enormous range of experiences . . . The truth, surely, is that just as Christianity has abandoned the dietary laws which once occupied a prominent position in religion so now it can shed it adhesion to exclusive views of human sexuality. Those views took their origin in distant societies where the frail existence of semi-nomadic peoples required that sexual energy should never be expended on anything that did not potentially add to their numbers. They are scarcely needed when an overcrowded planet, and a desiccated culture, yearn for human affection . . . the fact is that the lives of very many homosexual Christians down the centuries have disclosed spiritual gifts in astonishing abundance.

Edward Norman, Anglican clergyman and Dean of Peterhouse, Cambridge, 1972–88, in
The Times, 7 May 1988

Dangerous Liaisons

It was during this period that he [a rent-boy called David] first met Harvey Procter [Conservative MP for Billericay in Essex]. Another rent-boy, who he knew by sight, asked if he wanted to go back to a punter's house. It was 'a very ordinary one-bedroomed flat in Fulham with this guy who was wildly into schoolboy scenes. He asked me out the next night, then he asked me to move in' . . . Having moved in with Harvey Procter, life became – mostly – more comfortable. 'Every day he'd give me £20 and I'd go out and do another punter – just an hour job and get very, very slaughtered . . . He liked having a real situation to punish me for, so the next morning it would be "David, you've been a very bad boy, haven't you? What did you do last night?" "Come in drunk, sir." He liked me, I'd been at public school, I knew what I had to do.

'There was no sex involved at all. He'd start off with his hand, then move on to his slipper, then the cane. And it was horrendous. It brought back being at school to me in a big way . . . Once I actually enjoyed it and that scared me as well. But generally I didn't' . . .

[This life] continued for three months. It was then that he went to the *Sunday People* with his story. They couldn't believe their luck – having followed Procter on a round-the-world tour in an unsuccessful attempt to nail him . . . David's mother rang him up the morning it came out: 'I want to die today' . . . 'There was this feeling of climax and going as far as you could go . . . I spent £20 in a bar on my own and literally drank myself sick. The ridiculous thing is that three days after that I went and sat an English A-level . . . I went in and wrote a story about prostitution.'

from the Guardian, 5 November 1988

Stars, Stories and Videos

Only very recently have pornographic magazines been subjected to serious study . . . During the period from September 1970 thru December 1984, this researcher periodically purchased every fifth homosexual pornographic magazine available in adult bookstores in two major cities in the United States. Magazines published during the previous decade were also acquired through the purchase of a private collection and from a commercial source of secondhand material . . . One-hundred-fifty-eight gay pornographic magazines were subjected to a quantitative content analysis . . . The age range of models narrowed significantly over the span of the study period. The youngest-appearing models in the 1960s magazines appeared to be preadolescents in 23.7% of the magazines, adolescents in 31.6%, and in their late teens or twenties in 44.7%. In the early 1970s the distribution was: preadolescents in 4.8%, adolescents in 39%, and late teens and twenties in 56.1%. In the late 1970s, the youngest models appeared to be adolescents in 8.8% and late teens or twenties in 91.1%. All of the models in the 1980s magazines appeared to be in their late teens or twenties . . . there was no significant change in the race of the models appearing in the magazines. The overwhelming majority of the models in all four periods were white . . .

In the 1960s sample many of the models who were shown in multiple photos were identified by name (not necessarily, of course, their true name) and some appeared in numerous magazines, achieving a sort of 'star' status. In the early 1970s sample very few models were referred to by name. In the late 1970s models were occasionally referred to by name, but in several cases the same model was identified by different names in different magazines. In the 1980s a majority of the magazines identified the models by name and a 'star' system had clearly emerged once more. Also of interest regarding models' names in the 1980s was the frequency with which two models were referred to by the same last name and were portrayed (factually or not) as brothers. In some cases these 'brothers' are shown engaging in sex acts with each other, thus adding an element of incest which was not displayed in materials from the previous decades.

Perhaps the best-known of the gay porno stars of the 1980s is Kip Noll. In the largest of these real of 'fictional' families, Kip Noll is represented in various magazines as having three brothers and two cousins sharing the name Noll, who are all gay porno models. He is portrayed in one magazine (and video) having sexual relations with one of his purported brothers and in two magazines (and two videos) having sexual relations with one of his purported cousins.

In the 1960s, 60.5% of the magazines contained an essentially random assortment of photographs, while in 39.5% there was some grouping of photos, most often simply grouping together multiple photographs of the same model. In the early 1970s, 75.6% contained assorted photos and 22.4% showed some grouping. In the late 1970s, a majority (61.8%) were assorted pictures, 26.47% grouped photos of the same model or models, 8.8% had groups of photos which showed some progression or told a story, and in 2.9% all of the pictures in the magazine showed some progression or storyline. Of the 1980s magazines, 35.6% contained simple groupings, 15.6% contained groupings with a storyline, and in 48.79% all of the pictures followed some progression or storyline. The growing importance of videotapes in the gay pornography market of the 1980s seems to have played a part in this development. In 57.3% of the magazines sold in the 1980s the content was composed of still pictures taken in conjunction with the making of a video . . .

The pictures in 89.5% of the 1960s magazines showed only simple nudity without any sex acts, 7.9% showed masturbation and 2.6% included pictures of other sex acts. In the early 1970s 41.5% showed only nudity, 43.9% showed models with erections, 7.3% showed masturbation, and 7.3% showed other sex acts. In the late 1970s, 23.5% showed only nudity, 35.3% showed erections, 23.5% showed masturbation, and 17.6% showed other sex acts. In the 1980s, 17.8% showed models with erections, 44.4% showed models masturbating, and 37.8% showed other sex acts. This showed a significant increase in the overt sexual content of the magazines.

from David F. Duncan, 'Trends in Gay Pornographic Magazines: 1960 through 1984', in Social Science Review, vol. 73, January 1989

Our Struggle

[Paul] Gambaccini sees Aids as the major challenge facing our generation, just as fighting a war or surviving a depression was the challenge for his parents' generation. And he pulls no punches when attacking those who have spread lies and panic about the disease: 'I myself personally feel that the owners and editors of many of the tabloid newspapers on the British streets will be directly responsible for the deaths of tens of thousands of people in this country, because they will have given them a false idea about AIDS – that it was a gay disease which they didn't have to worry about.'

from Gay Times, January 1989

Chatwin

The death of Bruce Chatwin at the age of only 48 has caused widespread sorrow. But, for those who saw his wizened appearance when he was interviewed at the time of the Booker Prize last November (for which his novel *Utz* had been shortlisted), the reports that he had died of AIDS can't have come as much of a surprise.

Chatwin himself had said that he was suffering from a little-known Chinese bone disease, and my first impulse was to regret his reticence. Openness and honesty are among the few weapons that could be of some use in the public campaign against the disease, and it's a poignant fact that neither of the two most famous people to have died of the disease, Rock Hudson and Liberace, ever felt able to admit they had it . . . Bruce Chatwin was obsessed with myths and tales. As his various obituarists testified, his best work consisted of turning fact into potent fiction. Both *The Viceroy of Ouidah* and *On the Black Hill* began as true anecdotes told to friends but he wrote them down as fiction. *The Songlines* began as a work of anthropology but Chatwin tore it up and rewrote it as a novel.

One effect of Aids has been to break through the fluidity and playfulness of these different roles like a secret policeman, brutally classifying people who have previously escaped the simplicity of classification. I suspect that Chatwin's fictitious Chinese disease was another gallant myth, a way of escaping being pinned down to the very end.

Sean French in the New Statesman, *27 January 1989*

A Matter of Honour

One of the Navy's more notorious recent examples of what O. Henry called 'mental apparition' involves handsome Joseph C. Steffan, once a cadet at the U.S. Naval College at Annapolis until they discovered he was gay and drove him out two months before graduation . . . [his] life fell apart, he was a senior midshipman . . . and in the top tenth of his class – actually one of the top ten individuals in his class. Steffan had even been selected as a battalion commander, which made him responsible for one-sixth of the academy's brigade. And he was about to graduate with honours and enter the U.S. Navy as a commissioned officer . . . But two months before his graduation in 1987, Steffan was ordered either to resign or be discharged because he was gay. Under the school's honour code (which states that a cadet does not lie, cheat or steal), when the commandant asked him point blank whether the rumours were true, Steffan hesitated less than a second before he said yes. He could have lied, could have declined to answer, but chose not to do so. Instead he hesitated a tiny fraction of a second and answered, 'Yes.' Why? 'I think I felt a little pride,' he said . . . Did Steffan lie when they asked him, when he first applied at the age of 17 or so, whether he was gay? No. Although he had some awareness of his feelings in high school, he tried to suppress them. He became student body president and earned three letters each in track and wrestling . . . Steffan says that he did not know that he was gay until his second year as a midshipman . . . Even so there was never any allegation that his orientation had affected his training or performance . . . What happened was that Steffan confessed his feelings to some close friends and one of them betrayed him . . . Among his extra-curricular activities, he joined the school glee club, toured with them, and even sang the national anthem at the Army–Navy football game in both 1984 and 1986.

'I cannot explain the emotional trauma,' Steffan said, 'I literally went from the absolute pinnacle of my life to the lowest point within a matter of hours'. . . . Not only was there the shame of not graduating when everyone in his small hometown was watching his progress, but there was a telephone call I can only partially imagine in which he had to tell his mother and father not only that there would be no graduation – but why.

from Him, *no. 23, 1989*

Revenge

'I was looked upon at the house as a nonentity', the 35-year-old musicologist [Marc Christian] said in a telephone interview. 'The friends of Rock Hudson saw me as a piece of toilet paper, as something to be thrown away. The [law] suit was my way of saying that I wasn't going to be treated that way. Everybody has a right to be treated with respect . . . They wouldn't have treated someone who was seen as Rock's equal that way.'

from the Los Angeles Times, *19 February 1989*

Out of This World

The astronomer and former leader of the United Country Party, Patrick Moore, accuses the Inner London Education Authority of being as 'guilty as drug pushers' for recommending a book about a teenager's 'progress to a positive gay identity' to schools.

Moore denounced the book, innocently titled *The Milkman's On His Way*, at a recent education committee meeting in the Lords, hosted by Baroness Cox. The novel, by David Rees, has been placed on the ILEA positive images list sent out to school libraries, and Moore claimed at the meeting: 'Our children are being corrupted and depraved by it' . . . Moore describes it as 'pure sexual perversion'. 'Children will read it and try it out and get Aids,' he rages.

from the Evening Standard, *30 March 1989*

Kissing I

Scenes of men kissing [on TV] do not seem to promote tolerance; they were invariably commented on unfavourably, sometimes with sharp hostility.

Lord Rees-Mogg, Chairman of the Broadcasting Standards Committee, in the Independent, *18 April 1989*

Self-Help

Tak Yamamoto, a 51-year-old [Japanese-American] . . . stopped going to gay bars in West Hollywood two years ago because he said they catered to a white clientele. 'No one wanted to meet people like me in the bars . . . They wanted to meet blondes with blue eyes and big, beautiful bodies.' So Yamamoto organized a social group for gay Asians and Pacific Islanders to allow its 200 members to openly discuss their homosexuality and cultivate their cultural identity.

from the Los Angeles Times, *30 April 1989*

Safe Distances

A Los Angeles superior court judge ordered R. James Babbitt, the former business manager and current housemate of diver Greg Louganis, to stay at least 500 feet away from Louganis after the athlete said he feared Babbitt would hurt him.

Louganis, who sought the restraining order, told superior judge Dzintra Janavs on March 28 that he 'could no longer tolerate [Babbitt's] abuse' and said that Babbitt had threatened to reveal intimate information about him to news reporters.

Louganis won gold medals for springboard diving at the 1988 summer Olympic Games. He and Babbitt have shared a home in Malibu, Calif., for four years, and gays have long speculated that Louganis might be gay.

Louganis has calmly declined to answer questions about his sexuality, saying they don't pertain to his public life as a sports figure.

In recent weeks, the gay press created a small brouhaha after a Madison Avenue advertising executive said that Louganis was rejected for contracts to endorse Wheaties cereals and many other products after his Olympic win because he was not sufficiently macho.

'I fear for my life,' Louganis wrote in a sworn court statement. 'I believe that Babbitt is unstable and capable of violent acts of aggression. I sincerely believe that he intends to harm me.'

Louganis fired Babbitt as his manager after six years on March 13. Louganis claimed that Babbitt responded to the dismissal by threatening to reveal 'confidential and private facts' about Louganis unless the athlete either rehired Babbitt as his manager on new financial terms dictated by Babbitt or paid Babbitt 50% of his present and future earnings and signed the deed of the Malibu house over to Babbitt.

Louganis alleged that Babbitt told him, 'I made you, and I can destroy you. I can make things and your life ugly.'

Babbitt, in a sworn statement presented to the judge by his lawyer, said he has never harassed Louganis. Janavs's order allowed Babbitt to withdraw a lump sum of $5,000 in living expenses from the two men's joint account and to continue living at the Malibu house. Louganis said he is the sole owner of the house.

Louganis claimed in court that Babbitt's presence threatens his work because it makes him unable to prepare for personal appearances. He said Babbitt held him 'hostage' in the house for four months after he returned from the Olympics.

from the Advocate, *9 May 1989*

Kissing II

An astonishing court case was reported in *The Hampstead and Highgate Express* (14 April 1989) concerning two men who were kissing in a King's Cross street. Apparently, the two had been arrested by a police officer who 'realised how offensive this can be to ordinary members of the public'. The men were bound over for £100 each after charges of 'gross indecency' against them were dropped. The judge, Thomas Pigot QC, told them they were lucky to escape a prison sentence: 'This kind of thing is intolerable,' he said, 'and you had better tell your friends that they risk a prison sentence if they do it . . . People are fed up of watching performances of this kind.'

Mediawatch, Gay Times, *June 1989*

A Parade

Veteran CARES, a group of gay veterans representing all branches of the military, led 257 floats and contingents in the pageant. The parade was sponsored by Christopher Street/Los Angeles . . . [An estimated 200,000 people] watched 10,000 marchers, ranging from the elegant to the extraordinary, waved and shouted to those who jammed the sidewalks. Assemblywoman, Maxine Walters (D[emocrat] – Los Angeles), the parade's grand marshal, and Los Angeles Mayor Tom Bradley received warm ovations as they rode in vintage Cadillacs.

A character called 'Kaptain Condom', dressed in a red, white and blue superhero suit, was also cheered as he cruised by the grandstand on an old military tank decorated with balloons and streamers. Not far behind were the West Hollywood High Cheerleaders, a group of female impersonators sporting pompoms, false breasts, wigs and mustaches.

'This is our day to be free,' said Steve Pounds, 29, who has been attending the parade with his mother for 10 years. 'It is about time we can be ourselves.'

Pounds' mother, JoAnne Wright, was equally enthusiastic. 'I don't believe gays belong pushed away in the closet,' Wright said. 'The parade is a very positive thing – I think more parents should support their children.'

from the Los Angeles Times, *26 June 1989*

Buggery Kills

The message to be learned – that the Department of Health should now be urgently propagating – is that active homosexuals are potentially murderers and that the act of buggery kills.

George Gale in the Daily Mail, *21 July 1989*

Change

'We say that AIDS is a moral problem sent by God. We tell the boys [male prostitutes] you should not have sex with another man, you should rehabilitate yourself and have sex only within the sanctity of marriage' said Pro-vida [a Catholic pro-life group in Mexico] President Jorge Serrano, adding that he would like homosexuals incarcerated.

from a report by Chris McGreal in the Independent, *23 September 1989*

Persecuted Opinions

Toleration is widely praised but rarely practised . . . When it comes to fashionable causes it is . . . positively dangerous, to dissent from them . . . The world is full of indignation against homosexuals and those who proselytise on behalf of them. But it is an indignation which dare not speak its name. 'Heterosexism', as it is called by our enlightened educationists, is neither an opinion nor a morality but a sin, to be rooted out if necessary by full-time censors, charged with policing our schools. Probably the Comment page of the *Sunday Telegraph* provides the last remaining place where you can criticise homosexuality in print – the last place where toleration will be extended to the heterosexist . . .

'In the long run,' he said, 'we are all dead.' Keynes was talking of economics, justifying his policy of paying the debts of the living by mortgaging the capital. But his is the authentic voice of Bloomsbury homosexuality. It is precisely this disenfranchising of the future generations which is the primary consequence of homosexual indulgence, and of the new morality which licenses it . . . why should we trust the future of our society to those who have no interest in reproducing it? . . . From Lytton Strachey to Adam Mars-Jones it has been a favourite pastime of the literary homosexual to hold our society and its decencies to scorn, to make a mockery of ordinary people in their ordinary ways, and to imply that the old-fashioned values by which so many people live are far too dowdy for their more sophisticated contemporaries . . . We can see it in the leisured hedonism of Bloomsbury, in the 'exile' posturing of Auden, Isherwood and Norman Douglas, in the sentimental Arabism (so disastrous for our foreign policy) of T. E. Lawrence, and in the climate of rebellion that flourished between the wars, and which injected our country with the languorous pacifism which was such an encouragement to Hitler.

Homosexuality places loyalty between the living above the duty to the dead and the unborn . . . this lack of 'moral shock' – or, to give it its proper name, this shamelessness – may well contain the doom of us all.

Roger Scruton in the Sunday Telegraph, *24 September 1989*

Big Guns

Kathy Kubicina, a 36-year-old Ohio housewife . . . is the sister of Clayton Hartwig, a 24-year-old artilleryman who earlier this month was accused by an official inquiry of setting off the gun turret explosion aboard the Second World War battleship USS *Iowa* last April. It killed 47 sailors, Hartwig among them.

Kubicina says her brother was wrongly accused of murdering his shipmates and committing suicide, and that the navy smeared him by leaking the allegation that a homosexual tiff had led to the explosion. She maintains that the navy needed a scapegoat . . . The navy said a $4m (£2.5m) investigation, which included 20,000 scientific tests, had failed to turn up any evidence of accidental causes. On the other hand, Hartwig was in a position to have caused the accident and unidentified 'foreign' residue was found in the gun barrel wreckage after the explosion. Navy investigators also said that they also found 'significant circumstantial evidence' that Hartwig had an irregular 'lifestyle and thought patterns' in the months before the accident . . .

Kubicina acknowledges that she may have caused navy investigators to focus on her brother. At the memorial service for the victims, Kendall Truitt, a survivor and Hartwig's former best friend, informed Kubicina and her parents that Hartwig had taken out a $100,000 life insurance policy and named Truitt as the beneficiary. Kubicina says Truitt promised to turn over half the insurance money to her parents. When he failed after a week to contact her and confirm this offer, she wrote to President Bush and the *Iowa*'s senior officers asking for help.

The ship's officers turned over Kubicina's letters to navy investigators, who immediately opened a criminal inquiry. Investigators leaked suspicions that Truitt and Hartwig may have been homosexual lovers. The suggestion was that Hartwig decided to blow up his ship after he broke up with Truitt and was rejected by another sailor. Truitt, who recently married, has vehemently denied homosexual tendencies. Kubicina has produced several letters sent by Hartwig in the months before his death to girlfriends in Cleveland.

from an article by Mark Hosenball in the Sunday Times, *1 October 1989*

The *Sun* Says

> Straight Sex Cannot Give You Aids – Official
> Aids – the hoax of the century
> *from the* Sun, *1989*

Mr Angry

I saw the rage in action at lunch with him [John Junor] in Dorking, when I tried to argue that his view of Aids as appropriate punishment for sodomy was wrong-headed and cruel. Immediately the eyes bulged, the skin marbled – it was as if someone had shot purple dye into his veins – the voice curdled into a snarl . . . But why did he hate homosexuals so much? 'Unhappily,' he intoned, 'some men are born in a certain way and with those people I have great sympathy. It's the proselytisers I object to; the people who flaunt their homosexuality and try to subvert and convert other people to it. These are the people I have an utter hatred for, because I think they are spreading filth.'

By now the voice was booming round the walls of the genteel Dorking restaurant, the face was deep indigo, and an unfortunate waiter who had come to collect our plates stood paralysed like a rabbit in a car's headlights. 'Filth, Miss Barber. I regard buggery' – he paused to savour the word – 'buggery as the putting of a penis into shit. Don't you, Miss Barber? Don't you?'

from an interview with John Junor by Lynn Barber in the Independent on Sunday, 4 *February 1990*

Slots

I don't mind if telly poofs are OUT ON TUESDAY – as long as they're locked up the rest of the week.

Garry Bushell in the Sun, 7 March 1990

Justification

After one of my son's teachers died of Aids, I told a school governor how grieved I was: 'But he was a homosexual,' she replied tartly, as though that made his death all right.

Claire Tomalin in the Independent on Sunday, 1 April 1990

American Values

. . . the real American values (divorce, abortion, homosexuality, consumerism) . . .

Jonathan Clark in the Sunday Telegraph, 15 April 1990

The Underclass

The persecution of homosexuals is spiritually akin to anti-Semitism. Hitler proved the point by despatching homosexuals as well as Jews and gypsies to the concentration camps. It is intolerable that people should be persecuted for not belonging to the same race as the majority. It is no less inexcusable that they should be vilified and assaulted because their sexual orientation differs from the norm. A report on our news pages, and a Press Council ruling which breaks new ground, come as a reminder today that in this particular form of aggressive intolerance the British are among the worst offenders.

The cause is not far to seek. It lies in the British educational system, which assumes that only the reasonably intelligent deserve further education, and fails to guarantee further training to those who leave school at 16. Despite belated attempts to plug the gap, Britain still lacks good technical schools and a flourishing industrial training system. The result has been the creation of a growing underclass of resentful youths whose lives seem to have no meaning. Left with only their maleness to believe in, their anger focuses on those who diverge from their own narrow view of the norm. Identifiable homosexuals are natural targets for such bullies. Gay rights activists believe that the existing legislation discriminates against them, and so seems to give the law's blessing to anti-homosexual prejudice. Crimes of violence committed against homosexuals are, however, fully covered by the existing criminal law. The police are suspected of being prone to homophobia themselves. They must take steps to eliminate that suspicion. Criminal acts against homosexuals must be investigated with as much zeal as those against young women or children.

The Press Council's condemnation of the *Sun* for referring to homosexuals as poofs or poofters suggests that its earlier rejections of similar complaints were wrong. Yet nothing has changed in the interim in public attitudes. The best remedy against such denigration lies in the hands of readers rather than the Press Council. If they find such terms offensive, they are at liberty to switch to another newspaper. Better education would hasten the trend.

from the Independent, *1990*

Lineker

I don't give a monkey's whether somebody's gay or not, to be honest.

Gary Lineker, 1991

Oxford Values

It is narcissism, turning to self-hatred: carried on with, it makes for trouble, and nowadays with AIDS, deadly trouble. But it is not, in a great number of cases, something that needs to go on . . . public decency, the family, are part of civilisation, and we should support them. The Eternal Feminine is jolly hard work. But she is a good thing and deserves support.

Professor Norman Stone in the Evening Standard, *7 February 1991*

Concerned Manxman

There is more than enough crime, disorder, cruelty and sickness in the world today without these types of people advocating to permit their type of crime and corruption and no one will convince me that these filthy creatures are not largely responsible for the spread of Aids. They are very sick people, even sick animals are put down . . . these abnormal people should be . . . shipped to a desert island where they can carry out their filthy and disgusting habits to their hearts' content, leaving we normal beings to live a cleaner, moral and Christian existence.

from the Isle of Man Examiner, *9 April 1991*

Backlash

The exclusion of gay scoutmasters from the Boy Scouts of America has prompted a bizarre backlash. Levi Strauss, the jeans maker, has withdrawn its $80,000 sponsorship, saying the ban on gays was at odds with the company's 'core values'.

from the Sunday Times, *7 June 1991*

Under Attack

It is a simple matter of the profound feeling that it is wrong to allow young men to be persuaded out of their role as husbands and fathers of the next generation by a practice that is the literal death of all that most parents have lived for and of all the treasures of temperament, intellect and talent that they have nurtured. This is not an idle fear to be dismissed as mere prejudice; it is the healthy response of families and of a society which know themselves to be threatened.

Lynette Burrows in the Sunday Telegraph, *4 August 1991*

Monastic Retreat

Three monks have died of Aids in the past three years in the all-male monastic republic of Mount Athos in Greece, officials confirmed yesterday.

from the Daily Telegraph, *20 September 1991*

Buddies

One of the lighter moments of the Gulf War was this letter that appeared in the problem page in the *People* under the title 'Secret Shame of the Desert Rat Buddies'.

I am a Desert Rat serving in the Gulf and my world is totally mixed up. Not only as a result of the present political crisis but because of a personal dilemma. We have no contact here with women and for the last few weeks out in the desert I've grown close to another soldier. We tend to spend a lot of time together.

I'm totally confused and think I'm starting to change my sexual inclination. It doesn't help when we are ordered on 24-hour guard duty together – half a mile from our main location.

I am sure my companion has previous homosexual experience but he has never exactly said so. Could I always have had these feelings towards men? Please tell me what to do because homosexuality within the Army is frowned upon.

I am sure everyone here would give me a severe beating if they ever found out. If this man and I feel the same way, should we be frank about it rather than letting it all get to boiling point?

from the People, *2 December 1991*

Norman

I chose to go public because, to misquote *Casablanca*, I'm not much at being noble but it doesn't take much to see that the problems of an old actor don't amount to a hill of beans in this crazy world.

There are many who believe this disease is God's vengeance. But I believe it was sent to teach people how to love and understand and have compassion for each other. I have learned more about love, selflessness and human understanding from people I have met in this great adventure in the world of AIDS than I ever did in the cut-throat, competitive world in which I spent my life.

Anthony Perkins, statement published after his death in September 1992

Tangled Emotions

An Irish grandfather was jailed for three years at the Old Bailey yesterday for accidentally strangling his lover's ex-husband during a bizarre sex act. James Duffy (60), from Dublin, and his best friend Frank Reilly (41), also a Dubliner, had secretly indulged in dangerous acts of bondage with each other for two years the court heard.

But in January this year their 'experiments' went tragically wrong and Reilly choked to death, said Mr Brian Barker, prosecuting. Reilly, who would get into fights because he enjoyed being beaten up, loved to strip naked and to be trussed up by his friend. The court heard that his favourite sexual thrill was to have a noose tied around his neck and slowly tightened. The sex games were kept secret from their close circle of friends.

Duffy was living with Reilly's former wife, Joan, who had no idea what the two men in her life were up to. But all was revealed last January, when Duffy accidentally tightened the noose around his friend's neck and strangled him . . . Mr Barker, prosecuting, said: 'The trussing up was consistent with the practice of semi-strangulation which apparently heightens some kind of sexual sensation or pleasure . . . This was a high-risk consensual homosexual act which tragically went wrong.' . . .

When first interviewed by detectives the grey-haired grandad was too ashamed to admit his secret gay games. The two men had been best friends for twenty years in East London's Irish community.

from the Irish Independent, *18 September 1992*

Portrait of the Artist

Tonight at the Théâtre des Champs-Elysées, in Paris, in the presence of the French Minister of Culture, Jack Lang, and a host of stars including Marcello Mastroianni, Catherine Deneuve, Jeanne Moreau and Jean Marais, the first feature film by Cyril Collard, *Les Nuits Fauves* (Savage Nights), will be in the running for the highest French cinema awards, the Césars. It has received no less than seven nominations: Best First Film, Best French Film, Best Original Screenplay, Best Musical Score, Best Young Actress, Best Director and Best Montage. Collard wrote the screenplay based closely on his own novel of the same name . . . He also directed it, acted the leading role and composed the music. A considerable achievement for a man of only 35. But he will not be present at the ceremony. He died of Aids last Friday.

Until almost the last moment Collard had been hoping to attend what is one of the great artistic events of the Paris season. For the last six years he had known he was HIV positive. But he fought his growing sickness with all the courage, energy, defiant spirit and positive faith in life of a man determined to leave his mark upon the world before it was too late. In one of his last interviews, he stated: 'I have three dreams. The first is to keep love alive in me. Next, that I should go on being well enough until they find a cure for Aids. And then, to make another film.'

His whole life had been a passionate, disorderly, sometimes violent confrontation with accepted professional and sexual behaviour . . . in the early 1980s, Collard formed his own rock group . . . He started making publicity clips for television. He wrote his first novel . . . [and] was introduced to directors like René Allio and Maurice Pialat, whose assistant he became on *Lolou* (1980), *A nos amours* (1983) – in which he had a love scene with Sandrine Bonnaire – and *Police* (1985).

He was a glutton for work, and for love. 'Within me there was this hunger for affection, for love. It was a craving that impelled me to satisfy immediately every passing lust, every aching desire, whether for boys or girls. My feelings were in total confusion. I was snatched up in a whirlwind of passion, but one in which I did not always find real love.' . . .

Cyril Collard's second novel, *Savage Nights*, was at once an immense success with both critics and public when it appeared in 1989. *France-Soir* called its author 'The spiritual child of Genet and Pasolini . . .'

During the making of the film, Collard had been afraid his sickness would ravage his dark good looks. But in fact his male beauty was miraculously spared.

He seemed to be working under a magic spell. The character he portrays is essentially his own – impulsive, generous, spiritually and emotionally extravagant, suggesting unplumbed depths of secret and ungovernable desires. He can be deeply touching in his love scenes with both boys and girls, but there is also in his brooding visage and prowling presence as he hunts for partners after midnight along the sinister Quai d'Austerlitz a moody subversive sexuality, a vicious predatory hunger for immediate, intimate casual contacts. One is reminded of Rimbaud's homosensual motto 'Anywhere, anyone, anyhow . . . ' And always we are conscious we are watching a condemned man.

from an obituary of Cyril Collard (1957–1993) by James Kirkup, in the Independent, *8 March 1993*

Wrong Word

He has a boy's face, but a man's body. He is a rap star, but he's white. He is street-tough, but the world's first male supermodel. He is adored by teen girls and gay men. He is Marky Mark – and he is in trouble.

People wouldn't believe it at first: this fresh, modern icon, just 21, has a criminal past and a deeply insulting attitude towards his fans.

Marky Mark's rise to fame seemed as effortless as his impish grin. He launched his pumped body at the world only two years ago; his debut album, *Music For The People*, reached No. 1 in the American charts . . .

In Britain readers of *Smash Hits* made his 'boy-Chippendale' status official by voting him Best Dance Act and Sexiest Man of the Year. Marky's erotic cabaret quickly became his trademark – and then his trade, as the media world beyond the pop magazines turned its lenses on his pneumatic flesh.

Last year *Interview* commissioned the photographer Bruce Weber to serve up choice cuts of Marky Mark to its readers, announcing that it was cool to gape at this urchin's pecs. *Rolling Stone, Vanity Fair* and *Penthouse* soon followed suit, and Gap exploited his now familiar features to promote its clothes. His 'respectable' fame spread to Britain, taking him out of the teenage market and on to the cover of the style magazine *The Face.*

His rap career was now eclipsed by his modelling . . . Last year he stepped up his own sexploitation, releasing a book of photos of his body by Lynne Goldsmith, dedicated 'to my dick'.

All this 'in-yer-face' sexuality prompted *The Face* to call him 'the Madonna of Rap'. 'He looks brilliant,' says Sheryl Garratt, the magazine's editor. 'Plus he's got such wide appeal: young women *and* gay men.'

It was the gay interest in Marky Mark that was to fuel the final stage of his launch into the media stratosphere. David Geffen, mogul of the gay media, suggested to Calvin Klein, whose business has long benefited from the spending power of gay men, that he sign up Marky Mark to promote – what else? – his line of men's underwear. It was a marriage made in heaven. Calvin Klein received devoted brand loyalty from the 'pink dollar' and priceless free publicity as the campaign became the most talked-about in years; Marky Mark got only

$100,000 for his sessions, but his image appeared on hoardings and television screens across the United States, making his the most famous male torso since Michelangelo's *David*.

Interviewers began to ask 'street tough' Marky Mark what he made of his phenomenal popularity with gay men, and his answers were liberal enough: no problem, he said, although he personally preferred the attentions of women. But eventually the ambiguity of being a rap star with a gay following proved too much.

Appearing last December on Channel 4's *The Word*, he refused to join the presenter in condemning a statement by his fellow guest Shabba Ranks that gays deserve to be 'crucified'. Instead he went on to perform with the Jamaican reggae star and to praise him for his 'candour'.

As news of this blunder filtered across the Atlantic, American gays began to sense that they had been robbed. The Gay and Lesbian Alliance Against Defamation (GLAAD) protested to Klein about his use of a homophobe to sell men's underwear, and threatened a boycott.

But worse revelations were to follow. The Committee Against Anti-Asian Violence (CAAV) revealed something Mark had been strangely bashful about: two convictions, dating from his mid-teens, for harassing black schoolchildren and assaulting two Vietnamese men.

Photographs of a demonstration by GLAAD and CAAV under the Calvin Klein poster in Times Square appeared in the *New York Times* and prompted a jittery Klein to issue a statement condemning homophobia and racism and offering the assurance that his model was 'a reformed young man who has grown way beyond his years as a result of a particularly difficult childhood' . . . [Marky Mark] issued an apology . . . He also announced that he would work with GLAAD and CAAV 'to help spread the word that bigotry and violence are wrong'.

from an article by Mark Simpson in the Independent, 10 May 1993

Star Turn

Last week, we were treated to a spectacle of a boarding party of senators headed by Sam Nunn, a conservative Democrat from Georgia who is chairman of the Armed Services Committee, prowling through ships of the US Atlantic Fleet to assess their suitability for homosexual habitation. At the huge naval base at Norfolk, Virginia, 200 miles south of the capital, the senators inspected the sleeping arrangements and lavatories on an aircraft carrier and three nuclear attack submarines.

Since the US Navy, like Senator Nunn himself and all but one of his companions, is vehemently opposed to Clinton's plan to allow undisguised homosexuals to enlist, they were not slow in providing the right picture opportunities for the accompanying press. Crouching senators were snapped with the grim faces of men who had stumbled on some awful crime as submariners demonstrated how close they slept in a space a Beirut kidnapper might have thought unkind.

A black petty officer told them he thought what homosexuals got up to was repulsive. He said he was fed up with people saying that the gays were being discriminated against like the blacks were once segregated, because they had a choice and black men did not. General Colin Powell, chairman of the Joint Chiefs of Staffs and the son of West Indian immigrants, is thought to agree.

The senators went back to Capitol Hill to listen to the testimony from senior officers from all three services. Both the Senate and Congress Armed Services Committees are supposed to be studying ways to implement the President's plan to admit homosexuals and to submit a draft executive order by 15 July. Congress could override the President's wishes.

The star witness was supposed to be the bull-necked Gulf hero, General 'Stormin' ' Norman Schwarzkopf. But the Marine Corps, to upstage the army, had a surprise in store in the form of Colonel Fred Peck, chief spokesman for the US forces in Somalia who has received so much television time he is almost as famous as Schwarzkopf himself.

The colonel scored a direct hit with his revelation that his son Scott was a homosexual and that he would do his utmost to keep him out of the military. As far as his new celebrity status was concerned, he seemed to have moved from the bulletins to something that sounded like the higher reaches of soap.

'A recruiter's dream come true,' the colonel told the senators in a hoarse voice. 'He is six-foot-one, blue-eyed, blond haired, great student . . . but if he were to go and seriously consider joining the military, I would have to . . . actively fight against it because my son is a homosexual.'

from a news report by Colin Smith in the Observer, *16 May 1993*

Safe Sex

Bulstrode was a banker in Louisville, Kentucky, and they had 'met' (if 'met' was the right word) one dreary winter Sunday when Walter was scanning the roster of names logged onto the gay channel in search of some sort of flirtation or dirty conversation. ('Interactive pornography' was how he described it to friends.) Among the Willing Slaves, Sweaty Jocks, Hung Studs, and Tight Ends who were jockeying for space and attention in that strange electronic gay bar of the mind, he had been amused to see for the first time his Louisville friend's aggressively offbeat handle, and since Bulstrode was one of his favorite characters in *Middlemarch*, one of his favorite books, he had dashed off a message, asking if indeed a literary allusion was intended. Bulstrode responded with a chat request; they retreated together to that little hypothetical private room, where Bulstrode acknowledged that Walter had recognized his source. He was Bulstrode because Bulstrode was, like him, a banker; also, he added, because the name had enough of a violent edge to interest the less literary. And who was this hunky lawyer, who recognized a name from *Middlemarch*? What was he doing in semiliterate compu-land? 'Information,' Bulstrode typed, 'we want information!'

In his past computer-enhanced communications Walter had been reluctant about divulging any true history, but Bulstrode for some reason put him at ease.

Walter admitted certain salient facts, being careful not to be too specific, then asked Bulstrode about himself, a subject on which he was less forthcoming not, Walter suspected, because he had anything to hide, but because the facts of his real life simply held no interest for him. 'Bulstrode's' biography, which he gave pieces of, was not, it quickly became clear, a thing of the real world. When Walter asked how old he was, he answered, 'Bulstrode is 32,' which made him suspect the banker in Louisville to be significantly older. In the meantime, Bulstrode admitted to several other alter egos: in moments of high-campy imaginativeness he was 'Rick-18', and in moments of extreme horniness he was 'Rough Master'. His real name was either George or Martin, depending on when you asked him. He said he was 6' 2" and weighed 175 pounds, had brown hair, blue eyes, a beard, a medium-hairy chest, and a seven-and-a-half-inch cock. All of this was probably a lie. Why not lie, after all, when there were so many barriers between you and the person you were speaking to? What harm could it do? And anyway, these particulars once they were dispensed never had much bearing on Walter and Bulstrode's conversations, even when those conversations took a decidedly sexy edge.

One cold Sunday evening Bulstrode asked Walter to call him. It seemed an inevitable progression, like sex on the third date. Walter was nervous and excited as he dialed the number, as if he were on the brink of doing something forbidden, but of course it was just ten digits, followed by a distant-sounding series of rings.

'Hello?'

'Bulstrode?' Walter asked.

'Walter? Hi!' And Bulstrode laughed. He had an appealing baritone with a slight southern lilt to it. 'I'm glad to be talking to you!'

'Me too.'

'You have a nice voice. Very masculine, very sexy.'

'Thanks. So do you.'

There were a few seconds of nervous breath, and then Bulstrode said, 'I can't believe it. Finally I'm hearing your real voice. And you know what? You sound just like what I imagined you would.'

Bulstrode was, it turned out, a veteran and an aficionado of the gay channel, the denizens of which he had maintained steady relations with for almost three years. 'I've had quite my share of adventures as a result of it too,' he told Walter. 'For instance, have you noticed a guy who comes on occasionally, not too often, with the handle Barracuda?'

'I'm not sure,' Walter admitted.

'Well, he's this kid up in Boston, a comp sci grad student at MIT. I had a pretty major love affair with him last year. We just broke if off a couple of months ago.'

'Really?' Walter said. 'Wow, I'm impressed. I guess I just never imagined people could really start a relationship this way.'

'I'd say this was just about the most serious gay relationship I've been in,' Bulstrode said. 'Jimmy – that was his real name – he and I were really in love. It was the best and the hardest thing I've ever been in.'

'Long-distance relationships are tough,' Walter said affably. 'Did you usually go up there or did he come to visit you?'

'Oh, we never met,' Bulstrode said.

For the space of a beat, Walter was silent. 'You never met?'

'Oh no. We just talked on the phone.'

'Oh.'

'Yes. Every day, sometimes two or three times . . . I've never had sex like that.'

'You mean phone sex,' Walter said cautiously.

'Yes of course. The most intense, incredible, horny, hot phone sex I have ever had. Sometimes we'd be on the phone five or six hours. He always came three or four times, but held back. I wanted to wait until the very end and then really make it big.' . . .

Bulstrode, it seemed, had ceased to believe in the barrier between imagination and act. And why not? What are we, after all, Walter wondered, but voices, synapses, electrical impulses? When one person's body touches another person's body, chemicals under the skin break down and recombine, setting off an electric spark that leaps, neuron to neuron, to the brain. Was that really all that different from what happened when fingers pushed down buttons on a keyboard that sent signals across a telephone wire to another keyboard, another set of fingers? Wasn't there, in all of that, something of a touch? All around him, Walter heard people complaining about how they wished they were different, wished they were bigger, smaller, smarter, sexier, thinner. Bulstrode had found a way round all that; he had found out how to become the self he imagined, the self his real life, apparently, constricted him from fully being.

from David Leavitt, Equal Affections *(1989)*

CHAPTER FOURTEEN

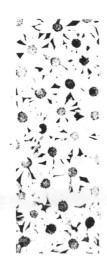

The Homintern

The word *Homintern*, which I coined in 1939, is attributed to Auden, who used it in an article in the *Partisan Review* about 1941, and has passed into the language. A takeoff on *Comintern* (Communist International), it was meant to convey the idea of a global homosexual community.

Harold Norse

'Some', he replied, 'it will be well to name,
The rest we must pass over, for sheer dearth
Of time – 'twould take too long to mention them.'

Dante

Anthony Powell suggested that his friend Jocelyn Brooke invented the term that Harold Norse tells us Auden stole from him. Whoever invented it provided us with a splendid word to explain the social and cultural power of homosexuality, the ability of this sexual allegiance to create networks and establish loyalties that do much to shape the imagination of the West. There is nothing in the homosexual act that makes its practitioner more artistic, but the fact that over centuries such men have had to conceal their intentions has supplied our culture with a source of much necessary ambiguity. Biographers have been tearing down these veils and showing us the artists of the past warts and all. What follows is an exercise in drawing on the biography industry to illuminate some of the important themes of the homosexual imagination and the legends upon which a homosexual identity has been constructed. It is an attempt to identify some elements of the homosexual clerisy.

Just as football managers say some players pick themselves, so no eleven playing for the cause could do without Wilde, Strachey, Auden, Isherwood or Orton. They will always command a place in the first team. Other members of the squad might find it difficult to maintain a run of first-team appearances, for competition in the squad is strong. Baldwin, Beaton, Behan, Bernstein, Blunt, Bowra, Cheever, Crane, Douglas, Housman, Howard, Jarman, Keynes, Leavitt, Maugham, Minton, Mountbatten, Nichols, Nicolson, Plomer, Porter, Sassoon, Scott, Welch, White and Wittgenstein are all players who with a different team manager might have found their name on the sheet.

CONSTANTINE CAVAFY (1863–1933), Greek Poet

Hidden Things

From all I did and all I said
let no one try to find out who I was.
An obstacle was there distorting
the actions and manners of my life.
An obstacle was often there
to stop me when I'd begin to speak.
From my unnoticed actions,
my most veiled writing –
from these alone will I be understood.
But maybe it isn't worth so much concern,
so much effort to discover who I really am.
Later, in a more perfect society,
someone else made just like me
is certain to appear and act freely.

Constantine Cavafy, 1908

He Swears

He swears every now and then to begin a better life.
But when night comes with its own counsel,
its own compromises and prospects –
when night comes with its own power
of a body that needs and demands,
he returns, lost, to the same fatal pleasure.

Constantine Cavafy, 1915

The Twenty-Fifth Year of his Life

He goes regularly to the taverna
where they met the previous month.
He made inquiries, but they weren't able to tell him anything.
From what they said, he gathered the person he'd met
was someone completely unknown,
one of the many unknown and shady young types
who dropped in there.
But he still goes to the taverna regularly, at night,
and sits there gazing toward the doorway,
gazing toward the doorway until he's worn out.
Maybe he'll walk in. Tonight maybe he'll turn up.

He does this for nearly three weeks.
His mind is sick with longing.
The kisses are there on his mouth.
His flesh, all of it, suffers from endless desire,
the feel of that other body is on his,
he wants to be joined with it again.

Of course he tries not to give himself away,
But sometimes he almost doesn't care.
Besides, he knows what he's exposing himself to,
he's come to accept it: quite possibly this life of his
will land him in a devastating scandal.
          Constantine Cavafy, 1925

In Despair

He's lost him completely. And now he tries to find
his lips in the lips of each new lover,
he tries in the embrace of each new lover
to convince himself that it's the same young man,
that it's to him he gives himself.

He's lost him completely, as though he never existed.
He wanted, his lover said, to save himself
from the tainted, sick form of sexual pleasure,
the tainted, shameful form of sexual pleasure.
There was still time, he said, to save himself.

He's lost him completely, as though he had never existed.
Through fantasy, through hallucination,
he tries to find his lips in the lips of other young men,
he longs to feel his kind of love once more.
          Constantine Cavafy, 1923

The Photograph

In this obscene photograph sold in the street
secretly (have to watch out for the police),
in this whorish photograph,
how could there be such a dream-like face?
How did you get in here?

Who knows what a degrading, vulgar life you lead;
how horrible the surroundings must have been
when you posed to have this picture taken;

what a cheap soul you must have.
But in spite of all this, and even more, you remain for me
the dream-like face, the figure
shaped for and dedicated to the Hellenic kind of pleasure –
that's how you remain for me
and how my poetry speaks about you.
            Constantine Cavafy, 1913

Two Young Men, 23 to 24 Years Old

He'd been sitting in the café since ten-thirty
expecting him to turn up any minute.
Midnight had gone, and he was still waiting for him.
It was now after one-thirty, and the café was almost deserted.
He'd grown tired of reading newspapers
mechanically. Of his three lonely shillings
only one was left: waiting that long,
he'd spent the others on coffees and brandy.
And he'd smoked all his cigarettes.
So much waiting had worn him out.
Because alone like that for so many hours,
he'd also begun to have disturbing thoughts
about the immoral life he was living.

But when he saw his friend come in –
weariness, boredom, thought all disappeared at once.

His friend brought unexpected news.
He'd won sixty pounds playing cards.

Their good looks, their exquisite youthfulness,
the sensitive love they shared
were refreshed, livened, invigorated
by the sixty pounds from the card table.

Now all joy and vitality, feeling and charm,
they went – not to the homes of their respectable families
(where they were no longer wanted anyway) –
they went to a familiar and very special
house of debauchery, and they asked for a bedroom
and expensive drinks, and they drank again.

And when the expensive drinks were finished
and it was close to four in the morning,
happy, they gave themselves to love.
            Constantine Cavafy, 1927

ANDRÉ GIDE (1869–1951), French Man of Letters

First Person

. . . dear, promise me from now on never to write I any more. In art, don't you see, there is no first person.

from a letter from Oscar Wilde to André Gide

Subtle Methods

Society knows very well how to go about suppressing a man and has methods more subtle than death.

from André Gide, 'In Memoriam Oscar Wilde' (1901)

Posterity

If I died today I would leave behind a one-eyed or totally blind image of myself.

from André Gide's journals for 1914

Preaching

Gide is hopelessly unapproachable. He gave a reading last night of his own works — in the most extraordinary style — like a clergyman intoning in a pulpit. It was enormously admired.

from a letter from Lytton Strachey to Dora Carrington, 26 August 1923

Honesty

In 1926 Gide published his memoirs, the confessional work *Si le grain ne meurt . . .* (translated into English in 1935 as *If it die . . .*). Edmund Gosse, by then the elder statesman of English letters, wrote to congratulate Gide on this courageous act but wondered if it had been prudent to expose his homosexual feelings so publicly.

What a fine letter I have from you, and how deeply I am moved by it! Why did I write this book? Because I thought I had to write it. What advantages do I expect from it? I expect nothing but consequence painful to me (and not only to me, alas). And of course the moral obligation had to be more than a little imperious to make me persist; but in truth it would have seemed to me cowardly to let myself be stopped by contemplation of the distress, or of the risk. I had the feeling that I could not have died in peace if I had kept all this locked up in me.

My dear friend, I abominate falsehood. I can't endure having a share in the customary camouflage that deliberately belies the writing of X, Y, and many another. I wrote this book to 'create a precedent', to set an example of candour;

to enlighten some persons, hearten others, and compel public opinion to reckon with something of which it is oblivious or pretends to be, to the immense impairment of psychology, morality, art – and society. I wrote this book because I had rather be hated than be beloved for what I am not. 'I would willingly come from the other world, to give him the lie, that should frame me other than I had been: were it meant to honour me,' Montaigne said.

I will add that I printed but one quickly exhausted edition of the book and that I am not minded to have it reprinted – at least, for a long time to come – except with the elimination of everything censurable. But I did not want to die without knowing that it is there.

I am talking to you without strain and without fear, and I am actually happy to be talking to you. Please do see in all I am telling you a testimony to my deep respect and steadfast friendship.

from a letter from André Gide to Edmund Gosse, 16 January 1927

Victims

We have had Wilde, Krupp, Macdonald, Eulenburg . . . Oh, victims! Victims as many as you please! But not a single martyr. They all deny it; they always will deny it . . . To try to establish one's innocence by disavowing one's life is to yield to public opinion. How strange!

André Gide

Observed

We found Gide sitting by an open window, and looking down at the Rue Michelet, up and down which GIs were endlessly passing, rolling their tight uniform trousers in a way which is very characteristic of North Americans . . . For Gide, the spectacle, for obvious reasons, held a special attraction.

from Malcolm Muggeridge, Chronicles of Wasted Time, Part 2: The Infernal Grove (1973)

Frisky

Taormina, in late April [1949] . . . I checked into the Albergo Timeo and went for a walk. In the main square, a promontory high over the sea, a group of men and boys were tossing coins. As I passed, André Gide came out of the crowd. Eighty years old, he wore a battered felt shepherd's hat, pulled straight down all around, and a cloak which looked as if it were made of an old horse blanket. A man in his late forties . . . was with him. They crossed the square to a large American limousine, got in, and were driven away by a chauffeur. Back at the hotel I wrote a note, reminding Gide of our meeting two years before . . . That evening in the dining room, midway of the meal, Gide came across to my table . . .

The next day when Gide and Herbart [his companion of the day before] invited me to ride to the beach with them in the afternoon, I had to decline. I had made an appointment to see the one person I had an introduction to in Taormina, an Englishman, Bobby Pratt Barlow. When Gide heard his name, he threw his hands up in mock horror. He had known Pratt Barlow in North Africa during the war and had run into him face to face the day before in the Greek theater. Gide had pretended not to recognize him; Pratt Barlow was the world's greatest bore; and I would be sorry if I kept my appointment.

Nevertheless, I kept it. That evening as soon as we encountered, Gide and Herbart wanted to know my impression. I had liked Pratt Barlow and said so; also, that the only servant who appeared all the time I was at the house was a boy of twelve or thirteen with the blond hair and perfect face of a Botticelli angel, who brought us vermouth, took away the glasses, opened and closed doors, etc. The minute Gide heard this he began to arrange a visit with as much enthusiasm as he had celebrated his escape the day before. We were in the lobby. The porter was asked to ring up Pratt Barlow; Gide got on the phone and said he had not recognized him in the Greek theater; his memory was fallible; but I mentioned his name and my visit and he would like to call and pay his respects.

We went the next morning. Gide was delighted with the little Beppe, who was as omnipresent as the day before, patting him on the head, complimenting his appearance, admiring his portrait by Oliver Messel . . .

The day after our visit to Pratt Barlow, Herbart accompanied Gide to the Taormina barber's, where a small boy lathered your face before a man shaved you. When the boy had finished lathering Gide, he said: 'No, you haven't done enough for me,' and made the boy continue lathering for nearly twenty minutes before he would let the man shave him.

from Donald Windham, Lost Friendships (1983)

MARCEL PROUST (1871–1922), French Novelist

Two Visits

Spent an hour of yesterday evening with Proust. For the last four days he has been sending an auto after me every evening, but each time it missed me . . . Yesterday, as I had just happened to tell him that I did not expect to be free, he was getting ready to go out, having made an appointment outside. He says that he has not been out of bed for a long time. Although it is stifling in the room in which he receives me, he is shivering; he has just left another, much hotter room in which he was covered with perspiration; he complains that his life is nothing but a slow agony, and although having begun, as soon as I arrived, to talk of homosexuality, he interrupted himself to ask me if I can enlighten him as to the teaching of the Gospels, for someone or other has told him that I talk particularly well on the subject. He hopes to find in the Gospels some support and relief for his sufferings, which he depicts at length as atrocious . . . I am taking him *Corydon*, of which he promises not to speak to anyone; and when I say a word or two about my Memoirs:

'You can tell anything,' he exclaims; 'but on condition that you never say: I.' But that won't suit me.

Far from denying or hiding his homosexuality, he exhibits it, and I could almost say boasts of it. He claims never to have loved women save spiritually and never to have known love except with men. His conversation, ceaselessly cut by parenthetical clauses, runs on without continuity. He tells me his conviction that Baudelaire was homosexual: 'The way he speaks of Lesbos, and the mere need of speaking of it, would be enough to convince me', and when I protest:

'In any case, if he was homosexual, it was almost without his knowing it; and you don't believe that he ever practised . . . '

'What!' he exclaims. 'I am sure of the contrary; how can you doubt that he practised? He, Baudelaire!'

And in the tone of his voice it is implied that by doubting I am insulting Baudelaire. But I am willing to believe that he is right; and that homosexuals are even a bit more numerous than I thought at first. In any case I did not think that Proust was so exclusively so . . .

Last night I was about to go to bed when the bell rang. It was Proust's chauffeur, Céleste's husband, bringing back the copy of *Corydon* that I lent to Proust . . . and offering to take me back with him, for Proust is somewhat better and sends a message that he can receive me if it is not inconvenient for me to come . . .

We scarcely talked, this evening again, of anything but homosexuality. He says he blames himself for that 'indecision' which made him, in order to fill out the heterosexual part of his book, transpose '*à l'ombre des jeunes filles*' all the attractive, affectionate, and charming elements contained in his homosexual recollections, so that for *Sodome* he is left nothing but the grotesque and the abject. But he shows himself to be very much concerned when I tell him that he seems to have wanted to stigmatize homosexuality; he protests; and eventually I understand that what we consider vile, an object of laughter or disgust, does not seem so repulsive to him.

When I ask him if he will ever present that Eros in a young and beautiful guise, he replies that, to begin with, what attracts him is almost never beauty and that he considers it to have very little to do with desire . . .

from André Gide's journal for May 1921

THOMAS MANN (1875–1955), German Novelist

Calculations

One cannot serve this Eros without becoming a stranger in society as it is today; one cannot commit oneself to this form of love without incurring a mortal wound.

Thomas Mann, quoted in Marcel Reich-Ranicki, Thomas Mann and his Family *(1989)*

Adolescence

The whole thing is metaphysics, music and adolescent eroticism; I shall never get over my adolescence.

from a letter from Thomas Mann to his brother Heinrich, 1901

Tadzio

Round a wicker table next him [Aschenbach] was gathered a group of young folk in charge of a governess or companion – three young girls, perhaps fifteen to seventeen years old, and a long-haired boy of about fourteen. Aschenbach noticed with astonishment the lad's perfect beauty. His face recalled the noblest moment of Greek sculpture – pale, with a sweet reserve, with clustering honey-coloured ringlets, the brow and nose descending in one line, the winning mouth, the expression of pure and godlike serenity. Yet with all this chaste perfection of form it was of such unique personal charm that the observer thought he had never seen, either in nature or art, anything so utterly happy and consummate. What struck him further was the strange contrast the group afforded, a difference in educational method, so to speak, shown in the way the brother and sisters were clothed and treated. The girls, the eldest of whom was practically grown up, were dressed with an almost disfiguring austerity. All three wore half-length slate-coloured frocks of cloister-like plainness, arbitrarily unbecoming in cut, with white turn-over collars as their only adornment. Every grace of outline was wilfully suppressed; their hair lay smoothly plastered to their heads, giving them a vacant expression, like a nun's. All this could only be by their mother's orders; but there was no trace of the same pedagogic severity in the case of the boy. Tenderness and softness, it was plain, conditioned his existence. No scissors had been put to the lovely hair that (like the Spinnario's) curled about his brows, above his ears, longer still in the neck. He wore an English sailor suit, with quilted sleeves that narrowed round the delicate wrists of his long and slender though still childish hands. And this suit, with its breast-knot, lacings, and embroideries, lent the silent figure something 'rich and strange', a spoilt, exquisite air. The observer saw him in half-profile, with one foot in its black patent leather advanced, one elbow resting on the arm of his basket-chair, the cheek nestled into the closed hand in a pose of easy grace, quite unlike the stiff subservient mien which was evidently habitual to his sisters. Was he delicate? His facial tint was ivory-white against the golden darkness of his clustering locks. Or was he simply a pampered darling, the object of a self-willed and partial love? Aschenbach inclined to think the latter. For in almost every artist nature is inborn a wanton and treacherous proneness to side with the beauty that breaks hearts, to single out aristocratic pretensions and pay them homage.

from Thomas Mann, Death in Venice (1912)

The Last Time

In advanced old age Thomas Mann was again overwhelmed and rejoiced by love, and this last erotic experience found direct expression in a literary essay. In July 1950, when he was seventy-five, a Bavarian waiter by the name of Franz caught his attention at a Zurich hotel: 'What beautiful eyes and teeth. What a charming voice,' he wrote in his diary. A few days later: 'My feeling for the boy goes deep. I think of him constantly and try to bring about meetings . . . ' Stammering with happiness and unhappiness, he recognizes that this is a great love: 'After an absence of twenty-five years, it was come to me one more time.' And 'Saw his face just for a moment while coming down in the lift. It won my heart. He wanted no part of me . . . World fame means a good deal to me, but it is nothing compared to a smile from him, the look in his eyes . . . ' Soon he would see the boy no more, he would forget his face, 'but not my heart's adventure' . . . This late love inspired the essay (*On the Erotic in Michelangelo*), which was published that same year. The outward inspiration for this essay was provided by the appearance of a bilingual edition of a selection of Michelangelo's poems in a new translation. From these poems Thomas Mann derived – so he tells us in his diary – 'a justification of love in old age', something he shared with Goethe, Tolstoy and, of course, Michelangelo, and that he interpreted as a sign 'of immense, tortured vitality'. He was deeply moved by 'this hopeless subjection of a mighty man, long after the seemly age limit, to the magic of the human face'.

from Marcel Reich-Ranicki, Thomas Mann and his Family *(1989)*

E. M. FORSTER (1879–1970), Conscience of the English Liberal Intelligentsia

Reactions

However gross my desires, I find I shall never satisfy them for the fear of annoying others.

E. M. Forster, 1910

Always Connecting

My defence at any Last Judgement would be 'I was trying to connect up and use all the fragments I was born with.'

from a letter from E. M. Forster to Forrest Reid, 1915

Instructions

When I die and they write my life they can say everything.

from a letter from E. M. Forster to T. E. Lawrence, 1928

Mother

[J. R.] Ackerley sometimes criticized Forster's reluctance to be more open about his homosexuality, pointing to the fine example set by André Gide, to which Forster would reply: 'But Gide hasn't got a mother!'

from Peter Parker, Ackerley *(1989)*

The Touch

Maurice dates from 1913. It was the direct result of a visit to Edward Carpenter at Milthorpe. Carpenter had a prestige which cannot be understood today. He was a rebel appropriate to his own age. He was sentimental and a little sacramental, for he had begun life as a clergyman. He was a socialist who ignored industrialism and a simple-lifer with an independent income and a Whitmannic poet whose nobility exceeded his strength and, finally, he was a believer in the Love of Comrades, whom he sometimes called Uranians. It was this last aspect of him that attracted me in my loneliness. For a short time he seemed to hold the key to every trouble. I approached him through Lowes Dickinson, and as one approaches a saviour.

It must have been on my second or third visit to the shrine that the spark was kindled and he and his comrade George Merrill combined to make a profound impression on me and to touch a creative spring. George Merrill also touched my backside — gently and just above the buttocks. I believe he touched most people's. The sensation was unusual and I still remember it, as I remember the position of a long vanished tooth. It was as much psychological as physical. It seemed to go straight through the small of my back into my ideas, without involving my thoughts. If it really did this, it would have acted in accordance with Carpenter's yogified mysticism, and would prove that at that precise moment I had conceived.

I then returned to Harrogate, where my mother was taking a cure, and immediately began to write *Maurice*. No other of my books has started off in this way. The general plan, the three characters, the happy ending for two of them, all rushed into my pen. And the whole thing went through without a hitch. It was finished in 191+ . . .

A happy ending was imperative. I shouldn't have bothered to write otherwise. I was determined that in fiction anyway two men should fall in love and remain in it for the ever and ever that fiction allows, and in this sense Maurice and Alec still roam the greenwood. I dedicated it 'To a Happier Year' and not altogether vainly. Happiness is the keynote . . .

E. M. Forster, from the 'Terminal Note' (September 1960) to Maurice

Sex

Nothing is more obdurate to artistic treatment than the carnal, but it has to be got in, I'm sure: everything has to be got in.

from a letter from E. M. Forster to Siegfried Sassoon, 1920

England

'And what's to happen to me?' said Maurice, with a sudden drop in his voice. He spoke in despair, but Mr Lasker Jones had an answer to every question. 'I'm afraid I can only advise you to live in some country that has adopted the Code Napoleon,' he said.

'I don't understand.'

'France or Italy, for instance. There homosexuality is no longer criminal.'

'You mean that a Frenchman could share with a friend and yet not go to prison?'

'Share? Do you mean unite? If both are of age and avoid public indecency, certainly.'

'Will the law ever be that in England?'

'I doubt it. England has always been disinclined to accept human nature.'

from E. M. Forster, Maurice (1971)

LYTTON STRACHEY (1880–1932), Historian and Biographer

Domestic Anthropology

Strachey planned he said in 1931 to write a book entitled *The Sexual Life of the English* modelled on the work of the anthropologist Malinowski's *Sexual Life of Savages in North-Western Melanesia*. 'It would be a remarkable book,' he added, 'but no doubt would have to be published in New Guinea.'

from H. Montgomery Hyde, The Other Love (1970)

Melting

. . . To be able to melt into a body literally twice as big as one's own . . .

from a letter from Lytton Strachey to Leonard Woolf

Boxing

. . . if I had ever been allowed to choose my life anywhere in my own age I should have been a stout athletic boxer.

Lytton Strachey, October 1902

Nothing But

We can't be content with telling the truth – we must tell the whole truth.

from a letter from Lytton Strachey to John Maynard Keynes, 8 April 1906

Odd

The world is damned queer – it really is. But people won't recognize the immensity of its queerness.

from a letter from Lytton Strachey to Duncan Grant, June 1908

Mallory

Mon dieu! – George Mallory! – When that's written, what more need be said? My hand trembles, my heart palpitates, my whole being swoons at the words – oh heavens! heavens! I found of course that he'd been absurdly maligned – he's six foot high, with the body of an athlete by Praxiteles, and a face – oh incredible – the mystery of Boticelli, the refinement and delicacy of a Chinese print, the youth and piquancy of an unimaginable English boy. I rave, but when you see him, as you must, you will admit all – all! The amazing thing, though, was that besides his beauty, other things were visible, more enchanting still . . . Virginia [Woolf] alone will sympathize with me now – I'm a convert to the divinity of virginity, and spend every day lost in a trance of adoration, innocence and bliss . . . The sheer beauty of it all is what transports me . . . To have sat with him in the firelight through the evening, to have wandered with him in the King's Garden among violets and cherry blossom, to have – no, no! for desire was lost in wonder, and there was profanation even in a kiss . . . For the rest, He's going to be a schoolmaster, and his intelligence is not remarkable. What's the need?

from a letter from Lytton Strachey to Clive and Vanessa Bell, 21 May 1909

Crossing Over

What a pity one can't now and then change sexes! I should love to be a dowager Countess.

from a letter from Lytton Strachey to Clive Bell, 21 October 1909

The Wanderer

Meanwhile, acting on what he called an 'inspiration', Lytton shouldered a knapsack and marched off alone to Salisbury. The next few weeks were spent trudging obstinately over the Wiltshire and Berkshire downs . . .

He was by this time sporting a conspicuous, bright yellow coat worn over a beautiful new suit of 'mouse-coloured corduroys' and an orange waistcoat; and his outlandish, heavily-haversacked figure caused some stir among the local populace as he stepped out gaily along the roads and fields, especially since he was wearing golden earrings. These, he told James [Strachey], were a great solace to him, though evidently outraging the good citizens of Wiltshire. 'They eyed me with the greatest severity,' he wrote . . . 'but I bearded them.'

from Michael Holroyd, Lytton Strachey (1967)

Jersey

After I left you I went to the Tube and saw there a very nice red-cheeked black-haired youth of the lower classes – nothing remarkable in that – *but* he was wearing a heavenly shirt, which transported me. It was dark blue with a yellow edge at the top, and it was done up with laces (straw coloured) which tied at the neck. I thought it so exactly your goût that I longed to get one for you. At last on the platform I made it an épreuve to go up to him and ask him where he got it. Pretty courageous, wasn't it? You see he was not alone, but accompanied by two rather higher-class youths in billycock hats, who I had to brush aside in order to reach him. I adopted the well-known John style – with great success. It turned out (as I might have guessed) that it was simply a football jersey – he belonged to the Express Dairy team. I was so surprised by that I couldn't think what other enquiries I could make, and then he vanished,

from a letter from Lytton Strachey to Henry Lamb, 20 February 1914

Substitution

The examination [to test his claim that he was a conscientious objector] could now commence. In the course of it the military representative attempted to cause him some embarrassment by firing a volley of awkward questions from the bench.

'I understand, Mr Strachey, that you have conscientious objections to all wars?'

'Oh no,' came the piercing reply, 'not at all. Only this one.'

'Then tell me, Mr Strachey, what would you do if you saw a German soldier attempting to rape your sister?'

Lytton turned and forlornly regarded each of his sisters in turn. Then he confronted the Board once more and answered with ambiguous gravity: 'I should try and come between them.'

from Michael Holroyd, Lytton Strachey *(1967)*

Modern Women

. . . a creature with a cunt . . .

from a letter from Lytton Strachey to James Strachey, May 1916

Fags

[He would] sit out on the village green surrounded by the village lads, dealing out forbidden cigarettes to them.

from Michael Holroyd, Lytton Strachey *(1967)*

POW

I had a curious adventure at the National Gallery where I went to see the Duveen Room – a decidely twilight effect: but spacing out the Italian pictures produces on the whole a fair effect. There was a black-haired tart marching round in india-rubber boots, and longing to be picked up. We both lingered in the strangest manner in front of the various masterpieces – wandering from room to room. Then on looking round I perceived a more attractive tart – fair-haired this time – bright yellow and thick hair – a pink face – and plenty of vitality. So I transferred my attentions, and began to move in his direction when on looking more closely I observed that it was the Prince of Wales – no doubt at all – a Custodian bowing and scraping, and Philip Sassoon also in attendance. I then became terrified that the latter would see me, and insist on performing an introduction, so I fled – perhaps foolishly – perhaps it might have been the beginning of a really entertaining affair. And by that time the poor black-haired tart had disappeared. Perhaps he was the ex-king of Portugal.

from a letter from Lytton Strachey to Dora Carrington, 10 June 1930

D. H. LAWRENCE (1885–1930), Poet and Novelist

Sane and Wholesome

Bawdy can be sane and wholesome,
in fact a little bawdy is necessary in every life
to keep it sane and wholesome.

And a little whoring can be sane and wholesome.
In fact a little whoring is necessary in every life
to keep it sane and wholesome.

Even sodomy can be sane and wholesome
granted there is an exchange of genuine feeling.

But get any of them on the brain, and they become pernicious:
bawdy on the brain becomes obscenity, vicious.
Whoring on the brain becomes really syphilitic
and sodomy on the brain becomes a mission,
all the lot of them, vice, missions, etc., insanely unhealthy.

. . .

D. H. Lawrence

Outlet

. . .
by instinct he's a sodomist
but he's frightened to know it
so he takes it out on women.

from D. H. Lawrence, 'The Noble Englishman'

The Suppressed Prologue

All the time, he [Birkin] recognized that, although he was always drawn to women, feeling more at home with a woman than a man, yet it was for men that he felt the hot, flushing roused attraction which a man is supposed to feel for the other sex. Although nearly all his living interchange went on with one woman or another, although he was always terribly intimate with at least one woman, and practically never intimate with a man, yet the male physique had a fascination for him, and for the female physique he felt only a fondness, a sort of sacred love, as for a sister.

from D. H. Lawrence

RONALD FIRBANK (1886–1926), Camp Novelist

Trip

I have found a most beautiful creature about sixteen with eyes like a gazelle, digging up the road. I take a taxi each morning at six to look at it.

Ronald Firbank

Facilities

The habit of putting glass over an oil painting always makes such a good reflection, particularly when the picture's dark. Many's the time I've run into the National Gallery on my way to the Savoy and tidied myself before 'The Virgin of the Rocks'.

Ronald Firbank

Camp Wisdom

I should have loved to live in the Bible period . . . How beautiful to have followed the Saints.

I am all design – once I get going.

All women are funny.

Ronald Firbank

Aesthete

Ronald Firbank was a customer of mine before the war. He was tall and slender in figure; his physique was almost feminine in its delicacy; he had the wasp waist affected by Victorian exquisites. His hair was dark and sleek and brushed flat to the head; his eyes were blue or bluish-grey; his features were oval in shape, the eyebrows thin and arched, the nose long, the chin weak; his complexion was fresh, with a delicate rosy blush on the cheek-bones. He was clean-shaven.

Firbank was always dressed in a dark, well-fitting lounge suit, and he wore a black bowler almost invariably tilted far back on his head. He carried gloves and a cane. His hands were white and very well kept, the nails long and polished, and what was unusual in a man is that they were stained a deep carmine. I might mention that before my wife and I learned his name we always spoke of him as 'the man with the red nails'.

He walked with a kind of leisurely saunter, as though time had no claims upon him. All his joints seemed to be loosely attached, like those of a marionette, and his movements in fact closely resembled those of a marionette, the controlling threads of which had been slackened. In short he was a decidedly limp specimen of mankind.

His tastes in literature were rather 'ninetyish', although he was interested in eighteenth-century French literature of the more frivolous type. His stock question on entering was: 'Have you anything in my line today; you know, something vague, something restful?' He was very fond of the word 'restful'; all the books he liked he termed 'restful'. Even a study in the baroque such as Beardsley's *Venus and Tannhauser* he would term 'restful', although the normal male would doubtless consider such a work, on the contrary, disturbing.

C. W. Beaumont, bookseller in the Charing Cross Road, in I. K. Fletcher, Ronald Firbank: A Memoir (1930)

Black Power

He was happy in watching Negroes.

from I. K. Fletcher, Ronald Firbank: A Memoir (1930)

RUPERT BROOKE (1887–1915), Poet and Bloomsbury Pin-Up

The First Seduction

We had hugged & kissed & strained, Denham [Russell-Smith] and I, on and off for years — ever since that quiet evening I rubbed him, in the dark, speechlessly, in the smaller of the two small dorms. An abortive affair, as I told you. But in the summer holidays of 1906 and 1907 he had often taken me out to the hammock, after dinner, to lie entwined there. — He had vaguely hoped, I fancy, — But I lay always thinking Charlie [Lascelles].

Denham was though, to my taste, attractive. So honestly and friendlily lascivious. Charm, not beauty, was his *forte*. He was not unlike Ka [Ka Cox, with whom Brooke had an affair], in the allurement of vitality and of physical magic – oh, but Ka has beauty too. – He was lustful, immoral, affectionate, and delightful. As romance faded in me, I began, all unacknowledgedly, to cherish a hope – But I was never in the slightest degree in love with him.

In the early autumn of 1909, then, I was glad to get him to come and stay with me, at the Orchard. I came back late that Saturday night. Nothing was formulated in my mind. I found him asleep in front of the fire, at 1.45. I took him up to his bed, – he was very like a child when he was sleepy – and lay down on it. We hugged, and my fingers wandered a little. His skin was always very smooth. I had, I remember, a vast erection. He dropped off to sleep in my arms. I stole away to my room: and lay in bed thinking – my head full of tiredness and my mouth of the taste of tea and whales, as usual. I decided, almost quite consciously, I *would* put the thing through the next night. You see, I didn't at all know how he would take it. But I wanted to have some fun, and, still more, to see what it was *like*, and to do away with the shame (as I thought it was) of being a virgin. At length, I thought, I shall know something of all that James and Norton and Maynard and Lytton know and hold over me.

of course I *said* nothing.

Next evening, we talked long in front of the sitting room fire. My head was on his knees, after a bit. We discussed sodomy. He said he, finally, thought it *was* wrong . . . We got undressed there as it was warm. Flesh is exciting, in firelight. You must remember that *openly* we were nothing to each other – less even than in 1906 . . .

Again we went up to his room. He got into bed. I sat on it and talked. Then I lay on it. Then we put the light out and talked in the dark. I complained of the cold: and so got under the eiderdown. My brain was, I remember, almost all through, absolutely calm and indifferent, observing progress, and mapping out the next step. Of course, I had planned the general scheme beforehand.

I was still cold. He wasn't. 'Of course not, you're in bed!' 'Well then, you get right in too.' – I made him ask me – oh! without difficulty! I got right in. Our arms were round each other. 'An adventure!' I kept thinking: and was horribly detached.

We stirred and pressed. The tides seemed to wax. At the right moment I, as planned, said 'come into my room, it's better there . . . ' I suppose he knew what I meant. Anyhow he followed me. In the large bed it was cold; we clung together. Intentions became plain; but still nothing was said. I broke away a second, as the dance began, to slip my pyjamas. His was the woman's part throughout. I had to make him take his off – do it for him. Then it was purely body to body – my first you know! I was still a little frightened of his, at any sudden step, bolting; and he I suppose, was shy. We kissed very little, as far as I can remember, face to face. And I only rarely handled his penis. Mine he touched once with his fingers; and that made me shiver so much that I think he was frightened. But with alternate stirrings, and still pressures, we mounted. My right hand got hold of the left half of his bottom, clutched it, and pressed his body into me. The smell of the sweat began to be noticeable. At length we took to rolling to and fro over each other in excitement. Quite calm things, I remember, were passing through my brain 'The Elizabethan joke "The Dance of the Sheets" has, then, something in it.' 'I hope his erection is all right' – and so on. I thought of him entirely in the third person. At length the waves grew more terrific; my control of the situation was over; I treated him with the utmost violence, to which he more quietly, but incessantly, responded. Half under him and half over, I came off. I think he came off at the same time, but of that I have never been sure. A silent moment; and then he slipped away to his room carrying his pyjamas. We wished each other 'Goodnight'. It was between 4 and 5 in the morning. I lit a candle after he had gone. There was a dreadful mess on the bed. I wiped it clear as I could, and left the place exposed in the air, to dry. I sat on the lower part of the bed, a blanket round me, and stared at the wall, and thought. I thought of innumerable things, that this was all; that the boasted jump from virginity to Knowledge seemed a very tiny affair, after all; that I hoped Denham, for whom I felt great tenderness, was sleeping. My thoughts went backward and forward. I unexcitedly reviewed my whole life, and indeed the whole universe. I was tired, and rather pleased with myself, and a little bleak. About six it was grayly daylight; I blew the candle out and slept till 8. At 8 Denham had to bicycle in to [Cambridge] to breakfast with Mr. Benians [his tutor], before catching his train. I bicycled with him . . . We said scarcely anything to each other. I felt sad at the thought he was perhaps hurt and angry, and wouldn't ever want to see me again. – He did, of course, and was exactly as ever. Only we never referred to it. But that night I looked with some awe at the room – fifty yards away to the West from the bed I'm writing in – in which I Began, in which I 'copulated with' Denham; and I felt a curious private tie with Denham himself. So you'll understand it was – not with a shock, for I am far too dead for that, but with a sort of dreary wonder and dizzy discomfort – that I heard Mr. Benians inform me, after we'd greeted, that Denham died at one o'clock on Wednesday morning, – just twenty-four hours ago now.

from a letter from Rupert Brooke to James Strachey, 10 July 1912

T. E. LAWRENCE (1888–1935), Romantic Hero

Misunderstanding

Dahoum was his other friend. He was then a boy of about fifteen, not particularly intelligent (though Lawrence taught him to take photographs quite well) but beautifully built and remarkably handsome. Lawrence was devoted to him. The Arabs were tolerantly scandalized by the friendship, especially when in 1913 Lawrence, stopping in the house after the dig was over, had Dahoum to live with him and got him to pose as model for a queer crouching figure which he carved in the soft local limestone and set up on the edge of the house roof; to make an image was bad enough in its way, but to portray a naked figure was proof to them of evil of another sort. The scandal about Lawrence was widely spread and firmly believed.

The charge was quite unfounded. Lawrence had in his make-up a very strong vein of sentiment, but he was in no sense a pervert; in fact, he had a remarkably clean mind. He was tolerant, thanks to his classical reading, and Greek homosexuality interested him, but in a detached way, and the interest was not morbid but perfectly serious; I never heard him make a smutty remark and am sure that he would have objected to one if it had been made for his benefit: but he would describe Arab abnormalities baldly and with a certain sardonic humour. He knew quite well what the Arabs said about himself and Dahoum and so far from resenting it was amused, and I think that he courted misunderstanding rather than tried to avoid it; it appealed to his sense of humour, which was broad and school-boyish. He liked to shock. Similarly he liked practical jokes, not least those which annoy, but his pleasure in them was so ingenuous that it was hard to take offence.

Leonard Wooley, in Lawrence by his Friends, *ed. A. E. Lawrence (1937)*

Demure

I was not much impressed by Lawrence's bombastic exaggerations . . . He is ambitious and makes preposterous claims while acting like a demure little schoolgirl.

from Richard Meinertzhagen's diary, 10 December 1917

Dedication

To S.A.
I loved you, so I drew these tides of men into my hands
    and wrote my will across the sky in stars
To earn you Freedom, the seven pillared worthy house,
    that your eyes might be shining for me
                    When we came.

Death seemed my servant on the road, till we were near
    and saw you waiting:
When you smiled, and in sorrowful envy he outran me
    and took you apart:
                    Into his quietness.

Love, the way-weary, groped to your body, our brief wage
    ours for the moment
Before earth's soft hand explored your shape, and the blind
    worms grew fat upon
                    Your substance.

Men prayed me that I set our work, the inviolate house,
     as a memory of you.
But for fit monument I shattered it, unfinished: and now
The little things creep out to patch themselves hovels
     in the marred shadow
                                        Of your gift.

from T. E. Lawrence, Seven Pillars of Wisdom (1926)

Desert Morals

The men were young and sturdy; and hot flesh and blood unconsciously claimed a right in them and tormented their bellies with strange longings. Our privations and dangers fanned their virile heat, in a climate as racking as can be conceived. We had no shut places to be alone in, no thick clothes to hide our nature. Man in all things lived candidly with man. The Arab was by nature continent; and the use of universal marriage had nearly abolished irregular courses in his tribes. The public women of the rare settlements we encountered in our months of wandering would have been nothing to our numbers, even had their raddled meat been palatable to a man of healthy parts. In horror of such sordid commerce our youths began to slake one another's few needs in their own clean bodies – a cold convenience that, by comparison, seemed sexless and even pure. Later, some began to justify this sterile process, and swore that friends quivering together in the yielding sand with intimate hot limbs in supreme embrace, found there hidden in the darkness, a sensual co-efficient of the mental passion which was welding our souls and spirits in one flaming effort. Several, thirsting to punish appetites they could not wholly prevent, took a savage pride in degrading the body, and offered themselves fiercely in any habit which promised physical pain or filth.

from T. E. Lawrence, Seven Pillars of Wisdom (1926)

Termination

Marriage contracts should have a clause terminating the engagement upon nine months' notice by either party.

from a letter from T. E. Lawrence to Edward Garnett, 1923

Weak Impulses

. . . the impulse strong enough to make me touch another creature has not yet been born in me.

from a letter from T. E. Lawrence to E. M. Forster, December 1927

Loud and Clear

Occasionally my eyes seem suddenly switched on to my brain, and I see all the more clear in contrast with the former mustiness, in these things nearly always shapes of rocks or trees or figures of living things – not small things like flowers . . . and in the figures always men. I take no pleasure in women. I have never thought twice or even once of the shape of a woman; but men's bodies, in repose or in movement – especially the former, appeal to me directly and very generally.

T. E. Lawrence, quoted in John Mack, A Prince of our Disorder: The Life of T. E. Lawrence (1976)

Bad Boy

A number of letters survive in which Lawrence, pretending to be his own uncle, wrote to his former batman, Jock Bruce, regulating and discussing the punishment that Bruce would administer to Lawrence. The uncle was supposed to be punishing his nephew for some misdemeanour.

Dear Sir,
Your letter showed me that I was perhaps being rather hard on Ted, by repeating that punishment at short interval. So upon reconsideration I informed him that it will be indefinitely postponed. I asked him to give you prompt notice that your help would not be immediately required. We will hold our hands and watch to see if the lad justifies this kindness. I need not say that I am very much obliged to you for being ready to take the further responsibility. I shall call upon you with confidence if Ted again makes it necessary. Please let me correct one misapprehension in your letter, however. Unless he strips, the birch is quite ineffective. The twigs are so light that even the thinnest clothing prevents their hurting. I fully understand your reluctance to strip him; so I was making up my mind to ask you to use either your friend's jute whip (which you mentioned to me in a former letter) or a useful dogwhip which I could send you by post. If the emergency arises, I shall agree to Ted's coming to you in flannels.

from a letter from T. E. Lawrence to Jock Bruce, 11 January 1935

Poor Boy

Another book I am reading is Richard Aldington's blistering, debunking attack on Lawrence of Arabia. I do not care for Richard Aldington's mind, and his malice is a little too apparent; nevertheless quite a lot of it – as far as I have read – sounds suspiciously like the truth. Lawrence was an inverted show-off and I have myself heard him talk the most inconceivable balls. Even at the time I was inwardly aware of this, but his legend was too strong to be gainsaid and I, being a celebrity snob, crushed down my wicked suspicions. He was charming to me anyhow, with a charm that could only be repaid by affection and a certain arid loyalty . . . All the same Lawrence is well out of it, poor dear. He would certainly not have enjoyed Richard Aldington's book. But then a sense of humour was never his strong suit.

from Noël Coward's diary, April 1955

Fraud

Richard Aldington has just published a book exploding the Lawrence Myth. It is a venomous book but true. Lawrence was the victim of his own desire for publicity but I blame the so-called Lawrence Bureau for pushing him into such an impossible position – men like Lowell Thomas, [Ronald] Storrs, and his own family. There are also men like Lloyd George, Winston Churchill, Allenby and Wavell who helped erect the myth and made the most extravagant claims for Lawrence's military genius. Lawrence had great charm, great ability and was in many ways a genius; he used all these virtues for deception. Not one single one of the men mentioned above had any first-hand knowledge of Lawrence's Arabian exploits, having gained their knowledge from Lawrence himself and from what he spread about, knowing it to be either false or exaggerated. Comparing him with Napoleon and Hannibal is just nonsense for Lawrence never commanded anything but a looting rabble of murderous Arab levies, he took part in no major military operation and his desert exploits had not the slightest bearing on Allenby's campaign. In his own words, his was a 'side-show of a side-show'.

I probably knew Lawrence better than any living man. We were attracted to each other when we first met in Sinai in 1917, we were much together in Paris in 1919, he laid bare his body and soul to me when he broke down in my room in Paris, we worked in the same room in the Colonial Office for almost two years and he often visited my house in London, playing with my children . . . There were no secrets between us and I believe I was the only one of his friends to whom he confided that he was a complete fraud. 'Some day I shall be found out' he said on more than one occasion. Poor little man . . .

Lawrence's love of speed and power was closely linked with his fascination for great big he-men such as Allenby, Dalmeny, Churchill and many others. He had no use for women, his sexual inclination being big strong men. He had little use for small men such as he was himself. I remember an occasion in the Majestic Hotel in Paris when he ran off with my knobkerry; I chased him, caught him and holding him tight gave him a spanking on the bottom. He made no attempt to resist and told me later that he could easily understand a woman submitting to rape once a strong man hugged her.

But, all the same, he had great charm and I was devoted to him. His obsession for publicity ruined his life; he got what he wanted, knew it was all false and got frightened. He found out that his life was an enacted lie.

from Richard Meinertzhagen's diary, 20 November 1955

J. R. ACKERLEY (1896–1967), Journalist and Writer

Hunting

Standing at the various bars with our token half-pints before us, we would eye each other surreptitiously, perhaps registering the fact that, with so many eagles about, if any Ganymede did arrive we would have to work fast.

from J. R. Ackerley, My Father and Myself *(1968)*

The Ideal Friend

Though two or three hundred young men were to pass through my hands in the course of years, I did not consider myself promiscuous, but monogamous, it was all a run of bad luck, and I became ever more serious over this as time went on. Perhaps as a reaction to my school, Army and Cambridge difficulties, the anxiety, nervousness, guilt that had dragged me all along the line (though I did not think of it then as guilt, if indeed it was), I was developing theories of life to suit myself: sex was delightful and of prime importance, the distance between the mouth and the crotch must be bridged at once, clothes must come off as soon as possible, no courtship, no nonsense, no beating, so to speak, about the bush, the quickest, perhaps the only, way to get to know anyone thoroughly was to lie naked in bed with him, both were at once disarmed of all disguise and pretence, all cards were on the table, and one could tell whether he was the Ideal Friend. What I meant by the Ideal Friend I doubt if I ever formulated, but now, looking back over the years, I think I can put him together in a partly negative way by listing some of his many disqualifications. He should not be effeminate, indeed preferably normal; I did not exclude education but did not want it, I could supply all that myself and in the loved one it had always seemed to get in the way; he should admit me but no one else; he should be physically attractive to me and younger than myself – the younger the better, as closer to innocence; finally he should be on the small side, lusty, circumcised, physically healthy and clean: no phimosis, halitosis, bromidrosis. It may be thought that I had set myself a task so difficult of accomplishment as almost to put success purposely beyond my reach; it may be thought too that the reason why this search was taking me out of my own class into the working class, yet still towards the innocence which in *my* class I had been unable to touch, was that guilt in sex obliged me to work it off on my social inferiors.

from J. R. Ackerley, My Father and Myself *(1968)*

Dog Lover

A great red lorry farts and groans among the trees at the edge of Siegfried [Sassoon]'s wood. Some workmen move about here putting chain tackle round the trunk of a felled tree. I think to myself as I watch Queenie roaming about after a rabbit in vain, 'The cunts! They have frightened all the rabbits to earth;

they are spoiling her sport!' Then I think to myself, 'Dear me! A few years back when there was no Queenie you would have put down your books and strolled (earlier still you would have hurried) up to that lorry to inspect the workmen; incurably romantic then, or so your intimates thought, you could not have rested until you had satisfied yourself that that small gathering of workmen, of country chaps, did not perhaps include the One, the Charmer, the Long Sought-For and Never Found Perfect Friend to Be, instantly recognizable, instantly responsive, the Destined Mate.' I smile to myself sadly, recollecting that discarded and almost forgotten past, those (were they not wasted?) twenty-five years of emotional fidget, when I could scarcely ever conclude or even start a journey, but must always be impulsively leaping off the bus as it went, or leaving the train at some intermediate station, or getting on to a train that was going heaven knows where, to follow, to get a closer look at, to make myself known to, that sailor, that soldier, that young workman, whom I had seen pass in the street below, or glimpsed on the station platform, or seated in some other train. Twenty-five years, at least . . . Now I do not move, I do not care, nor trouble: 'The cunts! They are spoiling Queenie's sport!' Is that then the epitaph upon my sex life?

from J. R. Ackerley's diary, June 1950, while staying as Sassoon's guest in the country

Elvis

If his [Elvis's] new film *Jailhouse Rock* reaches Cambridge I think you would not find the evening entirely wasted if you got one of your young friends to take you. He is a handsome boy and dances and sings most provocatively. A surprisingly good actor too. And the moral of the story good: love and honour win the day over ambition and the golden calf.

from a letter from J. R. Ackerley to his friend E. M. Forster, 1958

Flashing a Smile

He had never grown accustomed to wearing dentures and often carried them in his pocket. At the approach of a likely youth he would hastily insert his teeth and unleash a dazzling smile upon his prey. So alarming was this grimace that young men often hurried by, as if evading a lunatic.

from Peter Parker, Ackerley (1989)

FEDERICO GARCÍA LORCA (1898–1936), Spanish Poet and Playwright

Alive

The day we stop resisting our instincts, we'll have learned how to live.

Federico García Lorca, 1933

Tied to Mother

Rivas recalled that one day the poet [Lorca] failed to turn up for a rehearsal [of his play *Blood Wedding*, which was about to be performed in Barcelona] and that he found him sitting alone, deeply depressed, in a café, his head in his hands. It transpired that the previous night, after a binge in a downtown flamenco joint, Rapún [Lorca's lover] had left with a Gypsy girl and failed to return to the hotel where he was staying with Lorca. Federico was in despair, believing that Rapún had abandoned him; and, according to Rivas Cherif, pulled out a wad of Rafael's [Rapún's] letters out of his pocket to prove the passionate nature of their relationship . . . Lorca went on to relate his homosexuality to his early experience, saying that he had never recovered when, before he was seven, his best friend in Fuente Vaqueros school, slightly younger than himself, was taken away by his parents to another village. The poet also asserted that his close relationship with his mother made it impossible for him to feel heterosexual passion – a claim that Rivas dismissed as cheap Freudianism but that none the less the poet had made publicly in Montevideo two years earlier, when he said that while his brothers and sisters were free to marry, he belonged to his mother.

from Ian Gibson, Lorca (1989)

The Destruction of Sodom

Lorca confided his projects to Cardoza. He was going to write a play more daring than anyone had had the courage to attempt before him – by comparison, he said, Oscar Wilde (whom Lorca undoubtedly admired) would appear an out of date, fat and pusillanimous old queen. From the brief description Cardoza provides of the scenes from one of the projected works Lorca described for him, it is clear that this was to be *The Destruction of Sodom*, of which the poet later wrote at least one act (only the first page seems to have survived). The theme: the pleasures of the homosexual confraternity, who have made such a contribution to world culture.

from Ian Gibson, Lorca (1989)

Devotion

Maria Teresa Leon, the militant communist wife of Rafael Alberti, knew Rafael Rodríguez Rapún well and about the relationship that existed between him and Lorca. When Colonel Gonzalez Espinosa's reply to H. G. Wells [who had written a public letter to discover if the poet was still alive, and if rumours of his murder were false] was published in Madrid newspapers that October [of 1936], and it became clear that the poet had indeed been killed, that the appalling rumour was true, she saw Rapún again. 'Nobody can have suffered the way that quiet lad did on account of his death,' she wrote in her memoirs . . . 'Rapún went off to die in the north. I am convinced that, after firing his rifle furiously, he allowed himself to be killed. It was his way of recovering Federico.' Cipriano Rivas Cherif, who was arrested by the Nazis in France and handed over to Franco, heard a similar version when he was released from prison in 1945. Someone told him that Rapún, who had enlisted voluntarily in the Republican Army once he felt certain that the fascists had killed Federico, jumped out of the trench one day saying that he wanted to die. A few seconds later he was mown down. Rivas Cherif was never able to verify the truth of the account, which he admitted might merely be a legend. But it was substantially accurate. After taking an artillery course (in, of all places, Lorca, in Murcia) Rapún obtained the rank of lieutenant, and in the summer of 1937 was commanding a battery not far from Reinosa, in the north. One of his men has recalled that he was serious, cultured and talked little. These were the days of Franco's offensive against Santander, and the fighting in the area was intense. On the morning of 10 August the battery was in action against the rebel air force and, towards midday, faced with a strong enemy advance, Rapún left with two guns to find a new position. They stopped just outside the town of Barcena de Pie de Concha, where a sudden air attack caught them unprepared. Unlike the other men Rapún did not throw himself to the ground but remained sitting on a parapet. A bomb exploded nearby and he was mortally wounded. Rapún's death certificate states that he died on 18 August 1937, in the military hospital at Santander, from shrapnel wounds in the back and lumbar region. Lorca – and it seems impossible that Rafael could have been aware of this – had been assassinated a year earlier to the day . . . He [Rapún] was buried in Ciriego Cemetery, beside the Cantabrian sea. Eight days later Santander fell to Franco. Rodríguez Rapún had celebrated his twenty-fifth birthday that June.

from Ian Gibson, Lorca *(1989)*

NOËL COWARD (1899–1973), Performer, Playwright and Lyricist

Hollow Success

What are we left with? The picture, carefully incomplete, of a success; probably of one of the most talented and prodigiously successful people the world has ever known – a person of infinite charm and adaptability whose very adaptability however makes him inferior to a more compact and worldly competitor in his own sphere, like Cole Porter; and an essentially unhappy man, a man who gives one the impression of having seldom really thought or really lived and who is intelligent enough to know it. But what can he do about it? He is not religious, politics bore him, art means facility or else brickbats, love wild excitement and nervous breakdown. There is only success, more and more of it, till from the pinnacle he can look down to where Ivor Novello and Beverley Nichols gather samphire on a ledge, and to where, a pinpoint on the sands below, Mr Godfrey Winn is counting pebbles. But success is all there is, and that even temporary. For one can't read any of Noël Coward's plays now . . . they are written in the most topical and perishable way imaginable, the cream in them turns sour overnight – they are even dead before they are turned into talkies, however engaging they may seem at the time. This book reveals a terrible predicament, that of a young man with the Midas touch, with a gift that does not creep and branch and flower, but which turns everything it touches into immediate gold.

from a review by Cyril Connolly of Coward's autobiography, Present Indicative *(1937)*

No Jokes

Read the unexpurgated *De Profundis*. Poor Oscar Wilde, what a silly, conceited, inadequate creature he was and what a dreadful self-deceiver. It is odd that such a brilliant wit should be allied to no humour at all. I didn't expect him to enjoy prison life and to be speechless with laughter from morning till night but, after all, there are people even in gaol and he might have had a little warm human joke occasionally, if only with the warder. The trouble with him was that he was a 'beauty-lover' . . . [a] poor, podgy pseudo-philosopher.

from Noël Coward's diary, 11 November 1949

Fan

I went to see *En Plein Soleil* with Alain Delon in it. He looked handsome, as usual, and acted much better. He played a wicked, murderous little villain with charm. As he was in bathing trunks throughout most of the picture the charm was adequately displayed.

from Noël Coward's diary, April 1960

Wishful Thinking

I am neither impressed, nor frightened of death . . . the only thing that really saddens me over my demise is that I shall not be there to read the nonsense that will be written about me and my works and my motives. There will be books proving conclusively that I was homosexual and books proving equally conclusively that I was not.

from Noël Coward's diary, 9 March 1955

EVELYN WAUGH (1903–66), Novelist

Devoted Friends

The first friend to whom I gave my full devotion did not enjoy drinking and as a result we drifted apart.

He was Richard Pares, a Balliol Wykehamist, with an appealing pale face and a mop of fair hair, blank blue eyes and the Lear–Carroll fantasies of many

Balliol Wykehamists. I loved him dearly, but an excess of wine nauseated him and this made an insurmountable barrier between us. When I felt most intimate, he felt queasy. He withdrew, or was withdrawn, from our company and achieved many academic successes, university prizes, first-class Honours, an All Souls Fellowship, a professorship in the north; he would probably have been elected Master of Balliol had he not been tragically struck down by creeping paralysis . . .

His successor as the friend of my heart I will call Hamish Lennox, who was no scholar and soon went down to take a course in architecture in London; but he continued to haunt Oxford and for two or three years we were inseparable or, if separated, in almost daily communication, until like so many of my generation, he heard the call of the Levant and went to live abroad.

Hamish had no repugnance to the bottle and we drank deep together. At times he was as gay as any Hypocrite, but there were always hints of the spirit that in later years made him a recluse.

from Evelyn Waugh, A Little Learning (1964)

One-Way Traffic

. . . all roads lead to Sodom . . .
from a letter from Evelyn Waugh to Dudley Carew, 1924

Grimes

Grimes, as I may now call him, was conscientious in school; at dinner he treated Mrs Vanhomrigh with a benign condescension which left her dismayed but disarmed; after dinner he came with me to the village pub and drank copiously. The other habitués of the house spoke Welsh. Grimes and I spent many evenings together. At first he was something of a mystery to me. Not only was he paid more than the rest of us; he seemed to enjoy some private means and I was puzzled why he should choose to exile himself among us. But he was a man without deceit. His weakness (or strength) was soon revealed. After a week or two a whole holiday was ordained in honour of Mr Vanhomrigh's birthday. It was no holiday for the assistant masters. The whole school was packed into charabancs in the early morning and driven to the slopes of Snowdon, where games were played and a picnic luncheon devoured and scrupulously cleared up. Great licence was allowed; boys and masters chased one another and scuffled on the turf. At length at nightfall we returned wearily singing. When it was all over and the boys in bed we sat in the common-room deploring the miseries of the day. Grimes alone sat with the complacent smile of an Etruscan funerary effigy.

'I confess *I* enjoyed myself greatly,' he said as we groused.

We regarded him incredulously. '*Enjoyed* yourself, Grimes? What did you find to enjoy?'

'Knox minor,' he said with radiant simplicity. 'I felt the games a little too boisterous, so I took Knox minor away behind some rocks. I removed his boot and stocking, opened my trousers, put his dear little foot there and experienced a most satisfying emission.'

A memorable confession which, meeting him in after life, I found he had entirely forgotten. Such episodes were not rare in his chosen career.

from Evelyn Waugh, A Little Learning *(1964)*

Charles and Sebastian

Sebastian had gone to play tennis with his father and Cara at last admitted to fatigue. We sat in the late afternoon at the windows overlooking the Grand Canal, she on the sofa with a piece of needlework, I in an armchair, idle. It was the first time we had been alone together.

'I think you are very fond of Sebastian,' she said.

'Why, certainly.'

'I know of these romantic friendships of the English and the Germans. They are not Latin. I think they are very good if they do not go on too long.'

She was so composed and matter-of-fact that I could not take her amiss, but I failed to find an answer. She seemed not to expect one but continued stitching, pausing sometimes to match the silk from a work-bag at her side.

'It is a kind of love that comes to children before they know its meaning. In England it comes when you are almost men; I think I like that. It is better to have that kind of love for another boy than for a girl . . . '

from Evelyn Waugh, Brideshead Revisited *(1945)*

HAROLD ACTON (b. 1904), Aesthete

Discretion

Aquarium, my first volume of poems, was published during my second term, and its red, black and yellow striped cover met me everywhere like a challenge. For a book of poems it had a prompt success. Since I was free from false modesty, as from everything false, and possessed a resonant voice, I never faltered when I was asked to read them, but shouted them lustily down a megaphone. Nor would I tolerate interruptions. The megaphone could also be brandished as a weapon.

How many copies of *Aquarium* did I autograph with tender dedications! Where are they now, those witnesses of youthful passion? I think I know the answer. Not long ago I came across a copy in the Charing Cross Road and purchased it – for threepence . . . At least it had been well-thumbed and nicely battered. The fly-leaf was torn out. Had it compromised the owner? My thoughts returned to the bygone loves to whom I had given copies, to blue eyes, green eyes, eyes like black diamonds, to gentle struggles and showers of burning kisses. Could this have belonged to —? Perish the notion! Some of my inscriptions would have been embarrassing to explain. Nearly all my loves are married, and parents of children I have no desire to meet. Why distress the tranquil vegetation of middled-aged Darbies and Joans? No home-breaker I, no cuckoo in other nests. I culled the *prémices*, and it is a subtle satisfaction, even in retrospect, to have kindled flames in Elgin marble breasts. After many years, the breasts pretend to forget . . . Do they remember our ecstasies on the Thames and at Thame? Do they remember the poems they inspired? Let them blush as they read these words in their nuptial couches: I have not forgotten a single kiss. At the same time let them rest assured that with age I have learnt discretion.

from Harold Acton, Memoirs of an Aesthete *(1948)*

CHRISTOPHER ISHERWOOD (1904–1986), Novelist and Liberal Hero

Art and Truth

I think art is absolutely inseparable from truth. Any sort of concealments that you're putting up about your life injure you as an artist just as they injure you as a person.

Christopher Isherwood

Revenge

Looking back I wonder if I didn't do it a tiny bit to spite my mother.

from an interview with Christopher Isherwood in Gay News, *May 1976*

Dressing Up

Dressing up meant the excitement and safety of disguise. You had to transform yourself as much as possible, so it was natural that you should change your sex. Kathleen [Isherwood's mother] didn't discourage this at all.

from Christopher Isherwood, Kathleen and Frank *(1972)*

Inventive

If boys didn't exist, I should have to invent them.

Christopher Isherwood

Berlin

It was Berlin itself he was hungry to meet; the Berlin Wystan [Auden] had promised him. To Christopher, Berlin meant Boys.

from Christopher Isherwood, Christopher and his Kind *(1977)*

Brave New World

Waiting to greet them was George Davis, novelist and literary editor of a fashion magazine and their friend already; they had met him in London the year before. Small, plump, handsome, sparkling, he gaily stuffed into their pockets the wads of dollar bills he had earned for them by selling their travel articles to his own magazine and others. Utterly at their disposal as host, guide and fulfiller of all their desires, he was there to make them feel that New York was a theatrical performance staged expressly for them and that everybody in this city had been yearning for their arrival. He never left them for long throughout the nine days' wonder of their visit . . .

George also offered to make sexual introductions for them. 'All right,' said Christopher, half in joke, 'I want to meet a beautiful blond boy, about eighteen, intelligent, with very sexy legs.' Such a boy was instantly produced; he was almost too suitable to be true.

from Christopher Isherwood, Christopher and his Kind *(1977)*

Raiding the Cradle

Christopher Isherwood is here [in Key West] with the youngest-looking boy I have ever seen outside of school. They say he is twenty but he looks so young he has to order Coca-Cola in bars: somewhat embarrassing . . . They've been together two years so I guess it's okay.

from a letter from Tennessee Williams to Maria St Just, 7 November 1954

For Keeps

The thirty-year difference in our ages shocked some of those who knew us. I myself didn't feel guilty about this, but I did feel awed by the emotional intensity of our relationship, right from its beginning; the strange sense of a fated, mutual discovery. I know that, this time, I had really committed myself. Don [Bachardy] might leave me, but I couldn't possibly leave him, unless he ceased to need me. This sense of responsibility which was almost fatherly made me anxious but full of joy.

from Christopher Isherwood, My Guru and his Disciple *(1980)*

Mrs Strunk

Mrs Strunk . . . is trained in the new tolerance, the technique of annihilation by blandness. Out comes her psychology book – bell and candle are no longer necessary. Reading from it in sweet singsong she proceeds to exorcise the unspeakable out of George. No reason for disgust, she intones, no cause for condemnation. Nothing here that is wilfully vicious. All is due to heredity, early environment (shame on those possessive mothers, those sex-segregated British schools!), arrested development at puberty, and/or glands. Here we have a misfit, debarred forever from the best things of life, to be pitied, not blamed. Some cases, caught young enough, *may* respond to therapy. As for the rest – ah, it's so sad; especially when it happens, as let's face it it does, to truly worthwhile people, people who might have had so much to offer. (Even when they are geniuses in spite of it, their masterpieces are invariably *warped*). So let us be understanding, shall we, and remember that, after all, there *were* the Greeks (though that was a bit different, because they were pagans rather than neurotics). Let us even go so far as to say that this kind of relationship can sometimes be almost beautiful – particularly if one of the parties is already dead; or, better yet, both.

from Christopher Isherwood, A Single Man *(1964)*

Running for Cover

. . . against wicked bisexuals who break the hearts of innocent queens and then go waltzing back to Wifey.

from Christopher Isherwood, The World in the Evening *(1954)*

Minority

. . . A minority is only thought of as a minority when it constitutes some kind of threat to the majority, real or imaginary. And no threat is ever *quite* imaginary.

from Christopher Isherwood, A Single Man *(1964)*

Creativity

. . . breeding and bohemianism do not mix. For breeding you need a steady job, you need a mortgage, you need credit, you need insurance. And don't you dare die, either, until the family's future is provided for.

from Christopher Isherwood, A Single Man *(1964)*

Let Down

Oh, one always thinks one has dropped an H-bomb, and in fact one is lucky if it isn't mistaken for a burst tyre or a car back-firing.

Christopher Isherwood, May 1976

Happy Man

I remember Willie Maugham at a small luncheon at his villa in the south of France some time ago. He pointed to me and said: 'That young man down there held the future of English literature in his hands and he gave it up, he gave it up, he gave it up – for love.'

Christopher Isherwood, December 1974

California

A Paradise on earth: the climate can be marvellous, the scenery is lovely and the boys are so beautiful.

Christopher Isherwood, August 1976

TOM DRIBERG (1905–1976), Politician and Journalist

Charm

Driberg got into many scrapes, most dangerously when he was arrested by an Edinburgh policeman who caught him *in flagrante* with a Norwegian seaman. The policeman let him off, though, when Driberg promised to turn over a new leaf and revealed that he wrote the William Hickey column in the *Daily Express*, which the constable read every morning. Driberg sent the young man a number of books as a present afterwards, and received the following reply.

Dear Sir,
    I feel it would be presumptuous of me to approach you in your friendly style of dedication, but I never the less remain sensible to your great compliment.
    I confess, your recollection of me came as a very pleasant surprise; please accept my most sincere and grateful thanks for your kind letter and handsome gift. The book is invaluable in itself but I doubly esteem as a gift from you.
    My knowledge of Blake is decidedly limited, but I anticipate the pleasure of perusing his work, and comparing it with that of Burns.
    With the tokens, I obtained a History of the Borders, my native shire, also a work on the law of Scotland.
    I am still ploughing the lonely furrow of a Constable, patiently awaiting the day I get my feet on the promotion ladder, which in the past has proved most elusive. I am prompted to solicit your assistance in this respect, by your generous offer, and which I trust you will not view in the light of impertinence.
    Were I free to consult my own wishes I would be delighted and honoured to avail myself of your invitation and visit the House of Commons and renew our conversation. I have many times regretted the brevity of our meeting, but I assure you that it will remain a cherished memory and I will always feel indebted to your generous pen and kindness.

from Francis Wheen, Driberg *(1990)*

Semen

He believed that frequent consumption of semen kept one young, and had even persuaded himself that the age of the donor made a difference – an eighteen-year-old's was far more rejuvenating than, say, a twenty-eight-year-old's. Hence he recruited a number of eighteen-year-olds from the East End who agreed to be 'on call' for the spermophagous pensioner and pop round to the Barbican whenever he was feeling depleted; he paid them ten pounds a time for their trouble. One of these boys, Michael Duffy, got into the game through his uncle, a strange character called Ivor Powell who had once been an adviser to President Nasser but now lived at the Barbican and earned his living as a Tarot-reader and clairvoyant in West End clubs. 'Ivor basically never touched a woman in his life – he was well gay.' Duffy says. 'He said to me that Tom liked sucking boys' dicks because the chemical content would extend his life, and would I mind? I was on the fence of sexuality in those days, but I wasn't averse to earning a tenner through lying down on the chaise longue and having my dick sucked. Ten quid was a lot of money in those days.'

from Francis Wheen, Driberg (1990)

LUCHINO VISCONTI (1906–1976), Film Director

Horst

Horst, the son of small shopkeepers on the Judenstrasse of an obscure German town, needed only a few years to win admission to this circle of princes and millionaires eager to patronize the arts, a society in which talent and daring counted for more than titles and wealth. In 1936, on his return from New York, where he worked part of the year for *Vogue*, he was invited to lunch by the Viscountess de Noailles . . . this was his first meeting with the distant, incredibly handsome young Italian, Count Luchino Visconti di Modrone, still considered no more than an extravagantly rich playboy crazy about horses and racing cars.

Shortly before the luncheon Visconti had phoned Marie-Laure de Noailles and asked her if he could stop by for a moment and say hello before he caught the afternoon train for Rome. Beside a blazing fire in the great fireplace, the two men exchanged a few words – enough to start a compelling, instantaneous current flowing between the blond, wilful-looking 'little Kraut' and the Italian wrapped in Byronic gloom.

'He hung back,' Horst recalls, 'he didn't smile easily and seemed constantly to be reining in his Latin temperament . . . For some obscure reason, I was sure he was attracted to me. There was something mysterious in him, something simultaneously close and distant. I had lived long enough on the fringes of fashionable society to know that foreign aristocrats, even the English, as lordly and snobbish as they may be in their own country, tend to be far less cocky in Paris. And maybe the fact that I now lived mostly in America led me to affect a kind of indifference to European titles and customs.

'Whatever the reason, when Luchino apologized to Marie-Laure for having to leave to catch his train, I suddenly found myself interrupting their goodbyes to announce firmly to him: 'You're not leaving Paris this afternoon. Tomorrow at one o'clock you're lunching with me at the Crillon bar.' To Marie-Laure's somewhat amused surprise, and to my delight, he motioned his agreement and left. And the next day, when I reached the Crillon bar at one o'clock – without much hope, but you never knew – he was there, waiting for me. We lunched together, as agreed. Luchino remained at his hotel for a week or two, and we saw each other every day.'

Horst remembers that Visconti used to carry three books around with him everywhere. They were printed on bible paper and bound in red leather: a volume of Proust's *Remembrance*, *Death in Venice* and Gide's *The Counterfeiters*. The Mann story represented homosexual temptation, the Proust concerned roots and love of family, and the Gide, like an antidote, stood for alienation, praise of bastardy and hatred of family . . .

In those days, reports Horst, Visconti still kicked against his homosexuality. While he allowed himself what Oscar Wilde called the terrible pleasure of a double life, he feared gossip. Throughout the three years they were together – and that included frequent separations – he tried to keep their affair a secret. When they travelled to Tunisia together in the spring of 1936 . . . he was horrified to glimpse one or two appallingly familiar faces among his fellow passengers on the boat.

'To me,' says Horst, 'homosexuality was anything but a problem, but it wasn't the same for him. I made him more sure of himself, precisely because no one could have tormented him less on the subject than I did. He didn't talk about himself, didn't tell me his life story. Sometimes he tried to explain his character, which was prickly: he was always right, I was always wrong.'

Not even escape to Tunisia, which had overcome the puritanical scruples of many other homosexuals – beginning with Gide – seemed fully to still the skittish Visconti's inner torment . . .

[Horst says,] 'He had no sense of humour at all, and he couldn't laugh at himself.' An odd mixture of Latin sensuality and Prussian stiffness, born of his mother's stern ethics, a military and aristocratic sense of duty . . .

Horst was never with Visconti for long at a time. Yet, 'strangely enough, this only deepened our ties'. The war separated them, and they did not see each other again for ten years.

from Laurence Schifano, Visconti: The Flame of Passion *(1990)*

Callous

Maria [Callas] was deeply shocked, 'devastated', to learn that Visconti was a homosexual. Visconti himself brought the subject up, making no secret of his preference, and from then on Maria couldn't stand him.

from Laurence Schifano, Visconti: The Flame of Passion *(1990)*

Angel of Death

. . . an advertisement had been placed in the papers in Stockholm, Oslo and Helsinki as well as Copenhagen, to the effect that a youth, aged between thirteen and fourteen, was being sought to play an important role in his [Visconti's] forthcoming film, *Death in Venice*. The role of Tadzio.

Wrapped in furs, scarves, and wearing a huge fur hat with ear-flaps, he set off into the snowy wilderness of Scandinavia like a very chic Eskimo. He thought to be away a month. As it happened, the very first boy brought to his hotel in Stockholm by a hopeful grandmother was, in his opinion, the only person to play Tadzio . . .

In physical respects Bjorn Andresen was the perfect Tadzio. He had an almost mystic beauty. On the other hand he had a healthy appetite for bubble-gum, rock and roll, fast motor-bikes and the darting-eyed girls whom he met, tightly jeaned, ruby of lips, playing the pin-tables in the local hotel on the Lido.

The last thing that Bjorn ever wanted, I am certain, was to be in the movies.

What he did want was a Honda. The biggest and most powerful ever made. He spoke almost fluent English, but in that curious manner used by American disc jockeys. Which was perfectly reasonable, as he spent most of his time listening to the American Forces Radio.

Thus, almost every other word was punctuated with 'Hey!' or 'I dig!' or 'crazy' or, most often, 'man!'.

Fortunately, as Visconti said dryly, he would never be required to open his mouth as Tadzio, so that the 'enigmatic, mystic, illusion' which he appeared to have could be preserved . . .

[One evening] crossing the Piazza San Marco on the way to yet another make-up room, Bjorn came up to me, scattering pigeons and some Japanese tourists with their cameras.

'Hey man, I just read it.'

'You just read what?'

He fell into step beside me. 'The book. This film, I read it.'

'The book! Now look, for God's sake, you're not supposed to read it. It's strictly forbidden, no script, no book. You do just what Visconti tells you and no more.'

'I know that, man, but it's so crazy. Someone left a paperback in one of the rooms and so I read it.'

'So you read it. And so what?'

'Hell man, now I know who I am,' he said. 'I'm the Angel of Death, right?'

'In one,' I said . . .

Andresen returned to Sweden and bought a Honda on which he died soon afterwards.
from Dirk Bogarde, An Orderly Man *(1983)*

Necessary Pain

Accounts of the director's personal relationships with his most intimate friends, such as Zeffirelli and Berger, all agree on one point: each affair was one of constant confrontation, an interplay of cruelty, jealousy, reciprocal humiliation, a war of nerves with occasional brief truces. Visconti was in fact attracted to those who could stand up to him . . . Visconti could not contemplate pleasure or even beauty – as in *Death in Venice* – without pain and punishment, without a ritual death . . . For him, as for Wilde and Proust, love was always guilty; no matter how lucid he was, no matter how free he fancied himself, he had to overcome obstacles and taboos to love, had to pay for the terrible pleasure of transgression in money and/or pain.

He only attached himself to men he could not possess: men who were married, like Massimo Girotti, or 'committed', as Delon was to Romy Schneider, or who were flighty, frivolous and capricious like Berger. Love as Visconti depicted it was always forbidden love.

from Laurence Schifano, Visconti: The Flame of Passion *(1990)*

W. H. AUDEN (1907–1973), Genius and Poet

The Beginning

By 1922, when he was fifteen, he had begun to be sexually attracted to at least one of his schoolfellows . . . he did nothing – at least at first – to make his feelings known to the boy to whom he felt the attraction. This was Robert Medley, a year older than him, who had been absent from school for most of 1921 recovering from a road accident . . . Medley returned to Gresham's early in 1922 and joined the school's new Sociological Society, which had been formed ostensibly to study contemporary social and economic issues, but was really (as Auden said) an excuse to have 'a grand time visiting factories in a charabanc'. It was on one of these trips, on 22 March 1922, that Auden managed to get to know Medley (a slim, dark-haired boy), contriving to sit next to him on the bus . . . He and Auden had plenty to talk about. Medley's attitudes were largely a mixture of William Morris socialism and Blake–Shelley romanticism. It was this last topic that they discussed on the Sunday following the charabanc trip, going for a walk across fields near the school. Medley made an attack on the Church; Auden's drift away from religion had scarcely yet begun, and he surprised Medley by declaring himself to be a believer. 'An argument followed,' Medley remembered, 'and to soften what I feared might become a serious breach, after a pause, I asked him if he wrote poetry, confessing by way of exchange that I did. I was a little surprised that he had not tried and suggested he might do so.'

Auden's vision of himself and his future was at this time a little muddled. He was still toying with the idea of a career as a mining engineer, but he entertained other fancies – crazes for such things as motor-cycles and photography. Medley's casual question suddenly provided quite a different answer to the puzzle of what he ought to do with his life:

> Kicking a little stone, he turned to me
> And said, 'Tell me, do you write poetry?'
> I never had, and said so, but I knew
> That very moment what I wished to do.

from Humphrey Carpenter, Auden *(1981)*

Gossip

Let's be honest. When you open your newspaper, as soon as you have made sure that England hasn't declared war, or been bombed, what do you look at? Why the gossip columns . . . And as for books, if you had to choose between the serious study and the amusing gossip, say between Clarendon's *History of the Rebellion* and John Aubrey's *Scandal and Credulities*, wouldn't you choose the latter? Of course you would! Who would rather learn the facts of Augustus's imperial policy than discover that he had spots on his stomach? No one . . .

Gossip has fallen under a cloud because of the people who abuse it . . . The person who ruins gossip is the person who repeats it back to its victim. That's every bit as bad as writing anonymous letters . . . There are some kinds of people in whose presence you should shut up like an oyster: people with strong moral views, members of the Watch-Committees or Purity Leagues, natural policemen, schoolmasters . . .

How often I have worked off ill-feeling against friends by telling some rather malicious stories about them, and as a result met them again with the feelings quite gone. And I expect you've done the same. When one reads in the papers of some unfortunate man who has gone for his wife with a razor, one can be pretty certain that he wasn't a great gossip . . .

Gossip is creative. All art is based on gossip – that is to say, on observing and telling. The artist proper is someone with a special skill in handling his medium, a skill which few possess. But all of us to a greater or less degree can talk, we can all observe, and we all have friends to talk to. Gossip is the art-form of the man and woman in the street, and the proper subject for gossip, as for all art, is the behaviour of mankind.

from a radio talk by W. H. Auden published in the Listener, *22 December 1937*

The Wrong Blond

On the evening of April 6, 1939, the League of American Writers, one of those left-wing organizations that were popular in the thirties, had invited Auden, somewhat of a cult figure among young writers and college students, together with Isherwood, Louis MacNeice, and Frederic Prokosch, to give a public reading . . . In the audience that evening was a group of students from Brooklyn College who were on the college literary magazine, the *Observer*. Among the students were Walter James Miller . . . and Chester Kallman . . .

After the lecture, the lively group of students from Brooklyn College, along with more staid members of the audience, rushed backstage to meet the speakers . . . Auden was first attracted not by Kallman but by Miller, who was talking to Isherwood about poetic drama. Auden, overhearing the conversation, expressed a desire to read an essay Miller had written about modern poetic drama for the *Observer* called 'Aeschylus Returns'. While Walter was talking to Isherwood, Chester Kallman and another boy were concentrating on Auden. They asked for an appointment to interview him for the magazine, and Auden set a date for

Saturday, April 8, believing that Chester would bring Miller along. The handsome Miller, tall, blond, Anglo-Saxon, and heterosexual, probably reminded Auden of the schoolboy chums of his youth with whom he had been infatuated during boarding school years . . . [however] when Kallman arrived for the appointment with Auden, he arrived alone.

The young man who appeared at Auden's door on April 8, 1939, had just turned eighteen . . . He was naturally blond, about five feet eleven in height, slender, weighing 145 pounds, with gray-blue eyes, a pale, flawless skin, a Norse skull, Latin lips, and a straight, narrow nose. He had the touch of the gamin in his expression, and Auden would later describe him as an *ange gauche*, an awkward angel. Chester Kallman was a combination of an angel and a satyr, with the physical attributes of both: the coloring of a Florentine angel; the full lips of a satyr . . . Auden was not blinded by the first burst of light upon his life, for a moment after Kallman arrived at his door, Auden walked into another room where Christopher Isherwood was now working and said to him: 'It's the wrong blond.' Auden had expected to see Walter Miller. But if at first Chester was perceived to be the wrong blond, by the end of the afternoon he became the only right one . . . Wystan Auden was in love with Chester Kallman from that first afternoon in New York.

from D. J. Farnan, Auden in Love *(1984)*

The Making of a Poem

At the end of August, when Wystan and Chester returned, Chester and I spent our first night at the notorious gay bar called the Dizzy Club on West Fifty-second Street, three blocks from my room. The dive was the sex addict's quick fix, packed to the rafters with college boys and working-class youths under twenty-five. From street level you stepped into a writhing mass of tight boys in tighter pants. On those sultry August nights it was a sexual experience just getting a drink. Like the subway at rush hour you were crushed against one another. It was quite a feat to hold on to your drink and keep it from spilling on your shirt or pants, or someone else's, though nobody seemed to mind. Amid the laughter and screaming and ear-splitting jukebox music, it was like an orgy room for the fully clad. Everything but exposure and nudity took place.

Having decided that he must see it, we told Wystan, who loved sleazy dives, about the Dizzy Club. The next night, September 1, without our knowledge he went alone. I can only imagine what occurred there. With floppy shoelaces, creased suit and tie, ash-stained, he must have looked out of place, though with his rosy California tan and sun-bleached hair he could, in the right light, pass for twenty-five. He didn't go to pick up a boy; however, aware of age difference and quite shy, he would have selected one of the two unused corner tables at the rear of the bar, which was usually deserted except for those too drunk to stand, from which he could observe boys kissing and groping under the bright lights, packed like sardines pickled in alcohol. There he would begin to write the most famous poem of the decade. Surely he jotted notes, or even the first stanzas, for it begins with the immediacy of composition in situ. He did not write a detailed description of his immediate surroundings or his personal feelings but instead opened the poem outward into society at a historic moment, choosing the depressed mood of his isolation within the social drama. At precisely this moment, while Auden wrote tracing fascism and its 'Psychopathic gods' from Martin Luther to the birth of Hitler at Linz, the German Führer marched into Poland and started World War II. The poem was, of course, 'September 1, 1939'.

from Harold Norse, Memoirs of a Bastard Angel *(1990)*

Imperialism

He spent much of his time in the company of homosexuals – he did not deliberately seek them out as his friends, but he had become quite militant about homosexuality. In 1946 he annoyed Edmund Wilson by alleging that Eisenhower was a homosexual, and that Tristan and Isolde must really have been a pair of lesbians, 'because a man making love to a woman couldn't really get into that rapturous state'. This was no doubt meant to be outrageous, and was not to be taken seriously; on the other hand he did seem really to believe that any unmarried person who was a major artist must be homosexual. He was convinced, for example, not just of Shakespeare's homosexuality but of Beethoven's. He also continued to disapprove of homosexuals who married in order to hide their real nature, and to obtain the benefits of a home and family.

from Humphrey Carpenter, Auden *(1981)*

The Platonic Blow

It was a Spring day, a day for a lay, when the air
Smelled like a locker-room, a day to blow or get blown;
Returning from lunch I turned my corner and there
On a near-by stoop I saw him standing alone.

I glanced as I advanced. The clean white T-shirt outlined
A forceful torso; the light blue denim divulged
Much. I observed the snug curves where they hugged the behind,
I watched the crotch where the cloth intriguingly bulged.

Our eyes met. I felt sick. My knees turned weak.
I couldn't move. I didn't know what to say.
In a blur I heard words, myself like a stranger speak
'Will you come to my room?' Then a husky voice 'OK.'

W. H. Auden, quoted in Humphrey Carpenter, Auden *(1981)*

A Funny Pair: Two Letters

W. H. Auden to Chester Kallman, 21 February 1949, after receiving a jealous and angry letter:

Your lecture ill-received. I've never noticed, *darling*, any reluctance on your part to confine experiences, operatic, intellectual, etc., to me. (If you've never gone with a lover to *Tristan*, it wasn't because of me, but because Miss Butch preferred jazz. *Entre nous*, I would have minded that less than the great *gang* of chaps that always were at the Met[ropolitan Opera House].) If I'm anxious for you to approve of Keith [Callaghan] it's not because you are the Beatrice for whom I cherish a grotesque passion, but because you are the one comrade my non-sexual life cannot do without. Expressions like 'bowing out' and 'disappear' are twists of the knife which, as you know only too well, you beast, hurt. Still I adore you and I suppose you must deserve it.

W. H. Auden to Chester Kallman, 15 March 1949:

I know you won't believe it but there was honestly no malice, conscious or unconscious, in his [Keith's] being at 27th Street on Christmas Eve. He was Billy's friend (not in that sense) long before I met him, which was through Billy. Do you think I should have refused to take him with me?

As to our relationship, I'm sure you have a pretty good idea of how it is. I am Poppa to him; he unfortunately cannot be Big Brother to me, only Little Brother . . . I can talk to him and educate him – he cannot educate me. I'm not being catty about him, because you would realize at once if you met him, how decent he is. Once again, darling, what do you expect of me? One night stands with trade? I have neither the taste, the talent, nor the time. A chaste fidelity to the Divine Miss K[allman]? Miss God, I know, says that, but I haven't the strength, and I don't think you, sweetie, have the authority to contradict me. If it is wrong, at least I don't behave badly to him as I do to you. Enough. We're a funny pair, you and I.

from D. J. Farnan, Auden in Love (1984)

Displeased

In the autumn of 1962, travelling from New York to New Haven by train to lecture at Yale University, he sat in the club car and was eyed furtively for some time by two Yale students who finally sent a note to him which read, 'We can't stand it a minute longer: Are you Carl Sandburg?' Auden sent a note in reply: 'You have spoiled mother's day.'

from Charles Osborne, Auden (1979)

Magical Acts

Frank as he is, Mr Ackerley is never quite explicit about what he really prefers to do in bed. The omission is important because all 'abnormal' sex acts are rites of symbolic magic, and one can only properly understand the actual personal relation if one knows the symbolic role each expects the other to play . . . I conclude that [Ackerley] did not belong to either of the two commonest classes of homosexuals, neither to the 'orals' who play Son-and/or-Mother, nor to the 'anals' who play Wife-and/or-Husband. My guess is that . . . the acts he really preferred were most 'brotherly', Plain-Sewing and Princeton-First-Year.

from a review by W. H. Auden of J. R Ackerley's autobiography My Father and Myself, *1968*

At Home

No self-respecting Welfare Recipient would spend a night in this flat. A sad scene of sagging bookshelves, sprung-seat overstuffed chairs, a dusty and scarred 'cozy-corner' and everywhere litter, piles of paper and magazines, this morning's crusted dish of egg. I go to the toilet — not looking long into the kitchen — and switch on the light, they've *flocked* the walls! Then these move, a vertical nation of cockroaches shifting about uneasily. One of Chester's lesser dinners is set down on the dining room table. This, covered in glass, has a great crumb-filled crack running through it. We chat. 'Wystan, aren't you sad to be leaving New York?' Between spoonfuls he thinks; at last he answers — the tone, is it the poet's, the lover's fond oblivion to the work of time? There is a touch of a sigh. 'Yes, yes, particularly now that we've fixed the place up.'

from a memoir by David Jackson in The View from Christopher Street, *ed. M. Denneny, C. Ortleb and T. Steele (1984)*

A Nasty Unwed

Learning with glee that Cyril Connolly, weary of Wystan Auden's harping that toilets was an anagram for T. S. Eliot, had relettered Auden's own name as A nasty unwed.

from Ned Rorem, Nantucket Diary, 1973–1985 (1987)

CUTHBERT WORSLEY (1907–1977), Schoolmaster and Writer

Bad Luck

Scott, one of the intelligent and forward-looking Tutors on whose co-operation I depended, invited a well-known sexologist to come down and lecture to senior members of his Dormitory. This Scott was a most amiable, slightly muddle-headed man, full of the best intentions. He was also a good cricketer, that useful cover for advanced opinions, though his opinions were not perhaps really so advanced as those of his energetic and, some found, bossy wife, who was known to the school in general as Napoleon.

Between them they had organised this lecture and, in the circumstances of that time at College, the sense of outrage this produced was prodigious. But what made matters outrageously worse was that when the sexologist arrived he turned out to be a 'she'. To discuss sex in the open conspiracy of a lecture was bad enough; but to have it discussed by a woman passed all bounds. Not that Dr. Jameson was exactly a provocative figure herself. She was a sensible downright woman with spectacles who, naturally in her profession, prided herself on her plain speaking.

It was part of Scotty's arrangement that after the lecture she would make time for any boy or master who wanted to discuss their sexual problems with her, and for this purpose I took my place in the queue.

We walked round the garden together, and I tried to explain my problem, the difficulty being that I still had no language in which to pose it. I seemed to be gingerly confessing to being no more than over-fond of one of the boys. Dr. Jameson wasn't standing for any evasions of that kind.

'You mean you're in love with him?'

I still hadn't put it to myself in those terms, but faced with the question I supposed I was. Yes, that must be it.

'Well, then,' she went on with her brash and straightforward questioning, 'how far has it got?'

It had 'got' no distance at all, though this sounded, in front of so formidably progressive a woman, a feeble confession to have to make.

'You mean,' she went on disbelievingly, 'you haven't had his organ in your hand?'

Ugh! Ugh! Ugh! I was nearly sick at her progressive feet. Such a proceeding hadn't even entered my fantasies, much less had I contemplated it in real life. I was much too amazed by this totally unfamiliar suggestion to register even the repugnance which was to follow later.

'No, indeed not.' I rejected both her suggestion and the idea.

'Oh, bad luck,' she said encouragingly. 'Bad luck. Never mind, that will be the next step, won't it?' And she briskly rounded off the interview.

from Cuthbert Worsley, Flannelled Fool *(1967)*

GUY BURGESS (1910–1963), Spy

The Benefactor

Burgess spoke eloquently and with conviction about his political motivation, but revealed that he was wretchedly lonely in Moscow – 'starved not only of congenial non-political company but of sex'. Because of his official position he could not easily go out cruising as he had in London; in any case, he knew of nowhere to go. Here was Tom [Driberg]'s opportunity to do his old friend a good turn. When it came to 'cottages' he had the directional sense of a homing pigeon, and within days of arriving he had achieved what Burgess had failed to do in five years, locating the one gents' lavatory in central Moscow where pick-ups could be had. It was a large underground urinal behind the Metropole Hotel, open all night, and, according to Tom, 'frequented by hundreds of questing Slav homosexuals – standing there in rigid exhibitionist rows, motionless save for the hasty grope and the anxious or beckoning glance over the shoulder'. Burgess decided to risk a visit, which was more successful than he dared hope: among the Slavs in the stalls he found a young electrician named Tolya, who moved in with him shortly afterwards and cured him of his loneliness. Burgess could never thank Tom enough for this service.

from Francis Wheen, Driberg (1990)

Double Act

Although the duo had become as inseparable in the public mind as Waring and Gillow or Flanagan and Allen, they were not, in fact, particularly close. When Goronwy Rees sold his reminiscences of the Cambridge spies to the *People*, what most upset Burgess was the claim that he and Maclean had been brought together through some kind of homosexual association. 'The idea of going to bed with Donald!' he told Tom. 'It would be like going to bed with a great white *woman!*'

from Francis Wheen, Driberg (1990)

Without Inhibition

Everything about him was up-to-date. The innovation was not only to proclaim the paramount claims of eating, drinking and sex (if necessary auto-erotic), but accepting as absolutely natural open snobbishness, success worship, personal vendettas, unprovoked malice, disloyalty to friends, reading other people's letters (if not lying about, to be sought in unlocked drawers) – the whole bag of tricks of what most people think and feel and often act on, yet are themselves ashamed of admitting they do and feel and think.

from Anthony Powell, Messengers of Day (1978)

Bohemian Prince

. . . when acquaintances were asked whether Burgess had ever tried to recruit them, they recalled not the engaging young man of the thirties but the prince in Bohemia he became during the war. He used to cook, his friend Goronwy Rees recalled, in a heavy iron saucepan 'a thick grey gruel compounded of porridge, kippers, bacon, garlic, onions and anything else that may have been lying about in the kitchen', a dish which sustained him over every weekend. Chewing raw garlic was only one of his minor social disabilities: in his Foreign Office days a minute was circulated requiring him to desist. He kept in the shambles of his Bond Street flat a flitch of bacon outside the window which was hauled up when he needed to hack off a slice, and was then consigned again to outer space.

Grime covered everything. Every table, lampshade, sheet and blanket was scarred with burns, the stigmata of so many drunken evenings. The bath had no plug; in its place was a sock once white but by now dark grey with dirt into which a squash ball had been thrust. Screams rent the air at night in the building because his flat was sandwiched between two others inhabited by prostitutes, but it was a moot point whether the traffic in and out of their rooms was any heavier than that in and out of his. His habits were filthy, going far beyond those of negligent bachelors; in his Foreign Office days he was often sodden and sweaty. He had the appearance of a man who had just stepped off the Golden Arrow after a night in the Rue de Lappe. Maurice Bowra in a characteristically vigorous phrase used to complain that he had shit in his fingernails and cock-cheese behind the ears.

from Noel Annan, Our Age *(1990)*

JEAN GENET (1910–1986), French Criminal and Writer

Collaboration and Resistance

In 1944, as the Germans are retreating from Paris, Riton, a sixteen-year-old French boy, is raped by a party of retreating Germans, but he forms a connection with one German soldier, Erik.

In passing through all his flesh, the memory of the execution obliged Erik to greater humility toward the child. All his excitement receded. The executioner's hideous but hard face and sovereign build and stature, which he could see in his mind's eye, must be feeling freer, either the thought of them gave him greater pride in buggering Riton and caused him to beat and torture him so as to be surer of his freedom and his own strength and then to take revenge for having been weak, or else he had remained humiliated by past shame and finished his job with greater movements and reached the goal in a state of brotherly anguish. Riton, surprised at the respite of love, wanted to murmur a few mild words of reproach, but the vigour of the movements gave him a full awareness that great voluptuaries always retain in love. He said, almost sobbingly: 'You won't have me! No, you won't have me!' and at the same time impaled himself with a leap . . . The whole member entered in, and Riton's behind touched Erik's warm belly. The joy of both of them was great . . . Riton murmured: 'I now have the impression that I love you more than before.' Erik did not understand. No tenderness could have been expressed, for as their love was not recognized by the world, they could not feel its natural effects. Only language could have informed them that they actually loved each other. We know how they spoke at the beginning. Seeing that neither understood the other and that all their phrases were useless, they finally contented themselves with grunts. This evening, for the first time in ten days, they are going to speak and to envelop their language in the most shameless passion. A happiness that was too intense made the soldier groan. With both hands clinging, one to the ear, the other to the hair, he wrenched the kid's head from the steel axis that was getting even harder.

'Stop.' Then he drew to him the mouth that pressed eagerly to his darkness. Riton's lips were still parted, retaining the shape and calibre of Erik's prick. The mouths crushed against each other, linked as by a hyphen, by the rod of emptiness, a rootless member that lived alone and went from one palate to the other. The evening was marvellous. The stars were calm. One imagined that the trees were alive, that France was awakening, and more intensely in the distance, above, that the Reich was watching. Riton woke up. Erik was sad. He was already thinking of far-away Germany, of the fact that his life was in danger, of how to save his skin. Riton buttoned his fly in a corner, then quietly picked up the machine gun. He fired a shot. Erik collapsed, rolled down the slope of the roof, and fell flat.

from Jean Genet, Funeral Rites (1969)

TERENCE RATTIGAN (1911–1977), Playwright

Disease

During this period, although he never specified the exact date, Rattigan contracted venereal disease. He later claimed that this finally put him off women. A psychologist might interpret this as a rationalization frequently heard from homosexuals to justify the homosexuality they are reluctant to accept. In *Cause Célèbre*, Rattigan's last play, the boy Tony contracts a venereal disease from a prostitute and great play is made of the 'filthy, disgusting cure' he has to undergo as a result of this 'filthy, disgusting disease'. Rattigan claimed that he himself contracted VD as a result of an experiment with a prostitute. However, the radio and stage versions of *Cause Célèbre* are contradictory over this episode. In the earlier, and probably more autobiographically reliable, radio version, Tony tries but fails to make it with a prostitute. He leaves, ashamed and disillusioned. Whichever is closer to the true version of what happened, it is clear from what Rattigan said about the play that he had felt driven to try a sexual experiment with a woman, while attempting to come to terms with his sexual inclination. *Cause Célèbre* conjures up a picture of youthful desperation. The real-life consequences were disastrous, confirming feelings about himself which he wanted to avoid. In the long summer vacation of 1932, Rattigan had again been sent to a French crammer, this time at La Baule in Brittany. There is some evidence to suggest that the episode with the prostitute occurred while he was there.

from Michael Darlow and Gillian Hodson, Terence Rattigan (1979)

Strong Bonds

MARGOT: The friendship of young men can be very selfish.
DAVID: But so impregnable.

from Terence Rattigan, First Episode (1933)

The Calculator

Although he had sidestepped his father's efforts to put him into the Diplomatic Service, Rattigan was outwardly very much like the popular notion (as opposed to the usual reality) of a young diplomat: tall, good-looking, elegant in turnout, somewhat chilly in manner. He had been a cricketer of some eminence at Harrow. His homosexuality, which he made no particular secret, probably unswerving, was not at all obvious on the surface. Over a period of about three weeks Terry Rattigan and I were immured together with the purpose of producing a story between us. The brief collaboration added no classic to movie history, indeed professionally speaking was totally barren, but we laughed a lot over preposterous subjects discussed as possibilities.

One was always aware in Rattigan of a deep inner bitterness . . . He had a touch of cruelty I think, and liked to torment one of the male executives of the Studio, who showed signs of falling victim to Rattigan's attractions . . . He was a thrusting young man whose primary concern was to make himself financially independent, not interested in 'art' so much as immediate effect.

from Anthony Powell's memoirs

Chips

Chips Channon was the forty-eight-year-old Conservative MP for Southend. He entertained the high and the mighty – cabinet ministers and royalty – at his house in Eaton Square. He counted among his intimates the Duchess of Kent, the Duff Coopers, the Wavells (then Viceroy and Vicereine of India) and members of Churchill's cabinet. He knew about the courtship of Philip Mountbatten and Princess Elizabeth long before it was public knowledge, and was approached by Buckingham Palace to loan them his house as a first home after their marriage. He was married to, but about to be divorced from, Lady Honor Guinness, the eldest daughter of the second Earl of Iveagh. Tom Driberg continues: 'For Chips was one of the better known homosexuals in London, and he was rich enough to rent almost any young man he fancied – a handsome German princeling, a celebrated English playwright. His seduction of the playwright was almost like the wooing of Danae by Zeus: every day, the playwright found, delivered to his door, a splendid present – a case of champagne, a huge pot of caviare, a Cartier cigarette box in two kinds of gold . . . In the end, of course, he gave in, saying apologetically to his friends, "How can one *not*?"'

Rattigan, who was of course the 'celebrated English playwright', had met Chips Channon on 29 September 1944 when he was deeply engaged in writing *Love in Idleness*. The social world, the glamour which Rattigan described and sought to defend in that play, was the social world of Chips and his friends.

Rattigan resisted for some time. Here is how one close friend remembers it: 'It was pathetic really. Channon used to buy him these presents, which Terry could have bought six times over, but he was flattered by the social side, Princess Marina (the Duchess of Kent) and all that stuff. The trouble was he didn't want to pay the price. He would bring him here and he would say, "Oh, for God's sake get him drunk so that I don't have to go to bed with him." ' When *Love in Idleness* was published it was dedicated 'to Henry Channon', a fitting acknowledgement of his capitulation; Rattigan had surrendered more than his body. Chips Channon was a glittering social figure – 'the iron butterfly', as Rattigan and his friends called him behind his back. For all his gaiety and social poise, Channon was at heart a failure. His feelings for Rattigan were undoubtedly much stronger than for most of the young men he 'rented'; but they were not feelings Rattigan could reciprocate. He found Channon's demands increasingly difficult to meet. The consolation Channon might have found in Rattigan was not forthcoming.

After the completion of *The Winslow Boy*, but before finishing *The Browning Version*, Rattigan made up his mind to break off the relationship with Channon. He must have brooded on his decision for some time before telling Channon. The irony was that the feeling which he could not reciprocate for Channon he had begun to feel for someone else. He would himself soon be racked by the very possessiveness he resented from Channon.

Kenneth Morgan, the young actor who in 1939 had played Babe Lake in the film of *French Without Tears*, seems to have largely dropped out of Rattigan's life while he was in the Forces. Ken Morgan's post-war career in the theatre did not quite realize his early promise. He was seven years younger than Rattigan, and . . . Rattigan found himself very strongly drawn to him now. His role in the relationship with Chips Channon was now reversed: Rattigan became the pursuer, Morgan the pursued. And of course, relative to Ken Morgan, Rattigan was in the financial position of Chips Channon; he could now play Zeus to Morgan's Danae. Morgan moved in with Rattigan, who smothered him with gifts and affection. He had never felt so strongly about another person. But, like Rattigan with Channon, Morgan seems to have been unable fully to return his feelings. What Rattigan had observed in others he now began to experience in himself – the more desperately you try to make someone love you the less they do.

from Michael Darlow and Gillian Hodson, Terence Rattigan *(1979)*

Cruising

From Sturford Mead – where we are staying – I took Terence Rattigan over to Longleat . . . Henry Weymouth took us all over the house and showed us the famous Shakespeare folios of which they have the first, second, third and fourth. Terry was fascinated and impressed and I saw his face light up as he took one down from the shelf and fingered it . . . In the evening we drove to Ashcombe to dine with Cecil Beaton, a long melancholy drive through isolated country. The house is romantic and amusingly arranged, and Cecil received us in Austrian clothes. Also there, an uninteresting couple the Graham Sutherlands. He is a painter.

from Chips Channon's diary, 20 May 1945

Precious

To see yourself as the world sees you may be very brave, but it can be very foolish. Why should you accept the world's view of you as a weak-willed neurotic – better dead than alive? What right have they to judge? To judge you they must have the capacity to feel as you feel. And who has? One in a thousand. You alone know how you have felt. And you alone know how unequal the battle has always been that your will has had to fight?

from Terence Rattigan, The Deep Blue Sea *(1952)*

The Pretty Playwright

One distinction will probably never be wrested from him: I support it with a completely unauthenticated story. It was told me by a friend who arrived at a Knightsbridge party and was ushered upstairs to doff hat and coat. Pausing on the cloakroom threshold and peering through the crack of the door, he saw someone talking to the mirror. Rattigan had stopped in the middle of combing his hair to muse, with a little groan, 'If you're not very careful, Terry Rattigan, you won't be the prettiest playwright in London.'

from Kenneth Tynan, Curtains *(1961)*

Chums

Rattigan encouraged his friend Robin Maugham to publish his queer novel, *The Wrong People* (1967). Rattigan wrote a note on its publication:

Dearest Robin, your uncle thought you would never make a writer and I thought you would never make sixty. I am delighted we have both been proved so triumphantly wrong. Great love, Terry.

To another friend Rattigan expressed the following opinion:

Maugham! He couldn't write bum on a wall; and if he could, he'd spell it Baugham.

from Michael Darlow and Gillian Hodson, Terence Rattigan *(1979)*

Bed

. . . in the release of the bed there lies an ecstasy so strong and a satisfaction so profound that it seems that it is everything that life can offer a man, the very purpose of his existence on earth.

from Terence Rattigan, A Bequest to the Nation *(1970)*

The English Vice

Do you know what '*le vice Anglais*' – the English vice – really is? Not flagellation, not pederasty – whatever the French believe it to be. It's our refusal to admit our emotions. We think they demean us, I suppose.

from Terence Rattigan, In Praise of Love *(1973)*

TENNESSEE WILLIAMS (1911–1983), American Playwright

The Kindness of Strangers

Whoever you are – I have always depended on the kindness of strangers.

from Tennessee Williams, A Streetcar Named Desire *(1947)*

Happy

There are only two times in this world when I am happy and selfless and pure. One is when I jack-off on paper, and the other when I empty all the fretfulness of desire onto a male body.

Tennessee Williams

Magic

I don't want realism. I want magic! Yes, yes, magic! I try to give that to people, I misrepresent things to them. I don't tell the truth, I tell what ought to be truth. And if that is sinful, then let me be damned for it   Don't turn the light on!

from Tennessee Williams, A Streetcar Named Desire *(1947)*

Bent

What is straight? A line can be straight, or a street, but the human heart, oh, no, it's curved like a road through mountains.

from Tennessee Williams, A Streetcar Named Desire *(1947)*

On the Waterfront

I don't want to be involved in some sort of scandal, but I've covered the waterfront.

Tennessee Williams, 1970

Animal Passions

In those days I used to cruise Times Square with another young writer who would prefer to remain unmentioned by name in this context, and he would despatch me to street corners where sailors or GIs were grouped, to make very abrupt and candid overtures, phrased so bluntly that it's a wonder they didn't slaughter me on the spot . . . [usually] they would stare at me for a moment in astonishment, burst into laughter, huddle for a brief conference, and as often as not would accept the solicitation, going to my partner's Village pad or to my room at the 'Y'.

Surely this adequately covers, to say the least, the deviant satyriasis into which I was happily afflicted in those early Manhattan years of my life. Sexuality is an emanation, as much in the human beings as the animals. Animals have seasons for it. But for me it was a round-the-calendar thing.

I wonder, sometimes, how much of the cruising was for the pleasure of my cruising partner's companionship and for the sport of pursuit and how much was actually for the pretty repetitive and superficial satisfactions of the act itself. I know that I had yet to experience in the 'gay world' the emotion of love, which transfigures the act to something beyond it. I have known many gays who live just for the act, that 'rebellious hell' persisting into middle life and later, and it is graven in their faces and even refracted from their wolfish eyes. I think what saved me from that was my first commitment being always to work. Yes, even when love came, work was still the primary concern.

from Tennessee Williams, Memoirs *(1976)*

Free Men

For Oscar Wilde his homosexuality was, at least in part, like so much else in his life and work, a public gesture, a conspicuous and deliberate protest against the hypocrisy, complacency and mediocrity of his own day. Almost a century after Wilde's death, homosexuality may still be the only resort of the cultural refusenik who cannot or will not conform to the conventional masculine agenda: who has passed through all the manhood rites without wanting to adopt them as his personal rights . . . To the young Tennessee Williams the homosexual was potentially *'homo emancipatus'*, the only human type which might be completely free of dishonesty, perversion and the compulsion to play the crippling roles of happy husband and fond father. The 'free man' of Williams's philosophical and sexual fantasy finds its *beau ideal* in Stanley Kowalski, hero of Williams's masterpiece *A Streetcar Named Desire*: part noble savage, exalted above the common herd, unspoiled and untouched, part 'brute beast' blindly following his instincts in the 'pure animal joy' of his nature, Stanley is both above and below the life of his time, out of it on every level. Only through contact with such men, Williams wrote wistfully, could a man hope to break out of his 'little cave of consciousness' and find 'the moment of grace when a word, a gesture, raps out a code message on the walls of the prison': then, and only then, 'sometimes – there's God – so quickly.'

> from Rosalind Miles, The Rites of Man: Love, Sex and Death in the Making of the Male (1991)

Behaving Badly

Tennessee went to see *Bent*, a play about homosexuals sent to the Nazi concentration camps. It was directed by Robert Alan Ackerman, a young man whom Tennessee considered especially gifted and was anxious to have direct his work. In 1982 the play was running on Broadway, starring Richard Gere. After the performance, Tennessee and Maria St. Just went backstage to congratulate the actors on their performances. When Maria and he entered Gere's dressing room they found the actor lounging in a chair wearing only a pair of jockey shorts. Gere stared at them. Tennessee shyly introduced himself and Maria, and proceeded to compliment Gere on his performance. Richard Gere said nothing, simply sat there staring at Tennessee with a look of smug boredom. Maria, losing patience with what she knew was insulting behavior, told Gere that it was outrageous that he did not have the courtesy at least to stand when the nation's greatest playwright came backstage to compliment him on his acting. Gere said nothing, and Tennessee left in confusion.

> from Datson Rader, Tennessee Williams: An Intimate Memoir (1985)

Injured

His was a wounded life.

> Marlon Brando

JACK KEROUAC (1922–1969), Novelist

Light Relief

Jack had told Connie Murphy that his first homosexual experience had taken place in the merchant marine. Jack said that many of the crewmen had one another because they were driven by sexual need, and he found that deplorable. What he regretted most was being exposed to that way of life, because although it wasn't his 'cup of tea' he had been 'thirsty' and learned to drink it. The confession seemed particularly anguished, as if Jack needed to unburden himself of something shameful. and to affirm that he was normal. In between voyages, during the war years. Jack went to bed with numerous girls (in a bragging mood years later, he reckoned 250 such conquests). But he was occasionally having sex with men in the city, too, though probably only as a passive recipient of fellatio.

from Gerald Nicosia, Memory Babe *(1983)*

Roots

Jack was also upset by his homosexual tendencies; as well as fooling around with Allen [Ginsberg], he had spent an evening drinking with Bill [William Burroughs] and some of Bill's friends, ending up as a participant in a homosexual orgy, which he regretted the next day. 'It automatically repels me,' he wrote Allen, 'thereby causing a great deal of remorse and disgust.' However, it was also during this time that Jack went with Bill and Allen to the Everard Turkish Baths, where a group of French sailors blew him . . .

from Barry Miles, Ginsberg *(1989)*

Neal

By the time Jack walked in, the room was filled with men, but LuAnne noticed him right away, and Neal [Cassady] was immediately aware of his interest. Allen had just been telling Neal about Jack and hurried to introduce them. Automatically Neal had become tremendously jealous of Jack – of his male power and beauty – but simultaneously Jack appealed to him for some other reasons. After Jack got into the conversation, Neal couldn't help being drawn to him. As far as LuAnne could see, Jack was experiencing the same mixture of attraction and repulsion toward Neal. Neal was not as 'pretty' as Jack, but he was holding everyone's interest through sheer will, an act of bravado Jack could never match. On the other hand, Jack saw that Neal didn't know what he was saying, that he was using big words and intellectual phrases in a crass effort to impress them . . .

Lacking money, degrees, or any other tickets to society, Neal had to get by on his wits alone. That was a trait Jack admired greatly, and it didn't take long for him to see what Neal was really doing.

All the same, that meeting between Jack and Neal wasn't wholly successful. Jack didn't even choose to mention it in *On the Road*, the first complete book he wrote about Neal . . .

A few days later Jack came with Hal [Chase] and Ed [White] to see Neal again. Neal answered the door in the nude; behind him LuAnne jumped off the couch and disappeared. Standing unselfconsciously in the doorway, Neal asked them to wait outside for a minute until he was 'through'. It was Jack's first glimpse of the 'Nietzschean hero' Hal had been telling him about, the lover whom women adored: half slender-hipped cowboy like Gene Autry, half Greek athletic champion, with a sex organ big enough for both.

This time Jack stayed with Neal until dawn, drinking beer and talking. He was intrigued by how intently Neal listened to him, with his head down, bobbing and nodding like a boxer taking instructions, punctuating everything Jack said with a 'Yes' or 'That's right.' . . .

A few years later, when Jack wrote the final version of *On the Road*, he began with an accurate rendering of that scene in the Harlem flat – except that in the printed text, for the sake of propriety, Neal was dressed in a pair of shorts before he opened the door to a new season in Jack's life.

from Gerald Nicosia, Memory Babe (1983)

NED ROREM (b. 1923), Composer, Diarist and Philosopher

Recognition I

The phone: 'How will I recognize you?' 'I'm beautiful.'
from Ned Rorem, The Paris Diary of Ned Rorem (1966)

Learning a Language

Circa 1949, I had arrived in Europe and asked Norris Embry, 'How's the sex in Florence?' Shirley overhearing: 'You boys! You cross an ocean and all you wonder about is sex. Aren't there other wonders in Florence to interest you besides that?' No. The best way to learn a new language is in bed.
from Ned Rorem, Nantucket Diary, 1973–1985 (1987)

Recognition II

[9 May 1981] We attended, at one of those gentrified little stables on West 42nd, a review called *Ah, Men* based on the prose of some twenty authors and their depiction of 'the male condition'. Included was a soliloquy, the one on Turkish baths, from my *New York Diary*, the only token queerness on the bill. As we perused our programs we eavesdropped on three young men behind us perusing theirs. 'Who's Bertrand Russell?' asks the one on the left. 'Oh, he's you know, that pacifist,' answers the one in the middle, obviously the brains of the trio. 'Who's O'Casey?' asks the one on the right. 'An Irish playwright.' 'Who's Ned Rorem?' 'That faggot composer.' For this I have sculpted a long, long life. My feelings were hurt . . .
from Ned Rorem, Nantucket Diary, 1973–1985 (1987)

Last Words

Famous last words of Ned Rorem, crushed by a truck, gnawed by pox, stung by wasps, in dire pain: 'How do I look?' It's harder to maintain a reputation for being pretty than for being a great artist.

from Ned Rorem, The Paris Diary of Ned Rorem (1966)

Achievement

. . . slept with four *Time* magazine covers . . .

from Ned Rorem, Nantucket Diary, 1973–1985 (1987)

Loser

. . . recall a restless night, circa 1958, when towards 4 a.m. I took him home – the black hair and red lips – not, in my drunkenness, realizing until later that he had an artificial limb, which took ages to remove – no sooner accomplished than I asked him to leave, cowered under the blankets, and heard only his cursing as he clamped the leg back on and clanked down the stairs.

from Ned Rorem, Nantucket Diary, 1973–1985 (1987)

The Baths

A Turkish bath, like the Quaker service, is a place of silent meeting. The silence is shared solely by men, men who come uniquely together not to speak but to act. More even than the army, the bath is by definition a male if not a masculine domain . . . There are so many varieties of bath as of motel, from the scorpion-ridden hammams of Marrakech, where like Rimbaud in a boxcar you'll be systematically violated by a regiment, to the carpeted saunas of Frisco, where like a corpse in a glossy morgue you'll be a slab of flab on marble with Musak. There is no variety, however, in the purpose served: anonymous carnality. As in a whorehouse, you check interpersonal responsibility at the door; but unlike the whorehouse, here a ménage might accidentally meet in mutual infidelity. The ethical value too is like prostitution's: the consolation that no one can prove you are not more fulfilled by a stranger (precisely because there's no responsibility to deflect your fantasies – fantasies which now are real) than by the mate you dearly love, and the realization that Good Sex is not in performing as the other person wants but as you want. You will reconfirm this as you retreat through every bath of history.

from Ned Rorem, The New York Diary of Ned Rorem (1967)

History

The current *Advocate*, in the Gay Trivia Quiz, lies by saying I wrote that Francis Poulenc [the composer] used 'to chase pretty Arab boys through the back streets of French North Africa', and also that Poulenc & Pierre Bernac were lovers. Poulenc never chased, nor did I ever suggest that he chased, pretty boys, nor were Poulenc & Bernac ever more than professional colleagues. (Poulenc's taste ran to overweight gendarmes with handlebar moustaches and to middled-aged businessmen. Governor Thomas Dewey, Poulenc once told me, was his ideal.)

from Ned Rorem, Nantucket Diary, 1973–1985 *(1987)*

FRANCO ZEFFIRELLI (b. 1923), Film Director

The End

One morning I was woken by a servant who told me that there had been a burglary. I found the police already there, with everybody gathered in the main salon. The losses were considerable: gold dishes and works of art. The burglars had even got into Luchino [Visconti]'s bedroom and scooped up the wrist watches, Cartier for the most part, which lay around his bedside table. The house was like an unguarded boutique and the thieves had had a field day.

The scene that greeted me was like something out of a 'B' detective movie. A raincoated, gruff inspector fired questions at us about our movements the night before. There were even rather overdone clues in the yard, where the thieves had walked into the coalstore, then left obvious footprints as they made their getaway.

Luchino and two members of the family were standing apart, and as the questioning went on, I suddenly wondered why he didn't call me over to him and tell the police that I was all right and needn't be questioned. But he didn't, and to my intense horror I saw that I was going to be taken to police headquarters with the others. Luchino never said a word as we were led away . . .

[Questioned by the police and accused of the robbery or as acting as accomplices, s]omewhere nearby were Luchino's butler, manservant, maids and cooks – all his servants – and what I realized was that I had to count myself as one of them, nothing more nothing less . . . I sat in that dismal room and tried to weigh up the past five years: I had broken with my family, I had had some incredible chances in the theatre and had lived in a style and among people beyond my earlier imaginings, but what did it all add up to except that I was the gilded creature of a famous man? I had nothing of my own – no reputation other than as his assistant and no money, for he gave me none. I had been happy enough, because I had not questioned his attachment to me, but now the reality was all too clear.

I began to remember incidents in the past showing his temper and insensitivity that I had previously dismissed as merely the moods of a great man.

Now I saw them as indications of my lesser status. I recalled the time he had hit me during the rehearsals for *As You Like It*, the total absence of any recognition or appreciation of the work done for him, and a dozen other incidents . . .

Eventually the lawyers completed all the formalities and we were released . . . so I decided to look upon that prison interlude as the impetus to break free from Luchino . . .

Years later Luchino and I were reminiscing about old times when at one point he referred to the amusing incident of the burglary and the way I had been taken off to the police station. I was stunned. Hadn't he realized how I'd felt when he let me be taken away like that? He was genuinely shocked. How could I have thought like that? Didn't I realize what a scandal it would have been if it had got about that I was staying in his house as something more than an employee? His obtuseness was total. Hadn't he even wondered what had caused my sudden decision to leave his house? In the weeks between the burglary and his departure for his annual holiday in Ischia, I let it be known that I intended to move out, and he made no attempt to find out why or to stop me. Of course, that sort of aristocratic indifference was part of the armour he always used to protect himself from any emotional distress.

from Franco Zeffirelli, Zeffirelli: The Autobiography of Franco Zeffirelli *(1986)*

Romeo

I tested various combinations of boy and girl, trying to find a pair who worked really well together. The boy turned out to be less of a problem than I feared. Lila de Nobili, who was in London designing a production for Peter Hall at Stratford, told me to look out for a young actor called Leonard Whiting. I did so, and sure enough, he seemed ideal. He was beautiful in that Renaissance page-boy way that was revived during the 1960s; he could probably act; and, as was obvious when I met him, he was very ambitious . . . his looks were perfect for the role; he was the most exquisitely beautiful male adolescent I've ever met.

from Franco Zeffirelli, Zeffirelli: The Autobiography of Franco Zeffirelli *(1986)*

Hard

12 December 1979
Big dinner party chez Lenny Bernstein for Zeffirelli, whom I've not seen since writing the score for his *Lady of the Camellias* in 1963. I never admired him then, and I still don't: he tries for Latin sweetness but is hard beneath, like his productions.

from Ned Rorem, Nantucket Diary, 1973–1985 *(1987)*

Discovery

Bruce [Robinson] admits the predatory [character in his film *Whitnail and I*] is based on one Franco Zeffirelli. 'Anyone who knows anything about my own rather miserable suburban acting career will know that I was in *Romeo and Juliet* and why it was a nightmare for me, genuinely the most unpleasant experience I've ever had in my life apart maybe from an operation. It was like a sustained asthma attack! Zeffirelli is a man of great vision and medium talent who's made one or two watchable films and I have great affection for him now – if I met him today I'd be the first to open a bottle and give him a glass – but I didn't then because he was fucking vicious. The great tragedy of Franco and I was that he fancied me and I was scared. Had I been gay I'd have been scared. There I was, I'd just come out of drama school and hadn't even done a week on the boards in Shropshire or Hull even, and suddenly I was on a jet-plane, which I'd never been on in my life, going to Rome to be in a film by a world-famous director. I'd never been a very worldly boy anyway, so there were massive pressures and confusions in my mind because it all seemed so important at the time. Franco and I could've had an adorable relationship, because he was so bright and it was fun when we went out and he'd point out a building by Bernini. He could've been a wonderful teacher, except for what he did. And everyone knows what he did – he abused his power with a young kid, and gave me hell because of that power. Why didn't he just fire me? Instead he kept me there so he could be cruel to me. He was a son of a bitch and did some dreadful things to me, mentally very cruel. It's all forgiven and forgotten now, but after *Romeo* everybody in the business knew exactly what had gone on and I came back to England and had a nervous breakdown and literally ended up in hospital because of that experience. After that I couldn't get a job for ages because (a) I was talentless and (b) because the attitude was' – here Robinson adopts an Italian accent – 'Yes, he's a pretty face, but there's fuck all else.'

from an interview with Bruce Robinson in Gay Times, February 1900

TRUMAN CAPOTE (1924–1984), Writer

Character Sketch I

I'm an alcoholic
I'm a drug addict
I'm a homosexual
I'm a genius
Truman Capote

Character Sketch II

A Republican housewife from Kansas with all the prejudices.
Gore Vidal on Truman Capote

Visible Assets

I never had any problems with being a homosexual. I mean look at me. I was always right out there. I was really quite popular. I was amusing and I was pretty. I didn't look like anybody else. People start out by being put off by something that's different, but I very easily disarmed them. Seduction – that's what I do. It was: You think I'm different, well, I'll show you how different I really am.

from an interview with Truman Capote in the New York Times Magazine, *1978*

Closely Observed Queen

Lunch at the Plaza. Truman Capote is in the men's bar. His bangs are dyed yellow, his voice is girlish, his laughter is baritone, and he seems to be a conspicuous male coquette. This must take some doing, but on the other hand it must be a very limited way of moving through life. He seems to excite more curiosity than intolerance. Almost everyone these days drinks a special brand of gin – Beefeater, House of Lords, Lamplighter – and vodka. I hear the orders come over the bar. The bartender calls to a handsome Italian waiter and they disappear into a broom closet, to straighten out their racetrack bets, I hope. But to someone familiar with a rigorous and a simple way of life these scenes might seem decadent and final, like those lavish and vulgar death throes of the Roman Empire that we see in the movies.

from John Cheever's journals for 1959

GORE VIDAL (b. 1925), Writer

Manhattan Chase

'Gore was a handsome kid, about twenty-four [*sic*], and I was quite taken by his wit as well as his appearance.' Incidentally I am mesmerized by the tributes to my beauty that keep cropping up in the memoirs of the period [the 1940s]. At the time nobody reliable thought to tell me. In fact, it was my impression that I was not making out as well as most people because, with characteristic malice, Nature had allowed Guy Madison and not me to look like Guy Madison.

'We found that we had interests in common and we spent a lot of time together. Please don't imagine that I am suggesting that there was a romance.' I don't remember whether or not I ever told Tennessee that I had actually seen but not met him the previous year. He was following me up Fifth Avenue while I, in turn, was stalking yet another quarry. I recognized him: he wore a blue bow tie with white polka dots. I was in no mood for literary encounters. I gave him a scowl and he abandoned the chase just north of the Rockefeller Center. I don't recall how my pursuit ended. We walked a lot in the golden age.

Gore Vidal reviewing Tennessee Williams's Memoirs *in the* New York Review of Books, *5 February 1976*

Pink Triangle and Yellow Star

Jews, blacks and homosexualists are despised by the Christian and Communist majorities of East and West. Also, as a result of the invention of Israel, Jews can count on the hatred of the Islamic world. Since our own Christian majority looks to be getting ready for some great adventures at home and abroad, I would suggest that the three despised minorities join forces in order not to be destroyed. Unfortunately, most Jews refuse to see any similarity between their special situation and that of the same-sexers. At one level, the Jews are perfectly correct. A racial or religious or tribal identity is a kind of fact. Although sexual preference is an even more powerful fact, it is not one that creates any particular social or cultural or religious bond between those so-minded. Although Jews would doubtless be Jews if there was no anti-Semitism, same-sexers would think little or nothing at all about their preference if society ignored it. So there is a difference between the two estates. But there is no difference in the degree of hatred felt by the Christian majority for Christ-killers and Sodomites. In the German concentration camps, Jews wore yellow stars while homosexualists wore pink triangles. I was present when Christopher Isherwood tried to make this point to a young Jewish movie producer. 'After all,' said Isherwood, 'Hitler killed six hundred thousand homosexuals.' The young man was not impressed. 'But Hitler killed six million Jews,' he said sternly. 'What are you?' asked Isherwood. 'In real estate?' Like it or not, Jews and homosexuals are in the same fragile boat, and one would have to be pretty obtuse not to see the common danger.

from Gore Vidal, Pink Triangle and Yellow Star, and Other Essays (1976–1982) *(1982)*

ALLEN GINSBERG (b. 1926), American Poet

Many Loves

So gentle the man, so sweet the moment, so kind the thighs that nuzzled against
    me smooth-skinned powerful, warm by my legs
That my body shudders and trembles with happiness, remembering –
His hand opened up on my belly, his palms and fingers flat against my skin
I fell to him, and turned, shifting, put my face on his arm resting,
my chest against his, he helped me to turn, and held me closer
his arm at my back beneath my head, and arm at my buttocks tender holding
    me in,
our bellies together nestling, loins touched together, pressing and knowledgeable
    each other's hardness, and mine stuck out of my underwear.
Then I pressed in closer and drew my leg up between his, and he lay half on me
    with his thighs and bedded me down close, caressing
and moved together pressing his cock to my thigh and mine to his
slowly and slowly began a love match that continues in my imagination to this
    day a full decade.

from Allen Ginsberg, 'Many Loves' (1956) – a poem about his one-time lover Neal Cassady

ANDY WARHOL (1928–1987), Artist

Ingenuity

How did people ever think of doing this?

Andy Warhol on sex, from The Philosophy of Andy Warhol: from A to B and Back Again *(1975)*

Butch

Then we went over to Studio 54. Stevie introduced me to Roy Cohn who was with four beautiful boys, but butch-looking. A boy is 'butch' if he weighs over 170 and he's an all-American football-type, a spilling-out masculine man.

from Andy Warhol's diary, 7 October 1977

Alone

It's the long life-spans that are throwing all the old values and their applications out of whack. When people used to learn about sex at fifteen and die at thirty-five, they obviously were going to have fewer problems than people today who learn about sex at eight or so, I guess, and live to be eighty. That's a long time to play around with the same concept. The same boring concept.

Parents who really love their kids and want them to be bored and discontented for as small a percentage of their lifetimes as possible maybe should go back to not letting them date until as late as possible so they have something to look forward to for a longer time.

Sex is more exciting on screen and between the pages than between the sheets anyway. Let the kids read about it and look forward to it, and then right before they're going to get the reality, break the news to them that they've already had the most exciting part, that it's behind them already. Fantasy love is much better than reality love. Never doing it is very exciting. The most exciting attractions are between two opposites who never meet.

I love every 'lib' movement there is, because after the 'lib' the things that were always mystique become understandable and boring, and then nobody has to feel left out if they're not part of what is happening. For instance, single people looking for husbands and wives used to feel left out because the image marriage had in the old days was so wonderful. Jane Wyatt and Robert Young. Nick and Nora Charles. Ethel and Fred Mertz. Dagwood and Blondie.

Being married looked so wonderful that life didn't seem livable if you weren't lucky enough to have a husband or wife. To the singles, marriage seemed beautiful, the trappings seemed wonderful, and the sex was always implied to be automatically great – no one could ever find words to describe it because 'you had to be there' to know how good it was. It was almost like a conspiracy on the part of the married people not to let it out how it wasn't necessarily completely wonderful to be married and having sex; they could have taken a load off the single people's mind if they had been candid.

But it was always a fairly well-kept secret that if you were married to somebody you didn't have enough room in bed and might have to face bad breath in the morning . . .

I don't see anything wrong with being alone. It feels great to me . . . The biggest price you pay for love is that you have somebody around, you can't be on your own, which is always so much better.

from Andy Warhol, The Philosophy of Andy Warhol: from A to B and Back Again *(1975)*

The Age of Improvement

Walked to the office. Made some phone calls, had a little lunch. There was a crowd of models there and Barry McKinley was taking photographs of, mostly male models, they were so good-looking. Why are there so many to choose from now? Because there's nobody in the army? Wouldn't it be great to do a whole movie of nothing but good-looking kids – the butcher, the baker – all models

from Andy Warhol's diary, 30 August 1979

But tell me why it is that everybody is so good-looking now. In the fifties, there were really good-looking people and then all the rest who weren't. Today, everybody is at least attractive. How did it happen? Is it because there's no wars to kill the beauties.

from Andy Warhol's diary, 16 August 1982

The city is just teeming with beautiful kids who all look like models. They must come from everywhere.

from Andy Warhol's diary, 3 June 1983

Challenge

Bob and I were talking about how hard it was to find Ten Straight Men, and somebody said that that should be my next portfolio – ten men who've never had a homosexual experience.

from Andy Warhol's diary, 27 October 1980

Fame

The *Cock Drawings* were never reproduced, and I don't have any. They were done mostly through friends . . . Like if he met somebody at a party or something, and he thought they were fascinating or interesting, he'd say, 'Oh, ah, let me draw your cock. I'm doing a cock book.' And surprising enough, most people were flattered [when] asked to be drawn. So he had no trouble getting people to draw, and he did a lot of beautiful drawings.

from an interview with Ted Carey, artist, in P. S. Smith, Warhol: Conversations about the Artist *(1988)*

Easy

Then to a great club called Chaca – all young, good-looking kids. Tangos and old Elvis songs and it was just the greatest.

Chris and I took this adorable boy, Martin, back to the hotel. We got him to take his shirt off and then we got him to take his pants off, too, and he had the craziest sort of Op Art underwear on and we took pictures and he did the best poses and then we gave him the car to go home in. One thing I've learned from Chris is that if you tell anybody to do anything, they just do it. Especially actors and models.

from Andy Warhol's diary, Vienna, 9 April 1981

Scared

He was so scared of that – physical contact – with people. It's hard to touch him. It's really hard . . . I've been in Studio 54, where there has been two humpy, well-built numbers that just jumped all over Andy. Like 'I'll do anything for you, possibly.' You know? And it's like he just doesn't know what to do. He's just freaked out. He'd say to me tomorrow, 'Rupert, can you imagine anyone turning them down? I mean, they'll always say to me, "Your place or mine?" ' And Andy gets freaked out. They should beat each other or something – leave me alone – or watch.

from interview with Rupert Smith, Warhol associate, in P. S. Smith, Warhol: Conversations about the Artist (1988)

Recognition

Went to Dr. Bernsohn's and who should be there in the waiting room but the star of my movie *Blowjob*. I never did know his name. He goes to Bernsohn, too.

from Andy Warhol's diary, 12 December 1984

JOE ORTON (1933–1967), Playwright

The Discovery

SLOANE: You have a son, don't you?
KEMP: Yes, but we're not on speaking terms.
SLOANE: How long is it?
KEMP: Twenty years.
SLOANE: 'Strewth!
KEMP: You perhaps find that hard to believe?
SLOANE: I do actually. Not speaking for twenty years? That's coming it a bit strong.
KEMP: I may have exchanged a few words.

SLOANE: I can believe that.

KEMP : He was a good boy. Played some amazing games as a youth. Won every goal at football one season. Sport mad, he was. (*Pause.*) Then one day, shortly after his seventeenth birthday, I had cause to return home unexpected and found him committing some kind of felony in the bedroom.

SLOANE: Is that straight?

KEMP: I could never forgive him.

SLOANE: A puritan, are you?

KEMP: Yes.

SLOANE: That kind of thing happens often, I believe. For myself, I usually lock the door.

KEMP: I'd removed the lock.

SLOANE: Anticipating some such tendencies on his part?

KEMP: I'd done it as a precautionary measure.

from Joe Orton, Entertaining Mr Sloane *(1964)*

Smoothie

I like a lad with a smooth body.

from Joe Orton, Entertaining Mr Sloane *(1964)*

Danger Woman

Women are like banks, boy, breaking and entry is a serious business.

from Joe Orton, Entertaining Mr Sloane *(1964)*

Growing Up

Why conform to the standards of the cowshed? It's a thing you grow out of. With me behind you, boy, you'll grow out of it.

from Joe Orton, Entertaining Mr Sloane *(1964)*

Unchanging

The country's moral values, far from changing, seem to remain unnaturally constant.

from Joe Orton, The Good and Faithful Servant *(1967)*

Blondes

God is a gentleman. He prefers blondes.

from Joe Orton, Loot *(1966)*

Youth

No position is impossible when you're young and healthy.
from Joe Orton, What the Butler Saw *(1969)*

Variety

Try a boy for a change. You're a rich man. You can afford the luxuries of life.
from Joe Orton, What the Butler Saw *(1969)*

Reticence

PRENTICE: I don't approve of scientists who publicize their theories.
RANCE: I must say I agree with you. I wish more scientists would keep their ideas
to themselves.
from Joe Orton, What the Butler Saw *(1969)*

False Foundations

Civilizations have been founded and maintained on theories which refused to
obey facts.
from Joe Orton, What the Butler Saw *(1969)*

Cover

Marriage excuses no one the freaks' roll-call.
from Joe Orton, What the Butler Saw *(1969)*

Advantage

Boys cannot be put in the club. That's half their charm.
from Joe Orton, What the Butler Saw *(1969)*

The Orton Murder

9 March 1967
Long, neurotic argument. Kenneth [Halliwell] said, 'You're turning into a real
bully, do you know that? You'd better be careful. You'll get your deserts!'

18 March 1967
Exhausting wrangles over trivia. Kenneth, lying in bed, suddenly shouted. 'I
hope I die of heart disease! I'd like to see you manage then.' He talks a lot of *The*

Dance of Death. 'We're living it,' he suddenly said. 'This is Strindberg!' Soothed down the situation only to have it break out later. 'You're quite a different person, you know, since you had your success.'

23 March 1967
Kenneth H. and I went for a long trot and argued most of the way – traffic and heat aggravating the argument to fever pitch. The argument was about Ivan the Terrible. I forgot how it began or ended.

31 March 1967
Unpleasant day. Constant rowing over small things.

4 April 1967
Arguments continue spasmodically.

23 April 1967
Dreary day. Kenneth in an ugly mood. Moaning. I said, 'You look like a zombie.' He replied heavily, 'So I should. I lead the life of a zombie.'

30 April 1967
When we got home we talked about ourselves and our relationship. I think it's bad that we live in each other's pockets twenty-four hours a day, three hundred and sixty-five days of the year. When I'm away Kenneth does nothing, meets nobody. What's to be done? He's now taking tranquillisers to calm his nerves. 'I need an affair with someone,' he says. He says I'm no good. I'm only interested in physical sex, not love. 'Your attitude to sensitive people is Victorian,' he said, 'basically it's Dr Arnold "Get out on the playing fields. You won't be sensitive then." ' 'All you need,' I said, 'is some field of interest outside of me. Where you can meet people away from me.'

1 May 1967
Kenneth H. had long talk about our relationship. He threatens, or keeps saying, he will commit suicide. He says, 'You'll learn then, won't you?' and 'What will you be like without me?' We talked and talked until I was exhausted. Going round in circles.

5 May 1967
When I got home, Kenneth H. was in such a rage. He'd written in large letters on the wall, 'JOE ORTON IS A SPINELESS TWAT'. He sulked for a while and then came round. He'd been to his doctor's and got 400 valium tablets. Later we took two each and had the most amazing sexual session. I'd decided that I'd fuck him. But it didn't work out. 'I'm not sure what the block is,' I said. 'I can fuck other people perfectly well. But, up to now, I can't fuck you.' This is something quite strange. I had a big hard on. Yet, when I tried to put it up him, it just went off. Anyway we made love and came. He sucked my cock. I've got a mark on it now where he did it too hard.

27 June 1967
[In Morocco] Kenneth became violently angry . . . and attacked me, hitting me about the head and knocking my pen from my hand. He left the room and a short

time later, the house. I got back to the flat about 9.45. Kenneth was lying in his bed in a towel dressing-gown, looking tight-lipped. I realised that it was no good speaking to him, the 'sore' would come sooner or later. I'd just settled down for the night when the door opened and Kenneth entered. I was selfish, I couldn't bear to be the centre of attention, I was continually sneering at him for only wishing to be masturbated while I was 'virile' fucking boys. 'I saw you in Nigel's car,' he said, 'and I've never seen you at a distance before. I thought, What a long-nosed ponce.' The holiday had been perfect. He was determined to spoil it somehow. 'And when we get back to London,' he said, 'we're finished. This is the end!' I had heard this so often. 'I wonder you didn't add "I'm going back to Mother",' I said wearily. 'That's the kind of line that ultimately makes your plays ultimately worthless,' he said. It went on and on until I put out the light. He slammed the door and went to bed.

17 July 1967

Kenneth v. irritating today. Weather hot again. Blue skies. Kenneth's nerves are on edge. Hay fever. We had a row this morning. Trembling with rage. About my nastiness when I said, 'Are you going to stand in front of the mirror all day?' He said, 'I've been washing your fucking underpants! That's why I've been at the sink!' He shouted it out loudly and I said, 'Please, don't let the whole neighbourhood know you're a queen.' . . . I said, 'I can't stand much more of it.'

Orton and Halliwell died in the early hours of 9 August 1967. The right side of Orton's head had been staved with a hammer which lay on Orton's counterpane. His cranium carried the mark of nine hammer blows which, to the coroner, suggested a frenzy. Brain tissue and blood were at the head of the bed, the side of the bedding and on the ceiling. There were no marks on Orton's hands or arms.

Halliwell lay nude in the middle of the bedroom. He'd removed his soiled pyjama top which was lying across the desk chair. The top of his chest and head were splattered with blood. Near him on the floor was a glass and a can of grapefruit juice with which he'd swallowed twenty-two Nembutals. Halliwell died first. When they were discovered, rigor mortis had set into all but Halliwell's arms; Orton's sheets were still warm.

On the desk, police found a note:

> *If you read his diary all will be explained.*
> *K.H.*
> *P.S. Especially the latter part.*

from Orton's diary and a note on the murder provided by the editor of The Orton Diaries, *John Lahr*

No Regrets

When you are dead you'll regret not having fun with your genital organs.
from Joe Orton's diary

DAVID HOCKNEY (b. 1937), Artist

Inspiration

Later it was the Alexandrian Greek poet Constantine Cavafy who became a great influence. I'd read Lawrence Durrell's novels The Alexandrian Quartet; in the back of *Justine* there's Cavafy's 'The City' which impressed me. I read more of his poems and was struck by their directness and simplicity; and then I found the John Mavrogordato translation in the library at Bradford, in that summer of 1960, and I stole it. I've still got it, I'm sure. I don't feel bad now because it's been redone, but you couldn't buy it then, it was completely out of print. Mind you, in the library at Bradford you had to ask for that book, it was never on the shelves. If you had the intelligence to look it up in the catalogue and ask for it, then it would be all right. But if you were just a casual person who took it down from the shelves and read one of the poems, well it might be too wicked and you might go home and jerk off with the poetry. That's what they thought. Anyway, when I found the book I read it from cover to cover, many times, and I thought it was incredible and marvellous.

from David Hockney by David Hockney: My Early Years *(1977)*

America

I discovered physique magazines about 1960 and they were all American. I gradually began to get this fantasy about the country. In the summer of 1961 I'd started selling pictures and somehow or another I got the air ticket for £40 and went to New York. When I first came to London I thought London was incredible but New York made London seem like Bradford . . . To me America was unbelievably sexy and attractive . . . in America you can always find somebody else if it's just sex you're wanting.

David Hockney in Gay News, August 1976

Living Doll

At the end of 1965 I had to go to London for a show at Kasmin's. About a week before I left Hollywood I met in a gay bar a ravishingly beautiful boy. It was lust on my part, sheer lust, and I thought fantastic! And I took him home that night. It seemed unfair that I should meet him just as I had to leave because of the exhibition; I had to get all the pictures back. So I said Why don't you come to England? He'd never left California before. So he went and got a passport. Robert Lee Earles III was his real name, Bobby Earles, and he was beautiful, a real Hollywood, California boy, blond hair, marvellous. We drove off with Patrick [Prockter] in this big car to New York. Patrick and I kept having rows on the way. He said You've gone mad, David, you're crazy. I said Never mind, we'll make up for it at night, it's all right. And in New York – Bob, who'd never been before, didn't like it at all; he thought it was terrible. But I thought, you're going to love Europe. We came over on the *France*, and [John] Kasmin and a few friends met us at Waterloo Station and we had this big welcome . . . The first night we were back here, Kasmin said Come to a club that's opened in Jermyn Street. And I went with Bobby Earles and just by chance Ringo Starr sat at the table next to him. Bob thought that's what you should expect in London when you came there, that, naturally, he'd meet the Beatles; and I was amazed about all this. He was dumb; really very dumb. He'd no interest in anything at all; have some sex and that's it; absolutely no interest; all he was interested in, really, was Hollywood bars. After a week I said I think you should go back; I'll give you your ticket to go back. And I put him on a plane and sent him back. There is a drawing called *Bob, 'France'*, of a marvellous beautiful pink bottom, and that's really all he had in his favour, I suppose. But he's dead now; he died later on. Sad thing. I saw him for a year or two when I went back to California. He was a go-go boy dancing at a bar on Laguna Beach – and a few years later he took an overdose of drugs; tragic. He was a sweet boy and I felt very sad.

from David Hockney by David Hockney: My Early Years *(1977)*

Partners

David decided early in 1968 that he wanted to experiment with a large double portrait and, as his models, he chose his close friends Christopher Isherwood and Don Bachardy. This was no casual decision. It was convenient because they lived a few blocks down the street in Santa Monica. But much more important was the fact that they were a very successful gay partnership. They had met in 1953 when Isherwood was forty-eight and Bachardy was eighteen. Isherwood had given Bachardy support and confidence throughout his art training and early years of establishing himself, and was very proud of his later success. Isherwood in turn found real love and devotion with his much younger friend. They were to live together for thirty-three years until Isherwood's death in 1986, and during that time they were hardly ever apart. They were both strongly creative people who gave each other inspiration and encouragement. They provided the ideal role-models for Hockney and Peter [Schlesinger]. The painting, therefore, was not designed simply as an exercise in composition, but also as an examination of an intimate relationship.

from Peter Webb, Portrait of David Hockney *(1988)*

The Work Ethic

Lots of sex is fantasy. The only time I was promiscuous was when I first went to live in Los Angeles. I've never been promiscuous since. But I used to go to the bars in Los Angeles and pick up somebody. Half the time they didn't turn you on, or you didn't turn them on, or something like that. And the way people in Los Angeles went on about numbers! If you actually have some good sex with somebody, you can always go back for a bit more, that's the truth. I know a lot of people in Los Angeles who simply live for sex in that they want somebody new all the time, which means that it's a full-time job finding them; you can't do any work, even in Los Angeles where it's easy. I can go a long time without sex. A person came to see me in Paris from *The Advocate*, a gay newspaper, to do an interview. And I had to say The trouble is, it doesn't dominate my life, sex, at all. For some people it does, but at times I'm very indifferent to it; and when people like this man come along and go on as though sex was a pioneering thing, I say, Well, it's really very far from that.

from David Hockney by David Hockney: My Early Years *(1977)*

References

Introduction

1   M. Denneny, C. Ortleb and T. Steele (eds.), *The View from Christopher Street* (London, 1984), p. 295

2   N. Rorem, *Nantucket Diary 1973–1985* (San Francisco, 1987), p. 125

3   Ibid.

4   M. Barber, *The Trial of the Templars* (Cambridge, 1978)

5   D. Knowles, *Bare Ruined Choirs: The Dissolution of the Monasteries* (Cambridge, 1976), pp. 177–8, 184–5, 188

6   D. W. Cory, *The Homosexual Outlook* (London, 1953); published in the USA as *The Homosexual in America: A Subjective Approach* (1950)

7   M. Foucault, *The History of Sexuality* (3 vols., tr. R. Hurley 1978–88), and D. Eribon, *Michel Foucault* (London, 1992)

8   J. Katz, *Gay American History: Lesbian and Gay Men in the USA* (London, 1976), p. 11

9   L. Crompton, 'Gay Genocide from Leviticus to Hitler' in L. Crew (ed.), *The Gay Academic* (Palm Springs, 1978), pp. 67–91

10   Ibid., p. 67

11   T. Stehling (ed.), *Medieval Latin Poems of Male Love and Friendship* (New York and London, 1984)

12   P. Parker, *Ackerley* (London, 1989), p. 317

13   Katz, op. cit., p. 292

14   A. Hall, *Scandal, Sensation and Social Democracy: SPD Press and Wilhelmine Germany, 1890–1914* (Cambridge, 1977), pp. 163–7 and 173–87, and I. V. Hull, *The Entourage of Wilhelm II* (London, 1982), chs. 3–5

15   A. C. Kinsey, *Sexual Behavior in the Human Male* (Philadelphia, 1948), p. 512

16   A. Tardieu, *Étude médico-légale sur les attentats aux moeurs* (Paris, 1857)

17   J. L. Casper, *Traité pratique de médecine légale* (Paris, 1862), p. 216

18   J. C. Gonsiorek and J. D. Weinrich, *Homosexuality: Research Implications for Public Policy* (London, 1991), pp. 5–6

19   I. Bieber, *Homosexuality: A Psychoanalytic Study* (New York, 1962)

20   J. L. Casper, *A Handbook of the Practice of Forensic Medecine* (London, 1859–65), vol. 3, p. 331

21   L. Z. Hobson, *Consenting Adult* (London, 1975), p. 35

22   M. J. Bruccoli (ed.), *The Notebooks of F. Scott Fitzgerald* (London, 1978), p. 334

23   G. Steiner, *A Reader* (London, 1984), pp. 194–5

Chapter 1

1   W. H. Auden, *Collected Poems*, ed. E. Mendelson (London, 1991), pp. 188–9

Chapter 2

1   Peter Damian, *The Book of Gomorrah*, tr. P. J. Payer (Waterloo, Ontario, 1982)
2   J. Sheridan (ed.), *De Planctu Naturae by Alan of Lille* (Toronto, 1980)
3   J. Boswell, *Christianity, Social Tolerance and Homosexuality* (Chicago, 1980), and T. Stehling (ed.), *Medieval Latin Poems of Male Love and Friendship* (New York and London, 1984)
4   M. Musa (ed.), *Dante's Inferno* (Bloomington, Indiana, 1971), pp. 123–38 (Cantos XV and XVI)
5   M. Barber, *The Trial of the Templars* (Cambridge, 1978)

Chapter 3

1   I. Origo, *The World of San Bernadino* (London, 1963), R. C. Trexler, *Public Life in Renaissance Florence* (London, 1980), and G. Ruggiero, *The Boundaries of Eros* (New York, 1985)
2   J. Saslow, *Ganymede in the Renaissance* (London and New Haven, 1986)
3   A. Bray, *Homosexuality in Renaissance England* (London, 1982), pp. 60–7
4   S. Schoenbaum, *Shakespeare's Lives* (Oxford, 1970), pp. 69, 303–4, 441, 446–8, 453–6, 668, 675–6, 680, 738, 751
5   W. R. Dynes (ed.), *The Encyclopedia of Homosexuality* (London, 1990)

Chapter 4

1   C. Bingham, *James I of England* (London, 1981), R. Lockyer, *Buckingham: The Life and Political Career of George Villiers, First Duke of Buckingham 1592–1628* (London, 1981), and H. and B. van de Zee, *William and Mary* (London, 1973), pp. 144, 415–24
2   A. Ellis (ed.), *Sodom, or The Quintessence of Debauchery by John Wilmot, Earl of Rochester* (Los Angeles, 1966)
3   J. P. Kenyon, *The Popish Plot* (London, 1972), pp. 46–9
4   A. Bray, *Homosexuality in Renaissance England* (London, 1982), and R. Norton, *Mother Clap's Molly House: The Gay Subculture in England, 1700–1830* (London, 1992)
5   Norton, op. cit., pp. 54–69
6   For those mentioned in this paragraph, see biographical entries in W. R. Dynes, *The Encyclopedia of Homosexuality* (London, 1990)

Chapter 5

1   J. A. Symonds, *The Sonnets of Michelangelo* (1878)
2   For example, *Tarcissus, the Boy Martyr of Rome* (1880), *Ballade of Boys Bathing* (1888), *Stories Toto Told Me* (1898), *Hadrian the Seventh* (1904) and *The Desire and Pursuit of the Whole: A Romance of Modern Venice* (1934)

3   R. Hyam, *Empire and Sexuality: The British Experience* (Manchester, 1990)
4   B. Inglis, *Roger Casement* (London, 1973)

Chapter 6
1   J. M. Masson, *The Assault on Truth: Freud's Suppression of the Seduction Theory* (London, 1985), *Against Theory* (London, 1988), and *Final Analysis: The Making and Unmaking of a Psychoanalyst* (London, 1990)

Chapter 7
1   C. Wolff, *Magnus Hirschfeld: A Portrait of a Pioneer in Sexology* (London, 1986), pp. 57–9
2   A. Hall, *Scandal, Sensation and Social Democracy: SPD Press and Wilhelmine Germany, 1890–1914* (Cambridge, 1977), ch. 4
3   R. Plant, *The Pink Triangle* (London, 1987), ch. 4

Chapter 8
1   L. Trilling, 'The Kinsey Report', in *The Liberal Imagination* (London, 1950), pp. 210–28
2   A. Berube, *Coming Out under Fire* (London, 1990), ch. 6
3   J. Fishman, *Sex in Prisons* (London, 1936)
4   E. Cooper, *The Sexual Perspective: Homosexuality and Art in the West* (London, 1986), p. 233

Chapter 9
1   R. Davenport-Hines, *Sex, Death and Punishment: Attitudes to Sex and Sexuality in Britain since the Renaissance* (London, 1990), p. 3

Chapter 11
1   S. Kleinberg, *The Other Persuasion* (London, 1977)
2   A. Maupin, *Tales of the City* (London, 1978), *More Tales of the City* (London, 1980), *Further Tales of the City* (London, 1984), *Babycakes* (London, 1986), *Significant Others* (London, 1988), *Sure of You* (London, 1990)
3   P. York, *Style Wars* (London, 1980)

Chapter 12
1   See K. Anger, *Hollywood Babylon II* (New York, 1984)
2   S. Sontag, 'Notes on Camp', *Partisan Review*, 1964

Acknowledgements

Chapter One: Antiquity

p. 21, "The Desire and Pursuit of the Whole"   p. 23, "Fruitless Labours" Plato *The Symposium* trans. Walter Hamilton (Penguin, 1951). p. 26, "Contemptuous Partner" Xenephon *The Symposium* trans. Hugh Tredennick (Penguin, 1970).   p. 26, "Alexander and Hephaiston" R. Lane-Fox *Alexander the Great* (Allen Lane, 1975).   p. 26, "The Death of Orpheus" R. Lane-Fox *A Stylistic Commentary on Phanocles and Related Texts* Adolf Hakkert, (Amsterdam, 1988).   p. 27, "The Fragmentation of Greece" K. Dover *Greek Homosexuality* (Harvard University Press, 1978).   p. 28, "A Favour and a Threat"   p. 29, "Memories" *The Poems of Catullus* trans. Peter Whigham, (University of California Press, Berkeley and Los Angeles, 1969).   p. 29, "The Abduction of Ganymede" Ovid *Metamorphoses* trans. A. D. Melville (Oxford University Press, 1986) by permission of the Oxford University Press.   p. 30, "Telling Father" Petronius *The Satyricon* trans. William Arrowsmith, (University of Michigan Press, Ann Arbor, 1959).   p. 32, "Butch Bride"   p. 33, "Tell-Tale Glances"   p. 33, "Disappointed Shopper" P. Howell *A Commentary on Book One of the Epigrams of Martial* (Athlone Press, 1980).   p. 34, "Ceasar's Past"   p. 35, "Tiberius"   p. 35, "Caligula" Suetonius *The Twelve Ceasars* trans. R. Graver (Allen Lane, 1979 ed.) by permission of A. P. Watt of The Trustees of Robert Graves Copyright Trust.   p. 35, "The Vain General"   p. 35, "Unnatural Contracts"   p. 35, "Dishonest Romans"   p. 35, "Lament of the Ageing Hustler" Juvenal *The Satires* trans. P. Green (Penguin, 1967).   p. 38, "Toy Boy" R. Lambert *Beloved and God* (Viking, 1984).

Chapter Two: The Middle Ages

p. 46, "The Court of King Rufus" Oderic Vitalis *Ecclesiastical History* volume IV ed. M. Chibnall p. 189 (Oxford University Press, 1983) by permission of the Oxford University Press.   p. 46, "Clerical Crimes" Peter Damian's *Book of Gommorah* (1982) trans. P. Payer, (Wilfrid Laurier Press, 1982).   p. 47, "An Unsuitable Attachment" *Eneas* translated by John A. Yunck (Columbia University Press, New York, 1974).   p. 48, "Richard the Lionheart" J. A. Brundage *Richard the Lionheart* (Scribners, 1974).   p. 54, "Medieval Slang" J. Boswell *Christianity, Social Tolerance and Homosexuality* (University of Chicago Press, 1980).   p. 55, "The Trial of Arnold Verniolle" M. Goodich *The Unmentionable Vice* (ABC-Clio, 1979).

Chapter Three: The Renaissance

p. 61, "Renaissance Venice" G. Ruggiero *The Boundaries of Eros* (Oxford University Press, 1985).   p. 62, "Call to Arms"   p. 65, "A Marvellous Matter" J. Saslow *Ganymede in the Renaissance* (Yale University Press, 1986).   p. 62, "The Little Devil" R. Payne *Leonardo* (Robert Hale, 1978).   p. 63, "The Rule of Law" B. Pullan & D. S. Chambers (eds) *Renaissance Venice: a documentary history* (Blackwell, 1992).   p. 64, "Michelangelo" M. Walters *The Nude Male* (Penguin, 1978).   p. 66, "The Headmaster" H. Montgomery Hyde *The Other Love* (Little Brown, 1970).   p. 68, "Every Picture Tells a Story" H. Hibbard *Caravaggio* (Thames & Hudson, 1983).

Chapter Four: Seventeenth and Eighteenth Centuries

p. 78, "Boy George" R. Lockyer *Buckingham* (Longman 1981).   p. 80, "Fraternal Sermon" K. Fincham *Prelates as Pastors* (1990) Oxford University Press.   p. 81, "Restoration Rake"   p. 82, "A Restoration Season" *Lorenzo Magalotti at the Court of Charles II* edited and translated by W. E. Knowles Middleton (Wilfrid Laurier University Press, 1980).   p. 83, "Valencia During the Seventeenth Century" R. Bennassar *The Spanish Character* (University of Southern California Press, 1975).   p. 84, "Finding Sex in Eighteenth Century Paris" M. Rey '*Parisian Homosexuals create a lifestyle, 1700–1750: The Police Archives*' in R. P. Maccubbin (ed) '*Tis Nature's Fault: Unauthorized Sexuality during the Enlightenment* (Cambridge University Press, 1981).   p. 87, "Nursing the Bruises" R. Haslaband *Lord Hervey* (Oxford University Press, 1973) by permission of the Oxford University Press.   p. 88, "Murder of an Art Historian" H. Mayer *Outsiders* (MIT Press, 1982).   p. 89, "The Powderham Scandal" J. Lees-Milne *William Beckford* (1967) by permission of David Higham Associates, Century paperback edition.

Chapter Five: The Nineteenth Century

p. 93, "Exchanging Gifts" L. Crompton *Byron and Greek Love* (University of California Press, 1985).   p. 94, "Fairy Tales" W. B. Pomeroy *Dr. Kinsey* (Yale University Press, 1972).   p. 94, "A Danish Biographer Replies" E. Bresdorff *Hans Christian Anderson* (Scribners, 1975).   p. 94, "The Little Mermaid" H. Mayer *Outsiders* (MIT Press, 1982).   p. 95, "Scot-Free" H. Scharnhorst *Horatio Alger* (Twayne's United States Author Series, 1980).   p. 96, "A Grand Passion" H. Starkie *Arthur Rimbaud* (Faber and Faber, 1938).   p. 98, "A Double Life"   p. 100, "The Gondolier"   p. 101, "Taming the Wild Beast"   p. 102, "Unnecessary Enquiry" P. Grosskurth *The Woeful Victorian* (Holt, 1964).   p. 99, "Snaps" A. Thwaite *Gosse* (Secker & Warburg, 1984).   p. 103, "A Straight Friend" J. Kaplan *Walt Whitman: A Life* (Simon & Schuster, 1980).   p. 105, "Candid Camera"   p. 105, "Uncorrupted" M. Benkovitz *Corvo* (Hamish Hamilton, 1977).   p. 106, "Apologia" C. Tsuzuki *Edward Carpenter* (Cambridge University Press, 1980).   p. 115, "Sublimation"   p. 115, "Agony Ant"   p. 115, "Popular Album" T. Jeall *The Boy-Man* (Morrow, 1989).   p. 116, "A Different World" M. Seymour *A Ring of Conspirators* (Houghton Mifflin, 1988).

Chapter Six: Freud and the Doctors

p. 120, "For the Record" J. Wortis *Fragments of an Analysis with Freud* (Simon & Schuster, 1954).   p. 122, "Big Kids" D. Henderson & D. Gillespie *A Textbook of Psychiatry* (Oxford University Press, 1962) by permission of the Oxford University Press.   p. 123, "Crackers" J. Haley (ed) *Conversations with Milton Erickson* (Triangle Press, 1985).   p. 123, "Old Boar" J. Marmor *Sexual Inversion* (Basic Books, 1965).   p. 125, "A Mix-Up" E. Bergler *Principles of Self-Damage* (Grove/Atlantic Inc. 1959).   p. 126, "Bisexual II"   p. 126, "Re-Definition" J. C. Gonsiorek and J. D. Weinrich *Homosexuality: Research Implication for Public Policy* (Sage Publications, 1991).   p. 127, "Catholic Psychiatry" J. H. Van der Veldt and R. P. Odenwald *Psychiatry and Catholicism* (The Free Press, 1957).   p. 127, "Vegetables" R. Fine *The Psychoanalytic Vision* (Macmillan, 1981).   p. 128, "Telling the Difference"   p. 128, "Colluding Mother" D. Miller *The Age Between Adolescence and Therapy* (1983) Jason Aronson.   p. 129, "Homosexual Panic" A. E. Slaby, L. E. Tancredi and J. Lieb *Clinical Psychiatric Medicine* (Harper Row, 1981).   p. 130, "Spots" S. S. Turner (ed) *Adult Psychopathology and Diagnosis* (John Wiley & Sons Ltd., 1984).
*p. 130, "Applied Anthropology"
*p. 130, "The Menu" G. Herdt and S. Lindenbaum *The Time of AIDS* (Sage Publications, 1992).

Chapter Seven: The German Experience

p. 135, "The Krupp Scandal" A. Hall *Scandal, Sensation and Social Democracy* (Cambridge University Press, 1977).   p. 136, "Hirschfeld" C. Wolff *Magnus Hirschfeld: A Portrait of a Pioneer in Sexology* (Quartet, 1986).   p. 139, "A Progressive School" G. Mann *Reminiscences and Reflections* (Norton, 1990).   p. 140, "An Early Morning Call" Noakes & Pridham *Nazism 1919–1945* volume I, (Schocken Books, 1983). p. 141, "Frederick the Great" F. Kersten *The Kersten Memoirs 1940–1945* (Macmillan (USA) 1956).
*p. 142, "Personal Picture Schow" R. Hoess *Commandant of Auschwitz* (Weidenfeld & Nicolson, 1959).   p. 143, "Saved"   p. 144, "A Captive Audience" R. Plant *Pink Triangle* (Mainstream Publishing, 1987).

Chapter Eight: The American Century

p. 151, "Macho Man I" M. J. Bruccoli (ed) *The Notebooks of F. Scott Fitzgerald* (Harcourt Brace Jovanovitch, 1945).   p. 151, "Macho Man" E. Hemingway *The Sun Also Rises* (Scribners, 1926) E. Hemingway *Death in the Afternoon* (Scribners, 1932).   p. 152, "Exercises in Deception"   p. 168, "Uneconomic Activity" H. Benjamin & R. Masters *Prostitution & Morality* (Souvenir Press, 1965).   p. 153, "The War" J. Costello *Love, Sex and War* (Collins, 1985).   p. 153, "The Examination"   p. 154, "YMCA" H. Norse *Memoirs of a Bastard Angel* (Morrow, 1989).   p. 155, "Breakfast at Tiffany's" p. 157, "Cheating Wife" G. Clarke *Capote* (Random House, 1988).   p. 155, "Helpless Victim" D. J. Franan *Auden in Love* (Faber and Faber, 1985) by permission of the Rosalyn Targ Agency.   p. 156, "California Cruising I" J. Fryer *Isherwood* (Doubleday, 1977).   p. 156, "California Cruising II" L. Bergreen *James Agee: A Life* (Dutton, 1984).   p. 156, "Complacent Cardinal" J. Cooney *The American Pope* (Time Books, 1984) by permission of Random House Inc.   p. 157, "Anus Mirabilis" J. Cheever *The Journals* (Knopf, 1990).   p. 157, "Starting Point"   p. 158, "The Conclusion"   p. 158, "The Lesson to be Learnt" A. C. Kinsey *Sexual Behaviour in the Human Male* (W. B. Saunders Co., 1948) by permission of the Institute for Sexual Research, Indiana,   p. 159, "The First Touch" W. B. Pomeroy *Kinsey* (Yale University Press, 1972).   p. 160, "The American Dream" *The Athletic Model Guild* (GMP, 1987).   p. 164, "American Underworld Lingo" *The Dictionary of American Underworld Lingo* (Constable, 1950).   p. 165, "Denial" A. G. Theoharis & J. S. Cox *The Boss* (Temple University Press, 1988).   p. 166, "The Loving Eye" R. G. Powers *Secrecy and Power* (Free Press, 1987).   p. 166, "Defending American Values" B. Castle *The Castle Diaries* (Weidenfeld & Nicolson, 1984).   p. 167, "The Tormentor"   p. 167, "Lubrication" N. von Hoffman *Citizen Cohn* (1988) by permission of Abner Stein.   p. 168, "Uncle Tom" E. Cleaver *Soul on Ice* (Random House, 1969).   p. 168, "Bad Boys" J. Gagnon & W. Simon *Sexual Deviance* (Harper Row, 1967).   p. 169, "Restraint" B. Pronger *The Arena of Masculinity* (GMP, 1990).

Chapter Nine: British Aberrations

p. 176, "Buggers" B. Hillier *Young Betjeman* (1988) p. 11/John Murray   p. 176, "Feline" N. Nicolson (ed) *A Change of Perspective: The Letters of Virginia Woolf* volume III (Harcourt, 1977).   p. 176, "Unfortunate Creatures" K. Clarke *Another Part of the Wood* (John Murray, 1974)   p. 178, "On the Up" R. Graves *The Long Weekend* (Faber and Faber 1940) by permission of A. P. Watt Ltd on behalf of the Robert Graves Copyright Trust.   p. 179, "Deceptions" J. Miller *One Girl's War* (Brandon Press, 1986).   p. 180, "Crashing a Garden Party" Lady Aberconway *A Wiser Woman?* (Hutchinson, 1960).   p. 181, "Raining Men" J. Lees-Milne *Prophesying Peace* (Chatto & Windus, 1977).   p. 181, "The Duke of Kent" H. Thornton *Royal Feud* (Michael Joseph, 1985).   p. 181, "Mentor" P. Snow *Stranger and Brother. A Portrait of G. P. Snow* (Macmillan, 1982).   p. 182, "War Games" J. Costello *Love, Sex and War* (Collins, 1985).   p. 183, "Outrage"   p. 184, "The Great Purge"   p. 186, "British Justice" R. Davenport Hines *Sex, Death and Punishment* (Collins, 1990).   p. 184, "Tolerant Christian" J. Como (ed) *C. S. Lewis at the Breakfast Table & Other Reminiscences* (Macmillan (USA) 1980).   p. 189, "An Interesting Discussion"   p. 190, "A Day in the Life of an English Public Schoolboy"   p. 191, "Helping"   p. 192, "Long Night" R. Lambert *The Hothouse Society* (Weidenfeld & Nicolson, 1968).   p. 193, "Cottages" R. Lahr (ed) *The Orton Diaries* (Methuen, 1986).   p. 194, "A Hard Night"   p. 194, "Taking a Stand"   p. 195, "Sterling Service"   p. 196, "Consequences" B. Castle *The Castle Diaries* (Weidenfeld & Nicolson, 1984).   p. 195, "Unnecessary Gamble" R. Grossman *The Diaries of a Cabinet Minister* vol 2 (Hamish Hamilton and Jonathan Cape, 1976).   p. 196, "Gangland Pleasures" J. Pearson *Profession of Violence* (Saturday Review Press, 1972).

Chapter Ten: The Gay Movement

p. 203, "The Good Old Cause" J. D'Emilio *Sexual Politics. Sexual Communities: The Making of a Homosexual Minority in the United States* (Chicago University Press, 1983).   p. 203, "Against the Current" S. Coote (ed) *The Penguin Book of Homosexual Verse* (Penguin, 1983).   p. 204, "Label"   p. 211, "Passing" S. Kleinberg *The Other Persuasion* (Picador, 1977).   p. 213, "Horrors"   p. 213, "Experience" M. Mieli *Homosexuality and Liberation* (GMP, 1980).   p. 214, "The Gay Gaze"   p. 215, "The Good Games" B. Pronger *The Arena of Masculinity* (GMP, 1990).

Chapter Eleven: The Golden Age?

p. 222, "An American Lifestyle Before the Plague"   p. 224, "Advise from San Francisco"   p. 224, "A Way of Life"   p. 226, "Buying the Christmas Tree" A. Maupin *More Tales of the City* (1980). A. Maupin *Tales of the City* (1978). A. Maupin *Further Tales of the City* (1980). By permission of David Grossman Literary Agency on behalf of the author.   p. 223, "More Thoughtful"   p. 223, "Vanity" E. White *Travels in Gay America* (Dutton, 1980).   p. 224, "Rates of Exchange" S. Kleinberg *The Other Persuasion* (Picador, 1977).   p. 225, "Hot" L. Michaels & C. Ricks (ed) *The State of the Language* (University of California Press, 1980).   p. 227, "Murderous Thoughts" B. Masters *Killing for Company* (Cape, 1985).   p. 230, "Midnight Express" B. Hayes & W. Hoffer *Midnight Express* (Dutton, 1977).   p. 232, "Getting in Touch" J. Spada *The Spada Report* (New American Library, 1979).   p. 233, "Pin-Ups" M. Walters *Nude Male* (Penguin, 1978).   p. 240, "Beware" S. Kleinberg *The Other Persuasion* (Picador, 1977).

Chapter Twelve: Show Business

p. 245, "Energy" *Rock Hudson: His Story* (Morrow, 1986). p. 245, "Out in the Open" C. Higham & R. Moseley *Cary Grant* (Hodder & Stoughton, 1989). p. 246, "The Odd Couple" D. Spoto *Laurence Olivier: A Biography* (Harper Collins, 1991). p. 246, "Domestic Pleasures" P. & L. Gilman *Alias David Bowie* (Hodder & Stoughton, 1986). p. 247, "Creative Urges" p. 247, "Tease" R. Coleman *Brian Epstein* (McGraw Hill, 1989). p. 248, "Impresario" A. Motion *The Lamberts* (Farrar, Straus & Giroux 1986). p. 250, "Sell-by-Date" B. Thomas *Liberace: The True Story* (St. Martin's Press, 1987). p. 253, "High Energy" C. Higham *Errol Flynn: the Untold Story* (Doubleday, 1980). p. 253, "In Hiding" S. Callow *Charles Laughton: A Difficult Actor* (Methuen, 1987). p. 254, "Montgomery Clift and Innocence" P. Bosworth *Montgomery Clift: A Biography* (Harcourt Brace Jovanovich, 1978). p. 254, "Ambidextrous" G. McCann *Rebel Males: Clift, Brando and Dean* (Hamish Hamilton, 1991). p. 255, "Fags" K. Anger *Hollywood Babylon II* (Dutton, 1984). p. 256, "Camp I" W. R. Dynes *The Encyclopedia of Homosexuality* (Garland, 1990). p. 257, "Camp IV" C. Isherwood *The World in the Evening* (1954) reproduced with the permission of Curtis Brown Ltd. on behalf of the estate of Christopher Isherwood.
*p. 257, "Collaboration" D. Jarman *At Your Risk: A Saint's Testament* (Hutchinson, 1992).

Chapter Thirteen: Living in the Shadow of the Plague

*p. 264, "Adrian Mole" S. Townsend *The Growing Pains of Adrian More* (Metheun, 1984).
*p. 265, "Lies" T. Parker *The Trail of Rock Hudson* (Sidgwick & Jackson, 1990). p. 282, "Wrong Word" with permission of Mark Simpson p. 284, "Safe Sex" D. Leavitt *Equal Affections* (1989) Weidenfeld & Nicolson

Chapter Fourteen: The Homintern

p. 288, "Hidden Things" p. 288, "He Swears" p. 288, "The Twenty-Fifth Year of his Life" p. 289, "In Despair" p. 289, "The Photograph" p. 290, "Two Young Men, 23 to 24 Years Old" E. Keeley and P. Sherrard (ed) *The Collected Poems of C. P. Cavafy* (Princeton University Press, 1975). p. 291, "Posterity" p. 293, "Two Visits" A. Gide *Journals* translated, selected and edited by Justin O'Brien (Penguin, 1967). p. 292, "Observed" M. Muggeridge *Chronicles of Wasted Time* vol. 2 (Morrow, 1973). p. 292, "Frisky" D. Windham *Lost Friendships* (Morrow, 1983). p. 294, "Calculations" p. 295, "The Last Time" M. Reich-Ranicki *Thomas Mann and His Family* (Collins, 1989). p. 295, "Tadzio" T. Mann *Death In Venice* (1912) Penguin translation by H. T. Lowe Porter p. 297, "Mother" p. Parker *Ackerley* (Constable, 1989). p. 297, "The Touch" p. 298, "England" E. M. Forster *Maurice* (1971) by permission of the Provost and Fellows of King's College, Cambridge. p. 298, "Domestic Anthropology" H. Montgomery Hyde *The Other Love* (Little Brown, 1970). p. 299, "The Wanderer" p. 300, "Substitution" p. 300, "Fags" M. Holroyd *Lytton Strachey* (William Heineman 1967–1968) by permission of A. P. Watt Ltd. on behalf of Michael Holroyd. p. 306, "Demure" p. 309, "Fraud" R. Meinertzhagen *Middle East Diary* (Cresset Press, 1959). p. 308, "Loud and Clear" J. E. Mack *A Prince of Our Disorders: The Life of T. E. Lawrence* (Little Brown, 1976). p. 308, "Poor Boy" p. 314, "No Jokes" p. 314, "Fan" p. 314, "Wishful Thinking" G. Payn & S. Morley (ed) *The Noel Coward Diaries* (Little Brown, 1989). p. 310, "Hunting" p. 310, "Ideal Friend" J. R. Ackerley *My Father and Myself* (Dodley Head, 1960). p. 311, "Flashing a Smile" P. Parker *Ackerley* (Constable, 1989). p. 312, "Tied to Mother" p. 312, "The Destruction of Sodom" p. 312, "Devotion" I. Gibson *Lorca* (Pantheon Books, 1989). p. 315, "Devoted Friends" p. 316, "Crimes" p. 316, "Charles and Sebastoam" E. Waugh *A Little Learning* (1964). E. Waugh *Brideshead Revisited* (1945) by permission of Peter, Frasers & Dunlop Ltd. p. 316 Discretion H. Acton *Memoirs of an Aesthete* (Methuen, 1948). p. 317, "Dressing Up" p. 318, "Berlin" p. 318, "Brave New World" p. 318, "For Keeps" p. 319, "Mrs. Strunk" p. 319, "Running for Cover" p. 319, "Minority" p. 319, "Creativity" C. Isherwood *Kathleen and Frank* (1972). C. Isherwood *Christopher and his Kind* (1977) C. Isherwood *My Guru and his disciple* (1980) C. Isherwood *A Single Man* (1964). C. Isherwood *The World In the Evening* (1954) reproduced with the permission of Curtis Brown Ltd. on behalf of the estate of Christopher Isherwood. p. 318, "Raiding the Cradle" M. St. Just (ed) *Five o'clock angel: letters of Tennessee Williams to Maria St. Just 1948–82* (Andre Deutsch, 1991). p. 319, "Charm" p. 319, "Semen" p. 330, "The Benefactor" p. 331, "Double Act" F. Wheen *Driberg* (Chatto & Windus, 1990). p. 321, "Horst" p. 321, "Callous" p. 323, "Necessary Pain" L. Schifano *Visconti: the flames of passion* (Collins, 1990). p. 322, "Angel of Death" D. Bogarde *An Orderly Man* (Knopf 1983). p. 324, "The Beginning" p. 327, "Imperialism" H. Carpenter *Auden* (Houghton Mifflin, 1981). p. 325, "The Wrong Blond" p. 327, "A Funny Pair" D. Farnan *Auden in Love* (Faber and Faber, 1985) by permission of the Rosalyn Targ Agency. p. 326, "The Making of a Poem" H. Norse *Memoirs of a Bastard Angel* (Morrow, 1989). p. 328, "Displeased" C. Osborne *Auden* (Harcourt Brace Jovanovich, 1980). p. 329, "A Nasty Unwed" p. 341, "Learning a Language" p. 341, "Recognition II" p. 342, "Achievement" p. 342, "Loser" p. 342, "History" N. Rorem *The Nantucket Diary of Ned Rorem* (North Point Press, 1987). p. 329, "Bad Luck" T. C. Worsley *Flanneled Fool* (Hogarth Press, 1967). p. 331, "Without Inhibition" p. 334, "The Calculator" A. Powell *Messengers of Day* (Heinemann, 1978). p. 331, "Bohemian Prince" N. Annan *Our Age* (Random House, 1990). p. 332, "Collaboration and Resistance" J. Genet *Funeral Rites* (1977). p. 333, "Disease" p. 334, "Chips" p. 336, "Chums" M. M. Darlow & G. Hodson *Terence Rattigan* (Quartet, 1979). p. 333, "Strong Bonds" p. 336, "Precious" p. 336, "Chums" p. 336, "Bed" p. 337, "The English Vice p. 335, "Cruising" R. R. James (ed) *Chips: The Diaries of Sir Henry Channon* (Weidenfeld & Nicolson, 1967). p. 337, "The Kindness of Strangers" p. 337, "Magic" p. 337, "Bent" p. 338, "Animal Passions" T. Williams *Memoirs* (Doubleday, 1976). p. 338, "Free Men" R. Miles *The Rites of Man* (Grafton, 1991) by permission of Peter Frasers & Dunlop Ltd. p. 339, "Behaving Badly" D. Rader *Tennessee Williams: An Intimate Memoir* (Doubleday, 1985). p. 339, "Light Relief" p. 339, "Neal" G. Nicosia *Memory Babe* (Grove Press, 1983) by permission of G. Nicosia. p. 340, "Roots" B. Miles *Ginsberg* (Viking, 1989) by permission of Aitken, Stone and Wyile on behalf of the author. p. 341, "Recognition I" N. Rorem *The Paris Diary of Ned Rorem* (Barrie & Rockcliffe, 1966). p. 342, "Last Words" N. Rorem *The New York Diary of Ned Rorem* (George Braziller, 1967). p. 343, "The End" p. 343, "Romeo" F. Zeffirelli *Zeffirelli: the autobiography of Franco Zeffirelli* (Weidenfeld & Nicolson, 1986). p. 346, "Closely Observed Queen" J. Cheever *Journals* (Knopf, 1990). p. 347, "Pink Triangle and Yellow Star" G. Vidal *Pink Triangle and Yellow Start, and other essays (1976–1982)* (Heinemann, 1982). p. 347, "Many Loves" A. Ginsberg *Collected Poems* (Viking, 1985). p. 348, "Ingenuity" A. Warhol *The Philosophy of Andy Warhol: From A to B and back again* (Harcourt, 1975). p. 348, "Butch" p. 349, "The Age of Improvement" p. 349, "Challenge" p. 350, "Easy" p. 350, "Recognition" P. Hacket (ed) *The Andy Warhol Diaries* (Warner Books, 1989). p. 350, "The Discovery" p. 351, "Smoothie" p. 351, "Danger Woman" p. 351, "Growing Up" p. 351, "Unchanging" p. 351, "Blondes" p. 351, "Youth" p. 352, "Variety" p. 352, "Reticence" p. 352, "False Foundation" p. 352, "Cover" p. 352, "Advantage" p. 352, "The Orton Murder" from the plays of J. Orton with the permission of Methuen. p. 355, "Inspiration" p. 355, "Living Doll" p. 355, "The Work Ethic" *David Hockney* by David Hockney (Thames and Hudson, 1977). p. 356, "Partners" P. Webb *Portrait of David Hockney* (Dutton, 1990).

Index